SCOTTISH HISTORY SOCIETY

SIXTH SERIES

VOLUME 17

The Poems of Roderick MacLean

The Poems of Roderick MacLean
(Ruairidh MacEachainn MhicIllEathain)
(d. 1553)

Edited by
Alan Macquarrie and Roger P H Green

COLLIGITE FRAGMENTA NE PEREANT

SCOTTISH HISTORY SOCIETY
2022

THE BOYDELL PRESS

First published 2022

ISBN 978-0-906245-47-7

A Scottish History Society publication
in association with The Boydell Press.
The Boydell Press is an imprint of Boydell & Brewer Ltd
PO Box 9, Woodbridge, Suffolk IP12 3DF, UK
and of Boydell & Brewer Inc.
668 Mt Hope Avenue, Rochester, NY 14620–2731, USA

website: www.boydellandbrewer.com

A CIP catalogue record of this publication is available
from the British Library

The publisher has no responsibility for the continued existence or accuracy of URLs for external
or third-party internet websites referred to in this book, and does not guarantee that any content
on such websites is, or will remain, accurate or appropriate

This publication is printed on acid-free paper

Printed and bound in Great Britain by
TJ Books Limited, Padstow, Cornwall

In Memory of Richard Sharpe
1954–2020

Agus thubhairt mi, Och, nach robh agam sgiathan!
mar choluman theichinn as air iteig agus gheibhinn fois.
SALM LV, 6

CONTENTS

ILLUSTRATIONS

The editors and publisher are grateful to all the institutions and persons listed for permission to reproduce the materials in which they hold copyright. Every effort has been made to trace the copyright holders; apologies are offered for any omission, and the publisher will be pleased to add any necessary acknowledgement in subsequent editions.

ACKNOWLEDGEMENTS

It is a pleasant duty to acknowledge the help of the staff at various institutions where relevant materials have been consulted: in particular the staff of the libraries which hold the known copies of Roderick MacLean's works, the Wolfson Reading Room at Aberdeen University Library and the Biblioteca communale Augusta in Perugia, have been unfailingly kind, informative, and helpful in supplying access to, and copies of, the materials in their possession, and in giving permission for their publication. The University Archives of Halle-Wittenberg, the Universitäts- und Landesbibliothek Sachsen-Anhalt, Lady Angelika Campbell of Cawdor, and the Archivist of the Society of Jesus in Rome, have likewise been very helpful. Material from the Vatican Apostolic Archives has been consulted in the collection of material painstakingly collected over many years by the Department of Scottish History at the University of Glasgow.

Roger Green's translation of MacLean's paraphrase of Psalm 1 is reprinted, by kind permission of the Arizona Center for Medieval and Renaissance Studies, from his chapter 'Poetic Psalm paraphrases: Two versions of Psalm 1 compared', in *Acta Conventus Neo-Latini Budapestinensis*, ed. R Schnur (Tempe, 2010). The rest of the translation is very much a joint enterprise of the editors, incorporating many useful comments by Dr Betty Knott-Sharpe. The bulk of the introduction, notes, and commentary, and the appendix are by Alan Macquarrie, who has also compiled the index.

Many scholars have provided stimulating advice and suggestions; they are too numerous for all to be named. Mention should be made, however, of the Medieval and Renaissance Latin Reading Group at Glasgow University, led by Dr Steven Reid, and of Dr Ian Hazlett, Professor Dauvit Broun, Professor Roibeard Ó Maolalaigh, Dr Betty Knott-Sharpe, and Professor Christopher Black, all present and former teachers at Glasgow University, and Dr Janet Hadley Williams of the Australian National University in Canberra.

Roderick MacLean's poems greatly interested the late Professor Richard Sharpe of Oxford University, and he was a trail-blazer in the study of them. He expressed a warm interest in this work when it was in progress, and it is a matter of deep regret that his untimely death means that he has not seen it completed. It is fitting, therefore, to dedicate it to his memory.

ABBREVIATIONS

General

ADCP	G Neilson & H Paton, *Acts of the Lords of Council in Civil Causes* (Edinburgh, 1918).
ALI	J Munro and R W Munro, *Acts of the Lords of the Isles, 1336–1493* (Edinburgh, 1986).
Anderson, *ESSH*	A O Anderson, *Early Sources of Scottish History* (Edinburgh, 1922).
Anderson, *KKES*	M O Anderson, *Kings and Kingship in Early Scotland* (Edinburgh, 1973).
APS	T Thomson & C Innes, *Acts of the Parliaments of Scotland* (Edinburgh, 1814–42).
ATig.	W Stokes, *Annals of Tigernach* (reprinted Felinfach, 1993).
AU	S Mac Airt & G Mac Niocaill, *Annals of Ulster* (Dublin, 1983).
Boece, *SH*	Hector Boece, *Scotorum Historia*, ed. Dana F Sutton, http://www.philological.bham.ac.uk/boece/, 26 February 2010.
Chron. Bower	D E R Watt et al., *Scotichronicon by Walter Bower* (Aberdeen, 1987–98).
Chron. Fordun	W F Skene, *Johannis de Fordun Chronica Gentis Scotorum* (Edinburgh, 1871).
Chron. Pluscarden	F J H Skene, *Liber Pluscardensis* (Edinburgh, 1877).
CSD	*Concise Scots Dictionary* (1985).
Dilworth, 'Iona Abbey and the Reformation'	M Dilworth, 'Iona Abbey and the Reformation', *Scottish Gaelic Studies*, xii (1971), 77–109.

DMLBS	*Dictionary of Medieval Latin from British Sources*, ed. R E Latham et al. (London, 1975–2013).
Donaldson, *James V to James VII*	G Donaldson, *James V to James VII* (Edinburgh, 1971).
Dowden, *Bishops*	J Dowden, *The Bishops of Scotland* (Glasgow, 1912).
Durkan, 'Cultural Background'	J Durkan, 'The cultural background in sixteenth-century Scotland', *IR*, x (1959), 382–439 (reprinted in McRoberts, *Essays*).
Ford & Green, *Buchanan*	P Ford & R P H Green, *George Buchanan: Poet and Dramatist* (Swansea, 2009).
Green, 'Paraphrases'	R P H Green, 'Poetic Psalm paraphrases: Two versions of Psalm 1 compared', in *Acta Conventus Neo-Latini Budapestinensis:: Proceedings of the Thirteenth International Congress of Neo-Latin Studies*, ed. Rhoda Schnur, *Medieval and Renaissance Texts and Studies* 386 (Tempe, 2010).
HE	B Colgrave & R A B Mynors, *Bede's Ecclesiastical History of the English People* (Oxford, 1969).
Henry VIII Letters	J S Brewer et al., *Letters and Papers, Foreign and Domestic, of the Reign of Henry VIII* (London, 1862–1932).
Herbert, *Iona, Kells and Derry*	M Herbert, *Iona, Kells and Derry* (Oxford 1988).
IR	*Innes Review*.
Lacey, *Manus O'Donnell*	B Lacey, *The Life of Colum Cille by Manus O'Donnell* (Dublin, 1998).
Lorimer, *Patrick Hamilton*	P Lorimer, *Patrick Hamilton: The First Preacher and Martyr of the Scottish Reformation* (Edinburgh, 1857).
Macquarrie, *Legends of Scottish Saints*	A Macquarrie, *Legends of Scottish Saints* (Dublin, 2012).
McGinnis & Williamson, *Buchanan*	P J McGinnis & A H Williamson, *George Buchanan: The Political Poetry* (Edinburgh, 1995).
McRoberts, *Essays*	D McRoberts, *Essays on the Scottish Reformation, 1513–1625* (Glasgow, 1962).
Migne, *PL*	J P Migne, *Patrologia Cursus Completus Series Latina* (Paris, 1844–66).

NCLCL	A Harvey & J Power, *Non-Classical Lexicon of Celtic Latinity* (Turnhout, 2005).
OPS	*Origines Parochiales Scotiae* (Edinburgh, 1851–55).
Ó Riain, *CGSH*	P Ó Riain, *Corpus Genealogiarum Sanctorum Hiberniae* (Dublin, 1985).
Ó Riain, *Dictionary*	P Ó Riain, *Dictionary of Irish Saints* (Dublin, 2011).
Pennant, *Tour*	Thomas Pennant, *A Tour of Scotland and Voyage to the Hebrides in 1777* (London, 1790).
Pococke, *Tours*	Richard Pococke, *Tours in Scotland in 1747, 1750 and 1760* (Edinburgh, 1887).
RCAHMS	Royal Commission for the Ancient and Historical Monuments of Scotland.
RMS	J Maitland Thomson et al., *Register of the Great Seal of Scotland* (Edinburgh, 1882–1914).
RSCHS	*Records of the Scottish Church History Society.*
RSS	M Livingston et al., *Register of the Privy Seal of Scotland* (Edinburgh, 1908–82).
Scottish Correspondence of Mary of Lorraine	A I Cameron, *Scottish Correspondence of Mary of Lorraine* (Edinburgh, 1927).
Sharpe, 'MacLean'	R Sharpe, 'Roderick MacLean's Life of St Columba of Iona in Latin verse (1549)', *IR*, xlii (1991), 111–32.
Sharpe, *Adomnán*	R Sharpe, *Adomnan of Iona: Life of St Columba* (London, 1991).
Shorter OED	*Shorter Oxford English Dictionary,* revised edn (London, 1983).
SHS	Scottish History Society.
SRS	Scottish Record Society.
Steer & Bannerman, *Sculpture*	K A Steer & J W M Bannerman, *Late Medieval Monumental Sculpture in the West Highlands* (Edinburgh, 1977).
VC	A O Anderson & M O Anderson, *Adomnan's Life of Columba* (Oxford, 1991).
Watson, *CPNS*	W J Watson, *History of the Celtic Place-Names of Scotland* (Edinburgh, 1926).

Watt & Murray, *Fasti*	D E R Watt & A L Murray, *Fasti Ecclesiae Scoticanae Medii Aevi ad annum 1638*, revised edn (Edinburgh, 2003).
Watt & Shead, *Heads of Religious Houses*	D E R Watt & N F Shead, *Heads of Religious Houses in Scotland from Twelfth to Sixteenth Centuries* (Edinburgh, 2001).

Classical Authors

Augustine, *De Civitate Dei*	Aurelius Augustinus, *De Civitate Dei*.
Baebius Italicus, *Ilias Latina*	P Baebius Italicus, *Ilias Latina*.
Catullus, *Carmina*	C Valerius Catullus, *Carmina*.
Hor., *Epistles*	Q Horatius Flaccus, *Epistulae*.
Hor., *Odes*	Q Horatius Flaccus, *Carmina*.
Ovid, *Amores*	P Ovidius Naso, *Amores*.
Ovid, *Fasti*	P Ovidius Naso, *Fasti*.
Ovid, *Met.*	P Ovidius Naso, *Metamorphoses*.
Persius Flaccus, *Satires*	Aulus Persius Flaccus, *Saturae*.
Plautus, *Asinaria*	T Maccius Plautus, *Asinaria*.
Pliny, *HN*	C Plinius Secundus, *Naturalis Historia*.
Quintilian, *Inst.*	M Fabius Quintilianus, *Institutio Oratoria*.
Valerius Flaccus, *Argonautica*	C Valerius Flaccus, *Argonautica*.
Verg., *Aen.*	P Vergilius Maro, *Aeneis*.
Verg., *Ecl.*	P Vergilius Maro, *Eclogae*.
Verg., *Georg.*	P Vergilius Maro, *Georgica*.

Books of the Bible

1 Cor.	1 Corinthians
2 Cor.	2 Corinthians
1 Kings	1 Kings

2 Kings	2 Kings
1 Tim.	1 Timothy
2 Pet.	2 Peter
2 Sam.	2 Samuel
Acts	Acts
Deut.	Deuteronomy
Ex.	Exodus
Ez.	Ezekiel
Gen.	Genesis
John	John
Jon.	Jonah
Mat.	Matthew
Prov.	Proverbs
Ps.	Psalms
Rev.	Revelation
Rom.	Romans
Song	Song of Songs

Grammatical terms

abl.	ablative
acc.	accusative
adj.	adjective
CL	Classical Latin
dat.	dative
dec.	declension
fem.	feminine
gen.	genitive
Gk	Greek
imp.	imperative
inf.	infinitive
LL	Late Latin

loc.	locative
LXX	Septuagint
masc.	masculine
ML	Medieval Latin
neut.	neuter
nom.	nominative
pass.	passive
plu.	plural
pres.	present
sing.	singular
Vulg.	Vulgate

INTRODUCTION

The *Ionis* or *Ionidos Liber*, 'Book of the Song of Iona', was published in Rome in May 1549. The book is a paraphrase in neo-classical Latin verse of selected chapters from Books i and ii of Adomnán's *Vita Columbae* of *c.* 700. The book also includes a prose genealogy for Mary Queen of Scots, and has appended to it a paraphrase of Psalm 1 in elegiac verse. Only three copies of this very rare printed book are now known to survive, one in Aberdeen University Library and two (one incomplete) in the Biblioteca communale Augusta in Perugia.[1] One of the copies of *Ionis* in Perugia also has an additional gathering bound into it, seemingly unique, containing two other poems by the same poet under the title *Ad clarissimum virum d. Dauidem Lyndsaium a Monte equitem auratum, leonem heraldum de excellentia heroici ordinis epistola elegiaca.* [2] These are a flattering address to Sir David Lindsay of the Mount, dated 15 October 1548, and a short poem addressed to the Governor the Earl of Arran, dated 1 January 1549.

The author of these poems was Roderick MacLean of Iona, and these constitute the sum of the poems by him that are presently known to survive. We know, however, from what he tells us, that he wrote many other psalm paraphrases. Since two of these copies have only come to light recently, there is a possibility that other copies, and perhaps other poems, may come to light in future.

---

[1] The copies in Perugia were unknown in Scotland until recently. Cf. Sharpe, 'MacLean', 111; I Beavan, P Davidson & J Stevenson, *Library and Archive Collections of the University of Aberdeen* (Manchester, 2011), 115, 134–5, 306; Green, 'Paraphrases', 262. The editors are very grateful to Professor Sally Mapstone, principal of St Andrews University, and to the Universal Short Title Catalogue project based at the University of St Andrews for having drawn one of the Perugia copies to our attention. See 'Universal Short Title Catalogue: An open access bibliography of early modern print culture,' accessed 5 April 2022, http:// www.ustc.ac.uk/.

[2] Sir David Lindsay of the Mount was Lyon Herald at the court of James V. He is best known now for his anticlerical play *Ane Satyre of the Threi Estaitis*, ed. R Lyall (Edinburgh, 1989), but this was not published until after MacLean's poem.

THE AUTHOR

Biographical notes

Roderick MacLean was later commendator of Iona Abbey and bishop of the Isles; he died in 1553. On the title page of *Ionis* he calls himself *Rodericus Maclenius Hectorogenis*, that is, Roderick MacLean descendant of Hector. The family of MacLean of Kingairloch (in Morvern) was known as MacEachainn, 'descendant of Hector'. They were a cadet branch of the MacLeans of Lochbuie. On 6 January 1509 Eugenius filius Hectoris de Kilmalew (= Eoghan MacEachainn) had a crown grant of lands in Morvern previously held of John Lord of the Isles.[3] A tombstone and inscription relating to his father and uncles are at Kilcolmkill, Keil, by Lochaline in Morvern.[4] Roderick was probably a nephew of this Eugenius or Eoghan.

His family developed a close connection with Iona. His brother Farquhar MacLean was bishop of the Isles and abbot of Iona Abbey (1530–45).[5] Two of his female relatives, his cousin Anna or Agnes (fl. 1509; d. 1543) and his sister Maria or Marion (still alive in 1574), were successively prioresses of Iona nunnery.[6]

In papal documents of the 1540s he is usually described as 'clerk of the diocese of Ross', or occasionally as 'clerk of the diocese of Ross or of another diocese', indicating his place of birth, and the same documents call him MA and 'of noble birth on both sides'.[7] Of his origins he himself says *Nostri namque lares ibi sunt, patriique penates, / qua lacus illimi gurgite Noesus abit* ('Our place of origin and our parental home is there where Loch Ness runs out in a clear flood') (*Epistola*, **35–6**). He must, then, have been a member of the northern, Glen Urquhart, branch of the MacLeans of Kingairloch, as suggested by Mark Dilworth.[8] His early education, however, seems to have been largely at Iona, since he writes of *Ionae me nutricis insulae* ('of Iona, the island that nurtured me') (*Ionis*, P3.36). This might imply that he attended some sort of monastic school on Iona.[9] Governor Arran later wrote of him that he was *in insulis educatus*.[10]

---

[3]   *RMS*, ii, 3284.

[4]   Steer & Bannerman, *Sculpture*, no. 54.

[5]   Dowden, *Bishops*, 291–2; Watt & Murray, *Fasti*, 265-6; Watt & Shead, *Heads of Religious Houses*, 113; Farquhar died in June 1545: VA, RS 2664, f. 151r. Below, 332–3.

[6]   Steer & Bannerman, *Sculpture*, nos 29, 54; Watt & Shead, *Heads of Religious Houses*, 116; RCAHMS, *Argyll*, iv: *Iona*, 179 and n. 29 on p. 277.

[7]   Rome, VA, RS 2471, f.80r–81; 2474, f.32v–33; 2476, f.87r–v; 2478, f.23, etc. See Appendix, pp. 330–2. He also appears on occasion as 'clerk of the diocese of Sodor', probably erroneously: cf. n. 11 below.

[8]   M Dilworth, 'Iona Abbey and the Reformation', *Scottish Gaelic Studies*, xii (1971), 77–109, at 91–4.

[9]   There was also a burgh school in Inverness: see Durkan, *Scottish Schools and Schoolmasters*, 157 and n.

[10] See below, p. 8.

We do not know with certainty the exact year of Roderick's birth, or much about his early career. He cannot have been born too many years before or after 1500, but perhaps a few years after is more likely. What appears to be the earliest documentary record we have of him dates from 11 July 1529, when it was complained to the pope that the abbot and convent of Iona Abbey and a certain *Rodericus Hectoris Johannis alias Makilan*, clerk of the diocese of Sodor [sic], had detained certain parish churches without due title.[11] This Roderick is accused of detaining the parish church of St Columba *de Knok in Kynnallwadenech in Merwarma*, that is, Kilcolmkill in Morvern (near Lochaline).[12] The name *Johannis alias Makilan* could be for *Mac'Illeathain*, as *Hectoris* was certainly a Latinisation of *MacEachainn*. Since the minimum age for holding a benefice without dispensation was the twenty-fifth year, and no defect of age is mentioned, this might imply that Roderick was born no later than 1505; and since this is the first mention of him in connection with holding a benefice, he is perhaps unlikely to have been born too much earlier. If we suggest that he was probably born *c.* 1500 –1505, we will not be too far wrong.[13] If we speculate that this ambitious man began his clerical career at the earliest opportunity, and that his earliest appearance on record was at the beginning of this career, then possibly we can date his birth *c.* 1504-5.

This person must be the same as the *domino Rodorico Hectoris Joannis rectore de Morwarne*, who on 8 August 1532 was on Iona witnessing a charter of the bishop of the Isles and commendator of Iona and the chapter of Iona, feuing certain lands of the abbey to John Campbell of Cawdor, in the presence of the bishop, the prior and monks of Iona Abbey, the vicar of Iona, and one of the canons of Oronsay Priory.[14] The title *dominus* was usually applied to a clerk or priest who had not yet graduated with a master's degree. Clearly the attempt to remove him from Kilcolmkill in Morvern had been unsuccessful.

He is next heard of studying on the Continent in 1534, so he may have taken a first degree from a Scottish university by then: *Rodoricus Hector ex Hybernia* matriculated at Wittenberg in the winter semester of 1534–35.[15] The Wittenberg records do not tell us what subjects he studied, whether

[11] A Macquarrie, *Calendar of Entries in the Papal Registers Relating to Great Britain and Ireland: Papal Letters*, xxiii, 1 (Dublin, 2018), no. 447.
[12] For *Kynnallwadenech* as a name for Morvern, cf. Watson, *CPNS*, 122: 'Morvern was of old called Kinelvadon'.
[13] In the Middle Ages, the minimum age for consecration as a bishop was thirty, so Roderick must have been at least that age, and probably some years older, when he was elected bishop of the Isles in 1545.
[14] Cawdor Castle, Campbell of Cawdor Papers, 649/2; printed, with some inaccuracies, in *Book of the Thanes of Cawdor*, 156–8. The witness list on p. 158 should read: *coram hiis testibus: domino Bricio vicario Ione insule ac decano de Mull, domino Rodorico Hectoris Joannis rectore de Morwarne, Joanne canonico Mc duffe, cum diuersis aliis*. In the list of signatures that follows, for *tenta penna* read *tacta penna*.
[15] Halle, Universitäts- und Landesbibliothek Sachsen-Alhalt, Wittenberger Matrikel, 1, fo. 123v; see also Halle, Universitätsarchiv Martin-Luther-Universität Halle-Wittenberg, Album

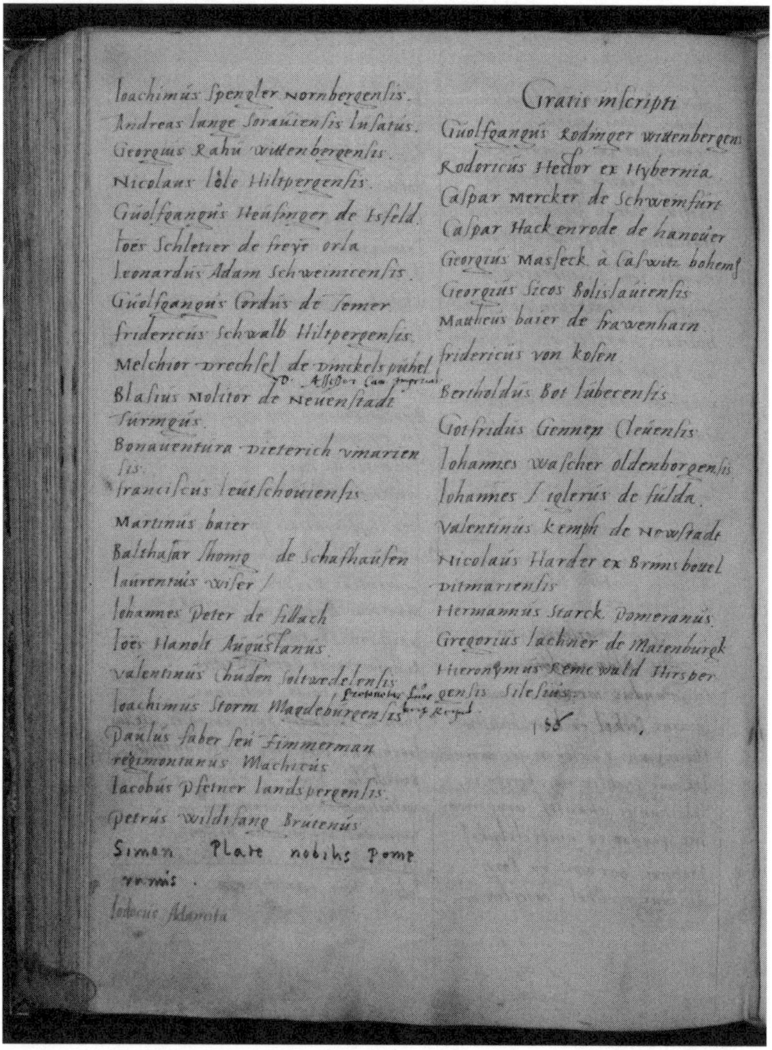

Figure 1. Wittenberg University matriculation album, showing names of students enrolled in 1534. The second name in the right-hand column, of students enrolled *Gratis inscripti*, is *Rodoricus Hector ex Hybernia*. The name added near the foot of the left-hand column, *Simon Plate nobilis Pomeranus*, is in Melanchthon's hand. Reproduced courtesy of the Martin-Luther-Universität Halle-Wittenberg under CC BY-SA 3.0.

he took a degree, or who his professors were.[16] They do tell us that he was enrolled *gratis inscriptus*, that is, without any registration fees: perhaps this was the equivalent of being awarded a scholarship. His name appears second in a list of those matriculating *gratis*, and the lists appear to have been made in chronological order, so his matriculation may have taken place at or soon after the beginning of the winter semester on 16 October 1534. The designation *ex Hybernia* probably simply indicates that he was a Gaelic speaker, though it is not impossible that he had studied in Ireland.

We cannot be certain where Roderick MacLean studied between his early education at Iona and his matriculation at Wittenberg. There is a possibility that he may have had some association with Aberdeen. In the *Ionis*, he twice (**2.4**, **2.22**) mentions places high up in the Mounth at the passes between Atholl and Braemar, and he gives a vivid description of a winter journey through this region; this possibly indicates a trip from Iona to Aberdeen *via* Atholl and Braemar. His version of the Queen's genealogy (**P6**) is drawn largely from the writings of Hector Boece, indicating that Boece had some influence on him. His brother Farquhar had some knowledge of the practices in Aberdeen Cathedral in 1529–31.[17] These faint indications cannot make it certain that he had studied at Aberdeen, but they may present such a possibility.

In 1536, as *magister Rodericus Farquhar Hectorissonne*, he was presented to the parishes of Barvas in Lewis, Kilmaluag in Trotternish in Skye, and Kilchoman in Islay.[18] Since he is described at this time as *magister*, having earlier (1532) been called *dominus*, it may be that he had completed his master's degree in between. This suggests that he took his master's degree at Wittenberg.

In 1542, he was appointed archdeacon of the Isles.[19] His predecessor in the post was Richard Lawson, who seems to have been archdeacon largely *in absentia*, working as a canon lawyer in Edinburgh.[20] Roderick was at court

Academiae Vitenbergensis, vol. 1, p. 157b/6; John Durkan, 'The cultural background in sixteenth-century Scotland', *IR*, x, 382–439, at 428.
[16] Information supplied by the Archivist of the Universitätsarchiv Martin-Luther-Universität Halle-Wittenberg.
[17] When Farquhar, a Benedictine monk, applied to the pope for permission to wear the clothes of a secular cleric as bishop, he cited the example of George Learmonth, coadjutor of Aberdeen, previously prior of Pluscarden: Rome, VA, RS, 2158, 93r.
[18] *RSS*, ii, 2045; Dilworth, 'Iona Abbey and the Reformation', 90.
[19] Rome, VA, RS 2471, f. 80–1; *RSS*, iii, 977; Watt & Murray, *Fasti*, 274. His successor as archdeacon, Donald Monro, also held the parsonage of Trotternish: see Munro, *Monro's Western Isles*, 18. For the development of the closely comparable archdeaconry of Argyll, cf. I G MacDonald, *Clerics and Clansmen: The Diocese of Argyll between the Twelfth and Sixteenth Centuries* (Leiden, 2013), 56–9. His predecessor as archdeacon had been Richard Lawson: see Watt & Murray, *Fasti*, 273. An attempt to unseat Lawson in favour of John Campbell in 1537 had been ineffective: Rome, VA, RS 2241, f. 173v. See below, Appendix, pp. 330–1.
[20] A Macquarrie, *Calendar of Papal Letters*, vol. xxiii, part I, *Clement VII*, part 1 (Dublin, 2018), nos 661, 875.

in February 1542, possibly in connection with this appointment, and had an encounter which was to have important consequences.

In the spring and summer of 1541, St Ignatius Loyola conceived the idea of sending Jesuit missionaries to Ireland to work with the Irish princes against Henry VIII.[21] The Jesuits chosen for the mission were a Frenchman, Paschasius Broët, and a Spaniard, Alphonsus Salmeron.[22] Armed with papal letters, they left Rome in September 1541, accompanied by a papal *scriptor*, Franciscus Zapata, and travelled first to Scotland. They arrived in Edinburgh after a stormy passage on New Year's Eve 1541, and early in the following year they met King James V and Queen Mary of Guise at Edinburgh. Salmeron reported back to Ignatius Loyola on 2 February that 'the response we were given was very gracious and favourable, namely, that he would give us letters of introduction to the Irish princes, and with them a man who would guide us there safely.'[23] This man, as it transpired, was Roderick MacLean, though he is not named in the Jesuit documents. Broët later reported to Loyola that 'In Scotland we consulted with many reverend men, firstly with the Archbishop of Glasgow, chancellor of the kingdom, and the Bishop of the Isles subject to the king of Scots which are nearest to Ireland', who gave them advice about the journey (which was not encouraging).[24] The king's letters of introduction to the Irish princes were dated at Stirling 13 February 1542 (n.s.). It was later reported that 'with them was sent for that purpose the bishop of the Isles' brother, that is Farquhard Farquhardson, which bishop lyeth at Icolm Kille, between Scotland and Ireland.'[25]

The Jesuits, with their guide, took ship from Irvine and arrived in the north-east of Ireland at the beginning of Lent 1542 (Ash Wednesday was 22 February). They later reported to Ignatius and to Cardinal Marcello Cervini (the future Pope Marcellus II) that the Irish were rude and uncultivated and largely devoid of pastoral guardianship, with few priests and bishops. Most of the Irish princes, they said, had accepted the king's Act of Supremacy, and had bound themselves to burn papal bulls and to arrest anyone found carrying them, and to send them in chains to the king or viceroy. They tried to arrange meetings with O'Donnell and O'Neill, but were unsuccessful. O'Donnell sent the bishop of Derry and the abbot of Derry to them, 'asking them to bring us secretly to him, lest it should come to the viceroy's ears and he should be

[21]   The chief sources for the Jesuit mission are printed in Alphonsi Salmeronis *Epistolae*, 1536–1565, vol. 1 (Madrid, 1906), and Paschasii Broëti et al., *Epistolae* (Madrid, 1903). There is a summary account in E Hogan, *Ibernia Ignatiana* (Dublin, 1880), 3–8.

[22]   The original leader of the mission was to have been Jean Cordure, but on his death Paschasius Broët replaced him as leader. He was a Frenchman and an early follower of Ignatius Loyola who went on to have a distinguished career among the Jesuits. Cf. J MacCaffrey, *History of the Catholic Church from the Renaissance to the French Revolution* (Dublin, 1914), i, 1127–9.

[23]   Salmeronis, *Epistolae*, vol. 1, 2–15, at 4.

[24]   Broëti, *Epistolae*, 23–31, at 24.

[25]   Hogan, *Ibernia Ignatiana*, 6–8.

condemned for violating his agreement.... We judged it was not to the honour of the Holy See that he should see and hear us secretly, who had been sent openly and publicly into the island, so we deferred visiting that prince until another time. After a few days we departed from there, with his knowledge, without him summoning or taking care of us.'[26] Similarly, O'Neill told them that he had given his son as a hostage to the king and would not put his life in danger. Their report is vague about other places they visited.

They resolved to leave Ireland lest anyone who associated with them should be put in danger. Back in Scotland at Easter, they tried to come to King James and to strengthen the Catholic cause; but they were hindered by the Scottish nobility, who were more concerned with the impending war against England, and so they could not arrange a fresh meeting with the king. So they decided instead to return to Rome according to their instructions, and took ship to Dieppe. From there they went on foot to Paris. At Paris they received a letter from the pope instructing them to return to Scotland, but they hesitated to do so until the pope had been made aware of the situation in Scotland, and decided to go on to Rome.

Roderick seems to have remained with them throughout their journey, as he had business of his own to transact in Rome. He may have had as his companion on his journey William Munro, vicar of the church of Lochbroom in Wester Ross: several supplications were submitted in the name of William Munro at the same time that Roderick was in Rome.[27]

In late July 1542, it was reported to Henry VIII by his informant in France, William Paget, that the brother of the bishop of the Isles was travelling through France with messages from the bishop of the Isles to the pope when he was detained at Lyons in company with 'two Spanish friars'. The Spaniards, Henry was told, had been sent by the pope *via* Scotland to the Irish rebels, with letters of introduction to James V. James had given them a safe-conduct to travel to Ireland *via* the Isles in February 1542, with the bishop's brother as their guide.[28] The Spaniards said they had achieved nothing because the king of Scots had broken his promise. The bishop's brother said he was on his way to Rome 'to receive instructions', and added that if Henry VIII invaded France, James would intervene.[29] He and the two Jesuits were released by the French and allowed to go on their way when the cardinal of Lyons intervened on their behalf: they were released honourably and given horses for their journey. (On this occasion, at least, James kept his promise, for he invaded England in November 1542.)

---

[26] Broëti, *Epistolae*, 26 7.

[27] Rome, VA, RS 2472, f. 235r; 2474, 29r–v; 2486, 259r–v. See below, Appendix, pp. 330–2.

[28] *James V Letters*, 435–6; *Henry VIII Letters*, xvii, no 102.; Hogan, *Ibernia Ignatiana*, 6–8.

[29] *Henry VIII Letters*, xvii, no 554.

By November 1542 Roderick was in Rome, and submitted a series of supplications to the pope for positions in the diocese of the Isles and for papal confirmation of positions which he already held by ordinary (i.e. episcopal) authority. In these he is mostly styled *Rodericus Ferquhardi* or *Rodericus Ferquhardi Hectoris*, clerk of the diocese of Ross (his place of birth) and MA. These supplications included petitions for the archdeaconry of the Isles, the church of St Mary on Arran united with it, the church of Barvas in Lewis, the churches of Kilmaluag (in Trotternish) and Trumpan (Kilchoman in Vaternish) in Skye, and the churches of St John the Evangelist (Kildalton) and of Kilchoman in Islay. He also petitioned for dispensation to read his breviary and hours privately following the recently published reformed breviary of Cardinal Francisco de Quiñones, and to hold up to four incompatible benefices.[30]

After the death of James V in December 1542, Scotland enjoyed a brief period of religious toleration during the governorship of James Hamilton, earl of Arran. In the early months of 1543, Arran encouraged the use of the vernacular Bible in Scotland, although his enthusiasm for religious reform turned out to be short-lived.[31] It is against this background that we must view the further rise of the Wittenberg-educated cleric Roderick MacLean. In November 1544, his brother Farquhar MacLean sought leave to resign the bishopric in his favour on grounds of age and infirmity.[32] In a letter under the name of Mary Queen of Scots (then aged nearly two), Governor Arran told the pope that Farquhar, bishop of the Isles and commendator of Iona, was elderly and wished to resign, and that Roderick MacLean was fitted for these offices. In a letter to Cardinal Carpi he added that Roderick was highly qualified, *quod is in Insulis educatus, pro more gentis satis habeatur literatus* ('because he has been brought up in the Isles, he is held to be very learned in the way of his race').[33] Farquhar, still bishop, was unable to attend the royal council in December 1544, probably due to infirmity.[34]

Farquhar MacLean was, however, still bishop at the time of his death in June 1545.[35] In August 1545 it was reported to Henry VIII that the governor had made a nomination to the bishopric;[36] Roderick himself claimed in the *Epistola* that he 'was nominated' to the post of bishop after his brother's death (*Epistola*, **151–2**).

---

[30] See below, Appendix, pp. 330–2. Cf. N Maclean-Bristol, *Warriors and Priests: The History of Clan MacLean, 1300–1570* (East Linton, 1995), 111–12.

[31] Donaldson, *James V to James VII*, 64–5; J E A Dawson, *Scotland Re-formed, 1488–1587* (2007), 158–60.

[32] *RSS*, iii, 977; cf. *TA*, viii, 338.

[33] *Henry VIII Letters*, xix, pt. ii, nos 640, 645. Maclean-Bristol, *Warriors and Priests*, 118–20.

[34] *TA*, viii, 338.

[35] VA, RS 2664, f. 151r. See below, Appendix, pp. 332–3.

[36] *State Papers Henry VIII*, iii, 532; *Henry VIII Letters*, xx, ii, 120. Since 1535 the papacy had accepted that the Scottish crown had the right of nomination to the highest church offices.

Roderick may have hoped that his progress to the bishopric would be smooth, but events in the Western Isles in 1544–45 had a complicating effect on the succession. Donald MacDonald (Dòmhnall Dubh), heir to the last MacDonald lord of the Isles, had been released from captivity by the governor in 1543, after thirty-seven years in prison, in accordance with James V's deathbed instructions on liberating prisoners.[37] The western chiefs quickly rallied to him, and soon he had assembled an impressive Council of the Isles, including MacLean of Duart, MacAllister of Clanranald, MacLeod of Lewis, MacLeod of Dunvegan, MacLean of Lochbuie, MacLean of Torloisk, MacIain of Ardnamurchan, MacLean of Coll, MacNeil of Barra, MacKinnon of Strathordell, MacQuarrie of Ulva, MacLean of Ardgour, Ranaldson of Glengarry, Ranaldson of Knoydart, and MacLean of Kingairloch.[38] This council supported the claims of Roderick MacAllister, brother of MacAllister of Clanranald, as bishop of the Isles, and of Patrick MacLean, brother of MacLean of Duart, as 'bailie of Iona', and sent them as commissioners to treat with Henry VIII in the summer of 1545.[39] Roderick MacAllister soon disappears from the record.[40] Patrick MacLean, by contrast, was to be a persistent rival to Roderick MacLean for a number of years. Dòmhnall Dubh was able to enlist the support of Henry VIII as part of the strategy of the 'rough wooing';[41] Dòmhnall's death in Ireland in December 1545 put an end to this brief but remarkable revival of the Lordship of the Isles, but the whole episode was to leave Roderick MacLean in a difficult position.

Roderick possibly still expected that after the death of Dòmhnall Dubh he would obtain the bishopric and commendatorship. On 12 December 1545, he was a witness to a marriage contract between the Campbell earl of Argyll and the daughter of MacLean of Duart.[42] In 1546 he was still archdeacon and acting as vicar-general during the vacancy when he confirmed the lands of Muckairn to Archibald Campbell of Cawdor.[43] In February 1547 Roderick MacLean, called 'elect of the Isles' on his brother's death, resigned the parish of Kilmaluag, evidently in anticipation of his promotion.[44]

37 Donaldson, *James V to James VII*, 61.
38 *Henry VIII Letters*, xx, pt. i, no. 1298.
39 Dilworth, 'Iona Abbey and the Reformation', 87–9; Watt and Murray, *Fasti*, 266. A Maclean Sinclair, *The Clan Gillean* (Charlottetown, 1899), 98–101; J Mackechnie, *The Clan Maclean: A Gaelic Sea Power* (Edinburgh, 1954), 9. The notary who drew up letters from Dòmhnall Dubh to MacAllister and Patrick MacLean was John Carswell, who eventually succeeded as bishop of the Isles and commendator of Iona in 1567 and who translated the reformed service book into Gaelic: see R L Thomson, *Foirm na n-Urrnuidheadh* (Edinburgh, 1970), pp. lxxix–lxxx.
40 Watt & Shead, *Fasti*, 266; Maclean-Bristol, *Warriors and Priests*, 121.
41 Dilworth, 'Iona Abbey and the Reformation', 87–8. The chief agent of Henry VIII's Scottish policy at the time was Matthew Stewart, fourth earl of Lennox.
42 Maclean-Bristol, *Warriors and Priests*, 121.
43 *OPS*, ii, 133, 377.
44 *RSS*, iii, 2164.

He was not immediately able, however, to gain possession of the offices to which he had been elected. On 7 August 1547, presumably to placate the rebels in the Isles, the governor granted the temporalities of the abbacy of Iona to Patrick MacLean until such time as the pope should make provision to it.[45] This must have been a serious disappointment for Roderick. In his *Epistola* he bitterly attacks Patrick MacLean as *petulcus, atrox, maiestate reus laesa, bastardus, adulter, caupo, rapax praedo, prorsus amusus, iners* ('wanton, savage, guilty of *lèse majesté*, a bastard, an adulterer, a huckster, a rapacious thief, totally uncultivated, slothful') (*Epistola*, **155–8**). He denounces Patrick's mother as promiscuous, and casts doubt on his paternity. The accusation of treason may relate to MacLean of Duart's involvement in Dòmhnall Dubh's uprising.

It was anticipated in March 1548 that Roderick would resign the archdeaconry of the Isles in favour of sir Donald Monro,[46] and on 25 August 1548, Donald Munro petitioned the pope for the archdeaconry as vacant by the resignation of Roderick MacLean.[47] Donald Munro, author of a description of the Western Isles of Scotland which probably reflects an archidiaconal visitation, was a nephew of Farquhar and Roderick MacLean: his mother Janet MacLean was their sister.[48]

At some point, probably in late 1547 or 1548, the prior and convent of Iona Abbey summoned Roderick before the commissary court of the archbishopric of St Andrews, as metropolitan, over certain moveable goods belonging to the abbey 'and other matters'. Doubting the competence and fairness of the commissary of St Andrews (John Spittal, official of St Andrews, 1546–53), he refused, and because of his non-appearance the commissary caused him 'to be removed and perhaps excommunicated'.[49] We do not know the exact date of this action; the vacancy at St Andrews lasted between the murder of Cardinal Beaton on 29 May 1546 and the summer of 1549, and Roderick is not mentioned in the surviving *Liber Sententiarum* of the official court of St Andrews.[50] What is most likely is that Roderick had been reluctant to comply with the governor's grant of the temporalities of the abbacy of Iona to Patrick MacLean in August 1547, and had to be legally compelled. In the *Ionis* he complains bitterly about those who prey upon St Columba's lands: *O Pater, duros utinam tyrannos, / qui tuos semper populantur agros, / uindices fato simili,*

---

[45] Ibid., 2367.
[46] Ibid., 2660; *Monro's Western Isles*, 15–16; Watt & Murray, *Fasti*, 274.
[47] Rome, VA, RS 2639, f.56v–57. Below, Appendix, p. 332.
[48] *Monro's Western Isles*, 11, 16–17.
[49] Rome, VA, RS 2672, f.38r. Below, Appendix, p. 335. The supplication is dated 1 Oct. 1549.
[50] Dowden, *Bishops*, 42–3; Watt and Murray, *Fasti*, 386–7. The records in question are Liber Sententiarum Officialis S Andree Principalis 1541–1553 (Edinburgh, NRS CH5/2/1) and the much more miscellaneous Liber Actorum Officialis S Andree 1546–1548/9 (Edinburgh, NRS CH5/2/3). See also S Ollivant, *The Court of the Official in Pre-Reformation Scotland*, Stair Society 34 (Edinburgh, 1982), at 8–9; G Donaldson, 'The Church Courts', in *An Introduction to Scottish Legal History*, Stair Society 20, (Edinburgh, 1958), 363–73.

et ruina, / Aliger, atra. ('O Father, winged One, would that you were avenged on harsh tyrants, who are always preying upon your lands, by a similar fate and dark ruin!') (*Ionis*, **2.13.41–4**)

Late in 1548 and in January 1549 we find MacLean writing flattering letters in verse to Sir David Lindsay of the Mount and to the earl of Arran, currying favour with them to win their support in his legal battle for the bishopric and commendatorship. He angrily denounces Patrick MacLean, begs Lindsay to speak up on his behalf (*te praecor in causa parce tacere mea*), and tells him that he will either be in the far west or in the eastern heat: *Atque ego seu fuero, qua uespertinus Iberno / Tytan flammigeros aequore tingit equos, / luthea seu roseas aperit qua Aurora fenestras, / urget ubi aeoos torrida zona lares* ('I, however, will either be where Titan at evening dips his flame-bearing horses in the Irish sea, or else where golden Dawn throws open her rose-coloured windows, where the scorched region oppresses the eastern homelands') (*Epistola*, **193–6**). In other words, he will either be in his rightful place in the Isles or else in Rome litigating for his rights.

The latter turned out to be the case. By April 1549 Roderick was back in Rome litigating for the bishopric and commendatorship.[51] Clearly, he still had, or had regained, the governor's support. On 8 June 1549 the pope responded *motu proprio* to a supplication in the name of Mary Queen of Scots (the petition therefore emanating from Arran), granting Iona Abbey *in commendam* to Roderick.[52] On 16 August 1549, a rival claimant, John Hay, the Scottish ambassador to France, abandoned his suit for the commendatorship in return for a pension, admitting Roderick's suitability because of his skill in the local language, which John lacked (*ob idiomatis loci peritiam que ab ipso Ioanne abest ac dicto Roderico inest*).[53] John Hay had probably never seriously expected to be provided to the commendatorship, but his application for the post was a means for him to obtain a pension from the fruits of the church while acting as ambassador to France.

In July and August 1549 a series of petitions was submitted to the pope in the names of the parsons of a number of churches in the Isles for canonries and dignities in the chapter of the cathedral of the Isles, 'while the dignities, canonries and prebends annexed to the said church have been detained by the English for about 100 years'.[54] These would have provided the cathedral with a chapter consisting of a dean, subdean, chancellor, treasurer, precentor, and

---

[51] The title page of the *Ionidos Liber* is dated May 1549. Appendix, p. 332.
[52] Rome, VA, RS 2664, f.151r. Below, Appendix, pp. 332–3.
[53] Rome, VA, RS 2668, f.185r. Below, Appendix, p. 335. For an analysis of the motives behind supplications which claim lack of Gaelic as a factor in the unsuitability of applicants for benefices, cf. I G MacDonald, '"That uncouth Dialect": English-speaking clergy in late medieval Gaelic Scotland', *RSCHS*, xliii (2014), 1–29.
[54] Rome, VA, RS 2664, f.155v; 2667, 298v–300r. Below, Appendix, pp. 333–5.

succentor, as well as an archdeacon.[55] These petitions can only have come from Roderick, who was perhaps now feeling more confident and aiming to develop a chapter of secular clergy for his cathedral.

The cathedral of Sodor or the Isles had had a rather shadowy existence for much of the fourteenth and fifteenth centuries. After the English had seized the Isle of Man in 1331, an episcopal election was held at Snizort on Skye,[56] but it was not until after the Great Schism of 1378 that there was a regular succession of Scottish bishops of the Isles, which continued after Scotland had accepted the obedience of Martin V in 1419. By 1433 they were using the church at Snizort as a cathedral,[57] and although canonries are occasionally mentioned, there is little evidence for a full chapter of cathedral dignitaries.[58] In 1499 the bishop, John Campbell, was granted the abbacy of Iona *in commendam*, and thereafter the abbey church was possibly used as a *de facto* cathedral, but without the Benedictine monks ever forming a cathedral chapter.[59] Donald Monro in 1549 claimed, somewhat inaccurately, that Iona Abbey 'was the Cathedral Kirk that the Bischoppis of the Ilis had sen the time thai were banist out the Ile of man be the Inglismen'.[60] Although Monro had been parson of Snizort, he had no knowledge of its previous use as a cathedral church. Roderick's actions in the summer of 1549 can be seen as the beginnings of an attempt to reorganise his cathedral and diocese, even before he had secured a final legal victory, and also to reward his own supporters.

Meanwhile, at the end of August 1549, there was a suggestion that Roderick should be provided to the bishopric of Clonmacnoise in Ireland.[61] This was possibly a legal ploy to give Roderick other options, without him ever seriously expecting to be provided to Clonmacnoise. In October 1549 Roderick successfully appealed to the Holy See in the case that the prior and convent of Iona Abbey had brought against him before the commissary court of the archbishopric of St Andrews, requesting that papal judges-delegate should

---

[55]   Below, Appendix, pp. 333–5.
[56]   *Diplomatarium Norvegicum* (1848–1972), xviii, no. 10; Watt & Murray, *Fasti*, 268–9.
[57]   *CSSR*, iv, no. 105. The church was on an island in the River Snizort beside Skeabost Bridge (NG 4148). The foundations of a substantial medieval church, about twenty-four metres in length, are visible, with smaller chapels or burial aisles and several late medieval West Highland gravestones: cf. RCAHMS, *Inventory of the Outer Hebrides, Skye and the Small Isles* (1928), 192–3.
[58]   Watt & Murray, *Fasti*, 268–9.
[59]   The best account of this complex subject is in Watt & Murray, *Fasti*, 257–69; cf. also Dilworth, 'Iona Abbey and the Reformation', 89.
[60]   *Monro's Western Isles*, 62. Monro's statement may reflect what was widely believed in the mid-sixteenth century.
[61]   Watt & Murray, *Fasti*, 266. With Ireland now firmly under the control of the Tudors, papal appointees could not have expected to get much or any revenue from their sees.

be appointed to hear the case.[62] The way was now clear for him finally to obtain the bishopric and commendatorship.

A further delay supervened, however, with the death of the eighty-one-year-old Pope Paul III on 10 November 1549. His death was followed by a long conclave deadlocked between French and imperial interests, during which the papal chancery was at a standstill; the new pope (Julius III) was not crowned until 8 February 1550. Thus, it was not until 5 March 1550 that the see of the Isles, described by the pope as vacant by the death of Farquhar Hectoris, was finally provided to Roderick by apostolic authority, and he resigned any claim he might have had to Clonmacnoise.[63]

Having obtained bulls of papal provision, however, he still had to make his way home and make his provision effective. In September 1550 he was described in a supplication to the pope as 'elect of the Isles', indicating that he had not yet been consecrated.[64] He still had to litigate before the Lords of Council against Patrick MacLean, brother of Hector MacLean of Duart, who was evidently resisting his papal provision. On 31 July 1551 he brought an action against Patrick MacLean before the Lords of Council. He finally won this action in Edinburgh on 16 January 1552, on the grounds that Patrick had failed to prove his right.[65] Six and a half years after the vacancy had first arisen, during which he had been forcibly exiled from Iona and required to make the long trip to Rome, Roderick finally vindicated his right to the bishopric of the Isles and commendatorship of Iona.

A few days later, on 26 January 1552, a provincial council of the Scottish bishops and clergy was held in Edinburgh. The records of this council do not include a list of those in attendance, but since business relating to the diocese of the Isles was discussed at the meeting, it is virtually certain that Roderick MacLean was present in his newly confirmed post as bishop of the Isles.[66] He may also have sat in Parliament in Edinburgh on 1 February 1552, but again the *sederunt* for this meeting does not survive.[67] His consecration probably took place round about this time.

He seems then to have held his bishopric in peace. He is found exercising his ordinary authority on 6 December 1552, now described as 'bishop' rather

---

[62] Rome, VA, RS 2672, f.38r. Below, Appendix, p. 335.

[63] Rome, VA, RV 1791, f.114r–116v. Below, Appendix, pp. 337–40. Cf. W M Brady, *The Episcopal Succession in England, Scotland and Ireland, A.D. 1400 to 1875* (Rome, 1876), i, 163; Dowden, *Bishops*, 292; Watt & Murray, *Fasti*, 266.

[64] Rome, VA, RS 2704, f. 210r–v. Below, Appendix, p. 336.

[65] *ADCP*, 610, 614; Watt & Shead, *Heads of Religious Houses*, 113–14. Cf. Munro, *Monro's Western Isles*, 14–15.

[66] D Patrick, *Statutes of the Scottish Church, 1225–1559* (Edinburgh, 1907), 135–48. Among its deliberations, the council enacted a statute stating that the register of testaments for the diocese of Sodor or the Isles should be made to conform to the practice of the rest of the kingdom: ibid., 137–8 and n.

[67] *APS*, ii, 483–9.

than 'elect'.[68] His consecration must therefore have taken place between 16 January and 6 December 1552, probably near the beginning of that period. He was present in the Privy Council at Perth on 19 June 1553.[69]

Sadly, however, he enjoyed peaceful possession of the bishopric for less than two years. On 26 November 1553 it was reported that he had died, probably shortly before that date.[70] His peaceful tenure of the bishopric was short, but by the time of his death he had triumphed over all adversity.

Internal evidence about MacLean's career within the poems

MacLean's long legal dispute over his right to the bishopric was not entirely sterile, however, as it provided a stimulus to him to write and publish poetry. The *Ionis* was published in Rome in May 1549. The only direct internal evidence given within the book itself (in **P 6**) is that it was composed after the death of James V and the accession of Mary on 14 December 1542. In *Ionis* Roderick MacLean describes himself as *exul in aeqora / qua Noesus nitido gurgite defluit* (**1.38**), 'an exile where Ness flows into the sea in a bright stream.' This is a poetical Latin rendering of Gaelic *Inbhir Nis*, Inverness. He seeks to return *postliminio*, 'to his rightful place'.[71] The flattering *Epistola* to Sir David Lindsay, written in October 1548, casts further light on the position in which he found himself. He followed this on New Year's Day 1549 with a letter to Governor Arran himself, with a flattering aside directed at George Gordon earl of Huntly.

We have seen that he was still resident on Iona and acting as vicar-general during the vacancy in 1546. When he was subsequently being denied peaceful possession of his bishopric and commendatorship, by the intrusion of Patrick MacLean, or by the legal action of the prior and convent of Iona Abbey, or both, he could have described himself as an exile who was being denied his *postliminium*. The most likely period for the writing of the *Ionis*, then, is between August 1547 and the beginning of 1549. The journey from Scotland to Rome usually took about three months; we know that he was still in Scotland at the beginning of January 1549 and that he was in Rome by April.

The *Ionis* provides some evidence about places he had visited in Scotland. He gives a vivid description of the Butt of Lewis and the stormy islands beyond (*ultra Leusiacas cautes*), a fit dwelling only for a *delphinum socius* (*Ionis*, **1.1.20–1**). We are reminded that MacLean was parson of Barvas. We have seen that he knew Inverness, and he describes the River Ness and its mouth (*Ionis*, **2.18.1–8**). He knew Skye: he identified Artbranán's harbour with

[68] *RSS*, iv, 1791.
[69] *RPC*, i, 141.
[70] *RSS*, iv, 2253.
[71] Sharpe, 'MacLean', 113, 127. The spelling *postliminio* on 113 is correct.

Portree: *portus hac in insula / secundus unda et flamine / a rege quem neoteri / portum uocant Gathelici*, where *oram mari conterminam / salicta texunt annua* (*Ionis*, **1.28**). Timothy Pont's map shows thick woodlands in the vicinity of Portree Loch.[72] He was for a time parson of Kilmaluag in Trotternish in Skye. He had no knowledge of any inhabitants of Skye prior to the Norse invasion, and assumed that Artbranán, as a non-Gaelic-speaking pagan, was also a Norseman. He sets another incident (*Ionis*, **2.17**) on Skye, *qua iam nemorosa scabro / finditur fluctu Schya continente / Hebris ab ora* ('where now well-wooded Skye ... is divided by the rough waters from the mainland shore'): again, Timothy Pont's map shows woodlands along the coast between Kyleakin and Kylerhea.[73]

As has been mentioned, he twice (*Ionis*, **2.4**, **2.22**) mentions places in the central Highlands high up in the Mounth: the sources of the Dee (*qua praeceps Dya de niuoso / uertice torret*) and the hill of An Sgarsoch (*in Monte Scarsiaco*). Since there is nothing in Adomnán to support these identifications, they must come from MacLean's imagination, and they may suggest that he had at some time made a journey in winter across the Mounth *via* Rannoch, Atholl, and Glen Tilt. The most likely destination for such a journey would be Aberdeen.

Nearer to home, he shows familiarity with Argyll (*Ora ... Gathaelica*), contrasting the still waters of Loch Awe (*lacus ... piger*) with the swift River Awe at Bonawe (*praeceps Abae per hostia*) (*Ionis*, **1.26.1–4**).

Above all, he shows familiarity with Iona, speaking of *fama Ionae me nutricis Insulae* ('the fame of Iona, the island which nurtured me' [*Ionis*, **P.3.37**]). He knew that there were innumerable cairns on its southern beaches, (*innumeros lapidum ... aceruos*), and that its southern seaways were approached *per saxa latentia et arcus, frendentes scopulos* ('through hidden rocks and arches, and gnashing cliffs'), a reference to the cliffs and arches of Carsaig and the Torran Rocks (*Ionis*, **1.1.46–8**). He identified the hill on which Columba would sit watching the sea with Dùn Ì, which he calls *Mons Ionius* (*Ionis*, **1.25.4**) and *Collis ... Yaei* (*Ionis*, **2.4.1**). He knew that in early summer nursing animals were taken from spring pastures on Iona to shielings on the Ross of Mull (*Rossiae ... ad oram*) while the fields of the island were given over to corn (*Ionis*, **2.19.5–8**). Among the crops grown on Iona, he tells us plausibly, were *auena, faba, triticum, / ceresque et ordeacea* ('oats, beans, wheat, corn and barley') (*Ionis*, **1.30.7–8**). He mentions *Angeli Cliuus*, the hill that Adomnán calls both *colliculus angelorum* and *cnoc angel*, 'the angels' hill' (*Ionis*, **2.35.35**). This is traditionally identified with a gently sloping knoll at Sìthean (= 'fairy hill') overlooking the western Machair of Iona, which is now called *Cnoc nan Aingeal*: MacLean's word *cliuus* describes it well.[74]

---

[72] Stone, *Illustrated Maps of Scotland*, pl. 43, p. 89.
[73] Ibid.
[74] Cf. Sharpe, *Adomnán*, n. 385, 368.

There may be hints in *Ionis* of a familiarity with places in Ireland (which we know he visited in 1542), but these are faint. In **2.14** he mentions 'the city where the metropolitan cathedral stands' (*in urbe prominet qua metropolis* [**2.14.4**–5]), where the *Clyathus amnis* flows, perhaps a reference to the tower of Christ Church Cathedral near the Liffey. Strictly speaking, the name *Áth Cliath*, 'ford of hurdles', refers to a crossing point on the Liffey at Dublin rather than to the river itself. The place *qua leuat cultis Laginaeus aruis oppida campus* ('where the Plain of Leinster raises towns in cultivated fields') could be a reference to Kildare, with its towers rising above the fertile plains of the Curragh. The report by the Jesuit missionaries in 1542 is quite vague when it comes to geographical detail, so we cannot be sure what places in Ireland he had visited. On the other hand, in **2.4.6**–8, MacLean has totally misunderstood Adomnán's reference to *riuulo … Ailbine* as the River Delvin in the north of County Dublin and *uadum Clied* as the ford of the Liffey at Dublin itself. In **2.30.88 ff.** he mentions Derry, but the description is quite vague. It is possible that *euripo curuas celerante puppes* could refer to the narrowing of the Foyle downstream from Derry, but this is not certain. In **2.30** he confuses Durrow and Derry (whose Irish names are similar), in a way that suggests he had no knowledge of the former.

Roderick MacLean's relatives and Iona

Roderick's immediate predecessor as bishop of the Isles and abbot of Iona was his brother Fearchar or Farquhar MacLean. This brother had previously been a Benedictine monk of Iona, and was a natural son of Farquhar MacEachainn MacLean of Kingairloch. The legal wranglings surrounding his provision are complex and obscure,[75] but he seems to have been effectively bishop and commendator of Iona from 1530 until his death in 1545. Little is known about Farquhar or his period as bishop, and few documents relating to him survive.[76] He may have become ill in the last year or so of his life, prompting him to contemplate resigning in favour of Roderick, his younger brother. There is no surviving monument or memorial to him on Iona.

Among the funerary monuments preserved on Iona, however, is a stone commemorating Anna, daughter of Donald son of Tearlach, prioress of Iona, who died in 1543. It has been described as 'unquestionably the most remarkable tombstone of the entire West Highland series'.[77] It is of particular interest to us, as the Anna in question was a close relative of Farquhar and

[75] Dowden, *Bishops*, 291–2; Watt & Murray, *Fasti*, 265-6; Watt & Shead, *Heads of Religious Houses*, 113. T W Graham, 'Patronage, Provision and Reservation: Scotland and the Papacy during the Pontificate of Paul III' (Ph.D. thesis, Glasgow University, 1992), Chapter 2, pp. 29–30.

[76] Cf. *James V Letters*, 162–3, 209; Steer & Bannerman, *Sculpture*, 116–7; *Book of the Thanes of Cawdor*, 156–8; Dilworth, 'Iona Abbey and the Reformation', 85–6, 91–4.

[77] Steer & Bannerman, *Sculpture*, 70.

Figure 2. The tombstone of Anna MacLean, prioress of Iona Nunnery, who died 1543. She was cousin of Farquhar and Roderick MacLean; the stone was carved while Roderick was resident and active on Iona. From H D Graham, *Antiquities of Iona* (1850).

Roderick MacLean, and the stone was carved while Roderick was resident and active on Iona.

The stone is no longer complete: it formerly lay in the chancel of the nunnery close to the high altar, and was broken by the collapse of the vault *c.* 1830.[78] Fortunately, before this date the part of its main inscription which is now lost (placed here within square brackets) had been recorded by Edward Lhuyd in 1699 and by Martin Martin in 1703. The complete inscription read: **[hic iacet dña anna dona]ldi terleti filia quondã priorissa de iona que obit año mo. do. xl. iii eius / ãiam altissimo cõmendam(u)s**. A second inscription, across the middle of the slab, reads: **sancta maria ora pro me**. These can be translated: '[Here lies Lady Anna, daughter of Dona]ld, son of Tearlach, late Prioress of Iona, who died AD 1543. We commend her soul to the Most High. Holy Mary, pray for me'.[79]

Anna's grandfather Tearlach was also great-grandfather to Farquhar and Roderick MacLean, so the brothers were her first cousins once removed.[80] The three died within a few years of each other (1543, 1545, and 1553). Anna may have been relatively long-lived: an act of the Privy Council in 1509 mentions 'Agnes daughter of Donald MacLean, Prioress of Iona'.[81] This is undoubtedly the same person. We have seen above, however, that Roderick was probably born *c.* 1500–05.

There are several points worthy of note regarding Prioress Anna's tombstone. One of them is its quite personal nature. Anna is portrayed as a large, heavily built woman with a round face (in contrast with other effigies probably by the same sculptor,[82] and also in contrast to her portrayal on Tiree (for which see below). She is shown with two lapdogs, sitting one on either side of her monastic cloak. Above her head, which rests on a pillow supported by two angels, are a mirror and comb. These symbols occur frequently on Pictish sculptures of a much earlier period, but are most unusual on sculptures of this date and locality. Could this indicate an antiquarian interest in Pictish art on the part of the person or persons who commissioned the monument?

Another point is that this is the only inscription in the West Highland corpus which contains the modern form of the name *Iona*. Others have forms like *I*, *Y*, and *Hi*.[83] Since Roderick repeats several times the pun on Iona and Jonah, one is tempted to wonder if he played a part in popularising the form *Iona*, and perhaps in composing his cousin's inscription. (The misreading *Iona*, for

---

[78]   RCAHMS, *Argyll*, iv: *Iona*, 164–5, 232.
[79]   Ibid., 118–9, and Plate 27; RCAHMS, *Argyll*, iv: *Iona*, 232, and plates on 233; Martin, 262.
[80]   Cf. the family tree in Steer & Bannerman, *Sculpture*, 131.
[81]   *RSS*, i, 1797; Steer & Bannerman, *Sculpture*, 119.
[82]   cf. Ibid., Plate 27, A, C and D.
[83]   Ibid., 119; cf. Watson, *CPNS*, 87–90.

Adomnán's *Ioua*, is probably first found in manuscripts of Fordun's *Chronica*, completed *c*. 1385. It also appears in late manuscripts of *VC*.)[84]

The stone has points of detail which connect it with a number of stones at Oronsay Priory, and it is strikingly similar to a stone with an inscription commemorating **bricius canonicus macmurich**, Gille-Brigde Mac Mhuirich, canon of Oronsay.[85] These stones belong to what is called the 'Oronsay school' of stone carving. Thus, the MacLeans at Iona were able to patronise a highly skilled mason whose main centre of activity was Oronsay.

Anna MacLean also appears on another stone with an inscription. There is a cross-shaft at Soroby on Tiree which belongs stylistically to the first half of the sixteenth century. On one face there is an image of St Michael slaying the dragon and below it Death leads away a female ecclesiastic. In between there is an inscription which reads: **hic est crux michael' archangeli dei. anna priorisa de Y**.[86] The dress of the female ecclesiastic on the stone on Tiree is similar to that of Anna MacLean on her tombstone, though she is not so heavily built. We know of a close continuing connection between Iona and Tiree in the late medieval period.[87]

Anna was succeeded as prioress of the nunnery by Mary or Marion MacLean, a sister of Farquhar and Roderick. She had a precept of admission from the Privy Council in 1548, and was still prioress in 1567. She was still alive in 1574.[88] Female members of the family of MacLean of Kingairloch thus dominated the nunnery of Iona for over half a century. During part of this time Farquhar was monk of Iona then commendator and bishop of the Isles, while Roderick was archdeacon and then bishop of the Isles and commendator of Iona Abbey.

James Thorntoun and other persons mentioned in the book

There is a puzzling Greek inscription on the title page of *Ionis*.[89] The Greek name ΘΟΡΧΘΟΝΟΣ (gen.) is not found elsewhere. The second element is χθών, gen. χθονός, 'earth, ground'. In the context it seems to be used as equivalent to Scots *toun* or Gaelic *baile*.[90] The prefix θορ- is not Greek. His designation ΤΗΣ ΈΚΚΛΗΣΊΑΣ ῬΟΣΣΕΩΣ ὙΠΟΔΕΚΆΔΟΡΟΣ (gen.) indicates that James or

---

[84] Cf. Anderson, *VC*, lxxiii n.; Sharpe, *Adomnán*, 257–9.

[85] RCAHMS, *Argyll*, v: *Islay, Jura, Colonsay and Oronsay*, 247-51; Steer & Bannerman, *Sculpture*, Plates 26, 27.

[86] Steer & Bannerman, *Sculpture*, 102, and Plate 35B; RCAHMS, *Argyll*, iii: *Mull, Tiree, Coll & Northern Argyll*, 169, and Plate 34A-B.

[87] Steer & Bannerman, *Sculpture*, 102; *Collectanea de Rebus Albanicis*, 2.

[88] *RSS*, iii, 2861; *RSS*, v, 3255; Steer & Bannerman, *Sculpture*, 119: RCAHMS, *Argyll*, iv: *Iona*, 179 and n. 29 on 277.

[89] Sharpe, 'MacLean', 113–14.

[90] MacLean, having studied at Wittenberg, will have known that the element -χθών was used by Melanchthon to translate the second element in his German surname Schwartzerdt (= 'black earth').

his father was subdean of Ross. The subdean of Ross from *c.* 1525 was John Thorntoun; he had a son or nephew James who succeeded him until 1577.[91] John Thorntoun was for many years a Scottish procurator or solicitor largely resident at the Roman *curia*.[92] He also held the precentorship of Moray at this time, and was succeeded by James Thorntoun, who died in 1577 – evidently the same James Thorntoun.[93] John Thorntoun also had some connection to the provostry of Tain in 1544, and litigated also for other benefices.[94] James Thorntoun appears to have been in Rome in 1549 at the same time as Roderick MacLean, for he submitted a number of supplications regarding succession to his father's benefices in the summer of 1549.[95] It seems very likely, then, that John Thorntoun was acting as MacLean's solicitor and procurator in his legal case for the bishopric of the Isles at the Roman *curia* in 1549.

Can we identify the φίλεχθρος ἀνὴρ, 'man who loves enmity', with any certainty?[96] Since this person was σεμνοπροσωπός, 'of solemn countenance', he was probably a clergyman. We should most likely consider the clergy intruded at Iona during and after Dòmhnall Dubh's uprising: Roderick MacAllister, described as bishop elect of the Isles, and Patrick MacLean, brother of MacLean of Duart, 'bailie of Iona'. MacAllister was accepted as elect of the Isles by the Council of the Isles and Henry VIII in 1545–46, but he is not heard of thereafter,[97] and his claim passed to Patrick MacLean. Roderick expresses extreme bitterness and hostility towards Patrick MacLean in the *Epistola elegiaca*, calling him a traitor, bastard, and huckster, and casting doubt on his paternity (*Epistola*, **155 ff**.). He litigated successfully against Patrick MacLean before the royal council in 1551–52.[98]

Although Patrick MacLean is the most likely contender, Roderick also had other opponents. He had a dispute with the prior and convent of Iona Abbey in 1547–48 over a claim to certain goods of the abbey and other matters. He

---

91   Watt & Murray, *Fasti*, 368.
92   *Inchcolm Charters*, 198–200. Cf. also T Graham, 'Patronage, Provision and Reservation: Scotland and the Papacy during the Pontificate of Paul III' (Ph.D. thesis, Glasgow University, 1992), Chapters 4 and 5 passim, esp. pp. 139—42, 154. John Thornton appears frequently as a procurator in the papal registers of the period: cf. A Macquarrie, *Calendar of Entries in the Papal Registers relating to Great Britain and Ireland: Papal Letters*, xxiii, 1 (Dublin, 2018), index, s.n. Thornton.
93   Ibid., 225.
94   Ibid., 374. Cf. Donaldson, *Scottish Reformation*, 16–17, where Thorntoun is (perhaps unfairly) held up as a flagrant example of a pluralist. As a solicitor, he may have applied in his own name for benefices on behalf of others. The provostry of Tain may have been the prebend of the subdean of Ross.
95   Rome, VA, RS 2672, f.75r–v; 2675, f.121v–122r; 2675, f.137r–v; cf. also 2675, f.278v.
96   Rendered 'the man who likes to be at odds with his fellows' by Durkan, in McRoberts, *Essays*, xvi; 'a man fond of quarrelling', by Sharpe, 'MacLean', 119: ἔcqroς = 'hating, hostile'. A one-word translation might be 'quarrelsome'.
97   Watt & Murray, *Fasti*, 266.
98   Watt & Shead, *Heads of Religious Houses*, 114.

expressed hostility towards John Spittal, official of the commissary court of St Andrews, who summoned him at the instance of the prior and convent.[99] Another rival seems to have been John Hay, the Scottish ambassador to France, who resigned his right to the commendatorship of Iona in exchange for a pension in October 1549, conceding Roderick's skill in the local language (*ob idiomatis loci peritiam*). So there are a number of possible contenders; but of these Patrick MacLean, half-brother of MacLean of Duart, emerges as the most likely contender for the role of φίλεχθρος ἀνήρ.

A clergyman called John Forman wrote a few lines in recommendation of MacLean's book (**P4**). There was a John Forman, a student in logic at Paris before 1505,[100] later claimant to the precentorship of Glasgow Cathedral by 1509, who was still alive in 1543.[101] He was probably a kinsman of Robert Forman, dean of Glasgow 1505–30, who had previously been precentor of Glasgow 1500–05.[102] A John Forman tried to get provision to the abbacy of Kilwinning *in commendam* in 1512–14, but was ultimately unsuccessful.[103] A John Forman, clerk of St Andrews diocese, unsuccessfully sought provision to Coldingham Priory in 1523.[104] Forman's little verse shows that poems by MacLean had been circulating in Scotland before the publication of *Ionis* in Rome in May 1549. Whether these were psalm paraphrases, or drafts of *Ionis*, or other poems now lost, is uncertain.

THE POEMS

MacLean's Psalm Paraphrases

Before he turned to *Vita Columbae*, MacLean had, as he tells us, written many (*quamplurima*) verse psalm paraphrases. The only one known to survive is the paraphrase of Psalm 1 in elegiac couplets which he appended to these poems, as he says, to fill a blank page (*ne pagina remaneret uacua*). Although he says that it is only included to fill the page, and it does not form part of *Ionis*, it does make a fitting and satisfying close to the book as a whole.[105]

We know (title page, **P3**, **P4**) that MacLean had been criticised for some of his earlier poetry, and in **P3** he attacks his critics with some vigour. He complains that adolescents and children learning the alphabet speak with

[99] Rome, VA, RS 2672, f.38r.
[100] Durkan & Kirk, *University of Glasgow*, 195.
[101] Watt & Murray, *Fasti*, 206.
[102] Ibid., 201, 206. *Glasgow Registrum*, ii, 503–4.
[103] Ibid., 206; Watt & Shead, *Heads of Religious Houses*, 128–9; *CPR*, xix, nos. 596–600, 878, 894, 1416,
[104] Watt & Shead, *Heads of Religious Houses*, 39–40.
[105] Commentary in R P H Green, 'Poetic Psalm paraphrases: two versions of Psalm 1 compared', in *Acta Conventus Neo-Latini Budapestinensis*, ed. R Schnur (Tempe, 2010).

greater boldness than did the ancient philosophers, while some boast of knowledge because of their mature years, without having gained appropriate qualifications, and some who do have qualifications have bought them with money. (We know that MacLean had matriculated *gratis*, presumably the equivalent of a scholarship, at Wittenberg in 1534.) Some, he says, will pick a fight with anybody, while others are masters of the one-word put-down, 'generous with insults, never bountiful with praise'. His critics are rustics (*agrestes*), easily bewitched and uninspired. He dismisses them as perverse (*praeposteros*), and appeals to the reader not to be swayed by them.

John Forman (**P4**) also implies that MacLean had been criticised for his poetry, and challenges the critics to be forbearing *uestra in lucem carmina donec eant* ('until your own verses see the light of day').[106] It is clear from this that poems of MacLean's had previously been circulating in Scotland. We may guess that he had previously published poetry, possibly some of his psalm paraphrases. We do not know where these were published. The standard of accuracy in printing in Scotland, for example, of *Breviarium Aberdonense* in 1510, printed by Walter Chepman and Andrew Myllar, was not high.[107] There is little evidence about printing in the following years, apart from *Compassio Beate Marie* of *c.* 1520, printed, rather more carefully, by the otherwise unknown John Story.[108] It may be that, like the *Ionidos Liber*, MacLean's earlier poetry was printed abroad. We know that he was in France and Rome in 1542–43. It is speculation, but it might be suggested that he could have published a volume of poems, possibly psalm paraphrases, in Rome, or elsewhere on the continent, in 1542–43, which had had a poor reception in Scotland on his return. When he was excluded from Iona in late 1547 or 1548, he may have returned to writing poetry, hoping to vindicate his reputation for poetry as well as to enhance his chances of obtaining the bishopric, and perhaps also to fill his enforced idleness in Inverness. The *Epistola elegiaca* and *Straena gratulatoria* of 1548–49 are examples of MacLean using verse to try to gain favour.

Ionis: Metre

The rich variety of metres used by MacLean, especially in the first quarter of the *Ionis*, is remarkable. The preliminary materials, which (following Richard Sharpe) have been numbered **P1–P6**, show the following metres:[109]

---

[106] This shows that George Buchanan was not among his critics, as he had been publishing poetry earlier. Buchanan's psalm paraphrases appeared later, and they are unlikely to have influenced MacLean. Cf. R P H Green, *George Buchanan: Poetic Paraphrase of the Psalms of David* (Geneva, 2011), esp. 18–19.

[107] Macquarrie, *Legends of Scottish Saints*, pp. xxxiv–xxxvii.

[108] Ibid., 314–16.

[109] The edition of Horace whose classification has been used here is N Rudd, *Horace: Odes and Epodes* (Cambridge, Massachussetts, 2004). His system is not always in agreement with that used in Sharpe, 'MacLean', 120 ff. The symbols used here represent, by convention:

P1 Elegiac couplets

　_ ∪∪ _ ∪∪ _ | ∪∪ _ ∪∪ _ ∪∪ _ ∪
　_ ∪∪ _ ∪∪ _ | _ ∪∪ _ ∪∪ _

P2 Elegiac couplets

P3 Iambic trimeter (cf. Horace, Epodes 17)

　∪ _ ∪ _ ∪ | _ ∪ _ ∪ _ ∪∪ ∪

P4 Elegiac couplets

P5 Modified third Asclepiad: four Asclepiad lines + one Glyconic (see below)

P6 A genealogy in prose. (Not, strictly speaking, part of *Ionis*.)

Book 1 then begins with the use of a variety of Horatian metres. Following a paraphrase of Adomnán's i,1 in dactylic hexameters (1.1), for the next eight poems of Book 1 (1.2–1.9) MacLean uses the same metres in the same order that Horace uses in *Odes* 1.2–9.[110] These are preceded by MacLean's introduction to his subject (P5) in what has been described as a hybrid of the metres of *Odes* 1.1 (continuous Asclepiad lines) and of *Odes* 1.6 (three Asclepiad lines followed by one Glyconic). It consists of stanzas of four Asclepiad lines followed by one Glyconic, and is a form not used by Horace. Then follows the paraphrase of Adomnán's i.1 in hexameters.

Metre		Horace
1.1	Hexameter	Satires, Epistles

　_ ∪∪ _ ∪∪ _ | ∪∪ _ ∪∪ _ ∪∪ _ ∪

| **1.2** | Sapphic stanzas | Odes 1.2 |

　_ ∪ _ _ _ ∪∪ _ ∪ _ ∪
　_ ∪ _ _ _ ∪∪ _ ∪ _ ∪
　_ ∪ _ _ _ ∪∪ _ ∪ _ ∪
　　_ ∪∪ _ ∪

| **1.3** | Second Asclepiad | Odes 1.3 |

　_ _ _ ∪ _ ∪∪
　_ _ _ ∪ _ | _ ∪∪ _ ∪∪

| **1.4** | Fourth Archilochian | Odes 1.4 |

　_ ∪∪ _ ∪∪ _ ∪∪ | _ ∪ _ ∪ _ _
　　∪ _ ∪ _ _ | _ ∪ _ ∪ _ _

　_ = long; ∪ = short; ∪ = either short or long; ∪ ∪ = either one long or two short syllables. A vertical stroke | marks the caesura.

[110] R P H Green, 'Poetic Psalm paraphrases: two versions of Psalm 1 compared', in J P Barea et al., *Acta Conventus Neo-Latini Budapestinensis* (Tempe, 2010), 261–70; cf. Sharpe, 'MacLean', 112, 121–3.

1.5   Fourth Asclepiad   Odes 1.5

　　　_ _ _ U U _ | _ U U _ U U̲
　　　_ _ _ U U _ | _ U U _ U U̲
　　　　　_ _ _ U U _ U̲
　　　　　_ _ _ U U _ U U̲

1.6   Third Asclepiad   Odes 1.6

　　　_ _ _ U U _ | _ U U _ U U̲
　　　_ _ _ U U _ | _ U U _ U U̲
　　　_ _ _ U U _ | _ U U _ U U̲
　　　　　_ _ _ U U _ U U̲

1.7   Alcmanic   Odes 1.7

　　_ U̲U̲ _ U̲U̲ _ | U̲U̲ _ U̲U̲ _ U U _ U̲
　　　　_ U̲U̲ _ U̲U̲ _ U̲U̲ _ U̲

1.8   Greater Sapphic   Odes 1.8

　　　　_ U U _ U _ _
　　_ U _ _ _ U U _ | _ U U _ _

1.9   Alcaic   Odes 1.9

　　U _ U _ _ | _ U U _ U U̲
　　U _ U _ _ | _ U U _ U U̲
　　U _ U _ _ _ U _ U̲
　　_ U _ U U _ U _ U̲

For MacLean's **1.10–1.13** the correspondences with Horace are as follows:

MacLean   Horace
1.10 Hipponactean   Odes 2.18

　　　_ U _ U _ U U̲
　　　U̲ _ U _ U̲| _ U _ U _ _

1.11 Ionic *a minore*   Odes 3.12
A succession of ionic metra:
　　　U U _ _ etc.

The line division is uncertain. Sharpe comments that in MacLean's division, into lines of three feet, three feet, four feet, 'he was probably following the text of Horace familiar to him.'[111]

---

[111] Sharpe, 'MacLean', 123. The university library at Wittenberg in 1536 had a copy of an edition of Horace by Antonio Mancinelli printed at Venice in 1492–93: S Kusukawa, *A Wittenberg University Library Catalogue of 1536*, Medieval and Renaissance Texts and Studies 890 (Binghamton, 1995), 148.

1.12 First Archilochian   Odes 4.7

A dactylic hexameter followed by a hemiepes (i.e. half a dactylic hexameter):

_ U U _ U U _ | U U _ U U _ U U _ U
    _ U U _ U U U

1.13 Third Asclepiad   Odes 1.6
See **1.6** above.

At this point, about halfway through Book 1, the poet lapses into continuous octosyllabic lines, which he calls iambic dimeter.[112]

U _ U _ U _ U U

The printer has set these up in double column to save space. Horace uses strophes which incorporate an iambic dimeter in the *Epodes*, but always paired with longer lines (iambic trimeter in *Epodes*, 1–10, dactylic hexameters in *Epodes*, 14 and 15). The use of the continuous iambic dimeter is not found in Horace. Iambic metre is quite flexible, allowing for the substitution of a spondee in the odd-numbered feet. In Roderick's iambics (**1.14–37**), the third and penultimate syllables of each line are always short, the even-numbered syllables are (almost) always long, and no line ends in a monosyllable except in elision.

The final peroration at the end of Book 1 (**1.38**) is in the Third Asclepiad stanza, found in Horace, Odes I.6, previously used by MacLean in **1.6** and **1.13**.[113]

Book 2, by contrast, does not show the same rich variety of Horatian metres, but is paraphrased entirely in Sapphic stanzas (see above). The choice of Sapphic stanzas for what is largely narrative verse might be thought curious; but many of the Gaelic bardic metres with which MacLean would have been familiar, including those used for narrative verse, consisted of four-line stanzas, and this may have influenced his choice of metres.[114]

The paraphrase of Psalm 1 which is appended on the last folio, *ne pagina remaneret vacua*, is in elegiac couplets.

There is no obvious reason for the contrast between the complexity and variety of the Horatian poems at the beginning of Book 1 and the relative simplicity of the iambic verse that follows; to try to find a reason necessarily involves a degree of speculation. One possible suggestion might be that MacLean began drafting his poems in Book 1 in iambic dimeter, but then changed his plan (perhaps having studied Horace's *Odes*) and began reworking them in more varied Horatian metres until he ran out of time. At the end

---

[112] Sharpe, 'MacLean', 123. Cf. Gildersleeve & Lodge, para. 765.
[113] Quoted in Sharpe, 'MacLean', 127; the last line should read *postliminio* (cf. ibid., 113).
[114] Cf. E Knott, *Irish Syllabic Poetry*, 1200–1600 (Dublin, 1928, reprinted 2011).

of **1.1** he announces that he is going to continue the poem in iambic verse (**1.1.129**: *melius quoque fiet iambis*), but he does not in fact do so until **1.14**. Possibly, then, he changed his plan, but ran out of time.

That the poem was completed hastily may be suggested by the total absence of a paraphrase of Adomnán's Book iii. *VC*, iii contains some of Adomnán's finest and most inspired writing, and MacLean could not have failed to be impressed by it. His manuscript of *VC* must have contained Book iii, because he includes a (very loose) paraphrase of *VC*, iii, 1, and he mentions people and incidents in a way which implies a full knowledge of material in Book iii which he does not cover in his verses; he also echoes some of Adomnán's language from Book iii.[115] Yet his book is complete as it stands and nothing is missing. We know this because (as he tells us) once he saw the layout of the book with an almost completely blank folio at the end, he tacked on a suitable Psalm paraphrase in elegiac couplets (possibly from memory) as an afterthought to fill the blank space. If he had to hurry his poem to a completion to meet a deadline, this could explain the absence of a paraphrase of almost all of Adomnán's Book iii.

There is one example in *Ionis* of a passage from Adomnán being paraphrased in two different ways. After **1.19**, MacLean includes a short poem of twenty lines beginning *O mors beata uisio*. This is a brief meditation on the passage from death to eternal life, and it ends with an invocation of Columba as a mediator with the deity. (Such invocatory language is rarely used by MacLean, who mostly portrays Columba as a powerful holy man whose example is to be followed, rather than as a mediator of salvation.) It is a paraphrase of a passage from near the end of Adomnán's Book iii, 23, which may have formed the original ending of Adomnán's work.[116] This poem is then used as a refrain after sections **1.20**, **1.21**, **1.22**, **1.23**, **1.24**, **1.26**, **1.28**, **1.29**, **1.30** (with its opening four lines altered), **1.33**, **1.34**, and **1.35**.[117] In **1.5**, a poem in the Fourth Asclepiad stanza, MacLean ends with a similar peroration (though without invocation of Columba as a mediator), beginning *Foelix exilium*. These lines could be regarded as an adaptation of the 'Refrain' section to the more complex Fourth Asclepiad stanza. Alternatively, the 'Refrain' *O mors beata uisio* might be viewed as a simplification of the *Foelix exilium* passage into iambics. But the latter explanation is less likely: the 'Refrain' *O mors beata uisio* in iambic verse is considerably closer to the original Adomnán than is the *Foelix exilium* passage in asclepiad verse, which departs further from the original. For the most part, MacLean delights in metrical complexity and in

---

[115] For example: mea fata cernes, 2.21.10, referring to *VC*, iii, 23; uisu ... meridiano, 1.1.87, echoing *VC*, iii, 19; O mors beata uisio, etc., 1.19.17 ff., paraphrasing the end of *VC*, iii, 23.

[116] Anderson, 232.

[117] Sharpe, 'MacLean', 124.

showing off his skill. It must be admitted, however, that it is speculation to try to reconstruct the order in which MacLean composed his book.

MacLean's two surviving occasional poems, addressed to Sir David Lindsay and to the governor, are in elegiac couplets, like his one surviving psalm paraphrase. So, in all we see that he was skilled in hexameters, elegiacs, sapphics, iambics, and a variety of Horatian lyric metres.

Ionis: *Stylistic considerations*

Roderici Maclenii Hectorogenis Scoti Gathaelici Ionitae de intuitu prophetico D. Columbae Ionidos Liber: readers of this impressive and imposing declaration of Roderick's authorship might gain the wrong initial impression from its dignity and formality (and indeed from the following liminary pages), which arguably belie the remarkable freshness and simplicity of the *Ionis* and the novelty of its treatment of Saint Adomnán's reports of Columba's 'prophetic insight'. This title page is followed by various preparatory material, in classical verse of various kinds, which should not detain today's reader, though the *ad lectorem* ('to the reader'), distinctly modest in aim and in size (does anyone today other than the most devoted professional normally read a sixteenth-century *ad lectorem* to the end?), deserves a mention for the sake of at least one line: the last of its four neat couplets carries a warning: 'beware of the poison of new-fangled Minerva'. (Minerva was, among other things, the goddess of learning in the ancient world). This refers to nothing in MacLean's book but is a general warning of the 'new learning' which might well divert the reader from traditional piety. The poetics implied here are not unusual (such warnings about the classical tradition had been made so often since the beginnings of Christian verse over one thousand years before), but one detects a reference to something else called 'neoteric' or new, and this deserves a word.

Today, scholars busily engage (even in Scotland) with what is termed, for obvious reasons, neo-Latin. This movement could be said to have reached a climax (or one of its many waves or peaks) at the time Roderick wrote, shortly before the middle of the sixteenth century. The Latin in the remainder of the preface shows the fruit of this, and it could not have been written without a background of such study. This neo-Latin movement (the term is modern, the notion is not) had long been studied with two key notions – inspiration and imitation. The best-known exponent of such a world-view is perhaps Erasmus, with his eagerness to write top-class Latin of classical exactitude, but there were many Latin poets who imitated classical versification and ideas, and who sought inspiration therefrom. The one classical poet that concerns us now (and concerned many of MacLean's contemporaries) is Horace.

To use Horace (in part, it should be added) was an inspired choice, and the outcome in the *Ionis* was a surprising one. Horace was a prolific poet, and it is usual to divide his great and varied output into six main types of poetry, each strikingly different; but it is the hundred or so *Odes* that are relevant to MacLean. In general, Horace's vocabulary is rich (and sometimes unusually so for his day); his topics range widely – from political/eulogistic poems, to ones that apparently address concerns of simple people or popular philosophy. They may occasionally be religious in nature. MacLean may have read some Horace early in life: we cannot tell. In the *Ionis* he does not need classical inspiration, and imitation is not his line, except in relation to one, remarkable area, and that is metre. Each of the poems in the earlier part of the first of his two books is in a different metre, and these metres are all metres used by Horace for his *Odes*; some twenty in all, but MacLean saw the possibilities for the rhythms and verbal music of his own collection. (There is no sign of formal musical accompaniment). He is almost certainly a pioneer: it was several years before the Psalm paraphrases of George Buchanan were printed and known to readers; in any case, Buchanan varies his metres, sometimes repeats a metre, and even innovates in metre a little.[118]

With the singular exception of metre, then, Roderick's style, like his subject matter, is very different from that of Horace. He has his own style (quite unlike most of the perhaps forgettable writing in the prefatory material), and this facilitates readability. A typical one from among his odes (that is not his name, in fact) will be seen to contain a simple statement of the theme of a chapter of Adomnán, the *vaticinium* or prophecy, then a brief scene-setting – local place-names are an essential feature – and then the neat telling of the tale: someone is saved from the predicted storm; or the spilling of an inkpot in the monastery is put right at once. Within the boundaries of the metre the language flows easily (*ars celare artem*). As the two of us in our preliminary readings proceeded to identify and discuss our translations, the problems, whether due to the orthography of another age, the language (seldom but sometimes unclassical), the word order, or anything else, were not many.

Of course, one would like to know much more about the man's education, especially in his early years, and of opportunities that existed. Autodidaxis cannot be the complete answer; he learnt much in the monastic community, no doubt, but much, too, perhaps, in formal teaching at school, whether locally on Iona or nearby, or in Stirling or Glasgow.[119] No doubt he took with him a good knowledge of Latin to Wittenberg, and no doubt he developed it there in one way or another. That was an important time for him, but nothing in his German experience, or in early German neo-Latin or sacred Latin can be

---

[118] The latest critical edition is R P H Green, *Poetic Paraphrases of the Psalms of David* (Geneva, 2011). The question of whether Buchanan and MacLean ever met, or influenced one another, is briefly raised in R P H Green, 'Poetic Psalm paraphrases: two versions of Psalm 1 compared', in *Proceedings of the Thirteenth International Congress of Neo-Latin Studies* (Tempe, 2010), 261–70, at 270.

[119] The masterly study of John Durkan, *Scottish Schools and Schoolmasters, 1560–2013* (Edinburgh, 2013) may be supplemented by various articles of his relating the earlier period in *The Innes Review, passim.*

seen to have influenced the *Ionis*, and nothing in the 'Delights of German [Latin] Poets' (published in the next century) is comparable. MacLean's later Latin verse shows maturity and a breadth of skills, but nothing so fresh and astonishing as the poems on Columba.

Language and Vocabulary

Many of MacLean's renderings of Gaelic names are of names taken from Adomnán, and simply reflect a classicisation of Adomnán's spellings (cf. the section *MacLean's text of* Vita Columbae below). But there are some names which are of greater interest.

Names used for Iona

MacLean's names for Iona, both as nouns and adjectives, are quite inventive and show some fluidity. The following is a representative sampling, and it is not intended to be comprehensive.

Title page: Ionitae (= of Iona); Ionidos (gen. = of the song of Iona: see below).

Preliminaries: **P2. heading**, Ionam; **P2.1**, Iona (voc.). **P3.37**, Ionae (gen.).

Book 1: **1.1.30**, Ya ... insula (nom.); **1.1.38**, Ionaeos ... campos (acc. pl. adj.); **1.1.40**, Ionida. **1.2.9**, Ionae. **1.6.17**, gregis ... Ionii (gen.). **1.7.14**, coetus Ionius (adj.). **1.13.30**, patribus ... Ioniis (dat. pl.). **1.18.11**, Ionida ... insulam (adj. acc.). **1.24.5**, Ionide (abl.). **1.25.4**, Mons Ionius (= Dùn Ì). **1.26.8**, Ionidum Colonia (= community of monks of Iona). **1.27.3**, Ionide (abl.). **1.35.9**, Ionide (abl.); **1.35.24**, Ionam. **1.38.1**, lumen Ionidum (= of the people of Iona).

Book 2: **2.3.3**, Ionitae monachi; **2.3.12**, Yaeo (adj. dat.). **2.15.25**, Ionam. **2.19. heading**, Insulae Ionae; **2.19.5**, Ionitae ... coloni. **2.21.12**, Iona. **2.30.2**, Ionaeos ... penates; **2.30.32**, Ionae; **2.30.112**, limen Ionae; **2.30.124**, penates ... Yaeos. **2.31.7**, Ionaeo ... in aruo. **2.32.30**, Ionaeas ... oras; **2.32.60**, penates ... Yaeos. **2.35**, phani ... Yaei. **2.36.59**, Yaeos ... portus; **22.36.80**, littus ... Yuum (adj. n.). **2.37.96**, domate Yaeo.

(abbreviations: abl. = ablative; acc. = accusative; adj. = adjective; dat. = dative; gen. = genitive; n. neuter; nom. = nominative; pl. = plural; voc. = vocative)

He uses a Greek form, *Ionis*, gen. *Ionidos*, as the name of the poem. This involves a pun on the name of the prophet Jonah.

Thus, he uses both the 'modern' form in *Ion-* and the older Gaelic form based on a root *Y* or *I*. Use of the latter is more frequent in the latter part of Book 2, but it is not clear whether any significance can be attached to this. The earliest, and indeed only, use of the form in *Ion* is on the is on the tombstone, mentioned above, of Roderick's cousin Anna MacLean, prioress of Iona Nunnery, who died in 1543 at a time when Roderick was active and living on Iona, before his exile.

MacLean's Latinisations of other Gaelic names taken from Adomnán

The other Gaelic name which appears several times in MacLean's poem is the name of Columba's close friend and successor Baithéne. For the name that manuscript A always gives as *Baitheneus*, and B gives as both *Baitheneus* and *Baithenus*, we find in MacLean *Bathinaeus* (with short first syllable), *Boethenaeus*, *Baetheneus*, *Boethenaeus*, *Baethenus,* and voc. *Boetheneu* (on the model of Greek nouns like βασιλεύς). Here MacLean shows considerable flexibility in adapting the name, for reasons which probably include metrical considerations.

The following is a select list of proper names in MacLean's *Ionis*, with forms in Adomnán, from manuscripts A and B. (All forms are nominative unless indicated otherwise.)

	MacLean	MS A	MSS B (where different from A)
1.1.1	Falbaeus	Failbeus	
	Osiualdus	Ossualdus	
	Seginaeus	Segineus, Segeneus	
	Addamnanus	Adomnanus	Adamnanus
	Brudaeus	Brudeus, Bruideus	
	Bathinaeus	Baitheneus	Baithenus
	Diormitius	Dermitius	Diormicius
	Cathalo	Catlo	Cathlo
1.2	Manteus	Maucteus	Macteus
1.3	Ethnae, Ethneae (gen.)	Aethnea	Eithne, Aeithne
1.5	Fintenus	Fintenus	Fentenus
	Boethenaeus	Baitheneus	Baithenus
	Oesseus	Oisseneus	
1.6	Crasseni Filius	Filius Craseni	
	Clecense Sacellulum	Clonoense cenubium	

1.7	Coennicus	Cainnichus, Cainnechus	Cainnethus, Cainnechus, Cannethus, Cannecus
1.8	Columbanus	Colmanus, Columbanus	Columbanus
	Carybdis Breccana	Carubdis Brecani	Caribdis Brecani
	Caribreccana		
1.9	Cormachus Lethanides	Cormacus, Cormaccus	
		Nepos Lethani	
1.10	Aedanus	Aidanus	
	Artur	Arturius	Arturius, Arcurius
	Ethodius	Echodius	
	Donyngardus	Domingartus	
	Eugenes Ethodius	Echodius	
	Miathei	Miathi	
	Belgici	bellica	
1.11	Scanlanus	Scandlanus	
	Colemanus	Colmanus	Colmannus
	Oedo	Aidus	
1.12	Oedochomanus	filius Aido Commani	
1.14	Mœldanus	Meldanus	
	Glasdarcus	Glasdercus	Glasdercis
	Ernanus	Ernanus	
1.15	Trenanus	Trenanus	
1.16	Bærachus	Berachus	Berachus, Barachus
	Aethica	Ethica	
	Bœtheneus	Baitheneus	Baitheneus, Baithenus
1.17	Nemanus Cathyrida	Nemanus filius Cathir	
1.18	Lugædus	Lugaidus	Lugaidus, Lugadius

	Diormitius	Diormitius	
	Turtreis nepotes	nepotes Turtrei	
1.19	Baetheneus	Baitheneus	Baitheneus, Baithenus
1.20	Lugbeus	Lugbeus	Lugreus, Lugbeus
1.21	Diormitius	Diormitius	
1.22	Aedanus ortus masculi	Aidanus filius Fergnoi	
1.23	Lugbeus	Lugbeus	
1.24	Lasrianus filius Feradachi	Laisranus filius Feradachi	Laisranus filius Ferdachi
	Diormitius	Diormitius	
	Doeria		
	Ora Conalliae		
1.25	Faechnus	Fechnus, Feachnaus	Fechnus, Fectnus, Fechnanus
	Mons Ionius		
	Boethenaeus	Baitheneum	
1.26	Coelteanus	Cailtanus	
	Ora Gathaelica		
	Lacus Abae	stagnum Abae fluminis	Abae, ab ae
1.28	Artbrananus	Artbrananus	
	Hebrida		
	Schya	Scia	
	Geon cohors	Geonae cohors	Geone
1.29	Fynchanus	Findchanus	Findchanus, Findcanus
	Oedus Niger	Aidus Niger	
1.30	Baethenus	Baitheneus	
1.31	Brudeus	Brudeus	
1.32	Nemanus	Nemanus	
	Canile prouincia	regio Cainle	
1.33	Triorithi	Trioit	Triota

1.34	Munenses	Muminenses	Muminenses, Muginenses
1.35	Imba	Hinba	Hinba, Himba
	Imbica colonia		
	Ernanus	Ernanus	
1.36	Goreus	Goreus	
1.37	Lugbeus	Lugbeus	
	Ceilrois (sacellulum)	Cell rois	Ceilrois, Cellros
1.38	Noesus		
2.1	Fymbarrus	Findbarrus	Fendbarrus
2.4	Collis Yaei	Munition magna	
	Sileanus	Silnanus	
	Albionus	Ailbine	
	(Praeceps) Dya	(vadum) Clied	cleeth, deeth (B2)
2.11	Nesanus	Nesanus	
2.12	Columbanus	Columbanus	
2.14	Thyles, Thylaeus	Ilea	Ilia (B2)
2.15	Landers	Lam Dess	lamdes, laudes, lamdhes
	Domnaldi nepotes		
	Connaldus		
	Finleganus	Findluganus	Finducanus (B3)
	Cronanus	Cronanus	
2.16	Germanus	Gemmanus	
	Clyathus		
	Laginaeus	Laginenses	
2.17	Insulae Galdi		
	Schya	Scia insula	sua insula
2.18	Noesus	Nesa	Nessamus, Nessamius
	Lugbeus	Lugneus	
2.19	Rossia		

2.20	Moluag, Moluagus, Molocus	Molua	
2.22	Mons Scarsiacus		
	Callianinde	Kailli au inde	Kaillianfinde, Kaillianfind
2.24	Brochanus	Broichanus	Broichanus, Broicanus
	Melconis		
	Brudaeus	Bruideus	Brudeus, Brudenus
2.25	Noesus	Nisa	Nessa, Nesa
	Germanus	Germanus	
2.27	Brudaeus	Brudeus	
2.28	Duum ruris coenobitas	Monasterium duum ruris riuulorum	
2.30	Libranus	Libranus	
	Conachtus	de Connachtarum regione	
	Ethica	Ethica	
	Robur	Daire Calcig	
	Roboreti	Roborei campus	
2.31	Munya		
2.32	Cormachus	Cormacus	
	Brudaeus	Brudeus	
	Orchades	Orcades	
2.35	Angeli cliuus	Colliculus angelorum	
2.37	Genus Loerni	Genus Loerni	
	Sainea	Sainea	
2.38	Ausonae		
	Galli		
	Britones		
	Suaeui		
	Teuthones		

Celtiberi	
Picti	Pictorum plebs
Gathaeli genus	Scotorum
	Britanniae
Angli	Saxonia

Proper names in MacLean's other poems

Bound in with the *Ionis* in one of the Perugia copies is a gathering of eight folios containing two 'occasional' poems. One of these, entitled *De Excellentia Heroici Ordinis*, is a flattering begging letter, in elegiac couplets, addressed to Sir David Lindsay of the Mount, asking for his help at court in MacLean's dispute over the bishopric of the Isles. This begins with a potted history of the Western Isles under the Clan Donald, and explains MacLean's relationship with that august dynasty. The names are Latinised as follows:

Rodericus Maclenius	*Ruairidh MacIllEathain*, Roderick MacLean
Ioannes Danielis	*Iain Dòmhnallach*, John MacDonald
Daniel Rossius comes	Donald earl of Ross
Alexander cui dat celeberrima Thyle nomen	Alexander de Ile
Angusius	*Aonghas*, Angus
Ferquhardus	Fearchar, Farquhar
Fingola	Finguala, Fionnghuala
Danieligenum progenies	*Clann Dòmhnuill*, Clan Donald

To this is appended a short elegiac poem addressed to the governor the earl of Arran, dated 1 January 1549. It celebrates the escape from captivity of George Gordon earl of Huntly (22/23 December 1548), and the recapture of Hume Castle from English control (26 December 1548).[120] This must have been very fresh news on New Year's Day 1549. It has only one interesting place name: *Humnia Rupes*, the 'Rock of Hume'.

MacLean's Latinisations of Gaelic names not taken from Adomnán

There are a few of these:

---

[120] These are the dates given by Lesley. The *Diurnal of Occurrents* places the fall of Hume Castle on 16 December; possibly *xvj* in the *Diurnal* is a mistake for *xxvj*.

Book 1

Leusiacas (acc. plu.)	*Leòdhasach*, of Lewis
Doeria	*Doire*, Derry
Oram ... Gathaelicam	*Earra-Ghàidheal*, Argyll
Portum ... a rege	*Port Rìgh*, Portree
Munenses	People of Munster
Abae ... hostia	*Bun Obha*, Bonawe
in aequora qua Noesus ... defluit	*Inbhir Nis*, Inverness, 'where Ness flows into the sea'

Book 2

praeceps Dya	*Uisge Dhè*, (sources of River) Dee
Insulas Galdi	*Innse Gall*, the Western Isles (cf. Boece)
Rossiae ora	*Ros*, the Ross (of Mull)
Monte Scarsiaco (abl.)	*An Sgarsoch*
Munya	Munster

On occasion, MacLean is quite inventive in his adaptation of Gaelic names. A particularly good example is in **1.26.1–4**: *Oram lacus Gathaelicam / unda piger disterminat, / praeceps Abae per hostia / salo redundans hespero* ('A still loch divides the Gaelic Shore (Argyll) by its waters, rushing headlong to the western sea by the mouth of the Awe (Bonawe).'). Here *Ora ... Gathaelica* is an elegant Latinisation for Argyll, *Earra-Ghàidheal*, the 'Gaelic shore', and *Abae ... hostia* is a Latinisation of *Bun Obha*, Bonawe.

Roderick's names of plants, winds, and the signs of the Zodiac

As well as his inventive forms of Gaelic and other names, MacLean finds inventive and original ways of naming other things as well. His extraordinary list of aromatic plants (**1.30.33 ff.**), extending to thirty-six lines, has been described as 'an exercise in virtuosity'.[121] The list below contains the word used by MacLean in **1.30**, followed by the common English name and (in brackets) the scientific name of each plant. We have not attempted to trace MacLean's sources for all his names of plants, though it is worth pointing out that the name *mala Medica* for a citrus tree may possibly be unique to Pliny the Elder.

---

[121] Sharpe, 'MacLean', 116.

Thus	Incense, Frankincense (*Boswellia species (spp.)*)
Myrra	Myrrh (*Commiphora myrrha*)
Cedrus	Cedar (*Cedrus libani*)
Laurea	Laurel, Bay tree (*Laurus nobilis*)
Myrtus	Myrtle (*Myrtus communis*)
Cypressus	Cypress (*Cupressus spp.*)
Lilia	Lily (*Lilium spp.*)
Roseta	Rose-Beds, Roses (*Rosa spp.*)
Palmae	Palm, date palm (*Phoenix dactylifera*)
Balsama	Balsam (*Amyris balsamifera*)
Amomum	Cardamom (*Elletaria cardamomum* and other spp. of *Elletaria* and *Amomum*)
Anethum	Dill (*Anethum graveolens*)
Amaracus	Marjoram (*Origanum majorana*)
Pinus	Pine (*Pinus spp.*)
Uiror Buxeus	Box-Tree (*Buxus sempervirens*)
Costus	Costmary (?) (*Tanacetum balsamita*)
Crocus	Saffron (*Crocus sativus*)
Nardinus	Nard (*Nardostachys jatamansi*)
Cynnama	Cinnamon (*Cinnamomum spp.*)
Rosmarinus	Rosemary (*Rosmarinus officinalis* synonym *Salvia rosmarinus*)
Narcissus	Daffodil (*Narcissus spp.*)
Aiax Flosculus	Hyacinth (?) (*Hyacinthus spp.*)
Granata	Pomegranate (*Punica granatum*)
Mala Maedica	'Fruit of Media', Orange (?) (*Citrus spp.*)
Oliua	Olive (*Olea europaea*)
Passus Racemus	Cluster of dried grapes (*Vitis vinifera*)
Fistula	Uncertain: possibly Cassia (*Cassia fistula*) or sugar cane (*Saccharum spp.*)

Likewise, in **2.36** and **2.37**, he provides a list of names of various winds, mentioning *Aphricus, Nothus, Euronothus, Lybs* (= *Λίψ*), *Eurus, Boraeas, Iapyx, Uulturnus, Auster, Zephyrus, Caurus.*

Throughout the poems he sets incidents by the seasons of the year, and he locates these by their astrological signs. Here is a list of his inventive names for the signs of the Zodiac:

Aries	Uector Hellaeus (**2.35.1**)
Taurus	Bouis sydus (**2.35.1**)
Gemini	Laedae proles (**1.1.14**); Castor et Pollux nitidi gemellum sydus (**2.19.1–2**)
Cancer	Octipes (**2.32.54**)
Leo	Nemeaeus Leo (**2.14.13–14**)
Virgo	Innuba (**2.3.15**)
Libra	Bilanx (**1.30.1**)
Scorpio	Scorpius (**2.14.16**)
Capricorn	Capricorna (**2.22.5**)
Aquarius	Aquis urnae Ganymaedis (**2.22.6**)

A Selection of some other unusual words

Over and above his Latinisations of Gaelic words and proper nouns, his names of winds and of constellations of the Zodiac, and his extraordinary catalogue of aromatic plants, MacLean's poems contain a number of other words that call for comment. The following list is a selection of other rare and unusual words in the poems which are mostly not proper nouns. Some of them are rare classical (CL) words which have only a few examples in standard dictionaries (e.g. *OLD* and *L&S*), some of them are Late Latin (LL) or – rarely – Medieval Latin (ML), and a few of them (e.g., *ascella*) are taken from Adomnán's *VC*. They are mostly discussed in the Commentary, and there is a reference in the list below to their occurrence there.

The impression given is that MacLean's vocabulary is very eclectic. He delighted in odd words, and possibly collected them and made lists of them. He used words from early Latin (e.g. Plautus and Terence), rare words from Latin of all periods, and he coined a lot of inventive compounds. He used patristic language, including from early Christian poets, and words from the Vulgate. There are a few words from Adomnán, but there is relatively little medieval Latin.[122]

Where did MacLean learn his rich and unusual vocabulary? The words 'fama Ionae me nutricis insulae' (**P3.37**) imply study at a school at Iona Abbey. We do not know where he studied immediately thereafter, though

---

[122] I am grateful to Dr Betty Knott-Sharpe for comments on MacLean's vocabulary.

Aberdeen University has been cautiously suggested above as a possibility (pp. 5, 15). We know that he studied at Wittenberg from 1534, probably taking his master's degree there. We have a snapshot of the library of the University of Wittenberg at the time, in the form of a library catalogue dated 1536.[123] This gives us an idea of the books that were available to MacLean there during his period of study. Authors and works marked with an asterisk ★ in the list below are listed in the Wittenberg University Library catalogue.

In the alphabetical list below, the words are from *Ionis* unless noted otherwise (**P** = Preliminaries, **1.** = Book 1, **2.** = Book 2); **Ps.** = Paraphrase of Psalm 1, **Ep.** = *Epistola Elegiaca*, **St.** = *Straena Gratulatoria*. CL = Classical Latin, LL = Late Latin, ML = Medieval Latin. Most of them are all discussed in the Commentary *ad loc.*, with cross-references below.

Algedo **2.30.25** – The meaning, 'cold', is clear, though MacLean's form is not CL. Cicero, *Tusculanae Disputationes*★, 2.34, links cold with the labours and hunger (etc.) of a Spartan education, echoed here by MacLean. In *Ciceronis opera philosophica*★ (1511). See p. 313.

Alphabeticus **P3.12** – This is not a CL word, and it has possibly been coined by MacLean. Cf. *Hoc discunt omnes ante apha et beta puellae*, Juvenal, *Satires*★, 14.209. *Alphabetum* is found in Gildas, Bede★, and in ML. See p. 270.

Apodixis **P6.** – Aulus Gellius★ and Quintilian★. See p. 273.

Apriceps **2.18.30** – A compound probably coined by MacLean from *aper*, 'boar' + *-ceps* < *caput*. See p. 304.

Arundinetum **2.30. heading** – The CL form is *harundinetum*. This spelling is from Adomnán. See p. 313.

Ascella **2.33.5** – From Adomnán only. Cf. *NCLCL*, s.v., citing only Adomnán. The CL word is *axilla*. See p. 316.

Atramen **1.21.12** – Not CL. Perhaps MacLean has coined this word (from CL *atramentum*) for metrical reasons. See p. 285.

Atramentarium **1.21.4** – Not CL, but cf. Vulg.★ Ez. 9.2, 9.3, 9.11. See p. 284.

Aulicus **2.24.45** – CL, found in the historians Cornelius Nepos and Suetonius★.

Auricomus **1.1.29** – For *auricomus* referring to the dawn, cf. Valerius Flaccus, *Argonautica*, 4.92. Vergil (*Aen.*★ 6.141) uses it in a different context (the golden bough), and it is perhaps unlikely to have been MacLean's inspiration here. The *Argonautica* is not mentioned in the Wittenberg Library catalogue of 1536, but cf. *undisonus* below for another echo of it. See p. 274.

[123] S Kusukawa, *A Wittenberg University Library Catalogue of 1536*, Medieval and Renaissance Texts and Studies 890 (Binghamton, 1995).

Ausonae　　2.38.6 – An ancient southern Italian people, usually Ausones, Ausonides, or Ausonidae. The name came to be applied poetically to the Italians in general. MacLean's form is unusual, possibly coined for metrical reasons. See p. 319.

Bicolis　　2.18.29 – A compound probably coined by MacLean from *bi* + *caulis*, 'stalk, stem', to mean 'cloven-footed'. See p. 304.

Bipotens　　2.2.14 – A compound probably coined by MacLean from *bi* + *potens*, presumably referring to Christ's divine and human natures. See p. 295.

Bubalus　　2.9.3 – Pliny, *HN*★, links this rare word with the African gazelle, and says that it is improperly used of the bison or wild ox (*HN*, 8.15; cf. also Solinus, *Collectanea Rerum Mirabilium*★, 20.5). It is used in the Vulgate★ (Deut. 14: 5, 2 Sam. 6: 19), and (spelt *bufalus*) by Venantius Fortunatus (*Carmina*, 7.4.21). MacLean may have been thinking of the ancestors of modern Highland cattle. See p. 298.

Celtiberi　　2.38.7 – CL, a race in central Spain. Probably MacLean is applying it to all the people of the Iberian Peninsula.

Chalybs　　2.20.13 – A loanword from Gk χάλυψ into CL for iron or steel.

Character　　2.9.17, 2.33.12 – a rare loanword from Gk into CL. χαρακτήρ should mean a letter or image that is cut or stamped or impressed. MacLean uses it once to mean the sign of the cross made with the hand, and once to mean Columba's handwriting in a manuscript.

Charis　　2.21.15 – *Charitum* (gen. plu.), < χάρις, 'grace, one of the Graces'. It is rare in the sing. in CL. MacLean is using it to mean 'gratitude, thanksgiving'.

Cherubicos　　1.30.80 – Cherubim and Seraphim are mentioned in the Vulgate★ and in patristic writers. It is uncertain how MacLean has intended these words to be scanned, but some sort of syncope or adjustment is required to make them fit his iambic metre. See p. 291.

Cicutipota　　P3.10 – From *cicuta* + *potare*, 'hemlock drinker': this epithet for Socrates is probably coined by MacLean. See p. 270.

Clecense　　1.6.10. The episode is set at Clonmacnoise, called by Adomnán (twice) *in Clonoensi cenubio*. It is not clear why MacLean has used this form, when he could easily have re-shaped Adomnán's name to fit the Asclepiad metre. In MacLean's papal bull of provision to the see of the Isles, there is a reference to *ecclesia Cluanensis*, the usual medieval form.[124]

---

[124] Below, Appendix, p. 338.

Colonia   **1.5.1** – Usually, when MacLean uses this word, he means a
                 monastery dependent on Iona: **1.26.8, 1.26.18, 1.35.7, 1.35.14**.
                 But that cannot be its meaning in **1.5.1**, where it appears that
                 Columba is referring to his physical body. MacLean may be
                 thinking of 2 Cor. 5: 1, where the Vulgate★ uses *habitatio* and
                 aedificatio to refer to the physical and heavenly body. See p. 279.

Consinuarier   **P5.47** – From *con* + *sinuare*, 'to bend'. This term has possibly
                 been coined by MacLean. Cf. *consinuacio*, 'insinuation', in one
                 manuscript of *Chron. Pluscarden*, x, 20 (ed. F J H Skene, i, 346),
                 which may, however, be a mistake for *insinuacio* (Cf. *MLWL*,
                 DMLBS, s.v. *consinuacio*). For the present infinitive passive
                 form in *-ier*, cf. note on *experirier* **P3.5** in the commentary.
                 See p. 271.

Contulus   **2.29.7** – The word is found in Adomnán: *NCLCL* cites *VC*,
                 2, 37 and *VC*, 2, 27 'the length of a pole'. It is characteristic
                 of Adomnán's fondness for diminutives. In 2.29 MacLean uses
                 the CL form *contus* frequently. See p. 312.

Copallus   **2.18.18** – MacLean has taken this unusual word from Adomnán
                 and adjusted it to fit his metre: cf. *caupallus* in *VC*, ii, 27. The
                 (extremely rare) CL form is *caupulus*, which would not fit
                 MacLean's prosody. Cf. *Shorter OED*, s.v. *coble*; *DMLBS*, s.v.
                 caupulus, cobellus. NCLCL offers no examples except Adomnán.
                 See p. 304.

Dryas   **1.24.16** – Strictly speaking, Δρυάς (borrowed into CL) is a
                 wood-nymph. The word MacLean is thinking of here is δρῦς,
                 acc. pl. δρύας, 'oak-tree'. See p. 286.

Ennosigaeus   **Ep. 38** – A Homeric epithet for Poseidon or Neptune, the
                 'earth-shaker'. Very rare in Latin of any period: used once by
                 Juvenal★. See p. 322.

Eous   **P5.69** – A CL borrowing from Gk ἠώς, 'eastern, pertaining
                 to the dawn', used in Vergil's *Georgics*★ and in other poetry.
                 See p. 271.

Erro   **Ps.4** – A vagabond or truant. Green, 'Poetic Psalm Paraphrases',
                 266, describes it as 'rare'. See p. 320.

Fericida   **2.14.31** – From *ferus* + *cida* (< *caedo*), 'killer of wild beasts';
                 probably coined by MacLean as an epithet for Diana. See p.
                 300.

Ferresco   **2.35.22** – A verb possibly coined by MacLean, meaning
                 'to become like iron'. Adomnán is quoting from Lev. 26: 19
                 (*Daboque caelum vobis desuper sicut ferrum et terram aeneam*), and
                 MacLean follows him closely.

Goetus   **2.10.heading, 2.23.93, 2.24.12, 2.25.57** – The meaning of
                 this unusual word is clear from *Augures, mantae, druidae, goeti,*

/ *saga, medeae, quoque nicromantae*, **2.25.57**. Sharpe ('MacLean', 128–9) points to a Gk word γοήτης, 'sorcerer', and comments: 'I have no idea where MacLean may have learnt it'. The word seems to be extremely rare in Latin of any period, though Augustine, in *De Civitate Dei*★ 10.9, speaks of *goetia* ('sorcery, necromancy'). See p. 309.

Hellaeus **2.35.1** – An adjective apparently coined by MacLean, meaning 'pertaining to Helle' (i.e. Aries, the Ram). See p. 316.

Hinnus **2.18.16** – CL, but rare. A hinny, strictly speaking, is the offspring of a she-ass and a stallion; MacLean may use the word to indicate that his river monster is a hybridised horse-like creature. See p. 303.

Hippopotamos **2.18. heading**, 2.18.52 – A CL borrowing from Gk ἱπποπόταμος, 'river horse', found in Pliny, *HN*★. Sharpe ('MacLean', 130), comments that MacLean's version of Adomnán's monster in the River Ness has characteristics of the Gaelic *each uisge*. This may be a relatively early example of the *each uisge* in writing. See p. 303.

Incino **1.36.10** – A rare compound from *cano*, 'to sing'. The context implies singing incantations over noxious plants with murderous intent. Adomnán has *maleficio*, which (among other things) can mean 'enchantment, sorcery' (*L&S*). See p. 294.

Infacetus **P.3.4** – This word can also be spelt *inficetus*. Cf. Catullus, *Carmina*★, xliii, 8. See p. 270.

Innuba **2.3.15** – One of MacLean's inventive words for the signs of the Zodiac, 'unmarried woman' (i.e. Virgo). Ovid uses it with oblique reference to Daphne fleeing from Apollo, *Met.*★, x, 92. See p. 296.

Lacustris **2.36.9** – A very rare ML word meaning 'pertaining to a lake': cf. *DMLBS*, s.v. Where MacLean picked it up is a mystery.

Latreia **2.16.78** – A rare word from patristic Latin, < λατρεία.

Leusiacus **1.1.20** – Coined by MacLean from Gaelic *Leòdhasach*, 'pertaining to (the Isle of) Lewis'. See p. 274.

Maceratus **2.30.54** – This is an unusual word. The vowel in the first syllable is short, connecting it with *macer*, 'thin', *macresco*, etc. Cf. ML *macerativus*, 'that involves fasting' (*DMLBS*). Cf. *quaderet*, **Ep., 110**, where MacLean has added an extra syllable for metrical reasons. But he has also perhaps been influenced by *mācero*, 'to make wet' (which, however, has a long vowel). If Librán worked in reed-beds as a penitent for seven years, he will have become both thin and wet. See pp. 313–14.

Maechus, **1.18.40, Ep. 156** – The (not very common) CL word is *moechus*, *Moecha* *moecha, moechas (-ados)*, < μοιχός, μοιχάς, 'adulterer, adulteress'.

Mantae, Mantes **1.31.15, 2.23.6, 2.23.39** – From μαντεία, 'prophesying'. Cf. *mantis*, gen. *mantidis*, in *OLD*; seemingly very rare. See p. 308.

Maximati **2.32.17** – ML, from nom. *maximas* (*DMLBS*, s.v.); very rare, unknown in sing., modelled on *magnates*. See p. 315.

Molossus **2.18.54, 2.29.49** – Already in CL used for a hunting hound, which became its usual meaning in ML. See p. 304.

Mulsum **2.9.13** – 'Milk', from *mulgeo*. Cf. *mulctrum* for a milking pail, just before at **2.9.5**. The words are not common, but are used by Vergil★, Horace★, and other poets.

Natilem **2.36.14** – Probably a misprint for *nautilem*.

Nugo **Ps. 6** – Roger Green ('Poetic Psalm paraphrases', 266) describes this word as 'very rare', and cites Appuleius's *Metamorphosis*★, 5.29 and 5.30. These are possibly the only occurrences of this word. See p. 320.

Octipes **2.32.54** – Cancer, the 'eight-footed' crab: used by Propertius★ (iv, 1, 150) and Ovid (*Fasti*★, 1, 313).

Oedo, Oedus **1.11, 1.29** – The Irish name was Áed. MacLean's Latin forms are not consistent. In **1.11.3** and **4**, he has *Oedo* (nom.), with gen. *Oedonis* in the chapter heading. In **1.29**, on the other hand, we find acc. *Oedum*, nom. *Oedus* (**6**); dat. *Oedo* (**20**); but also nom. *Oedo* (**40**), which would imply gen. *Oedonis*.

Oenotria **1.23.18** – Originally Apulia, but applied poetically to Italy in general: cf. Verg. *Aen.*★ 7.85. See p. 285.

Penates **2.8.3** – Sharpe ('MacLean', 129) draws attention to this word. MacLean uses it here and elsewhere (**2.13, 2.15, 2.24, 2.30, 2.32**) as synonymous with *lares*. It is used frequently in Verg. *Aen.*★, as Aeneas tries to find a home for the tutelary gods of Troy.

Perreuerenter **2.27.16** – Possibly coined by MacLean from *per* (intensive) + *reuerenter*.

Perscius **2.23.76** – This word may possibly have been coined by MacLean; *perscītus* is rare but classical, but it would not fit the metre.

Phanaloga **1.1. heading** – Probably coined by MacLean, either from φαίνω, 'disclose', or from *fanum*, 'church, temple', + λόγος, 'discourse, narrative'. See p. 273.

Philautia **P3.35** – from Greek φίλαυτος, very rare in Latin of any period (cf. *DMLBS*, s.v.). See p. 270.

Poenextimam **1.28.2** – Seemingly either coined by MacLean from *paene* + *extimus*, or possibly a misprint for *poene extimam*. According to *L&S*, *extimus* is 'rare but classical'. See p. 288.

Popelli **1.1.3, 2.25.44** – Used by Horace (*Epistles*★, 1.7.65) and by Persius Flaccus (*Satires*★, 4.15, 6.50) as a somewhat contemptuous term for 'the rabble'. MacLean's two uses of this rare word, however, are not derogatory. See p. 273.

Postliminium **1.38.8, St. 14** – A legal term, used by Cicero★ and legal writers, referring to the resumption of rights and property following exile or imprisonment. MacLean uses it twice, once to refer to his own exiled situation, and once with reference to the return from captivity of the earl of Huntly. Cf. Sharpe, 'MacLean', 113, 127. See p. 294.

Praeceps **1.1.116, 1.26.3, 2.4.7** – MacLean uses this word three times in its adverbial meaning 'headlong'; in two of these he is referring to a rapidly flowing river.

Praestigiator **2.10.4** – Used by Plautus★ to mean 'a trickster', but otherwise very rare.

Quaderet **Ep. 110** – For *quadret*, adding an extra syllable for metrical reasons. Cf. *maceratus* above.

Quadrigae **2.15.38** and **2.29.69–70** – MacLean uses this word (meaning 'a four-horse chariot') twice, both times at the end of a chapter, and both times without any equivalent in Adomnán. It is not clear where he has got it from, or what his figurative sense is. For *quadrigis ... albicatis* in **2.29**, cf. *numquam ... quadrigis albis indipiscet postea* in Plautus, *Asinaria,*★ 2, 2, 13, as an image of something fast. But there could also be a sense of riding out in triumph: cf. also *uoce praeconis pietas triumphat / nuncia pacis,* **2.16.79–80**. See pp. 301, 313.

Repandrostrus **2.26.27** – The word *repandirostrus* ('with turned-up snout') is found once only, in Quintilian (*Institutio*★, 1.5.67), quoting the early dramatist Pacuvius, with the meaning 'dolphins', and with reference to Nereus. So there is no doubt where MacLean has got this strange word. He uses it with syncope to make it scan. See p. 311.

Repascor **2.21.1** – Not a CL word. There is a rare LL verb *repasco* (in *L&S*, not in *OLD*), used by Paulinus of Nola★. MacLean's form *repasta*, however, is deponent, and seems to echo Vergil's *Georgics*★, iii, 458: *cum furit atque artus depascitur arida febris*, where *depascitur* is deponent. Is it possible that MacLean's *repasta* is a misprint for *depasta*? See p. 306.

Reptilis **2.19. heading** – Not a CL word, it is used by Sidonius Apollinaris★ and in the Vulgate★.

Rogula **2.29.3** – A diminutive of LL *roga*, 'alms' (cf. *DMLBS*, s.v. *roga*), i.e. 'that which is requested'. Adomnán has *elimoysinam*. MacLean may have coined the diminutive. See p. 312.

Rumusculus **1.23.27** – *Rumor* + diminutive suffix. Possibly found only (and rarely) in Cicero★ in CL (cf. *OLD*), and occasionally in ML.

Salicta   **1.28.28** – Strictly speaking, this word should refer to willow groves. There are to this day thickets of mixed deciduous woodland around Portree Loch, including alder, birch and rowan, but willow trees are not obvious among them. Trees are shown around Portree Loch in Blaeu's map (Stone, *Illustrated Maps of Scotland*, Pl. 43). One may suspect that MacLean has used the word in a generic sense to mean 'thickets of deciduous trees'. See p. 289.

Scotis   **1.3.10, 2.24.36, 2.24.42, 2.24.54** – Although MacLean uses the word *Scotus* to refer to a Scotsman or Irishman, he also uses *Scotis*, gen. *Scotidos*, acc. *Scotidem*, abl. *Scotide*, to mean an Irishwoman. He also refers to her in **2.24** as *Scotam ... puellam* and *Scotae seruae*. It is not obvious where he has got this from.

Sepes   **1.2.14** – The CL is *saepes*, 'hedge'. MacLean's *paruulae sepis* (gen.) echoes Adomnán's *sepisculae* in the Second Preface. MacLean is paraphrasing Adomnán quite closely at this point.

Seraphicos   **1.30.80** – See *Cherubicos* above.

Solimus   **P5.31** – From LL adj. *Solimus*, 'of Jerusalem': cf. *DMLBS*, s.v. See p. 271.

Sophia   **1.5.10** – From σοφία, used infrequently in CL for *sapientia*, and commonly in Patristic LL and ML.

Stillula   **1.13.50** – The diminutive is not CL, but is found in ML (cf. *DMLBS*, s.v., for examples). MacLean is paraphrasing Adomnán, *VC*, i, 50: ... *quasi quaedam parua aliquando stillicidia ueluti per quasdam rimulas alicuius pleni uassis fermentissimo nouo distillabant uino.* See pp. 282–3.

Suaeui   **2.38.6** – In CL, the *Suebi* or *Suevi* were a group of eastern Germanic peoples. It is not clear what MacLean is thinking of here: possibly either eastern Europe or Scandinavia. See p. 319.

Supparum   **2.30.117** – *Siparum* or *sipharum* (< σίφαρος) means a small sail or topsail. It came to be confused in manuscripts with *supparum*, 'a linen garment'. (Cf. *L&S* and *OLD*, s. vv.)

Symbola   **1.4.11** – *Cumbula*, 'a small boat', is extremely rare in CL, confined to the Letters of the Younger Pliny*; *cumba* or *cymba* is classical (e.g., Verg. *Aen.* 6.303). For ML, cf. *DMLBS*, s.v. *cymba, cymbula, symba.* MacLean's form may possibly be a misprint for *cymbola*. See p. 279.

Synaxis   **1.34.6, 2.5.1, 2.30.51, 2.30.55** – LL < σύναξις, 'assembly'. Common in ML, but rare earlier. In 1.34 and 2.30, MacLean is clearly using it to mean the Eucharist; in 2.5 he uses it to paraphrase Adomnán's *misam*, by which Adomnán may have meant the night office (cf. *VC*, 102 n.), but which MacLean will have understood as 'Mass'.

Talentum   **1.27.35, 1.35.15** – In origin a specific quantity of silver. In ML the word had come to be associated with the parable of the talents, Mat. 25: 14–30, Luke 19: 11–27. MacLean's two uses of the word are cryptic allusions to the parable of the talents.

Theatrum   **1.1.66, 2.24.63, 2.25.3** – MacLean uses the word three times, each time in the sense of 'audience, onlookers', used by a number of CL authors.

Trimalis   **2.11.5** – The usual word for 'three years old' is *trimulus*. This word has possibly been coined by MacLean to fit his sapphic metre. Cf. *duālis*, etc. See p. 298.

Triuia   **2.23.7** – An epithet for Diana, whose shrines or temples were often found at the meeting of three roads. See p. 308.

Tytanis   **1.1.29** – From the context, it is clear that this is a reference to the sun at its rising. The Titan Hyperion was equated with the sun. Given his tendency to use classical forms, MacLean might have been expected to use the Gk gen. *Titanos*, but gen. *Titanis* is found in medieval writers (*DMLBS*, s.v.; cf. also *L&S*, s.v.). See pp. 274–5.

Undisonus   **1.1.49** – A very rare poetical word, 'wave-resounding'. Cf. Valerius Flaccus, *Argonautica*, 1.364 (mentioning Neptune, as MacLean has just done in **1.1.45**). Cf. also *Argonautica*, 4.44. Cf. *auricomus* above. See p. 275.

MacLean's Scholarship as shown by the poems

One impression which the *Ionis* gives very strongly is that its author was a man of wide Renaissance learning and deep scholarship. He knew classical Latin and could handle the main Horatian metres, especially the Sapphic stanza, with assured confidence. His prosody is mostly good, with very occasional absent-minded slips. He could vary his style: when he uses hexameter verse (**1.1**), he can adopt an epic, Virgilian tone; in his attack on his critics (**P3**) he uses the rapidity and vigour of the iambic trimiter to good effect. The freshness and simplicity of his re-telling of Adomnán's stories in Horatian metres has been commented on above. He uses Greek words and Greek declensional forms.[125] He knew the meaning of certain Hebrew personal names, though this may have been taken from Jerome or other patristic writers. He knew Gaelic, his native tongue, and found inventive ways of rendering Gaelic personal and place names in Latin. Refreshingly, he shows no diffidence about his Gaelic scholarship: the governor reported that he was *in Insulis educatus, pro more*

---

[125] Above, pp. 27–9. Green, 'Paraphrases', 260.

gentis satis habeatur literatus, while on the title page of the book he proudly calls himself *Scotus Gathaelicus*. There is no trace of Adomnán's apology for using some Irish words (*aliqua Scoticae uilis uidelicet ling(u)ae ... uocabula*),[126] or of the alleged diffidence about his native tongue of which MacLean's contemporary George Buchanan has been accused.[127] Gaelic words are quietly classicised and seamlessly incorporated into the narrative (e.g. *Leusiacus < Leodhasach*, 'of Lewis' (**1.1**); *Ora ... Gathaelica < Earra-Ghàidheal*, 'Argyll' (**1.26**); *Mons Scarsiacus <* Beinn Sgarsoch (**2.22**)). (See the section on *MacLean's Latinisations of Gaelic names* above.)

MacLean also includes some local traditions, and some of these are interesting. For example, he identifies the harbour in Skye where Columba encountered Artbranán (**1.28**) with Portree; it would be interesting to know if this perpetuates a late medieval tradition which MacLean knew as parson of Kilmaluag on Skye. An ancient dedication to Columba on Skye was at Skeabost, on an island in the River Snizort, which had been at one time the cathedral church of the diocese.

He identifies Adomnán's father Rónán with the saint of North Rona off the Butt of Lewis, within the parish of Barvas, of which he was also parson. He describes how Columba arriving on Iona *fessam linquens in littore cymbam / erexit cumulos lapidum quos cernerat aetas / postera* ('leaving the worn-out ship on the shore, he raised up heaps of stones which a future age will see'), thus explaining the boat-shaped hillock and the large number of cairns at Port na Curaich and Port an Fhir-bhreige at the south end of the island. We have seen that he also identifies some places on Iona with incidents in *VC*, mentioning Dùn Ì and Cnoc nan Aingeal.

One of the most intriguing of his identifications is that of the Isle of *Hinba* (**1.35**). MacLean describes an island due south of Iona, implicitly not far away, in the open western sea. There can be no doubt that he was thinking of the Colonsay-Oronsay group, and probably in particular of Oronsay Priory, which was dedicated to Columba. This is evidence of a tradition in MacLean's time linking *Hinba* with Colonsay-Oronsay, but how far back it stretches is uncertain. MacLean also records a tradition that *Hinba* was a very early foundation of Columba's (*lares priusquam deserens*).

Occasionally, he elaborates Adomnán's narrative in a way that shows an acquaintance with Gaelic literature and tradition. In **2.17**, Columba's encounter with a wild boar on Skye (based on *VC*, ii, 26), MacLean describes the boar as *uenenosus* and *spirans uenena*. There is nothing in Adomnán from which this reference to poison could be derived, but in Gaelic literature

---

[126] *VC*, 1st Preface.
[127] McGinnis & Williamson, *Buchanan*, 40. Buchanan describes his poems as *Britannis / nata in montibus horrida sub Arcto, / nec cœlo neque seculo erudito*: ibid., 117. For Buchanan's knowledge of Gaelic, cf. I D McFarlane, *Buchanan* (London, 1981), 19.

and throughout Celtic literature in general wild boars could be thought
of as poisonous and supernatural. In a Scottish version of the legend of
Diarmaid the boar-hunter found in the *Book of the Dean of Lismore*, the boar
is specifically described as poisonous.[128] Similarly, in the following chapter
(**2.18**, based on *VC*, ii, 27), he elaborates Adomnán's vague description of
a fierce water monster in the River Ness into a horse-like *each uisge* with
equine features, which he calls *hippopotamos* (river horse), showing off
his knowledge of the Greek word as well as an acquaintance with Celtic
legend.[129] In **2.12**, the miraculous multiplication of a poor man's cattle,
MacLean mentions that the herd was white, where Adomnán (in *VC*, ii,
21) had said nothing about their colour. In Gaelic mythology white cattle
were much prized, and this may be another example of the influence of
Celtic lore in MacLean's paraphrase.

There is no evidence of any kind of relationship between Roderick MacLean
and Manus O'Donnell (Maghnus Ó Domhnaill) of Tirconnell. It is likely that
they did not meet during MacLean's trip to Ireland in 1542, since MacLean's
Jesuit companions refused O'Donnell's clandestine invitation to them.[130]
O'Donnell had submitted to Henry VIII in June 1540, and remained in the
peace of the English crown until his death in 1563.[131] On his matriculation
at Wittenberg in 1534, MacLean is described as *ex Hibernia*, which could
possibly, but does not certainly, indicate that he had spent time studying at
an Irish centre of learning earlier. He mentions Dublin in terms which might
possibly imply acquaintance with the city (**2.16**), and he mentions Derry
several times. But contact with Manus O'Donnell can be almost certainly
ruled out, and there is no trace of any influence from O'Donnell's work on
MacLean's. O'Donnell's *Beatha Colaim Chille* in early modern Irish (1532)[132] is
of interest as a work of historical scholarship by a contemporary of MacLean's.
As a Gaelic scholar, MacLean may have been aware of O'Donnell's book,
but the two works have almost nothing in common. O'Donnell's *Beatha* is
based on a fusion of an abbreviated recension of Adomnán's *VC*[133] with the
twelfth-century *Betha Coluim Cille*,[134] and a sprinkling of later traditions.[135]

---

[128] Donald E Meek, 'The death of Diarmaid in Scottish and Irish tradition', *Celtica*, xxi (1990),
       335–61. Cf. also John MacInnes, 'Gaelic poetry and historical tradition', in *The Middle Ages
       in the Highlands*, ed. L MacLean (Inverness Field Club, 1981), 142–63, at 160; N K Chadwick,
       'The lost literature of Celtic Scotland', *Scottish Gaelic Studies*, vii (1953), 115–83, at 142–5.
[129] As pointed out in Sharpe, 'MacLean', 130.
[130] See above, pp. 6–7.
[131] B Lacey, *Manus O'Donnell: The Life of Colum Cille* (Dublin, 1998), 8–11.
[132] A O'Kelleher and G Schoepperle (eds), *Beatha Colaim Chille* (Urbana, 1918); more recent
       translation in Lacey, *O'Donnell*.
[133] Sharpe, 'MacLean', 115 and n. 24.
[134] Máire Herbert, ed., *Iona, Kells, and Derry: The History and Hagiography of the Monastic Familia
       of Columba* (Oxford, 1989), 218 ff.
[135] Lacey, *O'Donnell*, 13–14; Sharpe, *Adomnán*, 91–2.

MacLean's poems are based almost entirely on the full text of Adomnán's *VC*, with only a quite small amount of supplementary information and tradition known to the author.

Another work by a contemporary, written in the same location and completed in the same year that MacLean's poem was published, is Donald Monro's *Description of the Western Isles of Scotland*.[136] Monro was Roderick's nephew, the son of his sister Janet MacLean. His book describes the many islands off the west coast in varying degrees of detail in unadorned Scots prose. He came from the Gaelic-speaking lands of Kiltearn in Easter Ross (NH 6265), and the English translations he gives for most of the Gaelic island names in the Western Isles are correct and show a good and scholarly knowledge of Gaelic.[137] After MacLean's election to the bishopric, Monro became his archdeacon.[138] In Monro's book we see the sort of geographical knowledge of the Western Isles that MacLean, as his predecessor as archdeacon, would also have shared.

MacLean had access to some historical scholarship independent both of Adomnán and of local tradition. He knew, for example, that the Pictish king Bridei's father was called Mailcon (*Melconis*, 'son of Mailcon', **2.24**). Adomnán mentions Bridei several times, but nowhere gives his father's name. Bede calls him *Bridius filius Meilochon*;[139] Fordun and Bower use similar forms derived from Bede, possibly influenced by king lists. The Pictish king list in the Poppleton manuscript calls him Bridei *f.* Mailcon.

There is reason to credit MacLean with considerable biblical scholarship. He was familiar with Jerome's prefaces, and with some of his interpretations of Hebrew names. He knew some New Testament apocryphal writings (**2.23**). MacLean claimed to have written verse paraphrases of many of the Psalms. In this he is unlikely to have been influenced by his contemporary and fellow Gael George Buchanan, whose much more famous psalm paraphrases began to appear in 1556, seven years after MacLean's book. Melanchthon is perhaps

[136] R W Munro, ed., *A Description of the Western Isles of Scotland* (Edinburgh, 1961).
[137] It was later claimed before the General Assembly in 1570 that he was 'not prompt in the Scottish tongue': *Acts and Proceedings of the General Assemblies of the Kirk of Scotland, 1560–1618* (Maitland Club, 1839), i, 175. This, however, was perhaps a fictitious pretext for appointing an assistant commissioner to 'assist' him in his duties, and should not be taken at face value. Cf. *Monro's Western Isles*, 23; but cf. also the interpretation in J Bannerman, 'Literacy in the Highlands', in I B Cowan & D Shaw (eds), *The Renaissance and Reformation in Scotland* (Edinburgh, 1983), 214–35, at 220.
[138] A supplication to the pope was granted in favour of Donald Monro on 2 August 1549, when Roderick was in Rome. Rome, VA, RS 2667, 2991-v. It is one of a series of supplications on behalf of petitioners for chapter offices in Sodor diocese, which presumably show Roderick rewarding his friends and supporters. See below, p. 334.
[139] *HE*, iii, 4.

a more likely influence.[140] The only one of MacLean's psalm paraphrases presently known to have survived is the one included here.[141]

Another influence which has to be considered is that of Hector Boece. Boece (1465–1536), a native of Dundee, was a noted humanist scholar, graduate of the universities of St Andrews and Paris, professor of philosophy at the College of Montaigu, friend of Erasmus, and (from *c.* 1500) first principal of King's College Aberdeen. His two historical works, *Murthlacensium et Aberdonensium Episcoporum Vitae* (1522) and *Scotorum Historia* (1527), were very influential at the time, though the latter is not well regarded by modern historians. We can see Boece's influence in the king list inserted in MacLean's book (P6). We know that Boece corresponded with the monks of Iona and in 1520 persuaded them to let him borrow some of their ancient books,[142] as he says that William Elphinstone had previously done.[143] We have seen above that MacLean was acquainted with the high passes across the Mounth between Atholl and Braemar, possibly indicating travel to and from Aberdeen. King's College Aberdeen may have been the only place in Scotland where it was possible to study Greek.[144] It is worth considering the possibility (it is no more than a possibility) that MacLean had studied at Aberdeen under Boece before going to Wittenberg.

MacLean's religious views and the intended recipient of the poems

The book is not dedicated to a named individual. It is dedicated, rather, to the Isle of Iona (**P2**). It has been argued that the book was intended for consumption by the pope and *curia* at Rome,[145] and while this may well have been part of its purpose, it is remarkable that it contains no clear profession of loyalty to Rome, and the papacy is nowhere mentioned.

Dr Durkan suggested that 'by 1549 he had returned to the faith of his ancestors',[146] while Fr Dilworth also believed that he 'later returned to the

[140] Green, 'Poetic Psalm paraphrases', 269–70; idem, 'George Buchanan's Psalm paraphrases in a European context', in T Hubbard and R D S Jack, *Scotland in Europe* (Rodopi, Amsterdam, 2006), 25–38, esp. 30–2; cf. also idem, 'George Buchanan's Psalm Paraphrases: Matters of Metre', in *Acta Conventus Neo-Latini Sanctandreani: Proceedings of the Fifth International Congress of Neo-Latin Studies*, ed. I D McFarlane (New York, 1986), 51–60, at 54; cf. McFarlane, *Buchanan*, cap. 7, esp. 247–50.

[141] John Durkan credited MacLean as the first Scottish poet to write psalm paraphrases: J Durkan, 'Native influences on George Buchanan', in *Acta Conventus Neo-Latini Sanctandreani: Proceedings of the Fifth International Congress of Neo-Latin Studies*, ed. I D McFarlane (New York, 1986), 31–42, at 34.

[142] Boece, *Scotorum Historiae*, Preface and vii, 10.

[143] Boece, *Vitae*, 68

[144] Macfarlane, *Elphinstone*, 369; Durkan & Kirk, *University of Glasgow*, 263.

[145] For example, Sharpe, 'MacLean', 113.

[146] In McRoberts, *Essays on the Scottish Reformation*, xvi.

Catholic faith'.[147] Neither of them states on what evidence they base this statement, which implies a belief that MacLean had at some point deviated from traditional Catholicism. This is presumably because he had matriculated at Wittenberg in 1534.

It may be questioned, however, whether study at Wittenberg necessitated an unquestioning acceptance of Lutheranism, or on the other hand whether the absence of overt heterodoxy in his verses marks MacLean as rigidly Catholic.[148] It is true that many Scottish 'evangelicals' were fleeing abroad, to England and the Continent, in the early 1530s in the face of James V's persecution of heretics.[149] In October 1533, just a year before MacLean's arrival in Wittenberg, his fellow countryman Alexander Alane (Alesius) had enrolled at Wittenberg, and he was definitely a Lutheran.[150] Alane's time at Wittenberg may have overlapped with MacLean's. Another noteworthy Scot, John MacAlpine (Joannes Maccabaeus), a Gael like MacLean and a Lutheran like Alane, enrolled at Wittenberg in 1540, before going on to have a distinguished academic career in Lutheran Denmark.[151] Neither Alane nor MacAlpine returned to Scotland, whereas MacLean did. We have seen that MacLean's career in Scotland was promoted by the evangelical-leaning Governor Arran in 1543–44; but Arran's cautious interest in Protestantism was short-lived and wavered in the later 1540s, especially after the defeat of Pinkie in September 1547, when he found he required French help to beat off England's 'rough wooing': French help came at a price.

There is not very much within the *Ionis* itself to show MacLean as either a crypto-Lutheran or a staunch Roman Catholic. He says that he was wary of certain (unnamed) new developments, which he denounced. The words *Dira neotericae ne forte uenena Mineruae / Ammoueant ueteri te pietate, caue* ('Beware, lest perchance the deadly poison of a new Minerva (Wisdom) moves you away from ancient piety'), discussed above, could possibly be a warning against Calvinism, the *neoterica Minerua* which troubled the 1540s, and whose views on the saints were much more hostile than those of the Lutheranism MacLean had encountered at Wittenberg in the 1530s. The Lutheran attitude to the saints, as expressed in Article XXI of the *Augsburg Confession*, involved giving honour to saints and following their example, without invoking them as mediators of salvation. Such a view, indeed, was compatible with Adomnán's.

---

[147] Dilworth, 'Iona Abbey and the Reformation', 89–90.
[148] Green, 'Paraphrases', 270: 'Not all products of Wittenberg had the same anti-Catholic zeal as Luther.'
[149] J. Durkan, 'Scottish evangelicals in the patronage of Thomas Cromwell', *RSCHS*, xxi (1981–83), 127–56; J Durkan, 'The Cultural background in sixteenth-century Scotland,' *Innes Review*, x (1959), 382–439, at 427 ff.
[150] P Lorimer, *Patrick Hamilton, First Preacher and Martyr of the Scottish Reformation* (Edinburgh, 1857, reprinted 1957), 232; Durkan, 'Cultural Background', 428; cf. also *Dictionary of Scottish Church History and Theology* (Edinburgh, 1993), s.n. Alesius.
[151] Durkan, 'Cultural Background', 428.

There are, however, a few places where MacLean does embrace the 'Catholic' concept of saints as intermediaries who can pray efficaciously for the faithful. In the Introduction (**P5**), he writes: *Coelestes igitur quisquis in accolas / Christi municipes atque domesticos / non orat reuerens, sit uelut impius, / dignus supplicio perdier ultimo / consors manibus infimis* ('Thus, whosoever does not pray revering the heavenly inhabitants, the fellow-citizens and family of Christ, may he be like an impious one, worthy to be lost by the ultimate punishment, a companion to the souls of hell.'). He speaks in the same place of *sanctorum precibus gratia fusior* ('grace poured out more at the prayers of saints'). And in the 'refrain' sections towards the end of Book 1 (**1.19**), he writes: *Agni sedens ad nuptias, / O Ales ora supplicans, / ut nos tui superstites / polo fruamur coelites* ('O Dove, seated at the Lamb's wedding-feast, pray in supplication that we your survivors may enjoy the heavenly (feast) on high.'). His cousin Anna's tomb effigy invokes the prayers of St Mary.

MacLean's Renaissance learning would perhaps have appealed to the scholarship of Cardinal Carpi (to whom MacLean had a letter of recommendation from the Governor in 1544) and of the nepotistic art lover Pope Paul III. But as we have seen, the papacy is nowhere mentioned, and there is no overt profession of loyalty to Rome. On the other hand, there is no detectable heresy within the poems, and there are a few passages which are not compatible with Lutheranism. It may be that MacLean reflects the spirit of Erasmus more than that of Luther.

It must be remembered above all that MacLean was applying for a job in the established church, for which he was required, willy-nilly, to litigate at the papal *Curia*, while in the late 1540s, with the resurgence of Mary of Guise and the French alliance, persecution of heretics was resumed in Scotland. In the 1530s and early 1540s, MacLean's career looks very much like that of a typical Scottish humanist 'evangelical' with possible Lutheran leanings. By the later 1540s, his career has become threatened by Henry VIII's mischievous intervention in the Western Isles (part of the strategy of the 'rough wooing'), and he needed the support of the papacy and the Scottish court, by now more orthodox under Mary of Guise, to get his job back. We would therefore expect that if MacLean still harboured 'evangelical' views, he would be very guarded about them.[152]

The *Ionis* was presumably intended to be read by senior clergymen whose help could be instrumental in getting MacLean back to his rightful position. During his exile at or near Inverness, the bishop of Moray was Patrick Hepburn (1538–73), who seems to have been cautiously sympathetic towards reform; in

---

[152] One might compare Buchanan's career in the years following his brush with the Portuguese Inquisition, when from 1552 he was 'anxious to remain on the right side of orthodoxy': McFarlane, *Buchanan*, 249.

the late 1560s he agreed to repair Elgin Cathedral for Protestant worship.[153] The bishop of Ross at the time was David Paniter (1545–58), previously secretary to Governor Arran, and so also open to reforming thought.[154] He was frequently absent from the country as an ambassador to France. Another possibility might be John Hamilton, nominated archbishop of St Andrews shortly after Beaton's death in May 1546. He was a natural half-brother of Governor Arran. We have seen that Arran was promoting MacLean's career in the early 1540s. The inclusion of a pedigree for Mary Queen of Scots would have been flattering to a family which was directly descended from James II, the queen's great-great-grandfather, while the governor was also heir presumptive to Mary in the event of her dying childless. Archbishop Hamilton's own attitude to reformed opinion was notoriously indecisive.[155]

The *Epistola elegiaca*, addressed to the anti-clerical reformist Sir David Lindsay, presents a rather different picture, which calls into question whether MacLean genuinely had 'returned to the faith of his ancestors'. He tells Lindsay that *Est tibi libertas mores taxare prophanos, alter ut et Momus credier ipse queas* ('There is freedom for you to criticise profane ways, and you can be considered to be another Momus himself'). Clearly, he approves of Lindsay's fault-finding. He goes further: Lindsay, he says, has transcended the arts of men *cunctus ut agnoscet Numen, uereatur, adoret, / sic Euangelica clangis ubique tuba* ('so that all might know the Godhead, worship and adore Him, as you sound forth everywhere by the trumpet of the Gospel'). This seems to suggest a more 'evangelical' position than what is implied in the *Ionis*.

MacLean's text of Vita Columbae

MacLean's only written source for the *Ionis* is Adomnán's *Vita Columbae*.[156] The full text survives in two closely related manuscript traditions, conventionally known as A and B. A is primarily represented by a manuscript called the 'Dorbbéne codex', now in Schaffhausen.[157] It was written by a monk of Iona who died in *AU* 713. A second MS, believed to be a ninth-century copy of the 'Dorbbéne codex', is at Metz.[158] B is represented by three manuscripts, all now in the British Library.[159] At least one of them (B2) was written in Scotland,

---

[153] Dowden, *Bishops*, 171–2; Donaldson, *Scottish Reformation*, 56–7, 60.

[154] Dowden, *Bishops*, 226–8; Donaldson, *Scottish Reformation*, 55–6.

[155] Ibid., 55–8. The reformers at one time held out hopes for him, but his suspected involvement in the assassination of the Regent Moray (1570) turned them, and especially Buchanan, to bitter hostility: cf. Ford & Green, *Buchanan*, 62–3.

[156] Sharpe, 'MacLean', 114–15.

[157] This is the primary MS used in Anderson, *VC*. It can now be consulted online at: http://www.e-codices.unifr.ch/en/sbs/0001

[158] L Bieler, 'Review of *Adomnán's Life of Columba*, ed. A O & M O Anderson (1961)', *Irish Historical Studies*, xiii (1962–63), 177 ff.

[159] Cf. Anderson, *VC*, liv ff.

and it appears that John of Fordun had access to a copy of *VC* related to B. Some of Fordun's spellings of proper names are closer to those in the B manuscripts, and he includes the list of Columba's twelve companions, found in B but not in A, while omitting any reference to the passage attributed to *Cummeneus Albus* which is in A but not in B.[160]

It should be possible to get some idea of the character of MacLean's manuscript of *VC* from an analysis of his forms of proper names. On the whole, MacLean tends to adapt names in a way that makes them look more classical: typical examples would be *Falbaeus* < *Failbeus*, *Seginaeus* < *Segineus*, *Brudaeus* < *Brudeus*, *Aethica* < *Ethica*, etc. No special significance can be attached to forms like these. MacLean is not always consistent: we have seen above that for some names (like Iona and Baithéne), he shows a lot of flexibility. Again, no special significance can be attached to this. Neither can we read anything into MacLean's use of the form *Addamnanus* where A has *Adomnanus* and B has *Adamnanus*: the form *Adamnán* had become common centuries earlier and is used in the OI *Betha Adamnáin*.[161] The double consonant *-dd-* is a metrical device to make the first syllable long.

There are, however, a number of names in MacLean's *Ionis* which show a closer affinity to manuscript A than to the B manuscripts. Examples of these are:

MacLean	MS A	MSS B
Manteus (**1.2**)	Maucteus	Macteus

MacLean's form comes from misreading *u* as *n*. As *u* is absent in B, MacLean's form cannot be derived from it.

Fintenus (**1.5**)	A: Fintenus	B: Fentenus
Fymbarrus (**2.1**)	A: Findbarrus	B: Fendbarrus

In these two examples, MacLean is closer to A than to B.[162] (The Aberdeen Breviary has *Fymberrus*, *Fimberrus*.)[163]

Schya (**2.17**)	A: Scia insula	B: sua insula

The form *sua insula*, 'his island' (i.e. Iona), is found in B1 and B3. B2 (damaged in the Cottonian fire of 1731) is illegible at this point.[164] Here again MacLean is consistent with A rather than with B. This is perhaps the single strongest

---

[160] Cf. ibid., lix–lx; Sharpe, 'MacLean', 115; *Chron. Bower*, ed. Watt, ii, 221, note on cap. 27, l. 3.

[161] M Herbert and P. Ó Ríain (eds), *Betha Adamnáin: The Irish Life of Adamnán* (London, 1988).

[162] Cf. Anderson, *VC*, lxxviii, on the spelling of *find-* with *e* in B. MacLean's spelling may reflect the Gaelic orthographic rule of using *m* instead of *n* before the labials *b*, *f*, *m*, and *p*.

[163] Macquarrie, *Legends of Scottish Saints*, 234.

[164] Anderson, *VC*, 131 n.

piece of evidence that MacLean's manuscript was closer to A than to B: his form, which correctly represents Adomnán's words in manuscript A, could not possibly be derived from B. If MacLean's manuscript had read *sua insula*, he would have assumed that this was a reference to Iona.

Callianinde (2.22)   A · Kailli au inde   B: Kaillianfinde, Kaillianfind

MacLean's copy appears not to have had the (lenited) *f* which appears in B but not in A. Accepting the misreading of *u* as *n*, his form is closer to A than to B.

In *VC*, ii, 44, Adomnán sets an incident *Ante annos … ferme xuii*, 'nearly seventeen years ago' (manuscript A). The B manuscripts have *ferme quatuordecim*, having misread *xuii* as *xiiii*. MacLean (2.35.2) has *sedecem plusquam … annos*, 'more than sixteen years'. This could not possibly be derived from B, but is consistent with A.

More ambiguous is the following example:

Landers (2.15)   A: Lam dess, Lam des   B: Lamdes, Laudes, Lamdhes

The name in MacLean's exemplar appears to have ended with two consonants, the first of which he misread. Long *s* in Insular minuscule hand (of which the hand of manuscript A is an example) can look like *r* with the descender going below the line, and could easily be misread as *r*.[165] The archetype of the B manuscripts appears to have had *lamdes* or *lādes*, which could not have yielded MacLean's spelling. Manuscript A has both *Lam dess* and *Lam des*.[166]

There are no forms of proper names in MacLean which could not be derived from a copy very closely related to manuscript A. On the other hand, most of the forms listed above could not be derived from the B tradition as it survives.

There are also some examples of misreadings in B which are not in MacLean:

Lugbeus (1.20)   A: Lugbeus   B: Lugreus, Lugbeus

Lugreus is a misreading in B1 in *VC*, i, 24.

Munenses (1.34)   A: Muminenses   B: Muminenses, Muginenses

Muginenses is a misreading in B1 in *VC*, i, 44. (The intervocalic *m* in OI *Muman*, Munster, had become lenited centuries before MacLean's time.) These last examples are inconclusive: if MacLean had been working from a manuscript which had these misreadings he could probably have corrected them from knowledge or from forms found elsewhere in his source. But they are all consistent with use of a source closely related to manuscript A.

165 Cf. the facsimile pages in Anderson, *VC*, lxxxi ff., M P Brown, *A Guide to Western Historical Scripts from Antiquity to 1600* (London, 1990), 48–9 and following.
166 Here again, MacLean's spelling may reflect Gaelic orthography, with *n* before a dental consonant.

MacLean's text seems to have been a complete copy of *VC*. Even though he did not paraphrase Adomnán's Book iii, MacLean knew its contents. He knew that Columba's mother Eithne had an angelic vision (**1.3**);[167] and he knew that Diarmait was a witness to Columba's last hours (**2.21**).[168] In his summary narration (**1.1.77–89**), he echoes language found in *VC*, iii, 19. The 'refrain' after **1.19** *et seq.* echoes a passage in *VC*, iii, 23 (on 134b) which may have formed the original ending of Adomnán's work.[169] MacLean paraphrases a number of Adomnán's chapters which are not in the so-called 'shorter recension': **1.16**, **1.17**, **1.19**, **1.20**, **1.21**, **1.22**; **2.11**, **2.12**, **2.22**, **2.30**, **2.34**.

There are a few short passages in the B manuscripts which are not in A. A number of these are definitely by Adomnán,[170] and read like additions made after the bulk of the text, as represented by A, had been drafted. The longest of them is in ii, 20. It is not included by MacLean, whose sections **2.11** and **2.12** follow continuously, linked by *similiter* in the title of **2.12** and *sic* in the first line. The organisation of MacLean's **2.11** and **2.12** is thus the same as manuscript A's ii, 20 and ii, 21,[171] without the second part of ii, 20 found only in the B manuscripts. This can be taken as negative evidence (and, as such, not totally conclusive) that this passage from B was not in his copy. It is barely conceivable, however, that MacLean would have paraphrased his manuscript in the way that he does in **2.11** and **2.12** if it had had a contrasting section in between. There is no trace either of the additional sentence in B in ii, 44 in MacLean's **2.35**.

Manuscript A has a long addendum at iii, 5 of a passage from Cumméne's 'Book of the Powers of St Columba', which is not by Adomnán and is not in the B manuscripts. Since MacLean does not paraphrase Book iii, sadly we do not know whether the addendum was in his MS. There are, however, very few passages in Books i and ii of Adomnán which are in A but not in B.[172] One brief example is in ii, 26, Columba's encounter with a wild boar in Skye. Manuscript A mentions the boar *quem forte uenatici canes persequebantur* ('which it happened that hunting dogs were pursuing'), words that are not in the B manuscripts. There is no trace of them in MacLean's **2.17**. But MacLean departs quite considerably from Adomnán's simple narrative here, with an elaborate and vivid description of a vicious, poisonous creature (cf. his vivid description of the River Ness monster in **2.18**, where he elaborates on Adomnán's simple account). We cannot make any assumptions about MacLean's manuscript from the absence of any reflection of these five words.

---

[167] Cf. *VC*, iii, 1.
[168] Cf. *VC*, iii, 23.
[169] Cf. below, p. 284.
[170] E.g., in *VC*, ii, 20; ii, 44. Cf. Sharpe, *Adomnán*, 236–7.
[171] Cf. Anderson, *VC*, 120–3 and n.; Sharpe, *Adomnán*, 169–70 and n. 256, 327.
[172] Enumerated in Bieler, 'Review of *Adomnán's Life of Columba*', 179–80.

Thus, the accumulation of evidence strongly suggests that MacLean's source was a manuscript of the complete text of *VC* which was more closely related to manuscript A than to the B manuscripts. MacLean's poems show no trace of the additions in B; some of his name forms are closer to A than to B, and he has some forms which could not possibly be derived from B. It is not certain where MacLean found his manuscript. Iona is by far the most likely place, though he must have had it (or a copy of it) with him in Inverness while he was completing his poem. Thus, although the A tradition now only survives in manuscripts on the Continent, MacLean's text shows that a version of the text very closely related to it survived in Scotland, probably on Iona, in the sixteenth century.

MacLean also had a version of a king list of Gaelic Scotland, which he describes as coming *ex uetustissimis Gathaelicae nationis hystoriographorum libris*. It is not clear where he got it from, but it appears not to be as ancient as he claims, being largely confected from Boece's *Scotorum Historia*.[173]

THE SOURCES

Three copies of Roderick MacLean's *Ionidos Liber* are now known to survive. One (Copy A) is in Aberdeen University Library.[174] A second copy of the book (Copy P1), which has recently come to light, is in the Biblioteca communale Augusta in Perugia.[175] This copy also contains the only known copy of the *Epistola elegiaca* and *Straena Gratulatoria*. A third copy of the *Ionidos Liber* (Copy P2), missing the title page and first gathering, has also even more recently come to light in the same library in Perugia.

The title page states that the book was 'Excusum Typis Antonii Bladi Romae apud Campum Florae Mense Maio M.D.XLIX' (Printed by the press of Antonio Blado, Rome, at the Campo de' Fiori, May 1549). The printer Antonio Blado (d. 1567) is well known. Antonio Blado d'Asola set up a printing press in Rome near the Campo de' Fiori in 1516 and soon became successful. He printed Machiavelli's *Discorsi* (posthumously) in 1531. In 1548, he printed Ignatius Loyola's *Spiritual Exercises*. In 1549, the year of publication of MacLean's book, he was appointed printer to the Roman *curia*. Printed catalogues of Blado's publications make no mention of MacLean's works.[176]

---

[173] I am grateful to Professor Dauvit Broun for advice on this point. See pp. 272–3.

[174] R P H Green, P H Burton & D J Ford, *Scottish Latin Authors in Print up to 1700: A Short-Title List* (Leuven, 2012), 192, 345.

[175] It is listed in the Universal Short Title Catalogue: http://www.ustc.ac.uk/ . We are grateful to Professor Sally Mapstone for drawing this to our attention.

[176] G Fumagalli et al., *Catalogo delle edizioni romane di Antonio Blado Asolano ed Eredi, 1516–1593*, 4 vols (Rome, 1891–1961). Cf. Sharpe, 'MacLean', 111.

Copy A: Aberdeen University Library π³ 92211 Col M

This bears the shelf mark π3 92211 Col M (formerly Σ2 09(456) Mac) and
the date 1928. It is a small quarto volume with a modern binding of brown
leather boards, the pages trimmed to approximately 200 x 135 mm. The
book now contains fifty-three folios, including two blank folios at front and
one at rear. In between are fifty folios containing MacLean's printed poems.
These are (mostly) numbered in pen in a nineteenth-century hand. The title
page is numbered 231 and the folios are then mostly numbered consecutively
through to the last page of the poem, which is numbered 277. Three folios
have been left unnumbered in error: they are following folios numbered 240,
241, and 251. All the folios (apart from the three endpapers at front and rear)
have writing except 249 v and 277 v.

There is a printed bookplate on the inside of the front board: 'Read this
book, O reader, and be mindful of William Dey, who was born and lies buried
in Strath Aven: for it is he that gives the book to the University of Aberdeen
and to you.' Below is the old shelfmark Σ2 09(456) Mac, cancelled out, and the
date 1928 in pen, and the modern shelfmark π3 92211 Col M, also in pen. The
spine has in gold lettering: MACLENIUS (DE INTUITU PROPHETICO D.
COLUMBAE 1549. There is a tag on a string bearing the writing: π3 92211 Col M.

Dr William Dey (1836–1915) was a native of Kirkmichael in Strath Avon,
Banffshire, and a Gaelic speaker. He graduated from the University of Aberdeen
MA 1861 and LLD 1885. He was rector of the Grammar School of Old Aberdeen
from 1870 to 1887, and one of the assessors in the university court, elected by
the General Council, from 1889 until his death in Aberdeen on 15 November
1915. He represented the university on several educational committees.
He lectured locally on education and training, and was author of several
books and pamphlets on the subject. He left several generous bequests to the
university on his death, including his own books and funds for the purchase
of books for the university library and for the library's Celtic and education
departments.[177] It is not known how the book came into the possession of
William Dey, or indeed whether it was purchased by the university library
after his death out of his bequest.

From the foliation it is clear that the book was formerly bound in with
other material. The date 1928, thirteen years after the death of the donor
William Dey, could either indicate when it was separated from the other
materials and rebound, or the year of its purchase out of William Dey's
bequest. The present binding appears to be consistent with such a date. It
would be interesting to know if the university library has a printed book or
manuscript with foliation which ends at f. 230. The book's earlier history
before the time of William Dey has not been traced.

---

[177] Obituary in *Aberdeen University Review*, iii (1915–16), 185; see also ibid., 98–107, 108–14, 171;
http://archiveshub.ac.uk/data/gb231-ms0648; cf. also W Barclay, *Banffshire* (Cambridge,
1922), 114.

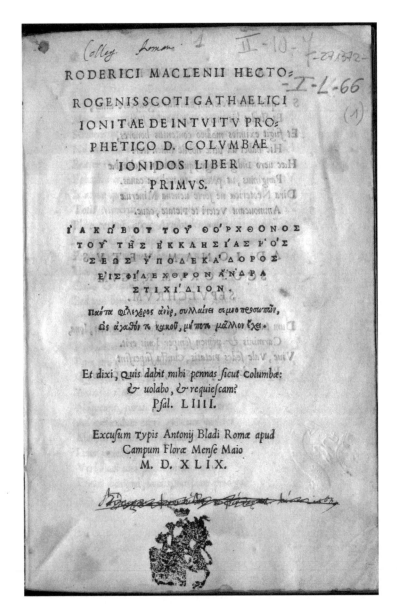

RODERICI MACLENII HECTO=
ROGENIS SCOTI GATHAELICI
IONITAE DE INTVITV PRO=
PHETICO D. COLVMBAE
IONIDOS LIBER
PRIMVS.

ΙΑΚΩΒΟΤ ΤΟῪ ΘΟΎΡΧΘΟΝΟΣ
ΤΟῪ ΤῆΣ ἘΚΚΛΗΣΙΑΣ Ῥ Ο΄Σ
ΣΕΩΣ ῩΠΟΔΕΚΑ ΔΟΡΟΣ
ΕΊΣ ΦΙΛΕ ΧΘΡΟΝ ἈΝΔΡΑ
ΣΤΙΧΙΔΙΟΝ.

Πᾶν τα φιλεχθρος ἀνὴρ, συ Μαίνει σεμνοπρσωπῶν,
ὡς ἀγαθὸὶ τε κακοῦ, μή πτε μᾶλλον ἔχει.

Et dixi, Quis dabit mihi pennas ficut Columbæ:
& uolabo, & requiefcam?
Pfal. LIIII.

Excufum Typis Antonij Bladi Romæ apud
Campum Floræ Menfe Maio
M. D. XLIX.

Figure 3. Title page of *Perugia, Biblioteca communale Augusta*, I-L-66 (1). The inscription *Colleg. Roman.* at the top shows that the book once belonged to the Jesuit College in Rome, founded by Ignatius Loyola in 1551. The stamp at the foot shows a crowned griffin holding an open book, the stamp of the Biblioteca communale Augusta in Perugia. By kind permission of the Biblioteca communale Augusta, Perugia.

Copy P1: Perugia, Biblioteca communale Augusta, I-L-66 (1–2)

This bears the shelfmark I-L-66. It is a small quarto volume, measuring 200 x 135 mm, bound in a soft flexible cover of purple leather. It now contains fifty-six folios. At the front is the *Ionidos Liber*, its folios numbered (1) 1–50 consecutively in pencil in a modern hand. It is followed immediately by the *Epistola elegiaca* addressed to Sir David Lindsay and the *Straena gratulatoria* addressed to the governor Arran, whose folios are numbered (2) 1–6 in the same hand.

On the spine is the number 99 (or possibly 66 upside-down) at top, and at foot an adhesive label marked: *Biblioteca Augusta Perugia: I L 66*. On the title page are two inscriptions in pen. At top are the words *Colleg. Roman.*, in a sixteenth-century hand. At the foot is a longer inscription of a single line extending across most of the page, which has been heavily scored through in pen several times. Beneath this is a stamp making a dark impression in ink. It shows a crowned griffin standing beside an open book, and is the stamp of the Biblioteca communale Augusta.[178] The griffin, having the hindquarters of a lion and the head and wings of an eagle, is prominent in the coat of arms of Perugia. In the top right-hand corner of the title page there is modern writing in pencil: II-10-7 (271372 (I (L (66 (1).

Bound into this copy at the end is the only known copy of the *Epistola elegiaca*. It is a gathering of six folios. The title page has -271373-1 (2) in pencil in a modern hand in the top right corner. It has no other inscriptions.

The inscription *Colleg. Roman.* indicates that this copy once belonged to the Collegium Romanum, now the Pontifical Gregorian University, founded by St Ignatius Loyola in 1551 (two years after the book's publication, and a year after MacLean's return to Scotland). It is believed, however, that the book was already in the collection which became the Biblioteca communale Augusta before its foundation in 1582, by which date the library had been mostly assembled.[179]

Near the foot, the second, longer inscription has been scored through several times and is now difficult to read. It is written in the Greek alphabet. A number of Greek letters are clearly visible, including phi, rho, delta, and lambda. It is probably therefore also in the Greek language. The inscription has been scored through at least three times. There is a heavy continuous stroke, more or less straight, and at least two zig-zag lines. One of the zig-zag lines does not extend across the whole inscription, but just over the first three words. There are acute accents, four in all, over certain letters. These letters

[178] Cf. Giovanni Cecchini, *La Biblioteca Augusta del comune di Perugia* (Rome, 1978), Plate XII; cf. also Plate XI.
[179] Information from Mr Paolo Renzi, Ufficio Fondo Antico, Biblioteca communale Augusta. We are grateful to the staff of the Biblioteca communale Augusta for their help during Alan Macquarrie's visits. Cf. also Cecchini, *Biblioteca Augusta*.

Figure 4. Greek inscription on the title page of the Perugia copy (P1). The words δεύτεραι φροντίδ[ες] [σ]οφ[ ]τερ[ ] λ[ ] 1565 can be made out. The date probably shows when the book was acquired by Prospero Podiani from the Jesuits in Rome. By kind permission of the Biblioteca communale Augusta, Perugia.

must then be vowels. The existence of four accents implies four words (unless there are enclitics).

At the right-hand end, where the zig-zag strokes are less heavy, is what appears to be a date in Arabic numerals. It looks like 1565, although the zig-zag stroke through it makes the last digit a little difficult to read. If the second and fourth digits are indeed 5, they are written as a single continuous stroke of the pen, which was characteristic of the time.

Reading through the zig-zag lines and the heavy continuous stroke, a number of letters can be made out with greater or lesser certainty. The inscription reads, as far as can be made out: δεύτεραι φροντίδ[ες] [σ]οφ[ ]τερ[ ] λ[ ] 1565.[180] The first two words thus appear to mean 'second thoughts'. The third word could be σοφίστερου, 'of a wise man', or its plural σοφίστερων 'of wise men', or possibly σοφώτεραι, 'wiser'. Only the first letter (lambda) of the last word is legible. It is followed by a vowel, which could possibly be epsilon or iota, with an acute accent. The word appears to have been of about five or six letters.

There is a line in Euripides' *Hippolytus*, κἀν βροτοῖς / αἱ δεύτεραι πως φροντίδες σοφώτεραι (435–6), 'among mortals second thoughts are somehow wiser', and the expression δεύτεραι φροντίδες, 'second thoughts', is used by a number of Renaissance writers.[181] Perhaps the inscription is suggesting that MacLean's 'second thoughts' were 'wiser' or more sophisticated than Adomnán's original?

---

[180] Thanks are due to Dr Evelyn Gillies of the Forensic Documents Bureau, Aberdeen, for supplying high-quality images of the inscription.

[181] It was used as the title of a book: *Δεύτεραι Φροντίδες, or, a Review of the Paraphrase & Annotations On All the Books Of The New Testament With Some Additions & Alterations*, By H[enry] Hammond, D.D. (London, 1656). It was also used, for example, by the French physician Samuel de Sorbière in his correspondence with Thomas Hobbes: in a letter (mostly in Latin) from the Hague in May 1646, he casually includes the Greek quotation, 'ταῖς δευτέραις φροντίδεσι σοφώτερων,' which the translator renders 'the second thoughts of wise men'. See Noel Malcolm, *The Correspondence of Thomas Hobbes* (Oxford, 1994), 128. Cf. also R van de Schoor, *Georgius Cassander's De Officiis pii Viri (1561)* (Berlin, 2016), 251; John Caius, *De Canibus Britannicis* (London, 1570), last paragraph. It may be guessed that the line from Euripides probably underlies these quotations.

If the date 1565 is correct, then the inscription cannot have been written by Roderick MacLean, who died in 1553.[182]

The Biblioteca communale Augusta was founded by a Perugian citizen, Prospero Podiani, in 1582.[183] Podiani (1535–1615) was a noted humanist and bibliophile, whose library contained some 7,600 works, including manuscripts and incunabula. In 1582 he gifted his library to the *commune* of Perugia. The library was opened to the public in 1623. It was housed first in the Palazzo dei Priori, then moved in 1623 to the university, the building which is now the Palazzo del Tribunale. It later moved to the Palazzo Conestabile della Staffa in the Via delle Prome, where it is presently located.

The first catalogue of books was made in 1617, by the then librarian Fulvio Mariottelli. It mentions: *Roderigo Maccleni De intuitu profetico Poesia Lat. Roma 1549*.[184] Thus the book was in the Biblioteca communale Augusta by 1617, which means it was almost certainly in Podiani's library before 1582. The date 1565 therefore probably indicates the date when it was acquired by Prospero Podiani, presumably from the Collegium Romanum. Podiani had a strong connection with Jesuits both at Rome and at Perugia, and is buried in the Chiesa del Gesù in Perugia. The most likely explanation is that Podiani acquired the book from the Collegium Romanum, probably in 1565, almost certainly no later than 1582, and certainly before his death in 1615.

Since Ignatius Loyola for his *Spiritual Exercises* used the same printer (Antonio Blado) in Rome in 1548 that Roderick MacLean used for *Ionis* in 1549, it is possible that MacLean met some of his Jesuit associates, or even Loyola himself, while he was in Rome in 1549–50, and gave them a copy of his book. We know that Roderick had earlier had an association with Jesuits, when he acted as guide to their mission to Ireland in 1542 and accompanied them back to Rome. It is possible, perhaps indeed likely, that he looked up some old acquaintances on his second visit to Rome in 1549. If the Jesuits had little interest in obscure Scottish hagiography, they could have passed it on to the bibliophile Podiani in 1565 within a few years of acquiring it.

---

[182] Prospero Podiani could write in Greek: C Dondi & M A Panzanelli Fratoni, 'Researching the Origin of Perugia's Public Library (1582/1623) before and after *Material Evidence in Incunabula*', *Quaerendo*, 46 (2016), 129–50, at 145. But the shape of some letters (e.g., *rho*, *lambda*) on the title page of *Ionis* is quite different from Podiani's Greek hand.

[183] For the background to the library's foundation, cf. C F Black, 'Perugia and Post-Tridentine Church reform', *Journal of Ecclesiastical History*, 35/3 (July 1984), 429–51, at 443. Cf. also C F Black, *The Italian Inquisition* (New Haven, 2009), 167 and 288, n. 37. Cf. also C Dondi & M A Panzanelli Fratoni, 'Researching the Origin of Perugia's Public Library (1582/1623) before and after *Material Evidence in Incunabula*', *Quaerendo*, 46 (2016), 129–50.

[184] Biblioteca communale Augusta, S. 3082, f. 129v.

Copy P2: Perugia, Biblioteca communale Augusta, ANT I-I-1255(8)

This is a miscellany in an eighteenth-century (?) binding, which is believed to have entered the library some time in the mid-nineteenth century, probably before the fall of the Papal States and the unification of Italy. It was not part of Prospero Podiani's collection, and does not appear in the earliest catalogue of the library (1617). The librarian believes it was acquired some time 1830–70, possibly *c.* 1840. Its earlier provenance is unknown.[185] Its copy of *Ionis* is incomplete, missing the first gathering.

Its contents are extremely miscellaneous. There are twenty-two items. All that they have in common is that they are all quartos, approximately 200 x 135 mm. Thirteen of the twenty-two items were printed in Rome, one was printed in Florence, and the rest do not state place of publication. In some cases Rome is the likely place of publication. They range in date from 1507 (no 5) to 1586 (no 1), though some are undated. The following list serves to indicate the extremely miscellaneous nature of the assembly:

1. *Discorso intorno all'origine, antichita, et virtu de gli Agnus Dei Dicera Benedetti. Di F. Vincentio Bonardo Romano, dell'Ordine de' Precatori, Maestro in Teologia. Con Licentia de' Superiori. In Roma, Appresso Vincentio Accolti, in Borgo, 1586.* (Thirty-two pages.)

2. *Theodoriti episcopi Cyri, Oratio Vere Aurea de Caritate sive Dilectione, ante hac nunquam Graece, nunc autem Graece simul et Latine recens edita, interprete Gerardo Vossio. Romae, in Aedibus Populi Romani 1580.* (Fifty-six pages.)

3. *Constitutiones et Decreta Synodi Dioecesanae Viterbien'. Romae, apud Antonium Bladum Impressorem Cameralem, 1564.* (Twelve folios.)

3A. *De modo et ordine deferendi sacramentum infirmis: De officio electorum pro capitibus parrochiarum: De celebranda missa et processione: etc.*

4. *Caesarei Edicti Wormatiae anno Christi MDXXI, Editi, Exemplar. Romae, 1545. Romae, apud Antonium Bladum.*

5. *Regule Ordinationes et Constitutiones Cancellarie S.D.N.D. Iulii divina providentia Pape scripte et correcte in Cancellaria Apostolica, 1507.* (Twenty-eight folios. No printer's name.)

6. *Hec sunt Acta Capituli Generalis Romae Celebrati, In Conventu S Mariae super Minervam in festo Sanctiss' Penthecostes, Anno Domini MDLIII, Die xxi Maii, Sub Rever' Patre F. Stephano Ususmaris Genuensi, Sac. Theologiae Professore, Magistro Generali Ordinis Praedicatorum, in eodem capitulo unanimiter electo, Diffinientibus communiter Rever. Provin. et Diffinitoribus ... Rome 1553.* (Sixteen folios.)

7. *Laurentii Gambarae Damastor et Daphnis. Romae apud Valerium et Loisium Fratres Doricos. MDLI.* (Four folios.)

---

[185] Information from Sgr Paolo Renzi, as above.

8.   *De Secundae in Vitam D. Columbae Praefatione quaedam de Virtutibus eius Summaria Enarratio. Phanaloga.* (Forty-six folios. The whole of *Ionis* and the paraphrase of Psalm 1, missing its first gathering.)

9.   *Lare* (sic) *sacre penitentiarie Apostolice incipiunt.* (Four folios. No printer's name.)

10. *Gregorius Magolatus Epis. Clus. Prov. Romand. et Exarc. Ravennae Pręses.* (Ninety-three numbered pages. No printer's name, but it looks similar to Blado's work.)

11. *Acta in Civitate Parisiensi a Rege Carolo Nono. Romae, apud Heredes Antonii Bladi impressores camerales. Anno MDLXXII.* (Four folios.)

12. *C. Cornelii Taciti Annalium ab excessu D. Augusti ad Imperium Galbae. Liber Primus A.M. Antonio Mureto emendatus. Permissu superiorum. Romae, apud Heredes Antonii Bladi impressores camerales MDLXXX.* (Forty pages.)

13. *Ordo servandis in processionibus fiendis in singulis diebus durante expeditione contra Infideles de mandato Sanctissimi D.N. Pauli Divina Providentia Papa III.* (Four folios. No printer's name.)

14. *In Processione fienda pro Victoria habita contra Infideles et Captione Regni Tunicis, per Serenissimum Carolum Imperatorem nostrum.* (Four folios. No printer's name.)

15. *Coronatio Ferdinandi regis Invictissimi.* (Four folios. No printer's name.)

16. *Epistola Stanislai Rescii, de Transitu et Dormitione Illustriss' et Reverendiss' d. Stanislai Hosii, S.R.E. Cardinalis, Maioris Penitentiarii et Episcopi Varmiensis. Romae, apud Heredes Antonii Bladi impressores camerales. MDLXXX.* (Twelve folios.)

17. *Capitula Statuta et Ordinationes Piae ac Venerabilis Confraternitatis Sanctissimi Corporis Christi in Ecclesia Minervae Almae Urbis Romae. Romae, apud Antonium Bladum impressorem cameralem. Anno Domini MDLXI.* (Sixteen folios.)

18. *Statuti et Ordini della Venerabile Arcicompagnia del Santiss' Crocefisso in Santo Marcello di Roma con l'Origine d'Essa.* (on last folio): *Rome apud Antonium Bladum Impress. Cam. MDLXV.* (Sixty-eight folios.)

19. *Bolla sopra la Institutione della Compagnia della Charità de Roma. Stampato in Roma MDXLVII.* (Six folios.)

20. *Diploma Caesareum Continens Erectionem Magni Ducatus Etruriae. Florentiae apud Iuntas MDLXXVI.* (Six folios.)

21. *Jacobus Cerrinus Guidoni suo S.P.D.* (Four folios. No printer's name.)

22. *Compendium terminorum pro novitiis Dialeticam sectantibus nuperrime editum.* (Four folios. No printer's name. The font and layout of nos 21 and 22 look very similar.)

Apart from no. 18, none of them has any marginalia or inscriptions. No. 18 has some marginalia in a late-sixteenth-century hand. The acephalous copy of Roderick MacLean's *Ionis* has no marginalia or inscriptions or any other clue about its provenance.

A hand-written catalogue card from an earlier library catalogue of the Biblioteca communale Augusta mentions Roderick MacLean and the printers Valerio and Luigi Dorico in Rome. This is erroneous, resulting from a confusion of items 7 and 8: the author of the card has wrongly assumed that item 7 is the missing head of item 8. In fact, the two are unrelated. He has got the name of Roderick MacLean from the title page of Liber 2 of *Ionis*.

Although the book's provenance cannot be determined beyond the middle of the nineteenth century, and the lack of marginalia or inscriptions provides no clue, it is of great interest to be able to identify another copy of this very rare book. It is certainly possible that further copies of MacLean's works will come to light in future: it would be very exciting to find more of his Psalm paraphrases.

Signatures

The title pages of MacLean's Book I and Book II (numbered f. 231 and 249 in Copy A, numbered f. 1 and 21 in Copy P) have no signatures, but the rest of the book has the following signatures.

Copy A: f. 232 = Aii: f. 235 = B: f. 236 = Bii: f. 239 = C: f. 240 = Cii: unnumbered folio between 241 and 242 = D: f. 242 = Dii: f. 245 = E: f. 246 = Eii: f. 250 = Fii: f. 252 = G: f. 253 = Gii: f. 256 = H: f. 257 = Hii: f. 260 = I: f. 261 = Iii: f. 264 = K: f. 265 = Kii: f. 268 = L: f. 269 = Lii: f. 272 = M: f. 273 = Mii: f. 274 = Miii. The discrepancy between the signatures and the folio numbers is accounted for by the accidental omission of the three folio numbers.

Copy P: f. 2 = Aii: f. 5 = B: f. 6 = Bii: f. 9 = C: f. 10 = Cii: f. 13 = D: f. 14 = Dii: f. 17 = E: f. 18 = Eii: f. 22 = Fii: f. 25 = G: f. 26 = Gii: f. 29 = H: f. 30 = Hii: f. 33 = I: f. 34 = Iii: f. 37 = K: f. 38 = Kii: f. 41 = L: f. 42 = Lii: f. 45 = M: f. 46 = Mii: f. 47 = Miii.

The book is evidently a quarto with an extra bifolium inserted into the last gathering (sig. M). The final folio has a Latin paraphrase of Psalm 1, included *ne pagina remaneret uacua*. Its verso is blank. This shows that there is nothing missing at the end, and that the book is complete as it stands. It also shows that the *Epistola elegiaca* is a separate book, and was not intended to be part of the *Ionis*.

The *Epistola elegiaca* has the following signatures: f. 1 (no signature: f. 2 = Aii: f. 3 = Aiii.

Most pages in both books have 28 lines of verse. The pages in iambic dimeter, with its short octosyllabic lines, are printed in double column. These are folios 241+1v - 248v in Copy A, folios 13v–20v in Copy P1.

EDITORIAL CONVENTIONS

The book is printed to a very high standard, in keeping with Antonio Blado's reputation: so only a relatively small number of textual notes are required at the foot of the page. Obvious misprints are corrected. Eccentric and hyper-correct spellings are retained, even where they distort the meaning of a word (e.g., *coetus* for *cetus*), or where they appear to disfigure the metre (e.g., *praece* for *prece*, *praemat* for *premat*, where these require a short vowel). In these cases, MacLean's intention is usually clear. Quotation marks have been added editorially to indicate direct speech, and punctuation is editorial, though as far as possible having regard for the original punctuation. Capitalisation has been modernised. Blado tended to capitalise most nouns, whether they be proper names or not, and to use capitals for the first word of a section or paragraph (where we might use an indentation). This is not, however, consistent. He used *v* in initial positions and in words that are capitalised, elsewhere *u*; here *u* has been used throughout except on the title pages. Initial and medial *f* has been changed to *s* throughout, and *ij* has been changed to *ii*. Blado used -*'q;* for -*que* and -*'q~;* for -*quam*. He very occasionally uses ~ over a vowel to indicate a following nasal. Once he uses *q* with a curving diagonal line through the descender to indicate *quod*. These are all silently extended. The ampersand & has been silently changed to *et* throughout; Blado is inconsistent in its use. Blado is not consistent in his use of the digraphs æ, œ, Æ, Œ; these have been changed to *ae, oe, Ae, Oe*, throughout. The original printing of the verse is in a handsome italic font; this has been changed to roman font, with chapter headings in bold.

The numbering of the sections of *Ionis* is adapted from Richard Sharpe's commentary.[186] These are numbered **P1–P6** for the preliminary matters, then **1.1–1.38** for the material from *VC* Book i, **2.1–2.38** for the material from *VC* Book ii. The psalm paraphrase is designated **Ps.**, the *Epistola elegiaca* is **Ep.**, and the *Straena gratulatoria* is **St.**

POSTSCRIPT

He was a career churchman from a family with a strong connection to Iona and its abbey. He was scholarly and learned in both Gaelic and Latin, which he wrote in a self-conscious, mannered style, imitating his best models while trying to show some originality. He took pride in his learning and he was ambitious, but in a way that was not out of keeping with his abilities. His biblical scholarship was of a very high standard, and he was widely read with a large vocabulary. He had a respect for tradition, especially the traditions of

---

[186] Sharpe, 'MacLean', 118–32.

Iona; he was at the same time also broad-minded and receptive to new ideas, widely travelled, and eager to learn from others. He admired the qualities which he found in Columba as described in the sources available to him, and he viewed Columba as a saintly example to be followed and admired.

This is a description that could apply equally to both Adomnán and Roderick MacLean. It is easy to see why MacLean was attracted to Adomnán's *Vita Columbae*. In temperament, in theology, in scholarship, Roderick MacLean was like a sixteenth-century Adomnán. To both men Bede's words could be applied: *Erat enim vir bonus et sapiens, et scientia scripturarum nobilissime instructus.*[187]

---

[187] *HE*, v, 15.

The Poems of Roderick MacLean

RODERICI MACLENII HECTOROGENIS
SCOTI GATHAELICI IONITAE
DE INTVITV PROPHETICO D<IVI> COLVMBAE
IONIDOS LIBER PRIMVS

ἸΑΚΩΒΟΥ ΤΟῦ ΘΟΡΧΘΟΝΟΣ ΤΟῦ ΤῆΣ ἘΚΚΛΗΣΊΑΣ
ῬΌΣΣΕΩΣ ῾ΥΡΟΔΕΚΆΔΟΡΟΣ ἘΙΣ ΦΊΛΕΧΘΡΟΝ
ἌΝΔΡΑ ΣΤΙΧΊΔΙΟΝ.

Πάντα φίλεχθρος ἀνὴρ συλλαίνει[1] σεμνοπροσωπῶν,
Ὡς ἀγαθόν τε κακοῦ, μήποτε μᾶλλον ἔχει.

Et dixi, Quis dabit mihi pennas sicut Columbae: et uolabo, et
requiescam?
Psal<mus> LIIII.

Excusum Typis Antonii Bladi Romae apud Campum Florae
Mense Maio MDXLIX

---

[1] *Sic*: read συλλαίνει.

Ionis

Book One

The Prophetic Knowledge of St Columba

by Roderick MacEachainn MacLean,

a Scottish Gael of Iona

Lines of James, son of [John] Thorntoun, subdean of the church of Ross, to
a man who loves enmity:

A man who loves enmity always mocks with a solemn countenance:
So he never holds to the good rather than the bad.

And I said, Who will give me wings like a dove? And I will fly
away and take my rest.
Psalm (Vulg.) 54

Printed by the Press of Antonio Blado, Rome, at the Campo de'
Fiori, May 1549

[f. P 1v; A 231v]

[P1] Ad lectorem

Si quis amat ueterum sanctas cognoscere uitas,
    et studet his mores aequiparare suos,
et fugit eximios modico contentus honores,
    hic habet ad uitae nobile limen iter.
5 Haec uero indigeti lege, qualiacunque Columbae
    pangimus, ut poteris, tu meliora canas.
Dira neotericae ne forte uenena Mineruae
    ammoueant ueteri te pietate, caue.

[f. P 1v; A 231v]

[P2] Ad Ionam uetus Scotorum regum sepulchrum

Dum tua templa manent, manet hoc tibi carmen, Iona,
    carminis et nomen semper 'Ionis' erit.
Uiue, uale sedes pietatis, cuncta supersint
    phana et reliquiae, sacra, sepulchra, cruces.

[f. P 2r; A 232r] A ii

[P3] Conciuncula scriptoris

Liuore mentes toxicante plurimas
mos poene nostro conualescit tempore,
scribens ut omnis liuorem metuat nimis.
Nil infaceto arridet isti saeculo,
5 praeter nephas, quis hoc uult experirier?
Ephoebus aequae rerum prodit arbiter,
is atque quem secreti fecit conscium
totis Minerua saeculis omniscia.
Plato peritus, atque Aristoteles uafer,
10 seuerus et cicutipota Socrates,
pronunciarent quidlibet uerentius,
hoc saeculo quam uel puer alphabeticus.
Canis et annis alii scire uenditant,
sed qui bonas nunquam attigere litteras.
15 Artes professi uegrandi Tonitruo
alii gradus redemptosque aere iactitant.
Pars litteras nil nisi in totum sibilant:

[P1] To the Reader

If anyone loves to learn of the holy lives of men of old and seeks to make his ways the same as theirs, and shuns high honours, content with little, here he has the threshold to a noble path of life. Yet read these things, such as they are; we compose them for our patron Columba; you may sing better things as you are able. Beware, lest perchance the deadly poisons of a new Wisdom move you away from ancient piety.

(*See notes, p. 269*)

[P2] To Iona, ancient burial-place of the kings of Scots

As long as your temples remain, Iona, this poem remains for you, and the name of the poem will always be *Ionis*, 'the Song of Iona / Jonah'. Live and flourish, seat of piety; may all your holy churches, relics, tombs, and crosses, endure for ever.

(*See notes, p. 269*)

[P3] Author's foreword

While envy is poisoning very many minds, the fashion almost grows stronger in our time, so that everyone who writes fears envy very much. Nothing is pleasing to this brutish age except wickedness – who wants to experience that? An adolescent comes forward as the arbiter of affairs, and he is just like someone whom all-knowing Wisdom made knowledgeable in deep secrets throughout all ages; skilful Plato and subtle Aristotle and grave Socrates the hemlock drinker would say anything at all more cautiously than a child learning his alphabet in this age. Others also boast of knowledge by virtue of their grey-haired years, yet who have never attained to good letters. Others boast of degrees bought with money, having professed the arts to a puny thunderer. Some will lisp nothing of their letters except the whole;

pars pro bonis accipiunt saepe pessimas.
Qui non fauent, plodunt, boant, exclamitant,
20 animique morbos dissimulare proprii
nequeunt, parati quauis de re dicere,
ad audiendum pigri, qui cum quolibet
manum libenter in re quauis conserunt.
Peior nouella quaedam nunc plantatio
25 uerbo uel uno pensat uires ingeni
probri benigna, laudis nunquam prodiga.   [f. P 2v; A 232v] A ii
Hanc, inter omnes, pestem credo maximam.
Ipse anteuerto iudices praeposteros:
solus meorum censor horum uersuum.
30 Nam sunt agrestes pauco rerum pondere
soli Sororum coetus quos Apolline
non concinente cursim praecentauerat.
Idcirco, lector, ex his non me iudices,
ut qui meas in hos uires consumerem.
35 Adeo fefellit me non haec philautia.
Zelus Columbae nostri patris optimi,
et fama Ionae me nutricis insulae,
nunquam sinebant immemorem sui fore,
omnino ne tacerem, tale protuli.

[f. P 2v; A 232v]

[P4] Io<annes> Formannus, Scotus

Carpitis hos factos quicunque ex tempore uersus,
        si ueniam uitio non datis, aequa date:
quas saltem efflagito inducias, date, parcite semper
        his, uestra in lucem carmina donec eant.

[f. P 3r; A 233r]

[P5]

Iam non caeruleos concinimus deos,
non Tritona ferum, Prothea lubricum,
candentesue choros Oceanitidum,
non argentipedem Dorida, Naereos
5   uel prolem canimus modo.
Tellurisue deos numina agrestium,

some often accept the worst for the good. Some who do not praise, applaud, roar, and shout approval, and cannot disguise the faults of their own soul, are prepared to speak of whatsoever thing, and are slow to listen; these will join battle readily with anyone in whatsoever cause. Now a certain new growth, even worse, esteems the strength of the intellect by a single word, generous with insults, never bountiful with praise – I think this is the greatest plague of all. I myself, the only critic of these verses of mine, prefer these perverse judges: for they are rustics, of matters of little weight, whom the company of Sisters had bewitched in passing, while Apollo was not singing in harmony with them.

So, Reader, you should not judge me by them, as one who should exhaust my strength against them: this self-love has not deluded me to such an extent. The zeal of Columba, our excellent father, and the fame of Iona, the island which nurtured me, never allowed me to become forgetful of them; I have brought forth this work so I should not be wholly silent.

(*See notes, p. 270*)

[P4] John Forman, Scotsman:

Whoever you are that read these verses made *ex tempore*, if you do not show forgiveness towards faults, show fairness: at least grant the truce which I beg: be always indulgent towards these, until your own verses see the light of day.
(*See notes, p. 270*)

[P5] [Introduction]

We do not now celebrate the gods of the sea, not fierce Triton or fickle Proteus, or the shining chorus of the children of Ocean; we do not now sing of silver-footed Doris or the children of Nereus. My heart does not move me to speak of the gods of the land or the deities of rustics,

faunos uel satyros, Panaue, Naiadas,
nympharum copias quas iuga montium
uel saltus retinent, uel uaga flumina,
10   fert mens dicere non mea.
Sed nec coelituum quos male Graecia
effinxit superos, ullaue numina
astrorum cupimus promere cantibus,
luxus, stupra, dolos[1], furta, homicidia
15   coelo non decuit frui,
incestumue Iouem, numen adulterum,
Martem, Mercurium, Pallada, Cypriam,
Saturnum ueterem, Lunam, et Apollinem,
nec quos[2] unda tenet, terra uel aethera,
20   fert mens dicere iam mea.
Unum sed colimus, coelica qui regit
Aeternusque Opifex regna, mare, aridam,
in Patrem Genitum Pneumaque credimus.
Tres unus Deus est, omnia in omnibus,
25   Finis principium facit.
Humani generis qui miserans uicem,
errores, tenebras, perdita saecula,
uisus Thareidae notuit Abrahae,   [f. P 3v; A 233v]
et Sarae genito, deinde nepotibus
30   Mosen exulibus dedit.
Quem uates Solimi Pneumate feruidi
uenturum Dominum carnis imagine
praedixere, homo qui temporis exitu
factus uera docens cuncta, tenebricas
35   ambages necat et necem:
Natos esse Dei qui dedit omnibus
in mundo genitis flumine et Halitu,
O foelix soboles, faustaque adoptio,
maiestate beans hos Deitateque,
40   Christi qui renitent fide.
Coelorum quibus et regna perennia
cum Christo pateant, nectare perfrui
quorum et perspicuum lumen amictus est,
uirtus, laus, requies, gloria, pax, honor,
45   sint possessio firmiter.

---

[1] doli, Blado.
[2] qaos, Blado.

fauns or satyrs, Pan or the Naiads, the crowds of nymphs which mountain ranges or forests or meandering rivers contain. But neither do we seek to promote in song the deities of the heavens whom Greece portrayed wickedly, or any of the gods of the firmament: it was not right for indulgence, debauchery, deceit, theft, and murder to enjoy the heavens. Neither does my heart now move me to speak of incestuous Jupiter, the adulterous god, of Mars, Mercury, Pallas, the Cyprian goddess, ancient Saturn, Luna, and Apollo, or those whom the waters contain, or land, or air.

But we worship the One, the eternal Maker, who rules the heavenly kingdoms, the sea, and land; we believe in Father, Son, and Spirit: He is Three and One God, all in all things; the End makes the beginning. Pitying the vicissitudes of the human race, their errors and darkness, the lost ages, when He was seen He became known to Abraham son of Terah and to Sarah's offspring; and later He sent Moses to their descendants the exiles.

He whom the prophets of Jerusalem foretold, burning with the Spirit, the Lord to come, who was made man in the image of flesh, teaching all truths, at the end of time He destroyed dark obscurity and death; He who gave to all those in the world, born by water and the Spirit, to be children of God: O happy progeny, fortunate adoption, blessing with majesty and the Godhead those who shine by the faith of Christ! May strength, praise, repose, glory, peace, and honour be firmly the possession of those to whom the everlasting kingdom of heaven is open, and whose garment is the clear light, to enjoy nectar with Christ.

Horum quis medio nostra piacula
solui, nosque Patri consinuarier
sensatus dubitet? Ira remissior
sanctorum precibus, gratia fusior,
50   coelo semita notior.
Coelestes igitur quisquis in accolas
Christi municipes atque domesticos
non orat reuerens, sit uelut impius,
dignus supplicio perdier ultimo
55   consors manibus infimis.
Omnes coelituum curia iam faue,   [f. P 4r; A 234r]
coetus angelici cuncta hierarchia,
primaeuique patres, Lotor, Apostoli,
attestante pii sanguine martyres,
60   uates, Uirgineum decus.
Tu cuius uarios pangere gestio
ortus, Sancte, lares, dicta prophetica,
uisus angelicos, craebraque praelia,
et magnalia, des carminis orsibus
65   uires aetherea domo.
Non ex pyeriis porrige fontibus
cantus, non hederam sertaue laurea,
sed Christi latices carmina condiant,
eoae foliis arboris exhibe
70   uitalem mihi lauream.
Tu da ueridicis gesta canoribus
aspirans facili scribere spiritu,
dici seu libeat Amathi filius,
in nostris laribus seu Felemitides,
75   Ionas, siue Peristhera.
Sed si quid[3] Latia uoce Columba iam,
Uates, te uocitem, labere mentibus
nostris, O uolucris nomen amabile,
qui[4] missus Niniuen pergere noluit,
80   quem coetus uomuit uagus.
O Ales reliquis una beatior,
de coelo uolitans cuius imagine
inspirauit aquis iura regignere
uerum[5] et nomen habet cuius et hospite   [f. P 4v; A 234v]

---

[3]   sed quid si, Blado.
[4]   quo, Blado.
[5]   ueri, Blado.

Who among those who are gifted with sense would doubt that our sins in this world have been forgiven, and that we are brought close to the Father? His anger is more remitted at the prayers of saints, His grace poured out more, the way to heaven is better known. Thus, whosoever does not pray, revering the heavenly inhabitants, the fellow citizens, and family of Christ, may he be like an impious one, worthy to be lost by the ultimate punishment, a companion to the souls of hell.

Be favourable now, O court of heavenly ones, all the angelic hosts, all the hierarchy, the ancient fathers, the Baptist, the Apostles, the holy martyrs with their blood witnessing, the prophets, the Virginal Glory! O Saint, you about whose various beginnings, whose home, prophetic words, angelic visions, frequent struggles, and great deeds I rejoice to compose, may you give strength to the beginning of the poem from your heavenly home! Do not put forth songs from the streams of the muses, nor ivy, nor garlands of laurel, but let the waters of Christ season my songs; give me a living laurel from the leaves of an eastern tree.

Grant me to write your deeds in my truthful songs with an easy spirit inspiring me; may it please you to be called either son of Amittai, or, in our homeland, son of Fedlimid, Jonah, or *Peristera*, the Dove.

But if I may call you something in Latin speech, O Prophet Columba, lovely name of a bird, the one who would not go when sent to Nineveh, whom the wayfaring whale spat out, glide now into our minds! O Bird, one more blessed than the rest, flying down from heaven, by whose image he inspired justice to regenerate from the waters, and from whose guest he also has his true name,

85   proles clara Sareptidos.
            Rerum causa ueni iam Sacer Halitus,
            formam cuius amas nomen et euehe[6],
            quae sanctis satagat laudis honoribus
            illustrem lyricis da Polyhymniam,
90   da cursum facilem rati.

[f. P 4v; A 234v]

[P6] Quo ordine Sereniss\<ima\> Maria Scotorum Regina descenderit, hic habes apodixin ex uetustissimis Gathaelicae nationis hystoriographorum libris decerptam.

Neolus. Gathaelus. Iber Scotus. Iber Candidus. Aesromius. Sromius. Taytus. Ogomanus. Nenoualus. Deatheus. Bratheus. Breogenes. Baelius. Mithlius. Erimon. Ptolemaeus. Mithlius. Symon. Phanduphus. Ethion. Glacus. Neothafilos. Rothesaus. Ferchardus. Fergusius. Mainus. Dornadilla. Reuther. Iosinas. Finnanus. Durstus. Dothanus. Ederus. Carranus. Europeia. Corbredus I. Corbredus II. Filia Cor\<bredi\>. Mogallus. Ethodius I. Ethodius II. Athirco. Chormachus. Finchormacus. Ethodius III. Erthus. Fergusius II. Domgardus I. Canranus. Aedanus. Eugenius I. Doneualdus. Dongardus II. Eugenius II. Eugenius III. Ethfinus. Achaius. Alpinus. Chennethus I. Constantinus. Donaldus. Malcolmus I. Chennethus II. Malcolmus II. Chennethus III. Beatrix. Duncanus. Malcolmus III. Dauid I. Henricus. Dauid II. Isabella. Robertus I. Rober\<tus\> II. Marioria. Rober\<tus\> III. Rober\<tus\> IIII. Iacobus I. Iac\<obus\> II. Iac\<obus\> III. Iac\<obus\> IIII. Iac\<obus\> V. Maria Dei gratia sereniss\<ima\> Scotoru\<m\> Regina MDXLII.

---

[6]   Eteuehe (capitalised and one word), Blado.

faithful child of the woman of Zarephath!

Come now, O Holy Spirit, cause of (all) things, and exalt the name whose beauty you love. Lend famous Polyhymnia, who is occupied with the holy honour of praise, to my lyric verses; give an easy passage to my ship.

(*See notes, pp. 270–2*)

[P6] The genealogy of her Serene Highness Mary Queen of Scots, taken from the books of the very ancient historical writings of the Gaelic race

Neolus. Gathelus. Iber Scot. Iber the White. Aesromius. Sromius. Taytus. Ogomanus. Nenovalus. Deatheus. Bratheus. Breogenes. Baelius. Mithlius [= Míl]. Erimon. Ptolemy. Mithlius. Simon. Panduphus. Ethion. Glacus. Neothaphilos. Rothesaus. Ferchard. Fergus. Mainus. Dornadilla. Reuther. Josinas. Finnán. Drust. Dothanus. Ederus. Carranus. Europeia. Corbredus I. Corbredus II. The daughter of Corbredus. Mogallus. Ethodius I. Ethodius II. Athirco. Cormac. Fincormac. Ethodius III. Erthus. Fergus II. Domangart I. Canranus [= Gauranus, i.e., Gabrán]. Áedán. Eochaid I. Domnall. Domangart II. Eochaid II. Eochaid III. Áed Finn. Achaius. Alpín. Kenneth I [= Cináed]. Constantine. Donald. Malcolm I. Kenneth II. Malcolm II. Kenneth III. Beatrice [= Beathag]. Duncan. Malcolm III. David I. [Earl] Henry. [Earl] David II. Isabella. Robert [Bruce] I. Robert II [= King Robert I]. Marjory. Robert III [= King Robert II]. Robert IV [= King Robert III]. James I. James II. James III. James IV. James V. Her Serene Highness Mary, by the Grace of God Queen of Scots, 1542.

(*See notes, pp. 272–3*)

Book I

The Prophetic Knowledge of St Columba

[f. P 5r; A 235r] B

[1.1] De secunda in uitam D<iui> Columbae praefatione quaedam de uirtutibus eius summaria enarratio. Phanaloga

'En Falbaee sacros quoniam persoluimus hymnos,
et silet in seros iam fratrum laxa sopores
fessa cohors, fragor omnis abest, murmurque popelli,
dissere quae retulit Seginaeo Rex Osiualdus,
5 audieras, comes huius eras, dicis, Seginaei.
Fusius enarra mihi Sancti gesta Columbae.
Claruit ede quibus inter mortalia signis
tam coelo datus, ut nunquam celestis origo
illum terrestri illecebra pateretur abuti.
10 Uirtutes animi refer, insuperabile pectus,
corpus et integrum, diuina oracula, signa,
instrue, quae calamo demandem posteritati.
Natalis quoque lux aderit nunc illius, ecce
iam Laedae, placidum sydus, nitidissima proles
15 in noua iam uitreas destillat gramina guttas.
Ipse ego nam memini, ut genitor meus ante Ronanus,
quam celebresque lares, castae thalamosque Ronatae
liquerat, et fluxi fugiens commertia mundi
auia deserto perquirens littora ponto
20 ultra Leusiacas cautes, Aquilonis ad iras   [f. P 5v; A 235v]
delphinum socius frigentem cessit ad Arcton,
plurima narrauit nobis miranda Columbae,
ut tam sancta pii me conuersatio Diui
euocet a luteis in phana dealia tectis.'
25 'Quod petis, Addamnane libet, nec iure negatur,
id iuuat, et potius cupio nihil, omnia princeps,
ut memini, nostro quae narrauit Seginaeo
ordine iam referam, tu fac recitata rescribas,
dum preit auricomos Tytanis Lucifer ortus
30 nec citat ad Primas sonitu campana canentes.
Haec, ubi phana uides, Ya multo daemone plena
insula dicta fuit, uariisque habitacula monstris
praebuit, Herculeos donec uirtute labores
mirifica, Stygias saeuum phantasma cateruas
35 corporeis oculis uisas, per inane, per auras,
per mare, per campos uates et athleta Columba
expulerat, nocuasque feras letale perurgens
agmen, Ionaeos sacrauit nomine campos,
atque suo nomen fecit de nomine terrae.
40 Cum posuitque solo fundamen Ionida dixit.

[1.1] Summary narration from the Second Preface of the Life of St Columba concerning his powers (*VC*, i, 1)

'Now, Faílbe, since we have completed the sacred hymns, and the weary company of brothers is now silent, relaxed in sleep of night, all tumult and the hubbub of the people is absent: describe what King Oswald told Ségéne; you heard it, you say you were this Ségéne's companion; tell me more fully the deeds of St Columba. Tell by what miracles did the one, now granted heaven, shine forth among human affairs, so much that his heavenly origins might never allow him to misuse earthly allurements. Tell me the strength of his soul, his indomitable breast, and his pure body, his divine prophecies and miracles; teach me what I may pass on to posterity by my pen. Where the light of his birth is now present, lo, now the most lovely progeny of Leda, the peaceful stars, distils transparent drops in fresh meadows. For I myself remember, that before my father Rónán left his celebrated ancestral home and the marriage bed of chaste Rónnat, fleeing the business of the unstable world, seeking pathless shores in the deserted sea beyond the rocks of Lewis, and as a companion of dolphins went to the fury of the north wind, to the cold north, he told us many miracles of Columba, so that such holy conversation of the pious Saint might call me away from muddy hovels into godly temples.'

'What you ask is good, Adomnán, nor is it right to refuse; it is pleasing, and I want nothing better. I will recount everything that the king told our Ségéne, in order as I remember; and you please do write down what is said, while Lucifer precedes the golden-haired arising of the Titan, and the bell does not yet summon the singers to Prime by its sound. Where you see churches, this isle, called Ia, was filled with many a demon, and provided dwelling places for all kinds of monsters, until the prophet and athlete Columba, (performing) Herculean labours with amazing power, expelled the Stygian crowds, a savage phantasm seen with bodily eyes, through empty spaces, through the air, through the sea, through the land, and, driving out harmful wild beasts, a deadly swarm, he sanctified the fields of Iona by his name, and made a name for the land from his own name: when he laid its foundation on the earth he called it Iona.

Fecit multoties et coram rege Brudaeo
uegrandes imo lapides a flumine sumptos
imperio Christi summas natitare per undas.
Qua ferus hesperio et fremebundus saeuit ab aestu,
45 et surdum horrifico Neptunus murmure littus
concutit, innumeros lapidum qua cernis aceruos,
insuetum per iter, per saxa latentia, et arcus,
frendentes scopulos, celeri rate uectus in istum [f. P 6r; A 236r] B ii
undisonum littus, sancta comitante caterua
50 appulit, et fessam linquens in littore cymbam
erexit cumulos lapidum quos cerneret aetas
postera, qui Christi seclis monimenta futuris
essent, atque fidem doceant seuisse Prophetam.
Hincque leuans unum coeli uirtute lapillum
55 fecit, ut omnigenis foret is medicatio morbis.
Unde eadem sequitur uirtus quoscunque calente
sumpseris inde fide, uulgi scelus ausa prophani
turba sed infido tam sanctam pectore famam
ridet, et hoc seclo fit cunctus fabula sanctus.
60 Tempora praetereunt mala, sed peiora sequentur.
Hic domuit rabidos irato sydere uentos,
cum praemerent tumido nauim freta concita fluctu.
In regione magos Pictorum uicit, opertas
detexit fraudes, et nil nisi numine Ditis
65 effecisse illos, signis, ratione probauit,
attonitoque iocos, plausumque dedere theatro.
Expositisque rati uelis, dedit obuia uentis
carbasa, ad optatas et uenerat ocyus oras.
Is lapidem Pictis tali uirtute beauit,
70 tactus ut omnigenos¹ depellat corpore morbos.
Pauperis et puerum defunctum a morte parenti
incolumem exhibuit, dum fleret funera nati.
Fecit aquae puros latices, dum sancta litaret
Fimbarrus, uini naturam ferre Leuites.
75 O ueneranda fides, longe meliore cothurno
dicenda, et leuibus minime referenda camaenis. [f. P 6v; A 236v]
Sed coeleste iubar de uertice sacrificantis
saepius effulsit, noctis quoque depulit umbras.
Aethereus splendor, radiosa et luce ministros
80 fecerat attonitos, mihi narrabant Bathinaeus
atque Diormitius se tali lumine tectos.

----

¹ omnigenas, Blado.

'Often, and also in the presence of King Bridei, he made little stones taken from the bed of the river to float on the surface of water by Christ's command. Where wild roaring Neptune rages from the western sea, and shakes the silent shore with terrible tumult, there where you see numberless heaps of stones, through unaccustomed paths, through hidden rocks and arches, and gnashing cliffs, he landed on that wave-resounding seashore, carried towards it by a swift ship, with a holy troop accompanying him; and leaving the weary ship on the seashore, he raised up heaps of stones which a subsequent age might see, which would be monuments of Christ to future ages, and may tell how the Prophet has sown the faith. Lifting one pebble, by the power of heaven he made it so that it would henceforth be medicine for all kinds of diseases.

'So the same power follows all those whom you will have raised up from there with glowing faith; but the crowd of the profane multitude, daring wickedness, mocks such a holy reputation with unbelieving breast, and every saint becomes a fable to this age: evil times are passing, but worse will follow.

'He overcame winds raging from an angry star, when seas stirred up by a swelling flood pressed against his ship. He defeated magicians in the lands of the Picts, he revealed hidden deceits, he showed by signs and reason that they had achieved nothing except by the god of darkness, and they presented tricks and applause for an astonished audience. When his ship's sails had been unfurled, he gave the exposed canvas to the winds, and came quickly to the desired shore. He blessed a stone with such virtue for the Picts that its touch drove away every kind of sickness from the body. He delivered the dead son of a poor man from death unharmed to his parent, while he was mourning the child's death. As a deacon, he made pure streams of water take the nature of wine, when Finbarr offered the sacrifice of holy things. O worthy faith, deserving to be declaimed in a far better tragic style, and not to be related in light verses!

'But often heavenly brightness poured forth from his head while offering the sacrifice, and also dispersed the darkness of night; the ethereal splendour made his attendants amazed by its radiant brightness: Baithéne and Diarmait told me they were covered over by such light.

Aligeris claro uolitantibus aethere diuis
admonitus Sagax animas in coelica sumi
tecta uidet laetas, superumque et in aere cantus
85 audiuit, summo fruitus terrae incola coelo.
Unum cum Domino fiet qui huic totus adhaeret.
Uiderat hic uisu, mihi credas, meridiano
Uates, effari quae nemo potest, calamoue
ferre, uel humano meditans attingere sensu.
90 Ipse creaturas et posteriora Tonantis,
quicquid et hac uastus cohibet testudine mundus,
collectum puro conspexit lumine totum.
Ut rebus Numen, sic res in Numine uidit.'
'Ne, uenerande pater, graue sit modo dicere, Numen
95 quo pacto uideas? Et eodem tempore uiuas?
Nemo Deum uiuens cernit, scriptura reclamat.'
'Nam mors ante Deum nimium preciosa piorum,
dicitur interitus, dum mens a corpore cedit,
uitaque cum Christo morientibus abdita constat.
100 Non animam corpus linquit, sed spiritus artus.
At neque praetereo quanam uirtute superbos
uicerit in bello et precibus truculenta tyrannis
cornua deiecit, fugitantia terga perurgens.
Narrantem audiui uetulo regem Seginaeo,   [f. P 7r; A 237r]
105 dum legeret fastos, haec inter caetera dixit:
"Sint Uobis Superi grates, sit gloria nostro
indigeti. Memini princeps[2] Osiualdus iniquo
dum Mauorte petor, saeuo Cathalone Britanno
insiliente, meos et iam prope conspicor hostes.
110 Apparet gelida mihi sanctus nocte Columba
angelico aspectu, qualemque fuisse recordor,
cum docuit nostra Christum leue uulgus in aula.
'Sis animosus,' ait, 'Christo confide, triumphos
acceptos Superis uictor refer, omnia uotis
115 successura tuis annuncio, crastinus ortu
Phoebus cum primo surget, gens praelia praeceps
et caeco impulsu nimium sitit, auxiliares
tu coelo expectes, ferus et Cathalo morietur,
barbarus ense cadet cunctus, uel turpiter actus
120 uulnereque auerso infamis morientia tractans[3]
membra fugit, semper iactis inglorius armis.

[2] prinseps, Blado.
[3] tractens, Blado.

Alerted by holy winged beings flying through the bright heavens, the Sage saw happy souls being taken up into the heavenly vaults, and heard songs of the high beings in the sky, a resident on earth, enjoying the highest heaven. He will become one with the Lord, who wholly cleaves to Him! Believe me, this Prophet saw, with the sight of midday, what no one can speak in words, or convey by the pen, or understand meditating with human sense: he himself saw the creation, and the back of God the Thunderer, and whatever the vast world holds in this shell, all collected together in a clear light: as he saw God in (earthly) things, so he saw these things in God.'

'Reverend father, may it not be grievous to say: in what way may you see God, and live at the same time? The Scriptures declare, no one living sees God.'

'Indeed, the death of holy men is very precious before God. It is called death when the soul departs from the body, and life taken away from the dying stays with Christ; it is not the body that abandons the soul, but the spirit the limbs.

'And I will not pass over by what power he defeated the proud in battle, and by his prayers cast down the fierce horns from the tyrants, smiting their fleeing backs. I heard the king speaking to elderly Ségéne, while he was reading from a chronicle; among other things he said this: "Thanks be to You, O Most High, glory be to our patron! I, King Oswald, remember, when I was attacked in unjust war, when savage Cadwallon the Briton invaded, I saw my own people, and the enemy now near at hand. In the frosty night St Columba appeared to me, of angelic appearance, and I remember, such as it was when he taught the fickle people about Christ in our court: 'Be bold,' he said, 'trust in Christ, and as victor ascribe the triumphs which you have gained to the Most High. I tell you that everything will go well by your prayers: tomorrow, when the sun arises at the first dawning, and the crowd greatly thirsts headlong for battle with blind haste, you may hope for aid from heaven; fierce Cadwallon also will die, every barbarian will fall by the sword or flee, shamefully driven back, dragging his dying limbs, defamed and disgraced forever, with wounds in his back, throwing away his weapons.

Imprimis uenerare Deum, fidei quoque semine terras
imbue subdendas, et religione supremum
perpetua Christum cole, nostramque camaenam
125 fac memorent pugiles et certatura iuuentus.'''
Addamnane parum chartas, calamumque repone,
en monet hora preces iam nunc octaua diurnas,
crastina, quod superest, aurora et suggeret omne,
quod tamen ut breuius, melius quoque fiet iambis.'

[f. P 7r; A 237r]

[1.2] De uaticinio Mantei ode prima [f. P 7v; A 237v]

Praescius Manteus Brito nascituri
dixerat: 'Uates agitante plenus
Spiritu, seris orietur annis
  aurea proles,
5 praesul, antistes, simul et propheta,
qui suo cunctas iubare occidentis
Insulas lustret, Scotiamque, toto
  clarus in orbe.
Hic Amathite, soboles Ionae,
10 tam Deo plenus puer aestimatur,
ipse praesagus patriam uocatus
  linquet, Ionas.
Eius et nostrum, spacioque, phana
paruulae sepis duo separantur.
15 Magnus hic coram Domino et coruschus
  lumine uitae.'

[f. P 7v; A 237v]

[1.3] Ethnae parentis uaticinium

  Centum lustra, biennium,
anni bisque decem, currere desinunt
  a partu retro Uirginis,
cum⁴ mundo rediere aurea saecula.
5   Fedhlaemita Nigellides,
qua sol hesperio tingitur aequore,
  tum rex omnis Iberniae

---

⁴ tum, Blado.

First praise God, then also imbue with the seeds of faith all the lands which will be subjected, and worship Christ supreme in perpetual devotion; do this, and fighters and youth about to give battle may tell our story.'"

'Adomnán, lay down your paper and pen a little while, for the eighth hour now announces the daily prayers. Tomorrow's dawn will also supply everything that remains, which, however, to be shorter, will also be better made in iambic verse.'

(*See notes, pp. 273–7*)

[1.2] First Ode: The Prophecy of Maucte (*VC*, 2nd Preface)

Prescient of the one about to be born, Maucte the Briton had said: 'A prophet, filled with the enlivening Spirit, will be born in later years, a golden child, a priest, abbot, and also a prophet, to enlighten all the Isles of the west, and *Scotia* (Ireland), with his radiance, shining in all the world: this descendant of Amittai, offspring of Iona, is esteemed a child so full of God, this prophet Jonah, with foreknowledge, will leave his homeland when summoned. His holy place and ours, the two are separated by the space of a little hedge. He is great in the sight of the Lord, and gleaming with the light of life.'

(*See notes, pp. 277–8*)

[1.3] Prophecy of his mother Eithne (*VC*, iii, 1)

A hundred times five years, twice ten and two, have finished their course since the Virgin birth, when a golden age returned to the world. Fedlimid Úa Néill is king of all Ireland, where the sun sinks in the western sea,

a clara ueterum gente Gathaelidum
    illustris, pius et potens.
Coniux connubio Scotidos Ethneae,   [f. P 8r; A 238r]
10   cui longum sterilis thori
moerorem genita prole leuauerat
    tam sancti pueri indoles.
Agnouitque parens coelitus editam
    frugis progeniem bonae.
15 Sic longaeua pia uoce prophetitat
    mater facta puerpera:
'En magno Superum non sine munere
    hic natalitius dies
festo transigitur in dyademate,
20   arae et thure calent sacro.
Hic coram Domino magnus erit puer,
    Christi miles, et Haelian
et Ionan referens uaticinabitur,
    Ionas ipse uocabitur.
25 Bisseptena cadet quando triaeteris,
    pontum traiiciet rate
Arctoi procul ad cardinis Insulas.
    Annis in puerilibus
coelestis sophiae se studio dabit.
30   Purus corpore et integer,
aspectu angelicus, consilio grauis,
    sanctus mentis in omine,
sermone nitidus, ingenio optimus,
    coelo dux populis erit.
35 Et fines Britonum perget in ultimos,
    pertaesus fera praelia
me nec respiciet, nec genus, aut domum.   [f. P 8v; A 238v]
    Una deget in Hebride.
Aras hic deicis condet honoribus.
40   Multos constituet bonos
tum diuersa uigil per loca praesules.
    Gratus nemo sit in sua
cum uates patria, sceptra perennia
    ardens, hic nihil arduum
45 splendorem larium suspicit, aut opes.
    Non poscet genialia.
Nolet regna patris Marte furentia
    nil mortale feret bonum.
Cum Pictisque Scotos pace resarciet.

from the famous race of the ancient descendants of Gathelus, illustrious, just, and powerful. He was spouse by marriage of Eithne, descendant of Scota, for whom the innate quality of such a holy boy relieved the long sorrow of a childless marriage when her offspring was born; and the mother acknowledged that her child of good promise was born from heaven.

So the elderly woman in labour, having become a mother, prophesied with pious voice: 'Lo, not without the grace of the Most High this birthday is enacted in a festal crown, and the altars burn with holy incense. This child will be great before the Lord, a soldier of Christ, he will prophesy, recalling both Jonah and Elijah, and he himself will be called Jonah. After fourteen times three years he will cross the sea in his boat far away to the isles of the northern pole. In his childish years he will surrender himself to the study of heavenly wisdom. Pure and whole in body, of angelic appearance, solemn in counsel, holy in mind in his prophecies, polished in speech, very good-natured, he will be a leader to heaven for the people. Wearied by their fierce wars, he will go to the furthest bounds of the Britons; he will not look back at me, or his people, or his house. He will dwell in one Hebridean island; there he will build altars to the honour of God. He will then watchfully appoint many good leaders in various places. Since no one is honoured as a prophet in his own country, burning for an everlasting sceptre, he thinks nothing of the lofty splendour or wealth of great houses. He will not seek for pleasures. He will refuse his father's kingdom, raging in wars; he will not endure any good thing that is transient; he will restore the Scots in peace with the Picts,

50   Et uirtutibus eminet
clarus prodigio non numerabili.
      Hic nam filius est satus
ut Sarae puer, ut uera Sareptidos
      proles, ut Samuel pius,
55 ut Baptista puer, flumine tingite
      iam sacro genus optimum,
et Ionan Latio nomine dicite:
      Ionae spiritus hunc reget.
Sic Manteus cecinit iam sene carmine,
60   sic uisus iubet angelus.
Salue nate, uale, uiue, Columba aue.'

[f. P 8v; A 238v]

[1.4] Concio autoris

Proposui lyricis perstringere uersibus Beati
      uitam Columbae, ast impari cothurno. [f. P 9r; A 239r] C
Cur breuis iste lyrae placuit canor, arduis in alis
      heroica dignis cani Camaena?
5 Plurima *Centaurus* retinacula, plurimos rudentes
      desiderat, nec absque uadit aura:
remige pigra legit, sublimibus imminet procellis,
      tenue[5] uadum timens, aquae per aequor
exit, in oceano fit deuia, luminis polique
10   egens lapilli ducis et iuuatu.
Littora tuta legit mea cymbola[6], quae minus pericli
      habent[7], minores dum uolat per undas.

[f. P 9r; A 239r]

[1.5] Uaticinatur Columba Fintenum ad Britaniam uenturum

'Postquam finierit ista colonia,
gaudensque in decimis orbibus egero et
      summi nectare[8] coeli
      laeter sorte perennium,

---

5   tenuis, Blado.
6   symbola, Blado.
7   habet, Blado.
8   neotare, Blado

and will shine with miracles, famous by innumerable prodigies. Thus, this child has been conceived like Sarah's son, like the faithful child of the woman of Zarephath, like pious Samuel, like the Baptist child. Now wash this excellent child in the sacred flood, and call him Jonah by a Latin name: the spirit of Jonah will rule him. Thus Maucte once prophesied by an old song, thus the angel that was seen commands: hail child, live long and flourish, hail Columba.'
(*See notes, p. 278*)

[1.4] A word by the author

I have set out to narrate the Life of St Columba in lyric verses, though inferior to a tragic style. Why did this brief lyric song seem good for lofty deeds on wings, worthy to be sung by a muse of heroic poetry?

The *Centaur* needs many mooring-cables, many ropes, and will not go without the wind; it traverses slow places by the oarsman; it comes up against towering storms; fearing the narrow shallows, it goes out over the breadth of the water; its wanderings are made in the ocean, wanting the help of the North Star and of a lodestone. My little boat chooses safe shores, which have less danger, while it passes through the lesser waves.
(*See notes, pp. 278–9*)

[1.5] Columba prophesies that Fintén will come to Britain (*VC*, i, 2)

'After this dwelling-place will come to an end, and I, rejoicing, will live in the tenth sphere, and may enjoy the portion of the immortal ones, the nectar of the highest heaven,

5   Fintenus ueniet unus Ibernici
    Toelchani genitus stemmatis, ut tibi
         subsit miles in isto,
       Boethaenaee, sacellulo.
    Hunc etsi iuuenem sancta peritia
10 diuinae sophiae coelitus erudit,
         coelo dux animarum
       fiet postea plurium.
    Boethaenaee, caue, ne sit in insula
    tam multis Scotiae finibus utilis: [f. P 9v; A 239v]
15   hunc in pace remittas,
       qua late patet Albion.'
    Grandaeuus retulit praesbyter Oesseus,
    Finteni comes haec audierat senis,
         uero tradidit ore
20   abbatique Ronanidae.

    Foelix exilium, mors, sopor, extasis,
    dum mens corporeis soluitur artubus,
         menti ac corpus adhaeret,
       et uita exanimi manet.
25 O mors clara, quies O uenerabilis,
    qua mens innumero lumine cingitur,
         qua tangit Deitatem, et
       se cernens uidet omnia.
    Quis mihi det pennas? Purus ut Alitis
30 huius more leuer limen in aetheris,
         in Christo requiescens
       tali ut lumine amiciar.
    Laus indiuiduae, gloria, pax, honor,
    sit semper Triadi, cuique sit et Trium
35   compar laus, honor idem
       nostri Uatis ob omina.

[f. P 9v; A 239v]

[1.6] Uaticinatur Columba Crasseni filium pium et religiosum fore

'Dum Uatis cuperem tangere pallium,
Crasseni genitus prendor, et "Impium,"   [f. P 10r; A 240r] C ii
clamat cuncta cohors, "hunc Pater abiice,
    Foedum tangere desine."

Fintén will come, one born of the progeny of Irish Tailchán, so that he can be subject to you, Baithéne, as a soldier in this little church. Holy knowledge of divine wisdom from heaven has enlightened this man: although young, he will afterwards become a leader of many souls to heaven. Beware, Baithéne, lest one useful to so many parts of *Scotia* (Ireland) should remain in our island; you should send him home in peace, where *Alba* spreads far and wide.' The old priest Oisséne recounted (that) as companion of elderly Fintén he had heard these things; and he told them by true word of mouth to the abbot, the son of Rónán.

Happy exile, death, sleep, ecstasy, when the spirit is separated from the body's limbs, and the body adheres to the spirit, and life remains for the dead! O bright death, O revered rest, where the soul is surrounded by limitless light, where it touches the Deity, and perceiving itself sees all things! Who may give me wings, so that, pure like this Dove, I may be raised up to the threshold of heaven, that I may be surrounded by such light, resting in Christ? Praise, glory, peace and honour be always to the undivided Trinity, to each of the Three be equal praise, and the same honour, on account of our Prophet's foretellings. (*See notes, p. 279*)

[1.6] Columba prophesies that Craséne's son will be pious and religious (*VC*, i, 3)

'When I wished to touch the Prophet's cloak, I, Craséne's son, was caught, and the whole assembly cried, "Cast this impudent one away, Father, do not touch the ugly one!"

5   Sic fatur, "Iuuenem mittite, mittite!
Sit quamuis puer abiectior hactenus,
increscet Superum munere de die
    prudens acriter in diem.
Olim grandis erit dux gregis optimus,
10   hoc Clecense reget nempe sacellulum,
et rursus Scotiam lucidat omnibus,
    fausto in dogmate, moribus."
Sic de me puero uaticinatus est
diuinus Scoticae filius Ethneae.
15   Euenit penitus cuncta prophetia,
    uos haec edite posteris.
Tu diuine gregis ductor Ionii,
hoc te non pigeat tradere posteris,
nec, Falbaee, tibi sit graue dicere,
20   si te quis rogitauerit.'

[f. P 10r; A 240r]

[1.7] D<iuus> Coennicum pium antistitem aduenturum uespere uaticinatur

'Ocyus hospitium uenientibus hisce parate,
    ponite aquam pedibusque lauandis.
Aequore iactatis [sit]⁹ coena parata: sub horam
    appellet ratis aduena littus.'
5   'Mira refers iam nunc, Pater,' unus de grege dixit.
    'Quis non his premeretur ab undis?   [f. P 10v; A 240v]
Quis furor iratum tam saeuo sydere pontum
    hoc tentare die tam sancta coegit
pectora? Nimbosis cernis freta percita uentis,
10   gurgitibus uada et eruta motis?'
Nec mora Coennicus rate uectus Iberide littus
    appulit, et cum sospite coetu.
Grato suscipitur laetanter sanctus honore,
    cui tum coetus Ionius infert,
15   'Per mare tam tumidum quo pacto appellitis oras?
    Diras uidistisne procellas?'
'Uidimus, et Superum dono non sensimus ullas,'
    aiunt, 'sed fuit aura serena.'

---

⁹   Ponite aquam sit pedibusque lauandis./Aequore iactatis coena parata: sub horam, Blado.
Cf. Sharpe, 'MacLean', 122, for this emendation.

He said, "Let the youth go, let him go! Although up to now the boy is quite base, he will quickly increase in the grace of the Most High from day to day, becoming prudent. Someday, grown up, he will be a very good shepherd of the flock: in fact he will rule this church of Clonmacnoise, and enlighten *Scotia* (Ireland) again in sound doctrines, in all goodness." Thus, the divine son of Eithne of the *Scoti* prophesied concerning me as a child. The whole prophecy has entirely come to pass; proclaim these things to those who come after. O you, divine teacher of the flock of Iona, let it not displease you to pass this on to posterity; neither, O Faílbe, should it be grievous for you to say it, if anyone should ask you.'
(*See notes, pp. 279–80*)

[1.7] The Saint Prophesies that the Holy Bishop Cainnech will arrive in the evening (*VC*, i, 4)

'Prepare the guesthouse quickly for these who are arriving, and set water there for the washing of feet. Let dinner be prepared for those tossed by the sea; within the hour, a visiting ship will arrive at the shore.'

One of the flock said, 'Now you are saying something amazing, Father! Who would not be overpowered by these waves? What madness has driven such holy hearts to brave the sea today, enraged by such an angry star? Do you see the straits aroused by stormy winds, the sea cast up by swirling whirlpools?'

Without delay, Cainnech reaches the shore, carried in an Irish ship, together with his unscathed crew. The saint is received joyfully, with welcome honour.

Then the assembly of Iona asks them, 'How did you come to shore through such swelling seas? Did you not see the terrible storms?'

'We saw them,' they say, 'and by the gift of the Most High we did not feel anything at all, but the breeze was calm.'
(*See notes, p. 280*)

Quis furor iratum tam fæuo fydere pontum
  Hoc tentare die tam fancta coegit
Pectora? Nimbofis cernis freta percita uentis?
  Gurgitibus uada & eruta motis?
Nec mora Cœnnicus rate uectus Iberide littus
  Appulit, & cum fofpite Cœtu.
Grato fufcipitur latunter Sanctus honore,
  Cui tum Cœtus Ionius infert,
Per mare tam tumidum quo pacto appellitis oras?
  Diras uidiflifne procellas?
Vidimus, & Superum dono non fenfimus ullas,
  Aiunt, fed fuit aura ferena.

Columbanum laborare in Carybdi Breccana præcinuit Columba.

EVRIPVS *eft proteruus,*
In Caribreccana furens uorticibus recuruis
Aequora, bullientum
Inftar ollarum cariofas perimens carinas.
Hic legit æftuofa
Iam Columbanus freta, & orans trepidat Carybdim,
Sicq; periclitatur,
Vt Deum femper roget attentius inuocando;
Huc uenietq; fofpes,
Et falutabit (referens ut timeat) Sodales.
Taliter allocutus
In domo fratres recitauit pios hæc Propheta.

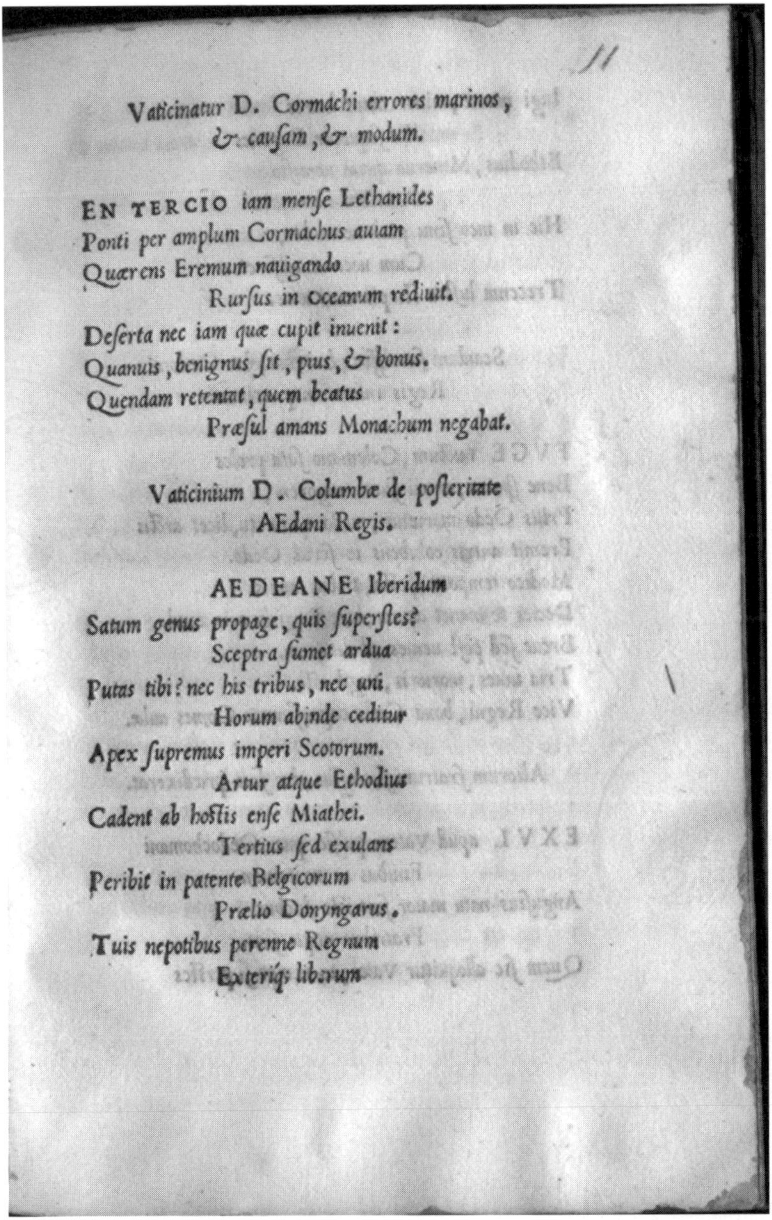

11

Vaticinatur D. Cormachi errores marinos,
& causam, & modum.

EN TERCIO iam mense Lethanides
Ponti per amplum Cormachus auiam
Quærens Eremum nauigando
            Rursus in oceanum rediuit.
Deserta nec iam quæ cupit inuenit:
Quanuis, benignus sit, pius, & bonus.
Quendam retentat, quem beatus
            Præsul amans Monachum negabat.

            Vaticinium D. Columbæ de posteritate
                        AEdani Regis.

                AEDEANE Iberidum
Satum genus propage, quis superstes?
            Sceptra sumet ardua
Putas tibi? nec his tribus, nec uni,
            Horum abinde ceditur
Apex supremus imperi Scotorum.
            Artur atque Ethodius
Cadent ab hostis ense Miathei.
            Tertius sed exulans
Peribit in patente Belgicorum
            Prælio Donyngarus.
Tuis nepotibus perenne Regnum
            Exteriq́s libarum

Figure 5.   Pages from the first part of *Ionis: Perugia, Biblioteca communale Augusta*,
I-L-66 (1), 10v–11r., showing the variety of metres MacLean uses in this section.
Ionis, 1.7–1.10. By kind permission of the Biblioteca communale Augusta, Perugia.

[f. P 10v; A 240v]

[1.8] Columbanum laborare in Carybdi Breccana praecinuit Columba

'Euripus est proteruus
in Caribreccana furens uorticibus recuruis
   aequora, bullientum
instar ollarum cariosas perimens carinas.
5   Hic legit aestuosa
iam Columbanus freta, et orans trepidat Carybdim,
   sicque periclitatur,
ut Deum semper roget attentius inuocando;
   huc uenietque sospes,
10 et salutabit, referens ut timeat, sodales.'
     Taliter allocutus
in domo fratres recitauit pios haec Propheta.

[f. P 11r; A 240+1r]

[1.9] Uaticinatur D\<iuus\> Cormachi errores marinos, et causam, et modum

'En tercio iam mense Lethanides
ponti per amplum Cormachus auiam
   quaerens eremum nauigando
      rursus in oceanum rediuit.
5   Deserta nec iam quae cupit inuenit:
quamuis[10] benignus sit, pius et bonus.
Quendam retentat, quem beatus
      praesul amans monachum negabat.'

[f. P 11r; A 240+1r]

[1.10] Uaticinium D\<iui\> Columbae de posteritate Aedani Regis

'Aedeane Iberidum
satum genus propage, quis superstes
   Sceptra sumet ardua
putas tibi? Nec his tribus, nec uni
5   horum abinde, ceditur

---

[10] quanuis, Blado.

[1.8] Columba prophesied that Colmán would struggle in the Whirlpool of Breccán (*VC*, i, 5)

'There is a wild strait, raging into the seas of Corryvreckan with twisting whirlpools like foaming cauldrons, smashing the leaky hulls. Here Colmán now traverses the billowy strait, and fears the whirlpool as he prays, and is in such danger that he prays constantly to God, invoking Him more earnestly. And he will arrive here unscathed, and will greet the company, describing how he is fearful.' The Prophet told these things at home, thus addressing the pious brothers.
(*See notes, p. 280*)

[1.9] The Saint prophesies Cormac's wanderings in the sea, both their cause and their extent (*VC*, i, 6)

'Now, in the third month, Cormac Úa Liatháin, seeking a pathless wilderness sailing through the breadth of the sea, has returned once again into the ocean. But he does not now find the solitary places that he seeks, although he is kindly, pious and good: he keeps someone with him whom a holy abbot, loving the monk, forbade.'
(*See notes, p. 280*)

[1.10] St Columba's prophecy concerning King Áedán's descendants (*VC*, i, 9)

'O Áedán, stock begotten from the progeny of the descendants of Iber, who, do you think, as your successor, will take up the exalted sceptre? Not to these three, not to any one of them hereafter,

apex supremus imperi Scotorum.
    Artur atque Ethodius
cadent ab hostis ense Miathei.
    Tertius sed exulans
10 peribit in patente Belgicorum
      praelio Donyngarus.
Tuis nepotibus perenne regnum
    exterique liberum   [f. P 11v; A 240+1v]
iugi manet; minor natus haeres
15   te sequetur, Eugenes
Ethodius, Minerua quem uenusto
    a colore nominat.
Hic in meo sinu puer recumbet,
    cum uocatus adforet.
20 Trecenta lustra stirpis eius aetas.'

[f. P 11v; A 240+1v]

[1.11] Scanlani successus et fata, et Oedonis regis interitum praecinuit

'Fuge luctum, Colemano sata proles,
bene speres, animi sume uigorem,
prius Oedo morietur modo quam tu, licet arctis
premit antris cohibens te ferus Oedo.
5 Modico tempore specta, tribus annis
decies te manet aeuum, lare regisque eris exul.
Breue sed post uenies ad ditionem.
Tria uiues, morieris, uigil esto.
Uice regni, bona coeli cape, summe comes aulae.'

[f. P 11v; A 240+1v]

[1.12] Aliorum fratrum successus et fata praedixerat

Exul apud Uatem pulsus puer Oedochomani
    finibus in Britonum.
Angusius natu maior fuit iste duobus
    fratribus atque suis.
5 Quem sic alloquitur Uates, 'Tu nempe superstes[f. A 241r; P 12r]
    frater eris reliquis.
In patria uiues, et longo tempore sceptrum

is given the highest pinnacle of the rule of the Scots. Artúr and Eochaid will fall by the sword of the enemy, of the *Miathi*; but the third, Domangart, going abroad, will perish in open battle with the *Belgici*. For your descendants there remains a lasting kingdom, free from foreign yoke: a younger son will follow you as heir, Eugenius (or) Eochaid, whom Minerva names from his fair colour. When he is here, having been summoned, this child will repose in my bosom. The age of his stock will be 300 times five years.'
(*See notes, pp. 280—1*)

[1.11] He predicted Scandlán's fortunes and death, and the death of King Áed (*VC*, i, 11)

'Depart from sorrow, child born of Colmán, be of good hope, put on strength of spirit: although fierce Áed restrains you in a narrow dungeon, confining you, Áed will die soon, before you. Wait for a short while, then a time awaits you of ten times three years, and you will be an exile (again) from the king's house; but after a short time you will come back to power. You will (then) live for three, and you will die – be watchful. Instead of a kingdom, receive the good things of heaven, O highest companion of the palace.'
(*See notes, p. 281*)

[1.12] He foretold the fortunes and death of other brothers (*VC*, i, 13)

A son of Áed Chommáin, having been expelled, was in exile with the Prophet in the land of the Britons. This Áengus was the eldest, and he had two brothers. The Prophet spoke to him thus: 'You will surely be the surviving brother of the rest; you will live in your homeland, and will wield the sceptre in prosperity for a long time.

      prosperitate reges.
  Pacifer inque manus nuncquam recides inimicas,
10   sed moriere domi.'

[f. P 12r; A 241r]

[1.13] Concio autoris

  Canetur dimetro nuda relatio;
  ne forsan cythara carmen iambica
  impar materiae dixeris arduae,
      causam consilii cape.
5 Rem per se nimio pondere fertilem
  et nostris humeris forsitan imparem
  malebam digito prodere posteris,
      primam et ducere lineam.
  Rerum sola nequit mystica uisio
10 efferri calamo, uindice nec sono,
  ipso quae satius proditur indice,
      solo clara silentio.
  Linquunt iudiciis abdita plurima
  pictores, operit ductio maximas
15 partes hystoriae, cerne tabellulae
      quantum lintea contegunt.
  Ut res eloquio parua nitescere,
  et sublima uehi uiribus ingeni
  extensis humilis materies solet;
20   dum nil dictio non beat,   [f. P 12v; A 241v]
  Thersites hominum dum lepidissimus,
  dum uastum modicus fit mare riuulus,
  et collis minimus Paelion eminet,
      linguae quidlibet euehunt.
25 Ignauis ita res ardua labitur
  attentata modis, dum nitor aureus
  dicentis facili pallet inertia
      plumbo tetrius ultimo.
  Iam digne poterit quis Felemitidae
30 sacramenta Senis dicere, Lugbeus
  quae sancte patribus scripsit Ioniis?
      Coeli non nisi conscius.
  Nam cedo ingenue, nulla prophetiae
  notescit ratio, praeter imagynes,

A bringer of peace, you will also never fall into enemy hands, but you will die at home.'
(*See notes, p. 281*)

[1.13] A word by the author (*VC*, i, 43; i, 50, f. 52a–b)

This bare account will be sung in dimetric verse. In case you say, a song in iambic lyric verse is unequal to such lofty material, understand the reason for this choice: I would have preferred to publish for posterity a fertile matter, of great weight in itself, and perhaps unsuited to my shoulders, and to trace the first outline with my finger.

A mystical vision is the only thing that cannot be brought forth by the pen or by speech from a proponent, which is better handed down by the revealer himself; it is clear only in silence. Painters leave many things hidden from discernment; the drawing out conceals the greater part of the story; see how much of the tablet linen cloths cover over. As a poor thing often shines by eloquence, and humble material is raised on high by a very great power of intellect – when no speech is other than praise, when Thersites is the most agreeable of men, when a little stream becomes the wide sea, and the lowest hill towers over Mount Pelion, and language can exalt anything at all – in the same way a high matter slips away when it is attempted in feeble fashion, when golden splendour fades through the facile laziness of the speaker, more vile than basest lead.

Who now will be able to tell worthily the mysteries of our Elder, the son of Fedlimid, which Luigbe wrote down in holy fashion for the fathers of Iona, except one who is conscious of heaven?

So, I freely concede, no account of a prophecy becomes known to the earthly senses of men beyond the external appearance,

35 terrenis hominum sensibus, ut docet
        gentis doctor Apostolus.
    Cum nullis hominum uocibus exprimi,
    sed nec coelituum famine ciuium,
    tam secreta queat celsaque uisio,
40   hanc uelamine teximus.
    Quin Sancti studio prorsus et abdere
    uisa archana solent, ne sibi gloriam
    querant, intuitus prodere coelicos
        ducunt praecipuum nefas.
45 Nolint siue uelint, hos aliquando sed
    illustrat Deus, et plurima gratiae
    argumenta patent, mole ita gloriae
        se prodente aliquapiam: [f. P 13r; A 241 + 1r] D
    ut scintilla foco paruula Sycano,
50 ut feruente mero stillula dolio,
    demanant cumulo ut grana superflua,
        plena ut nux cadit arbore.

[f. P 13r; A 241 + 1r]
[1.14] Duo rustici S<anctum> de uiuacitate et fato liberorum consulunt

    Moeldanus olim consulit
    Uatem Columbam, 'Filius
    qualis futurus,' inquiens,
    'praesens puer sit, obsecro?'
5   'Moeldane, crede firmiter,
    sol non ante delabitur
    lucente prima sabbati ut
    puer relinquet saeculum.'
    Glasdarcus inde consulit,
10 qualis sit eius filius.
    'Ernanus,' inquit, 'uiuior,
    gaudebit is nepotibus.'

as the instructor and Apostle of the Gentiles teaches. Since such a secret and lofty vision cannot be expressed by any voices of men, nor even by the speech of the heavenly citizens, we have covered it over with a veil. Indeed, the saints are accustomed to conceal their hidden visions completely from view, lest they should seek glory for themselves; they esteem it an especial crime to publicise heavenly visions. But whether they want it or not, God sometimes makes them known, and many signs of grace become clear when thus the vastness of their glory betrays itself in some way: as a tiny spark from the Sicilian fires, as a drop from a vat of foaming strong wine, as overflowing grain spills down from a heap, as a ripe nut falls from a tree.
(*See notes, pp. 282–3*)

[1.14] Two peasants ask the Saint about the life and death of their sons (*VC*, i, 16)

Meldán once consulted the Prophet Columba, asking, 'What sort of son will he be in the future, I beg you, this lad present here?'

'O Meldán, believe firmly, the sun will not set before, at first light on Saturday, the boy will leave this world.'

Glasderc then asked him what sort of son his would be. He said, 'Ernán, living longer, will rejoice in his grandchildren.'
(*See notes, p. 283*)

Talem dole ne remigem,
Qua pergis, I in Iberniam
Vtens secundo flamine.
Occurret unus obuiam,
Tibi ratim qui diriget,
Comes tui qui postea
Hucusq; nobis uenerit.
Electus, igne feruidus
Sacro, futurus præsbyter,
Hæc phana uise cætero
Nusquam relinquet tempore.

De ceto magno S. Vaticinium.

IVBE, Pater, me pergere
In pace postq; uertere,
Lucente iam diluculo
Sic frater inquit Bærachus.
Columba fatur Bæracho,
Frater uale tu prospere,
Time Deum, sed dilige,
Sæclo modestus utere.
Si pergis hinc in Aethicam,
Caue maris compendium,
Anfractus oræ tutior,
Trux cetus æquor occupat.
Oblitus iuit Bærachus,
Vatisq; dictum negligit,

Qui pæne sero pænitet,
Monstrosa cete approximas
Nautæ gemunt, & eminus
Velum ratis iam detrahunt,
Natantis undas execrant,
Salui retro uix remigant.
Dieq; eodem Bætheneus
Sic commeatum postulat,
Vates cauere bestiam
Monet petentes Aethicam.
Deo supremo subsumus,
Cetusq;, egoq; Bætheneus,
Clemente fidis Numine
Nihil timetur asperum.
In pace uade, Bætheneu,
Talis fides te liberet,
Ait Columba, fluctibus
Et Bætheneus se credidit.
Fauces patentes bestiæ
Horrent uidentes nauite,
Sed Bætheneus in nomine
Christi fugauit Dæmonem.

De Nemano ficte pænitente S. Vaticinium.

Iussit dari remissius
Alimenta pænitentibus,

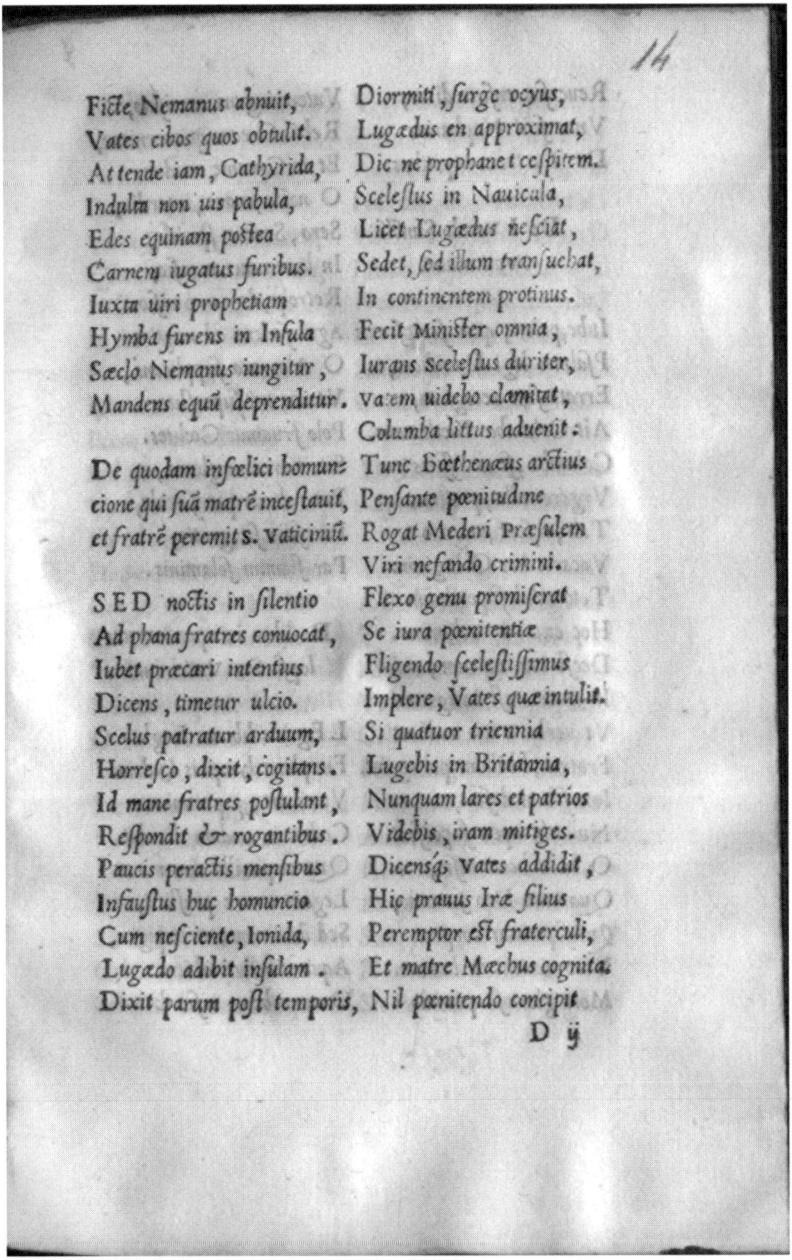

Ficte Nemanus abnuit,
Vates cibos quos obtulit.
Attende iam, Cathyrida,
Indulta non uis pabula,
Edes equinam postea
Carnem iugatus furibus.
Iuxta uiri prophetiam
Hymba furens in Insula
Sæclo Nemanus iungitur,
Mandens equu deprenditur.

De quodam infœlici homun:
cione qui suâ matrê incestauit,
et fratrê peremit s. vaticiniû.

SED noctis in silentio
Ad phana fratres conuocat,
Iubet præcari intentius
Dicens, timetur ulcio.
Scelus patratur arduum,
Horresco, dixit, cogitans.
Id mane fratres postulant,
Respondit & rogantibus.
Paucis peractis mensibus
Infaustus huç homuncio
Cum nesciente, Ionida,
Lugædo adibit insulam.
Dixit parum post temporis,

Diormiti, surge ocyus,
Lugædis en approximat,
Dic ne prophanet cespitem.
Scelestus in Nauicula,
Licet Lugædus nesciat,
Sedet, sed illum transuehat,
In continentem protinus.
Fecit Minister omnia,
Iurans Scelestus duriter,
va em uidebo clamitat,
Columba littus aduenit:
Tunc Bœthenæus arctius
Pensante pœnitudine
Rogat Mederi Præsulem
Viri nefando crimini.
Flexo genu promiserat
Se iura pœnitentiæ
Fligendo scelestissimus
Implere, Vates quæ intulit.
Si quatuor triennia
Lugebis in Britannia,
Nunquam lares et patrios
Videbis, iram mitiges.
Dicensq; Vates addidit,
Hiç prauus Iræ filius
Peremptor est fraterculi,
Et matre Mœchus cognita,
Nil pœnitendo concipit

D ij

Figure 6.   Pages from Book 1 of *Ionis: Perugia, Biblioteca communale Augusta,* I-L-66 (1), 13v–14r, showing MacLean's iambic dimeter set up in double columns. By kind permission of the Biblioteca communale Augusta, Perugia.

[f. P 13r; A 241 + 1r]
[1.15] Aliud uaticinium

Trenanus exit insulam
iubente Uate in Scottiam
festinus unum conquerens
sibi deesse remigem.
5 Columba fatur taliter: [f. P 13v; A 241 + 1v]
'Talem dole ne remigem,
qua pergis, i in Iberniam
utens secundo flamine.
Occurret unus obuiam,
10 tibi ratim qui diriget,
comes tui qui postea
hucusque nobis uenerit.
Electus, igne feruidus
sacro, futurus praesbyter,
15 haec phana uitae[11] caetero
nusquam relinquet tempore.'

[f. P 13v; A 241 + 1v]
[1.16] De ceto magno S\<ancti\> uaticinium

'Iube, Pater, me pergere
in pace postque uertere,
lucente iam diluculo,'
sic frater inquit Baerachus.
5 Columba fatur Baeracho,
'Frater, uale tu prospere,
time Deum, sed dilige,
saeclo modestus utere.
Si pergis hinc in Aethicam,
10 caue maris compendium,
anfractus orae tutior,
trux cetus aequor occupat.'
Oblitus iuit Baerachus,
Uatisque dictum negligit. [col. b]
15 Qui poene sero poenitet,
monstrosa cete approximans

---

[11] uite, Blado.

[1.15] Another prophecy (*VC*, i, 18)

Trenán leaves the island for *Scotia* (Ireland) in haste on the Prophet's orders, complaining that he lacks one oarsman. Columba spoke thus: 'Do not be regretful for this oarsman. Go into Ireland, where you are going, enjoying a favourable wind. Someone will meet you on the way who will guide your boat, who will afterwards, as your companion, come to us here. Chosen, burning with sacred flame, a future presbyter, for the rest of the time of his life he will never leave this church.'
(*See notes, p. 283*)

[1.16] The Saint's prophecy concerning a great whale (*VC*, i, 19)

'Father, bid that I may go in peace, and afterwards return, now as day is dawning,' so says Berach the monk.

Columba said to Berach, 'Farewell, brother, in prosperity. Fear God, but love Him, use the world circumspectly. If you go from here to Tiree, beware the shortcut across the sea. The circuit round the coast is safer: a savage whale dwells in the open sea.'

Berach sets out, having forgotten, and he ignores the Prophet's words. Almost too late he regrets it, as the monstrous whale approaches;

nautae gemunt et eminus
uelum ratis iam detrahunt,
natantis undas execrant,
20 salui retro uix remigant.
Dieque eodem Boetheneus
sic commeatum postulat:
Uates 'Cauere bestiam,'
monet, 'petentes Aethicam.'
25 'Deo supremo subsumus,
cetusque, egoque, Boetheneus,
clemente fidis Numine
nihil timetur asperum.'
'In pace uade, Boetheneu,
30 talis fides te liberet,'
ait Columba, fluctibus
et Boetheneus se credidit.
Fauces patentes bestiae
horrent uidentes nauitae[12]
35 sed Boetheneus in nomine
Christi fugauit doemonem.

[f. P 13v; A 241 + 1v]

[1.17] De Nemano ficte poenitente S\<ancti> uaticinium

Iussit dari remissius
alimenta poenitentibus,   [f. P 14r; A 242r] D ii
ficte Nemanus abnuit
Uates cibos quos obtulit.
'Attende iam, Cathyrida,
indulta non uis pabula,
edes equinam postea
carnem iugatus furibus.'
Iuxta uiri prophetiam
Hymba furens in insula
saeclo Nemanus iungitur,
mandens equum deprenditur.

---

[12] nauite, Blado.

the sailors cry out, and from afar they take down the boat's sail quickly, they curse the swimming creature's waves, they row backwards, barely saved.

The same day Baithéne likewise asks for leave. The Prophet warns, 'Beware the monster when you are heading for Tiree.'

'We are under God most high, both the whale and I, Baithéne; when God is merciful to his faithful people, nothing harsh is to be feared.'

'Go in peace, Baithéne, may this faith set you free,' said Columba, and Baithéne entrusted himself to the billows. Seeing the beast's yawning jaws, the sailors tremble; but Baithéne drove away the monster in the name of Christ. (*See notes, p. 283*)

[1.17] The Saint's prophecy concerning Nemán, a false penitent (*VC*, i, 21)

He ordered food to be given more generously to the penitents; Nemán feigningly refused the food which the Prophet offered. 'Listen now, son of Cathir: you do not want the food that is given, (but) afterwards you will eat horseflesh, together with thieves.'

According to the man's prophecy, being frantic in the island of *Hinba*, Nemán rejoined the world, and was caught eating horse. (*See notes, p. 283*)

[f. P 14r; A 242r]

[1.18] De quodam infoelici homuncione qui suam matrem incestauit et fratrem peremit S\<ancti\> uaticinium

Sed noctis in silentio
ad phana fratres conuocat,
iubet praecari intentius,
dicens, 'Timetur ulcio.
5 Scelus patratur arduum,
horresco', dixit, 'cogitans.'
Id mane fratres postulant,
respondit et rogantibus:
'Paucis peractis mensibus
10 infaustus huc homuncio
cum nesciente Ionida
Lugaedo adibit insulam.'
Dixit parum post temporis, [col. b]
'Diormiti, surge ocyus,
15 Lugaedus en approximat,
dic ne prophanet cespitem
scelestus in nauicula,
licet Lugaedus nesciat,
sedet, sed illum transuehat
20 in continentem protinus.'
Fecit minister omnia,
iurans scelestus duriter,
'Uatem uidebo,' clamitat.
Columba littus aduenit.
25 Tunc Boethenaeus arctius
pensante poenitudine
rogat mederi praesulem
uiri nefando crimini.
Flexo genu promiserat
30 se iura poenitentiae
fligendo scelestissimus
implere, Uates quae intulit.
'Si quatuor triennia
lugebis in Britannia,
35 nunquam lares et patrios
uidebis, iram mitiges.'
Dicensque Uates addidit,
'Hic prauus irae filius
peremptor est fraterculi,

[1.18] The Saint's prophecy concerning a wretched man who committed incest with his mother and killed his brother (*VC*, i, 22)

He calls the brothers together to the church, although at dead of night, and orders them to pray more intently, saying, 'Vengeance is to be feared. A terrible crime is being done; I tremble thinking of it,' he said. In the morning the brothers ask about it, and he replies to their questions: 'In a few months' time an ill-starred wretch will come here to the island, with an unknowing child of Iona, Lugaid.'

After a short period of time, he said, 'Diarmait, get up at once, see, Lugaid is approaching. Say to him, lest he profane our soil, that a criminal sits in his boat, although Lugaid does not know it; but he is to take him at once to the mainland (of Mull).'

His servant does all this, but the criminal, swearing hard, cries, 'I will see the Prophet!'

Columba comes to the shore. Then Baithéne asks the abbot to remedy the man's evil crime with a more demanding penance. On bended knee the most wicked man promised to fulfil the sentence of penance which the Prophet imposed as an affliction. 'If you lament in Britain for four times three years, and never see your ancestral home, you will assuage (God's) anger.'

Saying this, the Prophet added, 'This depraved child of wrath is the murderer of his own young brother,

40 et matre maechus cognita.
Nil poenitendo concipit;   [f. P 14v; A 242v]
reuersus, ense coeditur.'
Unus fuit nepharius
de Turtreis nepotibus.

[f. P 14v; A 242v]

[1.19] De I uocali Sancti uaticinium

'Iube pater, quos scripsimus
Psalmos legi Dauidicos,
errata sint recognita,'
ait Columbae Baetheneus.
5 Columba, 'Si necessitas
urgeret ulla, protinus
tali,' refert, 'negotio
uacaret hoc collegium.
Toto nihil superfluum
10 hoc extat in uolumine.
Deest iota unicum,
in caeteris est integrum.'
Ut uerba Uatis audiunt
fratres libellum perlegunt.
15 Iota solum defuit,
nullusque apex superfuit.

[f. P 14v; A 242v]

O mors beata uisio,
qua cum Deo sit unio,
qui separatur corpore
20 uero manens in lumine.
Mors gloriosa, praemio [col. b]
Uatem iugans omniscio,
rebus Creans qua cernitur,
et in Creante condita.
25 O nocte, mane, interdiu,
sero, serene spiritu,
in luce cuius mansio,
retroque et ante uisio.
Agni sedens ad nuptias,

and a fornicator, having known his own mother. He gains nothing by penitence; going back, he will be slain by the sword.' This wicked man was one of the Uí Thuirtri.

(*See notes, pp. 283–4*)

[1.19] The Saint's prophecy concerning the vowel *I* (*VC*, i, 23)

'Father, command that the Psalms of David, which we have written, be read over; let errors be detected,' said Baithéne to Columba.

Columba replied, 'If any necessity required it, at once this community would attend to this business. In the whole of this volume there is nothing superfluous; only one *iota* is lacking; it is complete in everything else.'

As they hear the Prophet's words, the brothers read through the book. Only an *iota* was missing, and not one letter was superfluous.

[Refrain] (*VC*, iii, 23, f. 134b)

O death, blessed vision where there is union with God, who is separate from the body, dwelling in the true light! Glorious death, joining the Prophet to his All-knowing reward, where the Creator is perceived by material things, and that which is made is perceived in the Creator. O serene in spirit, at night and in the morning, in the daytime and evening, whose dwelling-place is in light, a vision before and after: O Dove, seated at the Lamb's wedding-feast,

30 O Ales, ora supplicans
    ut nos tui superstites
    polo fruamur coelites.
    Sit Ternioni gloria,
    Patri decus per saecula,
35 par Filio sit gratia,
    par Flamini solaminis.

[f. P 14v; A 242v]

[1.20] De Libro in aquarium uas lapso S<ancti> uaticinium

    Legente librum Lugbeo
    fit plena lymphis hydria.
    Uates ait, quod protinus
    codex in undam decidat.
5   Quo coepit ille non minus
    legens tenore perstitit,
    sed dum moueret impiger,
    aquis libellus labitur.
    O mors beata uisio, etc.

[f. P 15r; A 243r]

[1.21] De Corniculo atramentario inaniter fuso S<ancti> praeuisio

    'Diormiti, qui clamitat
    ultra fretum, cum uenerit
    effundet hoc quod assidet
    nobis atramentarium.'
5   Is inde cornu sedulus
    perire nolens, efferum
    diu manebat hospitem
    iuxta fores cubiculi.
    Sed altero negotio
10 uocante, paulum cesserat;
    eo momento uenerat
    hospesque atramen fuderat.
    Crassis agrestis sensibus
    petens Columbam basio

pray in supplication that we your successors may enjoy the heavens as dwellers there. Glory be to the Trinity, honour to the Father throughout the ages, equal thanks be to the Son, equal thanks to the Spirit of comfort.
(*See notes, p. 284*)

[1.20] The Saint's prophecy concerning a book dropped in a vessel of water (*VC*, i, 24)

Where Luigbe is reading a book there happens to be a jar full of water. The Prophet said that the book would straight away fall into the water. He nonetheless continued reading in the same way that he had started; but when he moved suddenly, the book fell into the water.

[Refrain] O death, blessed vision, etc.
(*See notes, p. 284*)

[1.21] The Saint's foresight concerning an inkhorn suddenly spilt (*VC*, i, 25)

'Diarmait, someone who is shouting across the Sound (of Iona), when he comes here, will spill this ink-holder which sits beside me.'

So he, not wanting the horn to be upset, carefully awaited the rough guest beside the door of his chamber for a time; but when other business called him, he went away for a short while; at that moment the guest arrived and spilled the ink. When the rustic fellow with clumsy disposition approached Columba with a kiss,

15 uestis ruentis impetu
    humum nigredo leuerat.
    O mors beata uisio, etc.

[f. P 15r; A 243r]

[1.22] De Aedani hospitis aduentu et solutione ieiunii S\<ancti\> uaticinium

Sic luce Martis fratribus
Columba dixit, 'Crastina
soluetur hoc ieiunium [col. b]
urgente nobis hospite.'
5   Uenit die nam postera
    Aedanus 'ortus masculi',
    pius uir, ut praedixerat
    Uates, editque lautius.
    Inuitat hospes caeteros
10 fratres, ad esum compulit,
    cum gratiarum munere
    soluere sic ieiunium.
    O mors beata uisio, etc.

[f. P 15r; A 243 r]

[1.23] De Romani iuris ciuitate igne sulphuraeo combusta S\<ancti\> uaticinium

Ab horreo dum Lugbeus
tritis rediret frugibus,
ardore Uatis igneo
uultus rubentes auffugit.
5   Columba dixit Lugbeo,
    'Fili, mane, quid territat?'
    Mox mente seruus aequior
    audet Columbam poscere,
    'Horrore plena uisio
10 dic, qualis est? Quam uideras,
    scio, pater, te turbidat
    proteruitas spectaculi[13].'

---

[13]   spestaculi, Blado.

blackness stained the ground by the touch of his sweeping clothing.

[Refrain] O death, blessed vision, etc.

(*See notes, pp. 284–5*)

[1.22] The Saint's prophecy concerning the arrival of the guest Áedán and relaxation of the fast (*VC*, i, 26)

On a Tuesday, Columba spoke thus to the brothers: 'Tomorrow this fast will be relaxed, at the request to us of a guest.'

The next day, indeed, Áedán, 'Born of a Man', came, as the Prophet had predicted, a pious man, and ate quite well. The guest invited the rest of the brothers, (and) he urged them to eat with a gift of thanksgiving, thus to relax their fast.

[Refrain] O death, blessed vision, etc.

(*See notes, p. 285*)

[1.23] The Saint's prophecy concerning a city of the Roman jurisdiction burned up with sulphurous fire (*VC*, i, 28)

Once when Luigbe was returning from the barn, having threshed corn, he fled away from the Prophet's face, which was red with a fiery glow. Columba said to Luigbe, 'Wait, son, what frightens you?'

Presently the servant, calmer in spirit, ventures to ask Columba, 'Say, what manner of vision is this, filled with terror? I know, Father, the violence of the spectacle that you have seen troubles you.'

'Sic res habet iam, Lugbee,   [f. P 15v; A 243v]
ira Dei nam uindice
15 perit perampla ciuitas
cadente coelo sulphure.
Haec in remotis partibus
Oenotriae fit insita,
quae castra curat Martia
20 sub gente parens Romula.
Hic terna ferme milia,
pereunt uirorum, matribus,
puerisque cunctis obrutis,
Iouis micante spiculo.
25 Nec annus hinc implebitur,
cum nauis huc e Scotia
tales feret rumusculos,
ut uerba uerbis conferas.'
Paucis peractis mensibus,
30 in Albionem Lugbeus
Uatis comes, quo comprobet
praedicta, uenit percitus.
Nauclerus edit omnia
praescita; tum scit Lugbeus,
35 uidisse Uatem praedicat,
ut ciuitati contigit.
O mors beata uisio, etc.

[f. P 15v; A 243v]
[1.24] De Lasriano filio Feradachi S\<ancti> uaticinium

Iam Capricorni sydera
linquendo gaudet aureus
humente sol Aquario, et
hyems ferocit aspera.
5   Uates manens Ionide,
moerore fleuit eiulans;
rogat minister, lachrimae
Columba causas exhibet.
'En,' inquit, 'O Dyormiti,
10 hae iure fluunt lachrimae,
laesis oportet compati,

'Luigbe, the matter is like this: a great city just now is perishing with sulphur falling from heaven by the avenging wrath of God; it is situated in the distant lands of Italy, subject to the Roman people who keep its warlike strongholds. There some three thousand men have perished, with women and children, all of them overwhelmed, as Jupiter's thunderbolt has flashed. Neither will a year from now have passed when a ship from *Scotia* (Ireland) will bring these tidings here, so you may compare word for word.'

After a few months had passed, Luigbe came to *Alba* as the Prophet's companion, greatly excited to confirm what had been said: a ship's captain related everything that had been foreknown. Then Luigbe knew; he declared that the Prophet had seen it, as it befell the city.

[Refrain] O death, blessed vision, etc.

(*See notes, p. 285*)

[1.24] The Saint's prophecy concerning Laisrán mac Feradaig (*VC*, i, 29)

Now the golden sun rejoices leaving the stars of Capricorn for damp Aquarius, and bitter winter rages. The Prophet, residing in Iona, wept, groaning with grief.

His servant asks him, and Columba explains the cause of his tears: 'Lo, Diarmait,' he says, 'these tears flow for good reason: it is right that we should sympathise with the injured;

premit rigor nunc optimos.
Ora situm Conalliae
phanum frequente robore,
15 Pelasga uox contermina
Dryas sonatur, Doeria.
Querceta sacris caedua,
hic desecantur aedibus,
his Lasrianus milites
20 fatigat a laboribus.
Delubra iam nec incolunt
diuum, domum sed extruunt
graui peramplam fabrica
petente pompa saeculi.
25 Id iure flenti displicet,
enectat hos ieiunium,
furente nec dat ocium
bruma praecationibus.   [f. P 16r; A 244r]
Sed Lasrianum corripit
30 iam langor, isque aegrotitat,
cibos cohorti et debitos
iubet dari benignius.
Iubet maligno sydere
cessare de laboribus,
35 Deum praecari, et corpora
quassata iam quiescere.'
Tum flere Uates destitit,
talem beans antistitem:
laetanter et hoc fratribus
40 narrans dedit solatia.
O mors beata uisio, etc.

[f. P 16r; A 244r]

**[1.25] De Faechno sapiente, qu<omod>o is poenitens ad S<anc-
tum> Columbam diuinitus de aduentu praemonitum aduenerat**

Qua serus it fauonius,
est cliuus unde despicis
solis cubile uesperum,
dictusque Mons Ionius.
5 Huius Columba in uertice
fatur ministro talia,

bitterness now oppresses our dearest friends. Sited in Tír Conaill by the many oak woods, is a church, Derry; the Greek word sounds similar, *Dryas*. Here oak woods, ripe for felling, are being cut down for our sacred halls, and Laisrán is tiring out our soldiers by these heavy labours. Neither are they now frequenting the shrines of the saints, but they are building a great house with burdensome industry, while earthly glory drives them. This is rightly distressing to me as I weep. Fasting is wearing them out; neither does he give them time for prayer as winter rages. But now weariness affects Laisrán, he himself becomes faint, and he more kindly orders due food to be given to the company. He orders a halt from labour under the angry star, that they should pray to God, and then rest their worn-out bodies.'

Then the Prophet stops weeping, blessing this abbot; and recounting this happily to the brothers, he gives them comfort.

[Refrain] O death, blessed vision, etc.

(*See notes, pp. 285–6*)

[1.25] Concerning Fiachnae the wise, how he came as a penitent to St Columba, who was divinely forewarned of his coming (*VC*, i, 30)

Where the evening west wind blows there is a hill from which you see the setting of the sun in the west; it is called the Hill of Iona (Dùn Ì). On its summit, Columba spoke thus to his attendant:

'Miror, rati quid Scoticae,
qua hospes uehetur, accidit.
Uehendus huc est uir scius,
10 celebri Minerua prouidus, [col. b]
lapsuque pro nephario
ingente poenitudine.'
Austro secundo turgida
mox uela littus applicant:
15 'Surgamus,' inquit, 'ocyus
et obuiemus aduenae.
Huius fidelem suscipit
Christusque poenitentiam.'
De naue Faechnus exiens
20 pronus Columbae supplicat;
infit Columba lachrimans,
'Solare mentis aequior,
fient remissa plurima,
contritione, crimina.
25 Intremus,' inquit, 'optime,
uitae caue per caeterum.'
Ad Boethenaeum postea
in pace Faechnum destinat.

[f. P 16r; A 244r]

[1.26] De obitu Coelteani monachi S\<ancti> uaticinium

Oram lacus Gathaelicam
unda piger disterminat,
praeceps Abae per hostia
salo redundans hespero.
5   Ripe lacus adhaeserat
fratrum uetusta caellula,   [f. P 16v; A 244v]
cui Caelteanus praefuit,
Ionidum colonia.
Hic Caelteanus tempore
10 Columbae obedientia,
fratres regebat accolas,
Deum colens acerrime.
Binos ad hunc legauerat
fratres Columba cominus,

'I wonder what is happening to an Irish ship, by which a guest will be brought? A wise man is to be brought here, prophetic with famous Wisdom, with great penitence because of a sinful lapse.'

Presently the sails come to shore swelling with a favourable south wind. 'Let us arise quickly,' he said, 'and meet the newcomer; Christ accepts his faithful penitence.'

Disembarking from his ship, falling face down, Fiachnae besought Columba. Columba replied, weeping, 'Take comfort, be calm in spirit: many crimes will be remitted because of your contrition. Let us go in, dear friend,' he said, 'take care for the rest of your life.'

Thereafter he sent Fiachnae in peace to Baithéne.

(*See notes, p. 286*)

[1.26] The Saint's prophecy concerning the death of the monk Cailtán (*VC*, i, 31)

A still loch divides the Gaelic Shore (Argyll), by its waters, while it rushes headlong to the western sea by the mouth of the River Awe (Bonawe). An ancient cell of brothers clings to the shore of the loch, a community of monks of Iona, of which Cailtán was in charge. Here for a time Cailtán ruled the resident brothers, in obedience to Columba, worshipping God most strictly.

Columba sent two brothers together to him; he said,

15 'Ad Caelteanum pergite,
   hunc,' infit, 'huc adducere.'
   Iuere fratres protinus
   uisum suam coloniam,
   et Caelteanum congruo
20 honore ducunt impigrum.
   'Obedienter, Optime,
   uenisse te iam gaudeo,'
   Uates ait, 'quiescito,
   post, cur uocarim, percipe.
25 Idcirco te uocaueram,
   amans amicum, finiens
   cursum tui iam temporis
   in pace mecum ut manseris.
   Non finietur hebdomas
30 haec, ut relinques saeculum.'
   Id Caelteanus audiens
   amplexus illum fleuerat.
   Adit paratus cellulam,
   et nocte languet postera, [col. b]
35 hinc commeatu mystico
   coeli petiuit curiam.
   O mors beata uisio, etc.

[f. P 16v; A 244v]

[1.27] De duobus fratribus peregrinis S<ancti> uaticinium

Sacrae quietis tempore,
solis die iam septimo
Uates manens Ionide
uocem renouit per fretum.
5 'Duo peregre uenerant,
ultra fretum qui clamitant,
eos,' ait, 'adducite
cito, nec ab re uisitant.'
Uatem salutant hospites,
10 qui laetus illos excipit.
Ob quid, rogati, uenerint,
fantur Columbae talia.
'Unius anni circulo,

'Go quickly to Cailtán to bring him here.'

The brothers went directly to visit his community, and brought Cailtán eagerly back with due honour. 'I rejoice, dearest friend, that you have come obediently now,' said the Prophet. 'You will rest, and afterwards know why I have called you. I have called you for this reason, loving my friend, so that, finishing now the course of your time, you may remain with me in peace. This week will not be finished before you will leave the world.'

Hearing this, Cailtán wept while embracing him. Having been prepared, he went to a cell, and fell ill the next night, and went from here to the court of heaven by an inscrutable passage.

[Refrain] O death, blessed vision, etc.

(*See notes, pp. 286–7*)

[1.27] The Saint's prophecy concerning two pilgrim brothers (*VC*, i, 32)

At the time of sacred rest, on Sunday, the seventh day, the Prophet, staying on Iona, recognised a cry across the Sound. 'Two pilgrims have come, who call across the Sound,' he said; 'bring them quickly; their visit is not without purpose.'

The guests greet the Prophet, who joyfully receives them. When asked why they have come, they say this to Columba:

sit fas modo per gratiam,
15   hic esse tecum poscimus.
Audire Uatem uenimus.'
Tum sanctus infit, 'Non licet,
si non iugo monastico
repente uos submittitis.'
20   Fratres stupent instantia.[14]
'Si nos uides idoneos'   [f. P 17r; A 245r] E
aiunt, 'Pater, parebimus,
Sacro calere Spiritu
scimus tua haec oracula.'
25   'Ciues,' ait, 'domestici,
foelice fratres omine,
iam dico uos non hospites,
gaudete, sed attendite.
Uosmet dedistis hostiam
30   uiuam Deo, iam currite
toto, uiri, conamine
abest procul non terminus.
Nam sena uix per sydera
Diana complet cornua,
35   Heri talento duplices,
hinc cum petetis aethera.'
Grates agentes maximas
ambo locantur caellulis,
senex prius dissoluitur,
40   senem secutus iunior.
O mors beata uisio, etc.

[f. P 17r; A 245r]

[1.28] De quodam Arbranano Norico[15] gentili S<ancti> uaticinium

Arctous ambit Haebrida
unam sinus poenextimam;
Schyam uocarat Danica

---

[14]   Blado has: Tum sanctus infit, Non licet, / Fratres stupent instantia / Si non iugo monastico
/ Repente uos submittitis. The second line, interrupting Columba's speech, appears to have
been misplaced.
[15]   Nori-rico, Blado, with hyphen at the end of a line and the last syllable repeated in error at
the beginning of the following line. Cf. noricum, line 19 below.

'We ask to be here with you for the space of one year, by your grace, let this be good now; we come to hear the Prophet.'

The Saint then said, 'It is not allowed, unless you at once submit yourselves to the monastic yoke.'

The brothers are surprised at his insistence. 'If we seem suitable to you, Father,' they say, 'we will obey you: we know this word of yours is inspired by the Holy Spirit.'

'O household citizens,' he said, 'brothers, by this happy omen, now I do not call you guests; rejoice, but listen carefully. You have given yourselves a living sacrifice to God; now run, men, with all effort: the end (of your race) is not far away. For the moon will barely have filled her horns six times (as she goes) through the stars, when you, made double in the talent of your Lord, will go from here to heaven.'

Giving the greatest thanks, they are both placed in the (monastic) cells. The elder was released first, the younger followed the elder.

[Refrain] O death, blessed vision, etc.

(*See notes, p. 287*)

[1.28] The Saint's prophecy concerning Artbranán, a Norse pagan (*VC*, i, 33)

The northern gulf surrounds one Hebridean island, almost the furthest; the Danish people, ancient in origin, had called it Skye.

uetusta gens origine. [col. b]
5　Est portus hac in insula
　　secundus unda et flamine
　　a rege quem neoteri
　　portum uocant Gathelici.
　　Huc forte Uates applicans
10　in parte terramque atterens
　　ligni recurui cuspide,
　　'Res mira,' dixit, 'hoc die.
　　Gentilis unus hoc die
　　lauabitur baptismate,
15　actis lauacri ritibus
　　defunctus hic humabitur.'
　　Mox cymba portum penetrat,
　　senem uehens, primarium
　　Geon cohortis Noricum;
20　is ante Uatem ponitur.
　　Uerbo Dei abs interprete
　　senex recepto credidit,
　　lotus aquis renascitur,
　　hic functus atque conditur.
25　Nam quo lauatur flumine,
　　'Fons Ardbranani' dicitur,
　　oram mari conterminam
　　salicta texunt annua.
　　O mors beata uisio, etc.

[f. P 17r; A 245r]
[1.29]

Fynchanus olim praesbyter
Christi pugil perstrennuus, [f. P 17v; A 245v]
de Scotia ad Britanniam
assumpsit Oedum Cruthneum.
5　Qui regio de sanguine
　　Oedus Niger uocabulo,
　　athleta sanguinarius
　　regem peremit Scotiae.
　　Fynchanus illum clerici
10　amiciens indumine

There is a harbour in this island, favourable for tides and wind, which the more recent Gaels call 'Harbour of the King' (*Port Rìgh*, Portree).

Coming there by chance, the Prophet, striking the earth in part of it with the point of his curved wooden staff, said, 'An amazing thing (will happen) today. A single pagan today will be washed in baptism, and when the baptismal rites are finished, he will die and be buried here.'

Presently a boat entered the harbour, carrying an old man, a Norseman, leader of the Cohort of *Geon*; he was set down before the Prophet. When he had heard the word of God from an interpreter, the old man believed; baptised in water, he was reborn, and he died and was buried.

The stream in which he was baptised, indeed, is called 'Artbranán's Spring'; willow groves each year thickly cover the shore beside the sea.

[Refrain] O death, blessed vision, etc.

(*See notes, pp. 287–9*)

[1.29] [The Saint's prophecy concerning the priest Findchán] (*VC*, i, 36)

Findchán, once a priest and very active fighter for Christ, brought Áed of the Cruithne from *Scotia* (Ireland) to Britain; he was of royal blood, called Áed the Black, a bloody fighter, who killed the king of Ireland. Findchán, dressing him in clerical garb,

fecit suo in sacellulo
sacro Leuitam ordine.
Accitus atque pontifex
illum sacrauit unguine,
15   nolens manus imponere,
Fynchanus id ni fecerit.
Suam manum non impiger
Fynchanus huic accommodat,
solum sacer fit nomine,
20   Oedo abnuente Numine.
Egre tulit Nigellides
ludibriosos ordines,
praenunciauit horridam
ambobus et sententiam.
25   'Fynchane, qui nepharie
tuam Nigrum per dexteram
Oedum sacrari feceras,
haec ipsa dextra putreat.
Humata te superstite
30   fiat manus per dedecus [col. b]
ut mancus inde ecclesiae
poenam luas iniuriae.
Et ordinatus pristinam
tanquam canis reuertitur
35   ad faeditatem, saucius
mersus peribit flumine.'
Suo prophetae oracula
impleta sunt in tempore,
manum putredo inuaserat,
40   iugulatus Oedo mergitur.
O mors beata uisio etc.

[f. P 17v; A 245v]
[1.30]

Horas Bilanx rorantibus
equat diurnas noctibus
uindaemiantes demetunt
messes recuruis falcibus.
5   Tum coenobitas milites

made him a deacon in his chapel by sacred ordination. A bishop consecrated him with anointing, having also been summoned, not wishing to place his hands upon him unless Findchán did so too. Findchán, (although) not eager, applied his hand to him; he was made holy in name only, since God rejected Áed.

The scion of the Uí Néill bore ill this mockery of an ordination, and pronounced a terrible sentence upon both of them: 'Findchán, you who have wickedly caused Áed the Black to be consecrated by your right hand: may this same right hand putrefy. May your hand be buried while you live on in infamy as one deformed, so you may suffer the punishment of the church for this injury. The one who has been ordained will return like a dog to his former filth; wounded he will die, drowned in a river.'

The Prophet's oracles were completely fulfilled in their due time: putrescence infected the hand; Áed was slaughtered and drowned.

[Refrain] O death, blessed vision, etc.

(*See notes, p. 289*)

[1.30] [The Saint's spirit refreshes his monks in their labours] (*VC*, i, 37)

The Balance (Libra) makes equal the daylight hours with dewy night; the harvesters reap their crop with curved sickles.

fatigat in uindaemia
auena, faba, triticum,
ceresque et ordeacea.
Columba ne, fit anxius,
10 uiros praemat molestia,
quibus stupenda contigit
frugum diebus uisio.
Quam nemo narrat alteri,
alto sed in silentio,
15 arcana condit abdita,   [f. P 18r; A 246r] E ii
instanti messis tempore.
Rogare tandem Boetheneus,
qui praefuit laboribus,
audebat, 'An dieculis
20 sensistis his miraculum?
Ad phana sero uespere
a messe quando ceditis,
solamen a laboribus
si quod fuit, iam dicite.'
25 'Beate pastor Boetheneu,
fas propalare id accidens,
iussu tuo confidimus,'
ait senex humillimus.
'Sensi ferens non sarcinam
30 magno solutus gaudio,
calensque odores coeperam,
uerbis quibus quos exprimam?
Thus, myrra, cedrus, laurea,
myrtus, cypressus, lilia,
35 roseta, palmae, balsama,
illis minus fragrantia.
Amomum, anethum, amaracus,
pinus, uirorque buxeus,
costus, crocus, uel nardinus
40 liquorque odora cynnama,
illis minus fragrantia.
Sed rosmarinus Gallicus,
narcissus, aiax flosculus, [col. b]
Sabaea cuncta aromata,
45 illis minus fragrantia.
Amaena Tempe Thessala,
Persis calens, et India,
et Tmolus ipse odorifer,

Then oats, beans, wheat, corn, and barley make the monastic soldiers exhausted at their harvest. Columba becomes concerned lest the burden should oppress the men, for whom in these days of harvest a wonderful vision happens. No one tells it to another, but in deep silence keeps the secret hidden away in the urgent harvest time. At length Baithéne, who was in charge of the work, ventured to ask, 'Have you sensed a miracle in these few days? When you withdraw from harvesting to the church, late in the evening, if there has been some comfort from your toil, now tell me.'

'Blessed pastor Baithéne, we trust it is right to make known what is happening, by your orders,' said a very humble old man. 'I have sensed that I am not bearing a burden, having been released with great joy, and I have begun feeling warmth, and sensed fragrances; by what words may I express them? Incense, myrrh, cedar, laurel, myrtle, cypress, lily, rose beds, palm trees and balsam, are less fragrant than these. Cardamom, dill, marjoram, pine and green box tree, costmary, saffron, or the juice of nard and scent of cinnamon, are less fragrant than these. The French rosemary, the daffodil, the hyacinth, all the spices of Sheba, are less fragrant than these. Delightful Tempe in Thessaly, warm Persia and India, and sweet-smelling Mount Tmolus itself,

illis minus fragrantia.
50 Granata, mala Maedica,
oliua, mella Hymaetia,
passus racemus, fistula,
minus sapore dulcia.
Florum recens Alcinoi,
55 siluis opacis gratia,
et urna pigmentaria,
ualent minus fragrantia.
Sensi ferens nil sarcinam
magno solutus gaudio,
60 mirosque odores senseram,
uerbis nec his hos exprimo.
Aeous halans hortulus
quales odores exhibet,
quali dape et superstites
65 Enoch Helian recreat.
Uitalis arbor pabuli
quales respirat halitus,
cuius negato prandio
Adamus exul pellitur.
70 Audita fit melodia
canora, quam nec musula   [f. P 18v; A 246v]
humana, uoce aut organo
canendo possit assequi.
Urania, Terpsichore,
75 Clyo, sorores caeterae,
accomodarunt triplicem,
coeli canore iubilum.
Non illa fabulamina,
Homaericas musas loquor,
80 sed Cherubicosque Seraphicos
polo cantus audiueram.
Odor, sapor, melodia,
amica flamma innoxia,
fiunt leuamen omnium
85 laboris et molestiae.'
Grates agentes Numini
dixere sed conformiter
alii, 'Sed unde contigit,
iam, Boethenaee, edissere.'
90 'Quis nescit,' infit Boetheneus,
'nostrum senem nunc anxium

are less fragrant than these. The pomegranate, the fruit of Media, the olive, the honey of Mount Hymettus, clusters of dried grapes, *fistula*, are less sweet to the taste. The fresh grace of the flowers of Alcinous in shady woods, and vessels filled with aromatic plants, their fragrance is less strong. I have sensed that I am not bearing a burden, having been released with great joy, and I had sensed amazing odours; I do not express them (even) by these words. A fragrant eastern garden puts forth odours such as these; by such a feast also it refreshes the survivors Enoch and Elijah. The tree of lively nourishment breathes forth such aromas; Adam is driven forth in exile, when its fruit has been denied him. A sonorous melody is heard, which no human muse can come close to, by making music either with voice or instruments. Urania, Terpsichore, Clio, and the other sisters, have made way for a threefold joyful song by the harmony of heaven. I do not speak of those fabulous tales, of the muses of Homer; but I have heard songs from heaven of the Cherubim and Seraphim. The scent, taste, and music, the friendly, gentle warmth, these become an alleviation of the labour and burden of all.'

Others spoke, giving thanks to God, but (only) in agreement; 'But, Baithéne, explain now: where does it come from?'

Baithéne said, 'Who does not know that our Elder,

duro labore militum
fouere nos de spiritu?
Eius polo melodias,
95 et Tmolo odores coelicos,
ignes fauentes, spiritus
amplexus huc illexerat.'

Beata fratrum uisio,
qua cum Deo sint unio, [col. b]
100 dum separati corpore,
uero manent in lumine.
Mors gloriosa praemio, etc.

[f. P 18v; A 246v]

**[1.31] De tonitruo Psalmoediae, et confutatione nicromantarum
S\<ancti\> uaticinium**

Templi, canentis atrio
vox lata mille passibus
minor nec est absentibus,
maior propinquisue auribus.
5 Regnante Pictis Brudeo
coepit fides uigescere,
fraudes deum tenebricae
ploduntur atque idolatrae.
Adest uocatus Brudeo,
10 uerum Deum ut praedicet,
et fraudulenti numinis
ritus moueret impios.
Uates perosus augures,
druidas, magos, aruspices,
15 mantas uagos, ueneficas,
hos arguebat perfidos.
Delumbe sed collegium
matrum uolens auertere
regem Columba consule,
20 pernox[16] litat Proserpinae.   [f. P 19r; A 247r]
Uates retexit doemonum
artes, dolos, astutiam.

16 Per nox, Blado.

concerned in the hard work of his soldiers, supports us from his spirit? His embracing spirit has summoned here the melodies from heaven, the heavenly scents from Mount Tmolus, and the comforting fires.'

[Refrain] Blessed vision of brothers, where they are at one with God, they dwell in the true light when separated from the body! Glorious death, etc. (*See notes, pp. 289–91*)

[1.31] The Saint's prophecy concerning the thundering of his psalm singing and the defeat of wizards (*VC*, i, 37)

The voice of his singing in the court of the temple, carried a mile, is neither quieter to those far away nor louder to nearby ears. While Bridei reigned over the Picts the faith began to increase, (but) dark deceits of the gods and idolatry are (still) approved. He comes to Bridei when summoned, so that he might preach the true God, and remove the impious cults of a false godhead. The Prophet, loathing the seers, druids, magicians, soothsayers, wayfaring oracle mongers, and sorcerers, showed them to be faithless. But the wounded council of mothers (?), wishing to turn the king away from Columba as his adviser, meeting through the night, sacrificed to Proserpina. The Prophet unravelled the wiles, plots, and craftiness of the demons;

Fidem docebat unicam
in Ternione regiam.
25 Ne gens fidelis audiat
piam uiri psalmoediam,
magus procaci carmine
aures putat surdescere.
Munitionem regiam
30 exit Columba[17] tempore
ad mille passus deforis,
canat praeces ut uesperas.
Uates soni modestia
psalmis canendis utitur,
35 pauens remota ciuitas
audit uiri tonitruum.
Magus uerens exploditur,
fingit Columbae se obsequi
quaestus amore dilui
40 nolens aquis lustralibus.

[f. P 19r; A 247r]

[1.32]

Ferum Columba Cruthneum
Uates Nemanum corripit,
sermo Dei ludibrio
fuit Nemano perfido.
5 'Ex quo salutis semitam,'
ait Columba, 'deseris, [col. b]
Dei tibi iam[18] nomine,
Nemane, dico, pessime,
foeda litus libidine
10 incestuosae foeminae
infamis in cubiculo
fato peribis congruo.
Animam rapaces doemones
penas trahent ad inferas,
15 aquae Stygis, Cocytia
fluenta[19] fiunt praemia.'

---

[17]   Colnmba, Blado.
[18]   nam, Blado.
[19]   fluentia, Blado.

he taught the unique faith in the Trinity, worthy of a king. Lest faithful people should hear the man's pious psalm singing, a magician thought to deafen their ears with insolent song. At the time Columba left the royal hall, going outside to the distance of a mile, so he might sing Vespers. The Prophet used moderation of tone for the singing of the psalms; stricken with fear, the faraway city heard the man's thundering. The fearful magician is drowned out; he feigns to show himself obedient to Columba, (yet) because of his love of profit would not be washed in cleansing waters (of baptism).
(*See notes, p. 291*)

[1.32] [The Saint's prophecy concerning Nemán] (*VC*, i, 39)

The Prophet Columba rebukes fierce Nemán of the Cruithne; the word of God was as a joke to faithless Nemán. Columba said, 'Since you abandon the path of salvation, I say to you now, most wicked Nemán, by the name of God, you will perish by a fitting death, besmirched with filthy lust, of ill repute, in the chamber of an incestuous woman. Rapacious demons will drag your soul to the pains of hell; the waters of the Styx, the floods of Cocytus, become your reward.'

Parum recurrit temporis,
mortem Nemanus oppetit
ferro peremptus militis,
20 Canile de prouincia.

[1.33] De indigno praesbytero S\<ancti\> uaticinium

Dum luce prima sabbati
unus litat Triorithi,
bonum putant quem clerici,
horret Columba antistitem.
5   Mali sacerdos conscius
Uatem latere nescius,
foedi et sacri commercio,
denunciatur improbo.
Scelus sacerdos confitens
10 Uatis pedes et applicans   [f. P 19v; A 247v]
fletus amaritudine
foedo lauatur crimine.
O mors beata uisio etc.

**[1.34] Cognouit Columba fuisse episcopum quendam, admonitus
tempore Sacrificii**

Olim peregre uenerat
de finibus Munensium
sub ueste tectus pauperis
studens latere pontifex.
5   Uates sodalem coeperat
illum synaxis tempore,
panis sacri sodaliter
esum ut simul communicent.
Uates uidet tum perspicax,
10 caelauit id quod pontifex,
cuius prius sit nescius,
Sacer reuelat Spiritus.
Ut sciuit ergo praesulem,
cupit decenter obsequi,

A little while passed and Nemán met his death, slain by the sword of a soldier from the province of *Cainle*.
(*See notes, pp. 291–2*)

[1.33] The Saint's prophecy concerning an unworthy priest (*VC*, i, 40)

At the first light of the Sabbath, at Trevet, when one whom the clergy esteem to be good offers the sacrifice, Columba is horrified at this priest. The priest, aware of the evil, unable to hide from the Prophet, is denounced for immoral trafficking of the profane and the sacred. The priest, confessing his crime, and taking hold of the Prophet's feet with bitterness of tears, is cleansed of his filthy crime.

[Refrain] O death, blessed vision, etc.
(*See notes, p. 292*)

[1.34] Columba knew that a man was a bishop, warned at the hour of the Sacrifice (*VC*, i, 44)

Once a bishop had come on pilgrimage from the land of the people of Munster, dressed in the guise of a poor man, seeking to escape notice. The Prophet had chosen that companion at the time of the eucharist, so that as equals they might share the meal of sacred bread together. Then the perceptive Prophet sees what the bishop has concealed; the Holy Spirit reveals something of which he is ignorant before. So when he knew him to be a bishop, he wished to show obedience properly:

'Tu frange more episcopi,'
ait, 'uereri debeo.'
O mors beata uisio etc.

[f. P 19v; A 247v]

[1.35] S<anctus> Ernani auunculi fatum praedixit [col. b]

Qua fessus undas aureus
Phoebus colorat hesperas,
est Imba quaedam fluctibus
in estuosis insula.
Lares priusquam deserens
in Albionem uenerat,
fundauit hic coloniam
fratrum Columba Iberidum.
Quondam manens Ionide
praefecit huic auunculum,
quem diligens tenerrime
tali monebat famine:
'Ernane, te iam destino,
ut Imbicae coloniae
dux sis talento fructifer,
non est procul solutio.'
Postquam carina littore
abit, Boraeo flamine,
dixit Columba, 'Auunculum
non hoc uidebo in saeculo.'
Pauco relapso tempore
Ernanus arsit febribus,
uolens nepotem uisere
Austris Ionam uenerat.
Nepos cupiuit obuius
adire mox auunculum,
celer salutem is dicere
prius nepoti nititur. [f. P 20r; A 248r]
Senum quater uix passuum
intercapedo diuidit
eos, senex auunculus
cessit, piis ut manibus.
Duae cruces perenniter
testantur, una auunculi

'You break (the bread) in the manner of a bishop,' he said, 'I must show you respect.'

[Refrain] O death, blessed vision, etc.

(*See notes, p. 292*)

[1.35] The Saint foretold the death of his uncle Ernán (*VC*, i, 45)

Where the wearied golden sun colours the western seas is *Hinba*, an island in the foaming waves. When previously, leaving his home, Columba had come to *Alba*, he founded there a community of Irish brothers. Once, while staying on Iona, he put his uncle in charge there, whom he admonished in these words, loving him very dearly: 'Ernán, I am sending you now, so that, as leader of the community of *Hinba*, you may be fruitful in your talent: the due repayment is not far away.'

After the ship left the shore with the north wind, Columba said, 'I will not see my uncle (again) in this world.'

After a little while had passed, Ernán burned with a fever; wanting to see his nephew, he came to Iona with the south wind. The nephew wanted to come at once to meet his uncle, and he (Ernán) strove first quickly to give greetings to his nephew. A space of barely twenty-four paces separated them both, when the old uncle departed to the pious spirits of the dead. Two crosses bear witness forever:

35 fatum, locum quo restitit
Columba, signat altera.
O mors beata uisio etc.

[f. P 20r; A 248r]

[1.36] Aliud S\<ancti\> uaticinium de fato Gorei pugilis fortissimi

Rogat Columbam Goreus
quondam pugil fortissimus,
qua morte uitae terminus
sibi futurus uenerit.
5 Uates ait, 'Nec praelium,
mortem nec unda praeparat,
comes tui sed corporis,
de quo mali nil suspicis.'
'Nouis marita amoribus
10 illecta forsan incinet
herbis necem nocentibus,
uel unus ex pedissequis?'
'Non sic,' ait, 'nec indico,
quae tutius non audies, [col. b]
15 ne te iugis uel mentio
moerore turbet maximo.'
Certo peracto tempore
hastae uidens aeruginem
sicco ratis sub tegmine
20 cultro fricabat Goreus.
Tumultuantes audiens
surrexit, ut compesceret,
genu relapsus sauciat
culttellus infestissime.
25 Tunc ille cogitauerat
impleta, quae praedixerat
Uates, dolens et uulnere
expirat acto tempore.
O mors, beata uisio etc.

one marks the uncle's death, the other the place where Columba stood.

[Refrain] O death, blessed vision, etc.

(*See notes, pp. 292–3*)

[1.36] Another prophecy of the Saint, concerning the death of Guaire, a very powerful fighter (*VC*, i, 47)

Guaire, once a very powerful fighter, asked Columba by what death the end of his life would come to him.

The Prophet said, 'Neither battle nor water will bring about your death, but a companion of your body, from whom you suspect no evil.'

'Perhaps my wife, attracted to new lovers, will make incantations for my death by harmful plants? Or someone from my retinue?'

He said, 'It is not so; but I do not tell you, lest the constant calling to mind of that which you will not hear safely may greatly vex you with grief.'

After a certain time had passed, Guaire, seeing rust on a spear, was rubbing it with a knife, under the dry shelter of a boat. When he heard men fighting he got up to restrain them; his knife gashed his knee most grievously when he dropped it. Then he realised that what the Prophet had predicted had been fulfilled; and after the passage of time he died painfully of his wound.

[Refrain] O death, blessed vision, etc.

(*See notes, p. 294*)

[f. P 20r; A 248r]

[1.37] Aliud S\<ancti\> uaticinium de fato duorum nobilium qui mutuis uulneribus occubuere

Uates senescens corpore
sacra uirebat Pallade,
totus fuit propheticae
coelestis actu gratiae.
5 'Eheu!' gemescens, intulit,
'Quam dira mors hos abstulit,
horrent duos crudelia
inter propinquos uulnera.'   [f. P 20v; A 248v]
Audet rogare Lugbeus,
10 'Narra haec, Pater, diffusius.'
'Duo optimates,' intulit,
'plagis necantur mutuis.
Ceilrois apud sacellulum
regum sati propagine[20],
15 nobis et ex Hybernia
haec fama primum uenerit.' [col. b]
Octaua lux ut fulserit,
Columba sic praedixerat,
haec cuncta narrat nuncius,
20 praescita nouit Lugbeus.
'Fili caue charissime,'
inquit Columba Lugbeo,
'haec, quandiu sic uixero,
nulli reueles, obsecro.'

[f. P 20v; A 248v]

[1.38]

Haec utcunque tibi, lumen Ionidum,
Scotorum columen, et iubar aureum
coeli, praesidium, robur et omnium
            ad te confugientium,
5 descripsi Haectorides exul, in aequora
qua Noesus nitido gurgite defluit,
laetus sume, Pater, sisque mei memor,

---

[20]   pro pagine, Blado.

[1.37] Another prophecy of the Saint, concerning two noblemen who died by mutually inflicted wounds (*VC*, i, 43)

The Prophet, growing old in body, was vigorous in holy Wisdom: he was totally heavenly by the working of prophetic grace. 'Alas!' he cried with a groan, 'What a wretched death has carried them off! Cruel wounds are horrifying between two kinsmen.'

Luigbe ventured to ask, 'Father, tell this more fully?'

He said, 'Two noblemen of a fine race of kings are being killed by mutual wounds at the church of *Cell Rois*; and this news will first come to us from Ireland.'

As the eighth day dawned, as Columba had predicted, a messenger related all these things; Luigbe recognised what was foreknown.

Columba said to Luigbe, 'Be careful, dearest son; I pray you, as long as I am living thus, do not reveal these things to anyone.'

(*See notes, p. 294*)

[1.38] [Conclusion]

Light of the people of Iona, pillar of the Scots, and golden radiance of heaven, protection, and strength of all those who flee to you: I, MacEachainn, have described these things for you as best I can, an exile where Ness flows into the sea in a bright stream. Be pleased to receive them, O Father, and be mindful of me, sim ut postliminio redux.

Τέλος τῷ θεῷ χάριτας.

Soli Deo honor et gloria,
una Uni, unde, Deo[21], omnia.

Finis primi libri

---

[21] eo, Blado.

that I may return to my rightful place.

The end, thanks be to God.

Honour and glory be to God alone,
one (glory) to the One God, whence are all things.

End of Book One

(*See notes, pp. 294–5*)

Book II
The Powers and Miracles of St Columba

RODERICI MACLENII HECTOROGENIS
SCOTI GATHAELICI IONITAE
DE VIRTVTIBVS ET MIRACVLIS D\<IVI> COLVMBAE
ODAE SAPHICAE
IONIDOS LIBER SECVNDVS

καὶ ἔιπα, τίς δώσει μοί πτέρυγας ὡσεὶ περιστερᾶς, καὶ
πετασθήσομαι, καὶ καταπαύσω. νδ΄ .

Et dixi, Quis dabit mihi pennas sicut Columbae: et uolabo,
et requiescam?
Psal. LIIII.

Ionis

Book Two

The Powers and Miracles of St Columba

in Sapphic Verses

by

Roderick MacEachainn MacLean,

a Scottish Gael of Iona

And I said, Who will give me wings like a dove? And I will fly
away and take my rest.

Psalm (*Vulg.*) 54

[f. P 22r; A 250r] F ii

[2.1]

Christus orditur thalamos decorans
signa, quando eius Galilaea iussu
induunt uultus liquidi meraces
    flumina Bacchi.
5 Sancta sic clari soboles Nigelli,
inclytum Graio genus a Gathelo
primitus tales imitatur actus
    Numine pollens.
Forte Fymbarro celebrante, uinum
10 defuit, quod cum socios querentes
cerneret Christi[1] iuuenis leuita,
    percitus orat.
Urceo lymphas tulit e propinquo
fonte, quae pura prece tum Lyaei
15 more, natura laticis fugata
    uina rubescunt.
Gratias summo retulit Tonanti
pontifex tali monefactus orsu,
praesuli adscribi meriti Columba
20   dona iubebat.
Idque signorum reliquum Beati,
quae lyra Sapphus canere auspicamur
caetera illustrans praeeat coruschae
    lampadis instar.

[f. P 22r; A 250r]

[2.2]

Adfuit sacras prope phana quercus
malus, austeris opulenta pomis,
cuius infestat populos acerbus
    gustus edentes.   [f. P 22v; A 250v]
5 Implet umbrosis loca opaca ramis,
carpit ignauas puerile fruges
agmen, et pastum iuuenes senesque,
    turba queruntur.

---

[1] Cbristi, Blado.

[2.1] [Wine that was made from water] (*VC*, ii, 1)

Christ began his miracles while gracing a wedding, when by his command Galilean waters assumed the undiluted appearance of flowing wine. Thus this holy offspring of famous Niall, illustrious descendent from Greek Gathelus, imitated such actions first of all, strong in the Godhead. While Finbarr was celebrating (the Eucharist), it happened that there was no wine; when the young deacon of Christ saw his companions complaining, he prayed for this with great emotion. He drew water from a nearby spring with a pitcher, which then turned red like wine by his pure prayer, having put away the nature of water. The bishop gave thanks to God the Thunderer, warned by such a new event; (but) Columba ordered the gifts of his merit to be ascribed to the bishop. And may this, out of the remainder of the miracles of the Saint, which we begin to sing with the lyre of Sappho, go before the others, illuminating them like a shining lamp.
(*See notes, p. 295*)

[2.2] [The bitter fruit of a tree turned to sweetness] (*VC*, ii, 2)

At the church beside the sacred oak trees there was a fruit tree laden with sour-tasting fruit, whose bitter taste made ill the people who ate it. It filled the dark places with shady branches; a crowd of children gathered the useless fruit, and the crowd, both young and old, complained of its food.

Sanctus incassum miserans opimos
10 arboris foetus foliosae adultos
perdier, 'Cedas,' ait, 'hinc, amare
        gustus odorque.
Melleos coelo genimen sapores
ducat, in Christi bipotentis, atque
15 pabulum fiat modo dulce, cunctis,
        nomine, turbis.'
Nil morae, dicto citius proteruos
malus in suaues regerebat esus
melleo tum nectareoque succo
20   poma redundant.

[f. P 22v; A 250v]

[2.3]

Rusticus sylua doluit recisa
conquerens uirgis uiduata rura,
has Ionitae monachi ferentes
        aedibus aptant.
5 Ordei senos modios agresti
miserat Uates monachos[2] per ipsos,
serus aestiuo recidente ut astro
        mandet agellis.
'Gratias,' cultorque ait, ille reddat
10 maximas[3] Uati, 'Rogo quae serenti   [f. P 23r; A 251r]
post cadit quam solstitialis aestas,
        spes sit Yaeo?'
Nec minus seuit monitu Beati
farra, maturam sator unde messem
15 Innubae primum recipit sub ortum, ac
        horrea complet.
Martias passim sata sub Calendas
interim folles, tenerasque aristas
accolis spondet Ceres, obstupentes
20   signa renoscunt.

---

2   monacbos, Blado.
3   maximus, Blado.

The Saint, sorrowing that the excellent mature fruit of the leafy tree would be lost to no purpose, said, 'Begone from here, you bitter taste and smell! May your fruit bring forth the flavour of honey from heaven, in the name of doubly powerful Christ, and may there be sweet nourishment now for all these crowds!'

Without delay, almost before he had spoken, the fruit tree turned its bitter food into sweet, and its fruits then overflowed with the tastes of honey and nectar.

(*See notes, p. 295*)

[2.3] [A crop of grain sown after midsummer] (*VC*, ii, 3)

A peasant regretted when his woods were cut down, complaining that his fields were made bare of branches; the monks of Iona, taking them away, fashioned them for their buildings. The Prophet had sent six measures of barley to the peasant by the same monks, so that he could consign it late to his little fields, as the star of summer was declining.

'Thanks,' says the farmer, and he yields the greatest (thanks) to the Prophet; 'I ask, what hope is there for someone on Iona when he sows after midsummer's day has passed?'

Nevertheless, he sowed the grain on the Saint's instructions; from this the sower took in a mature harvest at the first rising of Virgo and filled his barns. When sown here and there at the beginning of March, Ceres promises sacks and a tender crop of grain to farmers in (due) time; the amazed people recognise a miracle.

(*See notes, pp. 295–6*)

[f. P 23r; A 251r]

[2.4]

Collis in summo residens Yaei
taliter fatur, 'Sileane frater,
cernis, ut saeua pluuiosa nubes
    turget ab Arcto?
5 Parturit morbos simul et uenena hic
imber australi ferus Albioni,
usque qua praeceps Dya de niuoso
    uertice torret.
Haec pecus nubes truculenta perdet,
10 noxio plures hominesque tabo
aggrauat, diro reuolans ab astro
    uespere manat.'
Colle descendens ita fatur, 'Ortu
tu para primo citus Albionem
15 aggredi, panis dabit hic salutem
    tinctus in unda.   [f. P 23v; A 251v]
Pane sacrato benedicta lympha
id malum sparsis fugat, imperante
protinus Christo; pete, crede, uentos
20   prosper habebis.'
Postero Phoebi Sileanus ortu
carbasum tendit Zephyris[4], et oram
nube uastatam reperit, beato et
    pane salutat.
25 Purus amoto nituit ueneno
aer, et laesae pecudes uigescunt,
plebs et armentum uegetatur illa as-
    pergine cunctum.

[f. P 23v; A 251v]

[2.5]

Decidit uirgo rediens synaxi
Doemenis sacro redimita peplo,
uirginis coxam grauiter ruina
    triuerat atrox.

---

[4]   Zepheris, Blado.

[2.4] [A pestiferous cloud and the healing of many people] (*VC*, ii, 4)

Sitting on the top of the Hill of Iona (Dùn Ì), he spoke thus: 'Brother Silnán, do you see how a rain cloud swells up in the bitter north? This fierce rain brings forth sickness and poison to the southern parts of *Alba*, as far as where the Dee descends headlong from snowy heights. This pestilent cloud will destroy cattle, it infects many men with noxious putrescence, it pours down moisture, flying from the deadly evening star.' He spoke thus as he came down the hill: 'At first light, get ready to go quickly to *Alba*: this bread dipped in water will give health. Water blessed by the sacred bread drives away this evil from the scattered people at once when Christ commands; pray and believe, and you will have the winds successfully.'

At the next rising of the sun, Silnán spread his sails before the west wind, and went to the shore stricken by the cloud, and healed it with the blessed bread. The clean air shone when the poison had been banished, and sick cattle became healthy; the people and all their flocks are made strong by that sprinkling.

(*See notes, p. 296*)

[2.5] [The healing of an injured virgin] (*VC*, ii, 5)

A virgin, daughter of Daimén, fell while returning from the assembly (in church), wrapped in her holy cloak; a serious fall gravely injured the virgin's hip.

5 Ingemit magno, 'Pater,' eiulatu,
    'adiuua sancta prece me, Columba!'
    Idque eo Uati patuit momento,
        isque medetur.
    'Uise Mauginam celer, O Lugoede,'
10 Uir Dei fatur; 'benedictionem
    hanc aqua tinges, madeatque tincto
        flumine coxa.
    Calculum uitae legat exigendae,
    uiuet a casu solidata sancte   [f. P 24r; A 251 + 1r]
15 cum tribus uotum et retinebit annis
        bis duo lustra.'

[f. P 24r; A 251 + 1r]
[2.6]

Ante diffusas Horeboea rupes
exhibet lymphas sitiente coetu
tacta praelustris dubiaeque uirgae
    Moseos ictu.
5 Postulat sancto puerum lauacro
tingier sicca ueniens eremo
dum parens, signo crucis ille saxo
    elicit undas.
Lauit oblatam fluitante prolem
10 riuulo, ueram et monuit latriam,
rite baptismo pueri et peracto
    fata prophetat.
'Tu diu uiues,' ait, 'O Lugoede,
deflues luxu iuuenis, senili
15 militas euo Superis, fruere et
    celsus Olympo.'

[f. P 24r; A 251 + 1r]
[2.7]

Fons erat lata celebrique fama
ante Pictorum populo uerendus
numen hunc plures habuere gentes

She groaned with great wailing, 'Father, Columba, aid me by holy prayer!'

This was known to the Prophet at that moment, and he sent healing. 'Lugaid, go and visit Maugín quickly,' said the Man of God; 'you will dip this blessing in water, and let her hip be moistened by the impregnated water. Let her read a reckoning of the life she will live: healed from her accident, she will live in holy fashion and will keep her vows for twice ten years and three.' (*See notes, pp. 296–7*)

[2.6] [Water produced from a rock at the Saint's prayers] (*VC*, ii, 10)

Previously the rock of Horeb brought forth profuse waters when the assembly was thirsty, touched by the stroke of the famous and changeable rod of Moses. When a parent asks that his child be dipped in the holy font, coming to a dry place in the wilderness, he drew water from the rock by the sign of the cross. He washed the child that had been offered in the flowing stream, and instructed him in true worship; and when his baptism had been duly performed, he prophesied the child's fate: 'You will live for a long time, Lugaid,' he said; 'as a youth you will sink low in luxuriance; in old age you will serve the Most High as a soldier, and being raised up, you will enjoy heaven.' (*See notes, p. 297*)

[2.7] [A spring which the Saint blessed in the lands of the Picts] (*VC*, ii, 11)

There was a spring, previously fearsome to the race of the Picts for its wide and great fame; many peoples held it to be a divinity,

doemone lusae.
5   Hac aqua tacti fierent leprosi,
    quopiam aut morbo caderent ibidem,   [f. P 24v; A 251 + 1v]
    unde diuinum tribuere honorem
            potibus atris.
    Strennuus Christi pugil at Columba
10 uenit ad fontem intrepidus lauatum,
    id repulsati druidae, magique,
            oppido suadent.
    Sustulit Sanctus Uolucerque coelo
    ter manus, signum crucis effugitque
15 caetero nunquam rediturus aeuo
            doemon ad undas.
    Utiles plebi latices beantur,
    hisce quae ferrent, mala iam repellunt,
    fonsque fit morbi bibitus leuamen,
20   antidotumque.

[f. P 24v; A 251 + 1v]
[2.8]

    Dum Columbanus parat ire in austri
    impiger tractus Aquilone, tendit
    Campilungaeos ratis in penates
            Boethenis Austro.
5   'Boetheneu,' Uates ita fatur, 'ortu
    crastino nigros tibi poscis Austros,
    sed Columbanus nebulam fugantes
            fert fore Cauros.
    Annuet uotis utriusque uestrum
10 summus immensi Dominator orbis,
    terra quem pontus, polus, astra adorant,
            Christus Iesus.'   [f. P 25r; A 252r] G
    Soluit aurora rutilante portu
    Boetheneus Austro fruitus secundo,
15 tertiam littus cupitum sub horam
            lucis adintrat.
    Mox Columbani, patrias, phaselum
    purus Arctoo Boreas ab axe
    sole iam seros recreante currus
20   egit ad oras.

deluded by a demon. Touched by this water they would become leprous, or fall ill there from some disease; wherefore they paid divine honours to the dark waters. But Columba, Christ's strong fighter, came fearless to the spring to bathe; the repulsed druids and magicians greatly encouraged this. The Saint and Dove held up his hands three times to heaven, and the demon fled from the sign of the cross, never to return to the waters for the rest of time. The waters were blessed, beneficial for the people: by them they now threw off any illnesses which they might bring. The spring when drunk becomes a comfort and remedy for sickness.

(*See notes, p. 297*)

[2.8] [Two men sail in different directions on the same day by the Saint's prayers] (*VC*, ii, 15)

While Colmán prepares to go swiftly into the regions of the south by the north wind, Baithéne's boat heads for his home in Magh Luinge with the south wind. The Prophet spoke thus: 'Baithéne, you ask for yourself for the dark southerly wind tomorrow morning, but Colmán says that there will be a north-west wind driving away the clouds. The supreme Lord of the vast world will hear both your prayers, Jesus Christ, whom earth, seas, and sky and the stars adore.'

Baithéne casts off from the harbour as dawn glows red; enjoying a favourable south wind, at the third hour of the day he comes to his desired shore. Next a clear north wind from the north pole drove Colmán's boat to his homeland shores, as the sun now revived his chariots at evening.

At Columbano benedixit, addens:
'Amplius non me rediens uidebis
hic.' Eo Sanctus requieuit anno
    aethere ciuis.

[f. P 25r; A 252r]
[2.9]

Dum Columbanus iuuenis beandam
atrii ad limen residi Columbae
bubalo plaenam citus obtulisset
    lacte metretam,
5   doemon in mulctri latitabat imo,
qui crucis signum quadriforme uitans
horrido strictum quatiens fragore
    rupit operclum.
Turbide uaso liquor ex aperto
10 funditur, parua remanente gutta,
auctior toto praece sed Columbae
    stilla recreuit.
Sic ait, 'Mulsum stolide prophano
uase fudisti, decuit dicari   [f. P 25v; A 252v]
15 uas, foret signo crucis auspicato
    tutius omne.
Hic triumphalis memori character
mente, res, actus, iter, auspicetur:
praeualet contra is fera multiformis
20   flagra tyranni.'

[f. P 25v; A 252v]
[2.10] Goetus quidam qui lac e masculo boue praestigiis emulxit, refutatur

Dissident olim duo rusticani
inuicem, Sancto referunt querelas:
doemonis quorum fuit alter astu
    praestigiator,
5   masculo iussus boue qui, niuali
exibet mulgens nitidum colore
lac, putant omnes fore tale magni

And he blessed Colmán, adding, 'When you return, you will not see me here anymore.' The Saint went to his rest that year, as a citizen of heaven. (*See notes, p. 298*)

[2.9] [The expulsion of a demon lurking in a milk-pail] (*VC*, ii, 16)

When young Colmán had swiftly brought a pail full of the milk of cattle to Columba, seated at the entrance of the *atrium*, for a blessing, a demon lurked in the bottom of the milk-pail, which, fleeing from the four-cornered sign of the cross, smashing the tightly closed lid with a terrible crash, broke it open. Liquid poured wildly from the open vessel, with a little drop remaining; but the small drop grew again by Columba's prayers, greater than the (original) whole.

He spoke thus: 'You have foolishly spilt milk from the defiled vessel; the vessel should have been dedicated; everything would be safer hallowed by the sign of the cross. Mindfully let this triumphant mark hallow (all) things, (all) deeds and journeys; it prevails against the cruel scourges of the many-shaped tyrant.'
(*See notes, p. 298*)

[2.10] A magician who drew milk from a bull by trickery is defeated (*VC*, ii, 17)

Two peasants once had a disagreement between themselves; they referred their dispute to the Saint; one of them was a trickster by the devil's cunning. He, when ordered, produced bright milk of snow-white colour from a male ox, milking it; all reckoned such a thing to be happening

numinis usu.
Spumeam iussit citius metretam
10   in manus[5] tradi sibi Sanctus, atque
doemonum lusu docuit cruorem
          lac simulantem.
Excutit nubes oculis Columba,
sanguis apparet ruber, et iacebat
15   saucius fuso uice bos cruore
          lactis anhelans.
Fraude confusus doluit retecta
dum magus cultor Stygiae Dianae,
credidit Christo populus docente
20   Alite signis.

[f. P 26r; A 253r] G ii
[2.11]

Hospitem pauper recipit Columbam
nocte, quam laute potuit, Nesanus.
Sanctus armenti rogitat Nesanum
          quam locuples sit?
5   'Quinque trimales mihi sunt iuuencae,'
laetior uultu retulit Nesanus.
'Duc citus uaccas,' ait, 'huc beandas,'
          Ales Iberus.
'Quinque sint uaccae, uigiesque quinque,
10   nec pecus foetu tamen augeatur,
grex nec hunc citra numerum minor sit
          tempore uitae.'
Sic crucis signo bouibus dicatis:
fatur, 'A taeda tibi iam iugali
15   haec nouellorum series nepotum,
          longa supersit.'

---

[5]   manns, Blado.

by the doings of a great godhead. The Saint ordered the frothing milk-pail to be given quickly into his own hands, and showed that blood was imitating milk by the devils' illusion. Columba drove away the clouds from their eyes: red blood appeared, and the bull lay wounded and gasping, its blood having poured out instead of milk. When his deception was revealed, the magician, worshipper of Stygian Diana, suffered in confusion; the people believed in Christ, when the Dove taught them by miracles.

(*See notes, p. 298*)

[2.11] [Nesán, a poor man] (*VC*, ii, 20)

Nesán, a poor man, received Columba at night as a guest, with the best fare that he could. The Saint asked Nesán how wealthy he was in cattle.

'I have five young three-year-old cattle,' answered Nesán, with quite cheerful countenance.

The Dove of Ireland said, 'Bring your cattle here quickly, that they may be blessed. May your five cattle be twenty times five: but neither will your cattle be increased in young, nor your flock be less than this number, during your lifetime.'

When his cattle had been thus consecrated by the sign of the cross, he said, 'May this succession of young grandchildren, which are now yours from conjugal wedlock, survive for a long time.'

(*See notes, pp. 298–9*)

[f. P 26r; A 253r]

[2.12] Similiter Sancti benedictione inopis Columbani armentum creuit

Sic Columbano pecus indigenti
quinquies deno duplicauit auctu,
maius accessu neque fit quotenni,
    nec minus album.
5 Integer centum numerus manebat,
pauit accessus pueros, domumque
quo peregrinos, inopes et aegros
    fouerat hospes.   [f. P 26v; A 253v]
Uictimas phanis dedit et sacellis,
10 usui aut cessit pietatis ali
seu perit casu, truce ui luporum
    siue abigente.

[f. P 26v; A 253v]

[2.13] Quomodo praedo, qui Columbani greges abegit, eadem die submersus fuit

Trux Columbani pecudes abactum
uenerat praedo, rabies habendi
dira quem solis stimulauit agris
    insidiari.
5 Uiderat praedam sacer Ales actam,
obsecrat diuos humili per omnes
uoce, ne cunctas abigat iuuencas
    depopulator.
Ille sed surdae furit anguis instar,
10 compulit curuas pecus ad carinas,
diripit tectum posito timore
    Numinis omni.
Sanctus obtestans sequitur phaselos
uuidus fluctu grauidas marino, et
15 pluribus nauim spoliis onustam
    caede boumque.
Sanctus Hebraeos Phariumque regem
plurimo suasu memorans minatur,
ille plus firma nihilo mouetur
20   ilice uento.   [f. P 27r; A 254r]

[2.12] Likewise the herd of Colmán, a poor man, increased by the Saint's blessing (*VC*, ii, 21)

Thus for poor Colmán he multiplied his herd of cattle by an increase to twice ten times five; it neither became greater with an annual increase, nor less white (in colour). The complete number remained one hundred; it fed his visitors, servants and his house, where the host cared for travellers, the poor, and the sick. He gave offerings to churches and chapels, or granted them for other works of piety, or else (one) died by accident, or by the savage attacks of wolves, or by theft.
(*See notes, p. 299*)

[2.13] How a thief who stole Colmán's herd was drowned the same day (*VC*, ii, 22)

A fierce thief had come to drive away Colmán's cattle, whom a deadly passion for possessions drove to lie in ambush on deserted fields. The holy Dove had seen the theft carried out; he begged with humble voice, by all the saints, that the despoiler should not drive away all his cattle. But he raged like a deaf serpent, he drove the cattle to his curving prows, he despoiled his house, having set aside all fear of God. The Saint, protesting, wet from the waves of the sea, followed the weighed-down boats, and the ship laden with many spoils and with the slaughtered cattle. The Saint threatened with much persuasion, calling to mind the Hebrews and the king of the Egyptians; (but) he was not moved, any more than a strong holm oak by the wind.

Quicquid orabat resupinus Ales
arguens saeuum[6] facinus piandum
morte, praedoni fuit id cachynno
    ludibrioque.
25 Prospicit uelis Aquilone tensis
loeniter plenas uolitare puppes,
tale praefatur sociis misertus
    nempe Prophetes.
'Proprios nunquam redit ad penates
30 hic miser, nostras neque perdet oras,
caerula uelox hodie peribit
    obrutus unda.'
Mox ferus nigra uenit imber Arcto
turbinem raucis[7] agitans procellis,
35 impetu, et puppes adigit scelestas
    cominus orco.
Caeterum ponti nituit sereno
sole tranquillum, facilique uento,
amplius uelo nocet aura nulli
40   praeter iniquis.
O Pater, duros utinam tyrannos,
qui tuos semper populantur agros,
uindices fato simili, et ruina,
    Aliger, atra.

[f. P 27r; A 254r]

[2.14] De repentino Thylaei praesidis, qui hospitem Pictum interemit, obitu
[f. P 27v; A 254v]

Gente Pictorum nitidus uetusta
exul ad Sanctum refugit Columbam,
praesidi Thyles dederat tegendum
    quem sacer Ales.
5 Ille crudeli iugulauit ense
perfidus Pictum, fideique iura
spreuit humano posito pudore,
    more Cyclopis.

---

[6] saeunm, Blado.
[7] rasis, Blado.

Whatever the Dove prayed, looking to heaven, asserting that the savage deed was deserving to be punished by death, it was laughter and derision to the thief.

He saw the full ships gently moving with sails stretched out to the north wind; the Prophet began to speak thus, having pity indeed on his friends: 'This wretched man will never return to his own home, neither will he waste our shores; swiftly he will perish today, overwhelmed by the blue-green waves.'

Suddenly fierce rain came from the black north, driving a whirlwind with raucous storms, and by its force it drove the wicked ships to death near at hand. The remainder of the sea shone tranquil, with a calm sun and a gentle wind; the breeze did no more harm to any ship except to the wicked ones.

O Father, winged One, would that you were avenged on harsh tyrants, who are always preying upon your lands, by a similar fate and dark ruin! (*See notes, p. 299*)

[2.14] The sudden death of a ruler of *Thyle* (Islay), who killed a Pictish guest (*VC*, ii, 23)

A distinguished exile from the ancient race of the Picts sought refuge with St Columba, whom the holy Dove had sent to a ruler of *Thyle* (Islay) to be sheltered. That faithless man murdered the Pict by his cruel sword, and despised the laws of trust, like the Cyclops, setting aside human shame.

Hospitis coedem, referente fama,
10 Sanctus[8] indigne tulit, omen atque
perfido infaustum recinit nefandi
          praemia laethi.
'Feruido saeuit Nemeaeus astro
iam Leo,' Uates ait, 'et priusquam
15 stringet effoetos gelidus pruinis
          Scorpius agros,
antequam carnes comedet suillas,
glande concussa recidente quercu
quas alit: pernix homicida Auernas
20   ibit ad umbras.'
Ut probet falsum stolidus Propheten,
exta nefrendis uerubus nouelli
torruit, tosta et puer offerebat
          lance tyranno.
25 Ille festinus rapit exta dicens,
'Num putas uerum cecinisse Uatem?'
dixit, et raptim moritur, caduco
          foedior apro.   [f. P 28r; A 255r]
Id fuit, quando segetes metuntur,
30 atque par luci tenebrescit hora, et
Luna cornutos fericida ceruos
          in Uenerem dat.
Hunc Deus signis ita gloriosum
fecit, hanc illi quoque claritatem
35 cessit, ut tanto celebremus omnes
          auspice Christum.
Christe sanctorum caput, et corona,
laus tibi in Sancto maneat Columba,
Flatui Sacro pariterque Patri
40   gloria compar.

[f. P 28r; A 255r]

[2.15] De fato Landers furiosissimi tyranni Sancti praeuisio miraculosa

Sanctus Hymbaeos recolit penates,
arguit, sacri et docuit rapaces

---

[8]   Sanstus, Blado.

When the news came to him, the Saint was angered by the murder of the guest, and pronounced an inauspicious omen on the traitor, the reward of a wicked death: 'The Nemean Lion now rages with a burning star,' said the Prophet, 'and before icy Scorpio binds up the worn-out fields with frosts, before he will eat the swine's flesh which he nourishes on the acorns which have fallen when an oak tree is shaken, the wicked murderer will go to the shades of Avernus.'

So that the brutish man could prove the Prophet false, he roasted the innards of a suckling young creature on spits, and his servant offered the roast to the tyrant on a plate. Quickly he took the innards, saying, 'Surely you do not think that the Prophet was foretelling the truth?' He spoke; and suddenly he died, more filthy than a falling pig.

It was while the fields are being harvested, and hours are dark in equal measure to the daylight, and Diana the Huntress gives over antlered stags to Venus.

Thus, God made him (Columba) glorious by miracles, and also granted to him this renown, so that we should all celebrate Christ by so great a prophet. O Christ, the head and crown of saints, may praise remain to Thee in St Columba, and equal glory to the Holy Spirit, and equally to the Father.

(*See notes, pp. 299–300*)

[2.15] The Saint's miraculous foresight concerning the death of Lám Dess, a raging tyrant (*VC*, ii, 24)

The Saint was dwelling again in his household of *Hinba*; he accused despoilers of sacred things,

Ditis[9] et seruos, Erebique ciues,
          atque anathema.
5   Unde Domnaldi Furiis nepotes
perciti Sanctum soboles prophani
dira Connaldi uoluere iacto
          figere telo.
Unus arrepta furibundus hasta
10   idque dum tentat, truciter minaci
impetu, Patris monachus cucullam
          sumpsit, ut obstet.
Uita cui patris melior cruore
proprio, custos pius, et fidelis,   [f. P 28v; A 255v]
15   hic erat patris uice Finleganus,
          sanctus et audax.
Ictibus ternis habitum recussit
impius, credit penitusque figi
Uatis exangues morientis artus
20   cuspide Landers.
Cessit illaesa is Sathanas cuculla,
sospes a telis quoque Fynleganus
asserit uestem officium loricae
          ferre uicesque.
25   Sanctus augustam rediens Ionam
postea elapsis aliquot diebus
taliter fatur simul audiente
          agmine toto.
'Quod mei, quantum potuit, proteruus
30   fixerat Landers, uice Fynleganum,
ecce bissenis reuolutus astris
          praeterit annus.
Nec minus Landers perit hoc momento
fixus emisso iaculo Cronani;
35   torsit id nostro iaculum Cronanus
          nomine miles.'
Bella cessarunt pereunte Landers,
alma pax altis equitat quadrigis,
multa libertas redit hoc sacratis
40   tempore phanis.

---

9   Ditiis, Blado.

and showed them to be slaves of Dis, citizens of the land of darkness, and excommunicate. As a result the Uí Domnaill, the fell progeny of impious Conall, roused by the Furies, wished to pierce the Saint with a spear-cast. When one of them, enraged, having taken up a spear, attempted this with a savagely threatening attack, a monk put on the Father's cowl to stand in his way. This was a pious and faithful guardian, for whom his Father's life was more precious than his own blood, Findlugán, in his Father's place, holy and brave. The impious one struck his habit three blows, and Lám Dess thinks that the dying Prophet's lifeless limbs have been deeply penetrated by his spear-point. This Satan withdrew with the cowl undamaged; Findlugán also, unscathed by spears, asserts that the shirt took on the function and place of a breastplate.

The Saint, returning later to famous Iona, after some days had passed, spoke thus, while at the same time his whole troop listened: 'Since violent Lám Dess transfixed Findlugán in my place, as far as he could, lo, a year has passed, having traversed through the twelve constellations. Nonetheless, at this moment Lám Dess is dying, pierced by Cronán's spear which he has thrown; Cronán the soldier has hurled this spear in our name.'

Warfare ceases when Lám Dess falls; health-giving peace rides out in a high chariot; at this time much freedom returns to holy churches.

(*See notes, pp. 300–1*)

[f. P 28v; A 255v]

[2.16] Quomodo iussu Colum\<bae\> subito e medio sublatus fuerit quidam sicarius
[f. P 29r; A 256r] H

Forte Germano sene iam tenellus
dum sacer quondam dyacon docente
castra diuinae coluit Mineruae
    Ales in urbe,
5 prominet qua metropolis, Columbae
patribus quondam lar amenus, ortu
qua fluit prono Clyathus per undas
    amnis Iberas,
Palladi incumbens ubi Christianae
10 croeber ad doctos rediit magistros
qua leuat cultis Laginaeus aruis
    oppida campus.
Accidit, quandam ferus ut puellam
in nephas luxu cuperet satelles,
15 casta complexum Ueneris perosa
    quae fugiebat.
Nisus ut Scyllam sequitur uolantem:
angit imbellem ut lupus acris agnam:
ut canis pernix leporem fatigat
20   cespite plano:
ardet exortem Ueneris puellam, ut
spumeus cursu furiens anhelo
hinnulus uisa uel equa petulcus,
    durus athletes.
25 Illa singultim cupiens asylum
lapsa Germani senis ante uultus
uoluitur, tales tremulo et quaerelas
    flamine promit.   [f. P 29v; A 256v]
'O Pater summo famulans Tonanti,
30 per Deos oro, miseresce, nostrae
cernis ut saeuit pietatis hostis
    sanguinolentus?
Ille nec nostrum rapiet pudorem
usibus tantum Cypriae nefandis,
35 sed solet stricto uiolata ferro
    fodere membra.
Is putat uanos Superum timores,

[2.16] How at Columba's command a murderer was suddenly slain (*VC*, ii, 25)

Once by chance, when the holy Dove, as a young deacon, was occupying a stronghold of divine Wisdom, while elderly Gemmán was teaching him, in the city where the metropolitan cathedral stands, once a lovely home to Columba's ancestors, where the River *Cliath* flows through waters of Ireland, down from its source, where he frequently returned to learned teachers attending to Christian wisdom, where the Plain of Leinster raises towns in cultivated fields, it happened that a fierce henchman desired a maiden for evil lustful purposes; she fled, chastely loathing the embrace of lust. As Nisus pursues Scylla as she flies, as a fierce wolf worries a defenceless she-lamb, as a swift hound tires out a hare over level ground, like a foaming, tossing stallion, going wild in its breathless chase when it has seen a mare, so the relentless pursuer burned for the maiden innocent of lust.

She, sobbing and begging for a place of refuge, falling down before the face of elderly Gemmán, tumbles down, and makes these entreaties with trembling breath: 'O Father, servant of the highest Thunderer, I beg you, by the Heavens, take pity! Do you see how the bloodthirsty enemy of my goodness is aroused?

'Neither will he only ravish my modesty by wicked practices of the Cyprian goddess, but it is his way to pierce the limbs which he has violated with his drawn sword.

He reckons that fear of the Most High is vain;

uirgines lusu necat ense castas
foedus, expleta ut fuerit libido,
40   Numinis expers.
Sexui nulli, teneris nec annis
parcit, immitis Sathanae minister
ante germanam perimit quadrimam
        trux inimicus.'
45 Inde quod sacras uereatur aras
fisus abdebat trepidam cuculla
hoste Germanus ueniente, iuuit
        idque Columba.
Nec ferox aras senis, aut moratur
50 ora tam sancti pueri, innocentes
sexies artus tenerosque ferro
        fixit acuto.
Flamen it coelo, iacuit cadauer
ante Germanum graue lachrimantem,
55 qui gemens sanctum comitem poposcit
        tale Columbam.   [f. P 30r; A 257r] H ii
'Quamdiu saeuum facinus tacebit
coelitum Rector? Quotus instat annus,
cum dabit poenas truculenta coedes?
60   Dic, puer Ales.'
Ille coelestes speculatur auras
Numen explorans, 'Erit hoc inultum
non diu,' fatur, sapiente plenus
        indole Uates.
65 'Unius coelos animus puellae
aduolat puncti spacio, superbus
atque damnatas Acherontis umbras
        hic adigetur.'
Mox ruit uerbo citius, cadentis
70 horror inuasit populos et urbes
plurimo et Christum uenerantur omnes
        thure litantes;
falsa sic, Petro stipulante, coniunx
nesciens lapsum, cecidit maritum,
75 qui Deo mendax meruit repente
        luce carere.
Templa fiebant celebris renatam
concio turmam docuit latreiam;
uoce praeconis pietas triumphat
80   nuncia pacis.

the filthy one slaughters chaste virgins by the sword for sport when his lust has been satisfied, mindless of the Godhead. The merciless servant of Satan spares no one, neither for their sex nor tender age: the savage enemy previously slaughtered my four-year-old sister.'

Trusting then that he should respect a sacred refuge, Gemmán covers the fearful girl with his cowl as the enemy approaches, and Columba helps this. The fierce one did not give heed either to the old man's refuge, or to the words of such a holy boy; he pierced the innocent tender limbs six times with his sharp sword.

Her spirit goes to heaven; her corpse lies before Gemmán, weeping bitterly, who, sighing, asks his holy companion Columba, thus: 'How long will the Ruler of the heavens keep silence at this cruel deed? How many years are there, until savage slaughter will pay the penalty? Tell me, my child, my Dove!'

He (Columba) looks to the airy heavens, exploring God's will; 'This will not be unavenged for long,' says the Prophet, full of innate wisdom: 'In the space of a single point in time, the soul of the girl flies to the heavens, and also this arrogant man will be dragged to the accursed shades of Acheron.'

Straight away he fell, almost before the word was spoken; dread of the fallen seized people and cities, and they all venerated Christ, offering copious incense; as the lying wife fell down at Peter's command, not knowing of the fall of her husband, who, as a liar to God, deserved to lose his life suddenly. Churches were built, much frequented; preaching taught the crowd renewed reverence; piety, the messenger of peace, triumphs at the voice of the herald. (*See notes, pp. 301–2*)

[f. P 30r; A 257r]

[2.17] De apro uenenoso qui iussu S\<ancti\> mortem occubuit
[f. P 30v; A 257v]

Quos premit Cauris hyemalis axis
tractibus Uates remoratur illis
Insulas Galdi, Cynosura mergi
    nescia ponto.
5 Inuius saltus, nimieque opacus
est ibi, qua iam nemorosa scabro
finditur fluctu Schya continente
    Hebris ab ora.
Sanctus oratum sinuosa saltus
10 intrat obscuri loca solus, horror
nec uetat purae precis aut tenorem
    aut animo obstat.
Interim facta prece fit tumultus,
fit fragor multus, nimiusque motus,
15 trux aper, pernix fera, senticoso
    prodit ab antro.
Frenduit curuo patulus molari
rictus, hirsutae steterantque setae,
ignei flammis radiant ocelli
20   perniciosis.
Faucibus spirans olidis uenena
impetu tendit: ratus esse praedam,
quo pater Sanctus uiridi sedebat
    gramine, uelox.
25 'Nulla, qua cuiuis noceas, potestas
sit tibi post hac, rabiosa pestis,'
sic ait, 'Christi morere imperante
    nomine ibidem.'   [f. P 31r; A 258r]
Tum ferus Christo cadit inuocato,
30 et solo indignans caput ingerebat
mortuus, monstrum nocuit uianti
    postea nulli.

[f. P 31r; A 258r]

[2.18] De Hippopotamo miraculose fugato

Praeterit quercus ueteres, genista
amnis apricas uiridante ripas

[2.17] A poisonous wild boar which fell dead at the Saint's command (*VC*, ii, 26)

The Prophet was staying in those parts which the wintry north pole oppresses with the north-west wind, the *Innse Gall*, where the Little Bear can never set in the sea. An impassable and very dark forest is there, where now well-wooded Skye, a Hebridean island, is divided by the rough waters from the mainland shore. The Saint went alone into winding places of the dark wood to pray; fear did not prevent the tenor of his pure prayer, or hinder his spirit.

Meanwhile as he prayed there came a tumult, a great crashing, a mighty commotion: a savage boar, a swift wild beast, emerged from a thorny cavern. Its yawning jaws gnashed with curved grinding teeth, its hairy bristles stood on end, its tiny fiery eyes flashed with vicious flames. Breathing poison from its stinking throat, it came forward with vigour, at speed, thinking there was prey where the holy Father sat on the green grass.

'You will have no power from now on to hurt anyone, you rabid pestilence,' he said; 'die on the spot, as the name of Christ commands.' Then, as Christ was invoked, the wild beast fell, and cast down its indignant head upon the ground; dead, the monster did not hurt any traveller ever thereafter. (*See notes, pp. 302–3*)

[2.18] A river horse miraculously driven away (*VC*, ii, 27)

The river Ness flows past ancient oaks, while the broom makes green its sunny banks,

Noesus illimi, uitreoque fundo
          flumine prono.
5   Exit aeoo per amena fluctu
hostia ad leuum Boream reflexus,
qua patet campo sinuosa apertis
          Albion Euris.
Huc Pater sancto comitante coetu
10 uenit, illustres tenuere Picti haec
arua, tum gentes sine christiano
          dogmate caecae.
Uidit ad ripam miseri cadauer
prendier curuis, ut humetur, uncis,
15 quem necat lymphis ferus innatantem
          hinnus aquosus.
Traiici Uates cupit in remotam
fluminis ripam, steterat copallus
iussus adduci comitis natatu
20   cymba biremis.   [f. P 31v; A 258v]
Lugbeus sancti monitu recinctus
ueste tranauit tenui, sub imo[10]
delitens motam fera sensit undam
          gurgitis atro.
25 Protinus summas per aquas uolutu
paruit monstrum exitiale, curuis
dentibus, dorso latere atque equino,
          crine leonis.
Ungulis pandi bicolis camaeli,
30 fauce portentumque apriceps aperta,
iridem multo retulit colore
          cauda coruscham;
mole uaegrandem superans asellum,
Lugbeum cursu petiit proteruo,
35 coede nec prima satiatur ardens
          sanguine praedam.
Horret informis trepidus caballi
coetus aspectu patriaeque gentes
execrant, cunctus prece uir salutem
40   nantis adorat.
'Non opus tanto,' Uolucer, 'tumultu,'
inquit, 'est omni uigor ad salutem
in fide, Christo faciles periclum

---

[10]   subimo, Blado.

with unmuddied glassy depths in its flowing stream. It goes out to the eastern sea through a fair river mouth, turned back towards the adverse north wind, where sinuous *Alba* spreads its plains, open to the east wind.

The Father came there, with a holy troop accompanying him; the famous Picts held these lands, at the time blind peoples without Christian teaching. He saw at the bank the corpse of a wretched man being taken out with curved hooks so it could be buried, whom a fierce water horse (had) killed swimming in the waters. The Prophet wanted to be taken across to the far bank of the river; a coble lay there, a two-oared boat; he ordered it to be brought by the swimming of his companion.

Luigbe, having undressed, swam across at the Saint's instructions, in a thin undergarment; the beast, lurking in the dark bottom of the stream, sensed the waters disturbed. Suddenly the deadly monster appeared, twisting through the upper waters, with curving teeth, its back and sides like a horse, with a lion's mane: a boar-headed monstrosity, with the cloven hooves of a hump-backed camel, and yawning jaws, its tail reflected a gleaming rainbow in many colours. Towering like a monster over a little donkey, it sought out Luigbe by a direct course; neither is it satisfied with its first slaughter, (still) yearning for prey by blood. The fearful company trembles at the appearance of the misshapen horse, and the people of the land curse it, and every man begs for the swimmer's safety by prayer.

The Dove said, 'There is no need for such a tumult; in faith there is strength for safety for everyone; we easily overcome every danger by Christ.

uincimus omne.
45 Triste, coniuro modo per Creantem
te ferox monstrum, ut redeas retrorsum,
nec noce seruo, tibi mando Christi
        nomine Iesu.'   [f. P 32r; A 259r]
Distitit paruo spacio, minarum
50 plenus, a Sancti monacho natante
hinnus, in lingua proprie Pelasga
        hyppopotamos.
Cessit at uerbo deicae Uolucris,
non[11] secus uiso lepus a Molosso
55 auolat, nunquam redit aut eodem
        aut nocet usquam.
Lugbeus sospes tulerat copallum,
coetus exultim celebrant Tonantem,
cogitur signo celebrare Christum
60   Noesicolum gens.

[f. P 32r; A 259r]

[2.19] Diem suae migrationis praedicens benedixit Insulae Ionae unde omne uenenosum reptile perit

Castor et Pollux nitidi gemellum
sydus, aestiuos aperit calores,
Flora uernantes reuirente campos
        gramine pingit.
5 Quando Ionitae satagunt coloni
saepibus seras cohibere fruges,
Rossiae effoetum pecus omne ad oram
        traiiciuntque.
Sanctus in plostris senio grauescens
10 ad laborantes uehitur diebus
proximis, coelos penetrat priusquam
        saecula linquens.   [f. P 32v; A 259v]
Sic salutatis ait, 'Incolatum
Conditor uestrum benedicat altus
15 qui creat coelos, mare et omne, sancto ex
        monte Syone.
Ut bonum pacis uideatis omni

---

[11]   Mon, Blado.

I charge you now severely, fierce monster, by the Creator, that you go back whence you came, and do not harm my servant: I order you in the name of Christ Jesus.'

The horse – it is properly called in Greek *hippopotamos* – full of threats, was only separated by a short distance from the Saint's monk while he was swimming; but at the word of the divine Dove it withdrew, just as a hare flees from a hunting hound when it has been seen; it never returned, nor did harm in that place or anywhere. Luigbe, unscathed, brought the coble; the crowd exultingly celebrate the Thunderer; the race of those dwelling beside the Ness is compelled by this miracle to celebrate Christ.

(*See notes, pp. 303–4*)

[2.19] While predicting the day of his departure, he blessed the Isle of Iona, so that all poisonous snakes should perish (*VC*, ii, 28)

Shining Castor and Pollux, the twin-born stars, usher in the warmth of summer; Flora paints the spring meadows, turning green with grass. Meanwhile the inhabitants of Iona are busy surrounding the late fruits of the earth with enclosures, and they bring across all the flocks that have produced young to the shores of the Ross (of Mull). The Saint, becoming weighed down with age, is brought in a cart to visit the labourers, in the days next before he enters heaven, leaving the world.

He spoke thus to those whom he greeted: 'May the high Creator, who made the heavens, the sea, and everything, bless your dwelling-place out of holy Mount Zion. So that you may see the benefit of peace in every

saeculo uitae, Ceres alma uestros,
et Pales foetu referant labores,
20   este beati.
Non ego post hac iterum reuertar
arua uisurus sata, carne cinctus,
corporis dempto repetens Olympum
          pondere migro.
25 Atque, ne nullo uiduata dono
munerer iam coenobialis arua
insulae, nunquam nocet hic ueneno
          uipera mordax.'
Inde solatur gemitus suasu
30 efficax, 'Omnes,' ait, 'incolamur,
sunt lares ueri, proprieque nostri
          regia coeli.'

[f. P 32v; A 259v]

[2.20] De ferro benedicto quomodo nocere non potuit

Forte scribenti Moluag minister
obtulit Uati rude fabricandum
frustulum ferri, sacer ut dicaret
          quod benedixit.   [f. P 32v; A 260r] I
5 Ille festinus tulit aes beatum,
inde cultellos fabricare acutos,
coedat ut pastos segetum iuuencos
          farra prementes.
Sic ait, 'Ferrum prece consecraui,
10 ut reor, sacrum satis est metallum
nemini infestum, pecori nec ulli
          tale nocebit.
Hic chalybs,' inquit, 'benedictus omni
utilis paci, nihil ad cruentos
15 conferet Martis furialis usus
          Auspice Christo.'
Nec minus facto pugione taurum
impetit crebro Moluagus ictu,
is fatigatus boue sed relicto
20   sospite uenit.
'Quid putas,' inquit Pater, 'O Moloce,

age of life, may kindly Ceres repay your labours with nourishment, and Pales with young creatures; may you be blessed. I will not come back here again after today clothed in this flesh, to see these sown fields; I depart, seeking heaven, having laid down the burden of this body. And now, lest I should bestow no gift on the fields of this monastic island when they are left bereft, the biting serpent will never do harm to anyone here by its poison.'

Thus, he effectively comforts their mourning by his persuasion; he said, 'Let us all be (His) dwelling-place; the true home, and ours especially, is the kingdom of heaven.'

(*See notes, pp. 304–5*)

[2.20] How iron that had been blessed could not do any harm (*VC*, ii, 29)

It happened that the servant Moluag presented a small unfinished piece of iron, ready to be worked, to the Prophet, while he was writing, so the holy man might consecrate it, and he blessed it. Quickly he took the blessed metal to forge sharp knives from it, so he could kill young pastured bullocks treading down the corn of the fields.

He (Columba) spoke thus: 'I have consecrated this iron by prayer; as I think, the metal is sufficiently holy, a danger to no one; such a thing will not harm cattle or anything (else).' He said, 'This blessed iron is useful for all things peaceful, (but) can do nothing for bloody uses of raging war, through the auspices of Christ.'

Nonetheless, Moluag struck a bull with the knife he had made, by continuous blows; but while the ox was left unscathed, he came back tired out.

The Father said, 'Moluag,

aere sacrato pecudes obesas,
siue quid uiuens animale fuso
          sanguine caedi?
25 Igne fornacis liqueat calentis
denuo mites habitura tactus,
secta per phani sacret aera nostri
          lamina sparsim.'

[f. P 33r; A 260r]

[2.21] Columba prece fugauit febres

Ferbuit quondam graciles repasta
militis chari fera febris artus,   [f. P 33v; A 260v]
proximus letho comes hic Columbae et
          aeger habebat.
5 Sanctus aegroto doluitque alumno,
obtinet multis precibus salutem,
quam nec in Phoebi potuit Machaon
          arte referre.
'Tu puer,' inquit, 'comes et senectae et
10 dulce solamen, mea fata cernes:
nam tibi plures Deus addet annos
          coelite Iona.
Hoc mihi donat miserens Iesus,
quem colo, Christus tibi ne superstes
15 sim recedenti, charitum sit illi
          gratior actus.
Tradite, uiuas bonitatis auspex
pluribus, uitae memor et futurae
surge, iam membris uigor imbecillis
20   coelitus insit.'
Corpus exili subito resultim
carne surrexit, uiguitque sensim,
gratias summo recinens Creanti
          munere in omni.

why do you think fat cattle can be killed by the blessed metal, or any living creature by bloodshed? Let it become liquid again in the flame of the hot furnace, to have a gentle touch; let the blade, cut up, consecrate the metals of our monastery in various places.'
(*See notes, pp. 305–6*)

[2.21] Columba drove away fevers by his prayers (*VC*, ii, 30)

Once a fierce fever burned, feeding on the weakened limbs of a dear soldier; this companion of Columba was near to death and sick. The Saint sorrowed for his sick fosterling, and by many prayers obtained his health, which not even Machaon could have restored through the arts of Phoebus. 'My child,' he said, 'you are both the companion and sweet comfort of my old age; you will witness my death: for God will add many years for you in heavenly Iona. Merciful Jesus Christ, whom I worship, grants this to me, that I shall not outlive you at your departing; let more grateful thanksgiving be to Him! May you live long, you seer of goodness, mindful of future life, having been entrusted to many; arise! Now may strength from heaven come into these feeble limbs.'

His body arose with a sudden leap in its weakened flesh, and he gradually became strong, giving thanks to the Highest Creator in all his works.
(*See notes, p. 306*)

[f. P 33v; A 260v]

[2.22] In Monte Scarsiaco iuuenem repentino morbo correptum prece liberauit

Montium nexus, parilisque tractus
Alpibus, limes secat Albionem   [f. P 34r; A 261r] I ii
peruius[12] Cauro medius sinistro,
  uertice celso.
5 Hac iter rarum niue Capricorna,
siue aquis urnae Ganymaedis astro,
mole pergentes subigente brumae
  funditus atrae.
Hac iter Sancto peragente coetus
10 languit quidam comitantis, umbra
mortis affini, quaerulique circum
  seminecem stant.
Ignea flauet cane tosta messis,
pacat austeros maris unda fluctus
15 frigus in Dorso mage fit remissum
  forte Britanno.
'Flectitur pura prece Numen,' aiunt,
'supplices ergo, Pater alme, Christo
pro tui nobis pueri salute
20 iam morientis.'
Orat intento Uolucer precatu,
indolis sanctae[13] puer hic superstes,
uiuat ut plures ualiturus annos
  hinc uegetatus.
25 Annuit Christus precibus Columbae,
unde praesagit uenerandus abbas
sospiti sanctam uegetante uitam
  religione.
'Clarus hic toto referetur orbe
30 editus coelo puer, auspicatur   [f. P 34v; A 261v]
moenia et primus sacra caenobitis
  Callianinde.'

---

[12] peruiae, Blado.
[13] sancte, Blado.

[2.22] He freed by his prayer a young man stricken with sudden illness on the hill of An Sgarsoch (*VC*, ii, 31)

There is a chain of mountains, a region like the Alps; the middle district divides *Alba* by its lofty summits, open to the inauspicious north-west wind. Here journeying is rare in the snows of Capricorn, or under the stars of Ganymede of the water jar (Aquarius), while the oppressiveness of dark winter completely holds back wayfarers; but here, while the Saint was making his journey, one of the accompanying group fell ill, close to the shadow of death, and those lamenting stand about the half-dead man.

A scorched harvest turns yellow at the burning Dog Star; the waves make calm the rough billows of the sea; perchance (winter) cold is made more mild on *Druim Alban*, the Spine of Britain. 'The Godhead is moved by pure prayer,' they said; 'therefore, bountiful Father, pray to Christ for us, for the health of your child who is now dying.'

The Dove prayed with intense supplication, that this boy of holy nature would survive, live, and be strong for many years, henceforth invigorated.

Christ heard Columba's prayers; then the reverend abbot prophesied a holy life for the one who had been healed, with his religion making him strong: 'This boy sent from heaven will be famous and reported in all the world; he first begins the sacred dwelling-place of the monastery of *Caille au Fhinde*.' (*See notes, pp. 306–8*)

[f. P 34v; A 261v]

[2.23] De Iuuene a morte resuscitato

Pluribus Pictos docuit diebus
dum fidem, multi renuere sacris
tingier lymphis, simulachra pronum
      uulgus adorans.
5 Impedit coetus Sathanae reluctans
plurimos mantae, druidae, magique,
augures et quae Triuiae litarant
      sanguine gentes.
Inuidens Plutho pia Christianae
10 phana successu fidei parari,
saeuit errores uarios per orbem
      dogmate iniquo,
mille diuersas reperire sectas
et potens album simulare fusco,
15 unde gens fluxit[14] methodo sub orcum
      mille meandris.
Uidit insignes cruce tot per urbes
deprimi regnum stygiale, cunctos
assequi Christum ueritus solutam
20   misit Erynnin.
Misit in Pictos uetulus Megaeram
anguis, infestae simul hae sorores
incitant uanos retinere ritus
      sacra deorum.   [f. P 35r; A 262r]
25 Una, nequicquam reprobante turba,
credidit Christo domus et maritus,
liberi, coniux, famuli, gregatim,
      foemina, masque.
Ille lustrali renouatus unda
30 dogmatis Christi et fidei peritus
cuncta quae coelum saperent, cupiuit
      auspice Iona.
Maximus natu bene Christianus
indolis clare iuuenis parentum
35 cura, solamen, moriens bonorum
      languit haeres.
Impius patri chorus exprobrare

---

[14] fluxat, Blado.

[2.23] A youth revived from death (*VC*, ii, 32)

When for some days he taught the Picts the faith, many people refused to be dipped in sacred waters (of baptism), and the common people bowed down worshipping images. The resisting company of Satan, oracle-givers, druids, magicians, soothsayers, and those people who had offered sacrifices in blood to Diana, prevented many. Pluto, envious that the holy church was being built up by the success of the Christian faith, sowed many errors throughout the world, with evil teachings, able to devise a thousand various superstitions, and to make white appear like black, whereby the people flowed in a thousand twists and turns to death by his teaching. He saw that the infernal kingdom was thrown down by the cross through so many great cities, and fearing that all would follow Christ, he sent unbridled Erinnys. The ancient serpent sent Megaera among the Picts; at the same time these angry sisters incite their vain cults to maintain the rites of the gods.

One household believed in Christ, while the crowd reproached them in vain: both husband and wife, children and servants together, men and women. He, renewed in purifying waters, and knowledgeable in the teachings of the faith of Christ, longed for everything that they might savour of heaven, by the prophet Jonah (Columba). The eldest son, firmly Christian, a youth of good disposition, the care and comfort of his good parents, their dying heir, lay sick.

The impious band,

coepit insultim fidei sacramen
et suos diuos celebrare, mantes,
40   augur, aruspex.
'Si uelis,' aiunt, 'opibus potiri,
et frui grato Ueneris cubili,
inde uitales habiturus ortus,
          et bona saecli,
45 quae satis diui patribus[15] dedissent,
crederes Christo minime, tulisti
morte iam nati precium, deorum
          uindice coetu.'
Huc celer uenit nimio laborans
50 Numinis zelo, dubiamque plebem
flagrat in Christo solidare, luctus
          intrat et aedes.   [f. P 35v; A 262v]
Aula ferali gemebunda planctu
egit assueto inferias praecatu,
55 lugubres sanctus monuit parentes
          credere firme.
'Fide, defuncti genitor fidelis,
arduum factu manui potenti
nil Dei, cuius facilis potestas
60   cuncta creauit.
Helias natum uiduae Sareptae
suscitans tactu tenero, fouebat
spiritu, nato mihi dante nomen,
          nuncupor Ales.
65 Nec Sunamitis sinit Helisaeum,
donec exangues animaret artus
prolis, et firmo iuuenis meatu
          pergere posset.
Lazarus Christo rediit iubente
70 institis uinctus, simul et sepultus,
foetuit cum quatriduano ab ortu
          lucis in antro.
Petrus et functam recitat puellam,
atque Ioannes Ephesum reuertens
75 suscitat uoto et prece Drusianam
          perscius ales.
Et licet nulli simulabor horum
sit fides nobis eademque et illis,

---

[15]   patri, Blado, leaving the line one syllable short.

oracle-giver, soothsayer, diviner, began to reproach the father insultingly for his vows of faith, and to celebrate their gods. They said, 'If you want to gain wealth, and to enjoy the pleasant couch of Venus, so that you may have living progeny thereby, and the good things of the world, do not credit to Christ that which the gods had amply given to your fathers; you have drawn this reward now in the death of your son by vengeance from the assembly of the gods.'

He (Columba) arrived there swiftly, greatly labouring with the zeal of God, and he inflamed the doubting people to be firm in Christ, and he entered the house of mourning. The lamenting hall brought forth funereal rites with mournful wailing, customary prayers; the Saint exhorted the mourning parents to believe firmly. 'O faithful father of the departed, be trusting, nothing is hard for the strong hand of God to do, whose simple power created all things. Elijah nurtured by his breath the child of the widow of Zarephath, reviving him by his gentle touch, while that child gives me a name: I am called the Dove. Neither did the Shunamite woman let go of Elisha until he had revived the lifeless limbs of her child, and the youth could proceed on a steady course.

'Lazarus returned as Christ commanded, having been bound in bandages and then buried, when he stank from daybreak of the fourth day in the cave. Peter summoned again the dead maiden; and John, the very wise bird, when he returned to Ephesus, revived Drusiana by his vow and prayer. And although I will be likened to none of these, let the same faith be ours as theirs;

omne praestabit nihil haesitanti
80   Christus abunde.   [f. P 36r; A 263r]
Mox adit solus loculum iacentis
mortui fusis lachrimis reclinans
sed nephas credo recitare uersu
     qualiter orat.
85 'O Deus, uotis gemituque nostro
esse opus nosti, miserescis ergo,
noteas signo, ut tibi credat omnis
     flumine lotus.
Annuis nostro melius rogatu,
90 corde sperantes neque derelinquis
suscitans istum fore te potentem
     Christe docebis.
En repulsati inspiciunt Goeti,
cunctus obseruat, tua quanta uirtus
95 ceditur nobis, iubeas resurgat
     ocyus, oro.
Surge tu Christo, puer, imperante!'
Fatus hunc uiuum tetigit, manuque
duxit ad laetos[16] obiter parentes
100   munere duplo.

[f. P 36r; A 263r]

[2.24] De Brochano mago Brudei regis familiari

Diuus obnixe druidam Brochanum
seruulae poscit manumissionem,
qui fero Scotam tenuit puellam
     iure coercens.   [f. P 36v; A 263v]
5 Ille Melconis duce pedagogus
impia errorum docuit Minerua
principis prolem iuuenem Brudaeum
     ludimagister.
Pro Scotae seruae manumissione
10 destinans Uates ita fatur Ales,
nil perorauit suadela postquam
     sonte Goeto.
'Antequam terris celer his recedam

---

[16]   letos, Blado.

Christ will furnish all things abundantly to him who hesitates in nothing.'

He then went alone to the place where the dead youth was lying, bowing down, with flowing tears; but I think it would be wrong to repeat in verse how he prayed. 'O God, You know that there is need for our sighing and prayers, and therefore You have mercy; may You become known by a miracle, so that everyone may believe in You, washed in the water (of baptism). You give better heed to our prayers, neither do You abandon those with hopeful hearts; O Christ, in reviving him You will teach that You are powerful. Now the rejected wizards are watching, everyone is looking to see how much of Your power is granted to us; I beg, command that he may quickly arise. Arise, thou child, as Christ commands!'

Having spoken, he touched him, living, and at the same time he led him by the hand to his joyful parents, by a twofold gift.

(*See notes, pp. 308–9*)

[2.24] Broichán the druid, friend of King Bridei (*VC*, ii, 33)

The Saint earnestly requested the druid Broichán for the release of a slave-girl; he held the Scottish girl by a harsh decree, keeping her prisoner. He, the teacher of the son of Maelchon by the guidance of Minerva, taught impiety of errors to young Bridei, child of the prince, as his schoolmaster.

The Prophet and Dove, determined for the release of the Scottish slave-girl, spoke thus, after pleading had achieved nothing with the wicked magician: 'Before I quickly leave these lands,

mortuus fies, fere nicromanta,
15 si tenes istam famulam Gathaeli
      stirpe renatam.'
Curia regis simul audiente
id, foras exit, socii sequuntur
ad pedem collis uiridesque ripas
20   Noesidos undae.
Inde candentem fluuio lapillum
sustulit dicens sociis, 'Beauit
hunc Deus multam populi ad salutem,
      ferte lapillum.'
25 Tale praesagus referens, 'In hora
hac magus dire quatitur, bibebat
uitreum et fregit calycem tremendo
      lapsus in aula.
Angelus summi quatit hunc Tonantis
30 uiribus fisum stygiae Dyanae,
barbara insontem quoque Christianam
      lege tenentem.   [f. P 37r; A 264r] K
Mox,' ait, 'binos equites uidebo
rege legatos, miser ut Brochanus
35 salueat nostro ualidus iuuatu
      Scotide missa.'
Ecce, legati regerunt fatentes
cuncta quae raptu Uolucer uidebat,
'Inclytus summa, bone, te Brudaeus
40   pace salutat.
Supplicat Christi uel amore princeps
ut iuues, mittet Scotidem paratus,
eius altorem miserans Brochanum
      mox moriturum.'
45 Aulico Uates ita nunciante
destinat binos simul, et lapillum,
fatus, 'Ex lympha lapidem rigante
      sic bibat aeger,
dum prius seruam modo liberabit,
50 sospes a potu ualidusque surget,
peruicax id si renuet, repente
      luce carebit.'
Perculit regem pauor et Brochanum
magnus, et Scotis data paciali
55 Uatis antiquos redit ad penates
      rege iubente.

you will be dead, cruel wizard, if you hold this reborn servant of the Gaelic race.'

While the king's court listened to this, he went outdoors; his companions followed, to the foot of the hill and to the green banks of the waters of the Ness. Then he lifted up a gleaming white pebble from the river, saying to his companions, 'Take this pebble; God has blessed this for the bounteous health of the people,' recounting thus in prophecy: 'the magician is struck hard at this hour; he was drinking, and broke his glass vessel when he fell down trembling in the hall. An angel of God the Thunderer has struck him with force, who trusted in Stygian Diana, holding a faithful and innocent Christian woman by a barbarous law.

'Soon,' he said, 'I will see two horsemen, messengers from the king, so that wretched Broichán may become well and strong by our help, when the Scottish woman has been released.'

Behold, confessing messengers repeated everything that the Dove had seen in rapture: 'Good sir, famous Bridei greets you in the most perfect peace. The prince begs, for the love of Christ, that, showing mercy, you will help his foster-father Broichán, who is presently about to die; he is ready, he will release the Scottish girl.'

When the courtier related this, the Prophet sent two men together with the pebble, saying, 'Let the sick man drink from water thus moistening the stone; when he first frees the slave-girl, then he will arise healed and strong by the drink; (but) if he obstinately refuses this, at once he will lose the light of life.'

Great dread overwhelmed the king and Broichán, and the Scottish woman, given safe-conduct as the king commanded, went back to the Prophet's ancient homeland.

Tingitur puris lapis inde lymphis,
qui natat summas per aquas uel instar
pomuli, nam res benedicta nauit
60   nescia mergi.   [f. P 37v; A 264v]
Poculo nantis rediit lapilli
morte sic Pictus ueges a propinqua,
credidit Christo et populus theatri
       uir, mulierque.
65 Conditus regis lapis ille gazis
expulit, summo miserante Iesu
innatans undis populi dolores
       tempore multo.
Mira res, aegris nequit inueniri,
70 terminus uitae quibus appropinquet:
nam die regis latuit Brudaei
       tegmine sueto.

[f. P 37v; A 264v]

[2.25] Sanctus uentis obnitentibus nauigauit uelis expansis

Nec minus tantae memor haud salutis
uertitur mantes magicas ad artes
ambiens plausum tenebris theatri[17]
       fraudis operti.
5 Prouocans Uatem stipulatus infit
taliter, 'Quando cupis, O Columba,
uela per pontum dare sibilantis
       flatibus Austri?'
Mitis aiebat Uolucer, 'Brochane
10 ut modo ueris pius acquiescas   [f. P 38r; A 265r] K ii
quod uiae nostrae rogitas dietam
       certus habeto.
Dum uelit Christus, comitante uita,
tertio solis dabimus sub ortu
15 nostra Neptuni per aquas secundis
       carbasa uentis.'[18]
Improbus mantes ait, 'Id nequibis:

---

[17] theathri, Blado.
[18] Mitis aiebat . . . . . . carbasa uentis.: the order of these two verses has been reversed: see
notes, p. 310.

Then the stone was dipped in pure water, and floated on the surface of the water like a little apple; for the thing that had been blessed floated, unable to be submerged. So the recovering Pict returned from near death by the draught of the floating stone; and the people in the audience believed in Christ, both men and women.

That stone, placed among the king's treasures, drove away the people's sicknesses, floating in water, for a long time, by the mercy of the great Lord Jesus. An amazing thing, it could not be found when the end of life came to someone sick: thus it was not found in its usual container on the (last) day of King Bridei.

(*See notes, pp. 309–10*)

[2.25] The Saint sailed against contrary winds with raised sails (*VC*, ii, 34)

Nonetheless, unmindful of such healing, the magician turned to magical arts, seeking the applause of his audience, covered over by the darkness of his deceit. Challenging the Prophet, demanding he asked: 'Columba, when do you intend to raise your sails upon the sea to the breezes of the sighing south wind?'

The Dove said gently, 'Broichán, so that you may now accept these truths as a good man, have certainty of the day's journey on our way which you ask: while Christ wills it, and while I have life, two days from now at sunrise, we will raise our sail with favourable winds, over the seas of Neptune.'

The wicked magician said, 'That you will not be able to do.

flamen aduersum faciam, caligo
et teget ponti faciem proteruis
20   humida nymbis.'
'At Dei numen dominatur omni,'
Diuus addebat, 'Duce quo mouemur[19],
res regit nostras, iter, acta, motus,
        Ternio Sanctus.'
25 Tertia Uates oriente luce
amnis ad Noesi spatiatur oram,
confluunt uisum uarii, sequatur
        quis modo finis.
Insolent plausu, facilique risu
30 tum magi obductas nebulas uidentes,
flamen et saeui Boreae fragosum
        aethere ab atro.
Quale Germano, ut legimus, beato
accidit, tantos operante motus
35 doemonum turba cupido Britannos
        uisere tractus.
Talis interdum datur et potestas
doemoni, ut coelo tolerante uentos
concitet, fulgur, tonitru, procellas,
40   fulmina et imbres.
Doemonum diuo legio per undas
multa Germano obstiterat salutis   [f. P 38v; A 265v]
ne uiam pandat fidei Monaeis
        ante popellis.
45 Ille sed Christi repulit minatos
spiritus, cunctum pelagi periclum
uicit appulsus cupitas ad oras
        Numine tutus.
Nec secus cernens elementa noster
50 mota se contra nequiter, retendens
inuocat Christum dominum, Boraeis
        lintea flabris.
Haesitant nautae dubii parumper,
quos fide cunctos animat Columba,
55 nauigant uento celeres reniso
        Auspice Iona.
Augures, mantae, druidae, goeti,
saga, medeae, quoque nicromantae,

---

[19] mouemnr, Blado.

I will make an adverse wind, and moist darkness will cover the face of the sea with angry clouds.'

'But the will of God rules in all things,' added the Saint, 'by whom we are moved as our Ruler; the Holy Trinity guides our affairs, our journeying, our deeds and thoughts.'

When day dawned two days later, the Prophet strode to the banks of the River Ness; many people came together to watch what result would then follow. The magicians became insolent with clapping and facile laughter, when they saw the overspreading mist, and ragged blasts of the savage north wind from the dark heavens.

In the same way, we read, it happened to St Germanus, eager to visit the British lands, when a crowd of demons worked such great disturbances. Sometimes such power is given to a demon, when heaven allows it, so that he may stir up winds, lightning, thunder, storms, thunderbolts and rain. The legion of demons previously greatly hindered St Germanus through the seas, lest he should open the path of salvation to faith to the people of *Mona*. But that man of Christ repelled the threatening spirits; he overcame all the dangers of the sea, brought to land at his desired shore, protected by the Godhead.

Just so, our man (Columba), seeing the elements moved against him wickedly, invokes Christ the Lord, unfurling the sails to the gusts of the north wind. The doubting sailors hesitate for a moment; Columba enlivens them all by faith; they sail swiftly while the wind is against them, through Jonah the Prophet. Augurs, soothsayers, druids, magicians, the sage, conjurers, necromancers too,

coetus errorum proprio pudescunt
60   numine uano.
Ales optatum properante portum
appulit cursu, populi fideles
Numen in Sancto[20] resonant Columba
        laudis honore.

[2.26] Sanctus rabidissimos aestus oratione sedauit

Forte[21] tempestas oritur, salumque
concitum crebris onerat carinam
fluctibus, quassae ut tabulae fathiscant
        aere soluto.   [f. P 39r; A 266r]
5   Saeuit irato rabiosa coelo
Tethys, eruptis cohibet nec antris
amplius murmur, domat haud canoros
        Aeolus Austros.
Clamitant nautae, et trepidant, crepantes
10 territant funes, superat recrescens
unda sentinae, uacuare et angit
        impote uulgus.
Quin manu Sanctus tenera iuuabat
uberes iactans latices lacunae
15 quae laborantes nimio fatigat
        foenore nautas.
Nauitae[22] Sancto, 'Quid agis, Columba?'
inquiunt; 'Prodes nihil hic, resultans
sic salum disco uacuans, precare et
20   Numen adora.'
Ocyus prora residens in uda
aerem ut ducta cruce signat, omnis
mox silet uentus, subitoque sidunt
        aequora lapsu.
25 Conuolant mergi pelago, sorores
ad choros ducit Galathaea, nactus
fit repandrostro pecori quietis
        pascua Naereus.

---

20   sansto, Blado.
21   EORTE, Blado (capitalised as the first word of the poem).
22   nauite, Blado.

the troop of error, are put to shame by their own false godhead. The Dove
lands at the desired harbour after a rapid voyage; the faithful people celebrate
the Godhead in St Columba with the honour of praise.
(*See notes, pp. 310–11*)

[2.26] The Saint calmed furious storms by his prayer (*VC*, ii, 12)

It happened that a tempest arose, and the aroused seas bore down on the ship
with constant waves, so that the battered timbers split open when the metal
fittings were loosened. Tethys raged, maddened by the angry heavens, neither
did she restrain any longer the roaring from the opened caves; Aeolus did not
tame the sighing south winds.

The sailors cried out and trembled; the creaking ropes were frightening;
the rising water in the hold overflowed, and it distressed the people who
were powerless to bail. Indeed the Saint helped with his tender hand, bailing
the copious waters in the bottom, which wearied the struggling mariners,
increasing excessively.

The sailors said to the Saint, 'What are you doing, Columba? You do no
good there, emptying out the returning sea thus with a shallow bowl! Pray
and worship God!'

At once, standing in the wet prow, when he signed the air, having drawn
the cross, at once all the wind was calm, and the seas subsided by a sudden fall.

The sea-birds flew together in the sea; Galatea led her sisters in the dance;
Nereus came to find pastures of tranquillity for his flocks (of dolphins) with
their turned-up snouts.

Obstupent nautae meritasque Christo
30 personant laudes, famulo precante
saluet a tantis homines periclis
            qui miseratus.

[f. P 39v; A 266v]

[2.27] Portae munitionis regiae ultro ad preces Columbae reseratae sunt

Lassus aduenit Uolucer peregre
prodiens urbem socia cohorte
inclyta ad magni properans Brudaei
            moenia regis.
5 Ianitor regis nimie superbo
longius cessit piger apparatu,
fecit et fastus, citus ut Columbae
            non aperiret.
Sanctus ad ualuas adiens restrictas
10 primitus signum crucis imprimebat,
mox manum apponens pepulitque seras
            sponte retrusas.
Ianuas intrat sacer hinc apertas,
obuiam sancto uenerans Brudaeus
15 uenit illustri nitidus senatu
            perreuerenter.
Signa perpendit reuerens benigne, et
dulciter sanctum alloquitur Columbam
debito mire recolens honore
20   tempore uitae.

[f. P 39v; A 266v]

[2.28] Simile quiddam

Sed duum ruris uice coenobitas
uisitans quadam penetrale phani   [f. P 40r; A 267r]
inuenit clausum nec eo reperta
            tempore claue,
5 dumque requirunt trepido tumultu
inuicem claues ita coenobitae,
ad fores pergit, 'Reserare Numen

The sailors were amazed, and sang merited praises to Christ, Who, being merciful when his servant prays, will save men from such great dangers.
(*See notes, p. 311*)

[2.27] The gates of the royal fortress were spontaneously unlocked at Columba's prayers (*VC*, ii, 35)

Exhausted, the Dove came on his journey, proceeding to the town accompanied by a worthy company, hastening to the famous fortress of the great King Bridei. The king's gatekeeper, with an excessive proud display, slowly delayed for a long time, and his pride caused him not to open up quickly to Columba. The Saint, coming to the closed gates, first imprinted the sign of the cross, and, placing his hand upon them quickly, struck the bars, which were spontaneously drawn back. As a result the Saint entered the open gates; Bridei, splendid with his illustrious council, came to meet the Saint, revering him very respectfully. He considered these miracles, kindly respecting him, and addresses St Columba humbly, revering him especially with due honour for (all) the time of his life.
(*See notes, p. 311*)

[2.28] A similar event (*VC*, ii, 36)

But also on one occasion, while visiting the monks of the land of *Duum*, he found the chapel of the sanctuary was closed, neither was the key found at that time. While the monks thus sought the keys together with anxious commotion, he came to the doors and said, 'God has the power to unlock.

est pote,' fatur.
'Qui potest caecos aperire ocellos,
10 ianuis clausis et inire portas
is potest istas reserare seruis
      claue sine ulla.'
Sic ait Uates, subito patescunt
ianuae motu sine ui uel ulla,
15 pessulis solum Deitatis actu
      sponte retrusis.
Praeuius portas iniit reclusas
Ales, hunc sancte hospitio receptant,
Numen in Sancto ueneratur omnis
20   concio fratrum.

[f. P 40r; A 267r]

[2.29] A S\<ancto\> sude tradita pauperi creuit ubertas, sed temere sude incisa eidem misero rediit egestas

Liberi et coniux fuerant alendi
pauperi, ac rerum tenuis facultas,
quamlibet Christi rogulam petenti
      nomine Ionam,   [f. P 40v; A 267v]
5 taliter Uates inopi locutus:
'Impiger syluas pete, fraxinumque
contuli fer materiam beandi, ut
      te locupletet.'
Fraxinum iussu miser ille Uatis
10 attulit, mox quam fabricauit Ales
contulum, signans benedictionis
      munere sanctae.
'Hoc ueru serua tibi diligenter,'
inquit, 'at nulli socio nocebit,
15 nec pecus figet cicur enecandis
      utile ceruis.
Apta figendis capreis, ferisque
caeteris, piscique sudis[23] premendo,
sit tibi, ut nunquam domui ferinae
20   copia desit.'

---

[23] sudes, Blado.

He who can open blind eyes, and go through closed doors, can unlock these gates of yours for His servants, without any key.' Thus spoke the Prophet; at once the doors opened up without movement or any force, when the bolts were spontaneously driven back by act of God alone. Going before them, the Dove entered the open doors; they welcomed him solemnly with hospitality; all the assembly of brothers revered God in his Saint.

(*See notes, p. 312*)

[2.29] Wealth came to a poor man from a stake given to him by the Saint; but when the stake was chopped up through fear his poverty returned to this wretched man (*VC*, ii, 37)

The children and wife of a poor man were in need of sustenance, and the quantity of his goods was slender, when he asked Jonah (Columba) for alms, howsoever small, in the name of Christ. The Prophet spoke thus to the poor man: 'Go to the woods quickly, and bring me ashwood timber of a pole for blessing, so that it may enrich you.'

The wretched man brought a stake of ash at the Prophet's instructions, which the Dove soon shaped into a pole, signing it with the power of a holy blessing. 'Look after this stake for yourself carefully,' he said, 'and it will not hurt any friend, neither will it pierce cattle or domestic animals, being useful in killing deer. May the stake be useful to you in hunting, for spearing goats and other wild animals and fish, so that plenty of wild game will never be lacking for your household.'

Iussa promissis alacer facessit
indigus, lustra et per opaca contum
fixerat, saltu procul in remoto
    nocte sed acta
25 postero Phoebi redeuntis ortu:
ut locum fixae sudis intuetur,
comperit mirans ibi mole caesum
    cuspide ceruum.
Sic et aurora redeunte semper
30 cerua uel ceruus sude figebatur,
fit domus ceruis, capreis, referta
    diues et ampla.   [f. P 41r; A 268r] L
Coniugis primum uetulus parentem
uicit ut serpens monitu, misello
35 stulta persuadet mulier prophanum
    tale marito:
'Tolle de terra uerulum, periclo
plena res nobis, homo uel iuuencus
si cadet, hasta et pereat, perimus
40   uel capiemur.'
'Non erit sic', uir retulit, 'beatus
ille qui contum dedit et dicauit:
pollicebatur pecori innocentem
    esse hominique.'
45 Destitit nunquam mulier, quousque
sustulit contum miser ille uaecors,
et penes uallum posuit propinquum
    domatis amens.
Utilis conto periit Molossus,
50 quo timens proli misere marito
uxor horrorem sudis instat extra
    limina poni.
Inuias tum uir repetendo syluas
abdita lustris sude senticosis
55 capream primo periisse fixam
    mane tuetur.
Inde sed contum remouens in amne
non procul ripam posuit, stupendum
mole qui piscem sude inhaesitantem
60   mane reprendit.   [f. P 41v; A 268v]
At miser sacrum tulit inde contum
collocans tecti superante parte
deforis, coruus uolitans adhaesit
    impete conto.

The poor man eagerly followed his instructions as promised; he fixed the stake in a dark forest far away in remote woodlands; when night had passed, afterwards, at the rise of the returning sun, when he saw the place of the fixed stake, amazed, he found there a stag of great size killed by the point. Thus every day as dawn returned, a stag or hind was impaled on the stake; his house became rich and plentiful, filled up with deer and goats.

As the ancient serpent overcame our first ancestor by the advice of his wife, so the stupid woman convinced her wretched husband of an impious deed, speaking thus: 'Take up the stake from the ground, the thing is full of danger for us; if man or beast falls and dies on the spear, we will be killed, or taken into captivity.'

'It will not be so,' replied her husband: 'that holy man who gave me the spear also told me, he promised, that it would be harmless to flocks or men.'

The woman never left off, until the foolish wretch, going frantic, took up the pole, and placed it beside the nearby wall of (his own) house. His helpful hunting hound perished on the spear; the wife, wretchedly fearing the danger of the stake for their children, insisted to her husband that it be placed beyond their bounds. Returning then to trackless forests, when the stake was concealed in thorny woods, in the early morning the man saw that a goat had died impaled. So then removing the spear to a river, he placed it not far from the shore; in the morning he found a fish of amazing size sticking to the stake. But then the wretch took the blessed stake, placing it outside on the upper part of his roof; a crow in flight became stuck to the spear by its forward motion.

65 Coniugis suasu fatuae maritus
    tum ueru tecto tulit, et securi
    dissecat frustis, proprium et cecidit
            saucius unguem.
    Nam sude incisa temere quadrigis
70 dura mendico redit albicatis,
    legibus stringens rigidis egestas
            tempora uitae.

[f. P 41v; A 268v]

**[2.30] De Librano arundineti genere Conachto, quomodo is liber-
tate donatus pie et sancte uixit usus S\<ancti\> Columbae consiliis**

    Nuper accinctus habitu, Conachtus
    gente Ionaeos adiens penates
    forte longinquis laycus peregre
            uenit ab oris.
5   Unde quaesitus lare, quae uiarum
    causa, cuiates habeat parentes,
    qua fide Christum coleret, quid optet,
            talia fatur.
    'Ales Achaei soboles Gathaeli,
10 et Dei cultor uenerande,' fatur,
    'Angor admissum scelus ut uiarum
            deleat, insto.'   [f. P 42r; A 269r] L ii
    Sanctus explorans ita, poenitudo
    qualis infestet, graue coenobitum
15 pondus ostendit, monachalis antri
            munus eremi.
    'Tu mihi leges dato poenitendi
    quamlibet duras,' ait, 'Auspicate,'
    confitens cunctum facinus piandum
20   poplite flexo.
    'Surge,' cui Uates ait, 'et sedeto:
    sitque septennis tibi poenitudo:
    pastus austerus, lachrimae, precesque,
            Ethica in ora.
25 Moeror, algedo, esuries, labores,
    rarior somnus, roga, solitudo,
    pallor oratus, scelus expianto,

At the persuasion of his foolish wife, the husband then took the stake from his roof and cut it into pieces with an axe, and, wounded, he cut off his own fingertip. For when the stake had been heedlessly cut up, harsh poverty returned to the beggar in a white chariot, binding the time of his life to its unbending laws.

(*See notes, pp. 312–13*)

[2.30] Concerning Librán 'of the reed bed' of the race of Connacht, how when he had been given his freedom he lived in a pious and holy manner by St Columba's counsel (*VC*, ii, 39)

It happened that a layman of Connacht by race, having recently put on the monastic habit, came from distant shores on pilgrimage, arriving at the house of Iona. Where his home was, what was the cause of his journeyings, where his parents were from, by what faith he worshipped Christ, what he sought, he told these things. 'Revered Dove, offspring of Greek Gathelus and worshipper of God,' he said, 'I beg that the anguish of journeyings should put away the crimes that have been committed.'

Investigating thus what kind of guilt assailed him, the Saint offered the heavy burden of monasticism, and the gift of a monastic hermit's cell.

'Give me the laws of repentance, however hard they be, O auspicious one,' he said, confessing with bended knee every deed to be expiated.

The Prophet said to him, 'Arise and sit. There will be seven years penitence for you, poor fare to eat, tears and prayers in the land of Tiree. Sorrow, cold, hunger, labour, only a little sleep, ashes, solitude, the paleness of prayer; let these expiate crime

Ethica in ora.
Usque septenus numeratur annus,
30 ambo uiuemus, Duce quo mouemur
Campilungeis maneas in oris,
          linquar Ionae.'
Tum Deo grates referens Conachtus,
'O Pater Uates,' ait, 'haec facessens
35 quomodo certum luo peieratum?
          Obsecro, dicas.
Nam reus mortis patrio statuto,
uinculis quondam fueram retentus
iudicor poenis, quod homuncionem
40   ense trucido.   [f. P 42v; A 269v]
Uir bonus quidam locuples paternae
me parentelae eripuit, redemptus,
seruiens illi officium et perenni
          iure paciscor.
45 Mensibus paucis iterum peractis
seruus indignor remanere semper,
saeculum taesus fugio peroptans
          uiuere Christo.'
'Septimo,' Uates ait, 'huc in anno
50 in quadragenis uenias diebus,
ipse paschali celeber synaxi
          te recreabo.'
Quid moror? Iussus alacer capessit,
Campilungaeo maceratus antro
55 septimo sanctam rediens synaxim
          sumpsit in anno.
'Nunc,' ait Uates, 'abeas oportet,
fitque carnalis dominus superstes,
te manent fratres, simul et parentes,
60   patria in urbe.
Pro tua munus manumissione
fulgidam argento capuloque eburno,
hanc, tuo heroi spatulam reporta,
          nec capietur.
65 Nec minus gratis precibus maritae
liber exibis, iubet illa solui
cingulum lumbis citius salubri
          saedula iussu.   [f. P 43r; A 270r]
Alteram uix effugies procellam,
70 negligis quicquid uetulo parenti

in the land of Tiree. Until seven years have passed we will both live where we are placed by the Lord: you will stay in the shores of Magh Luinge, I will remain in Iona.'

Giving thanks to God, the man of Connacht then said, 'O Father, Prophet, in doing this, how do I atone for a certain broken promise? Tell me, I beg. For I was judged guilty of death, by the law of our land; I was once held in chains in punishment, because I killed a man with the sword. A good and wealthy man of my father's family rescued me; when I was redeemed, I pledged myself to him in due service, by a permanent binding oath. After a few months had again passed, I was resentful of always remaining as a slave; having become weary of the world, I fled, choosing to dwell with Christ.'

'In the seventh year,' said the Dove, 'if you come here in the days of Lent, I myself, thronged at the paschal assembly, will make you new again.'

Why do I delay? When he was commanded, he quickly obeyed; becoming thin in the cell of Magh Luinge, returning in the seventh year, he resumed the holy sacrament.

'Now,' said the Prophet, 'it befits you to go away: it happens that your earthly lord is still living; there remain your brothers and also your parents, in your home town. As a gift for your liberation, take this shining sword, with a handle of silver and ivory, to your protector; and yet he will not accept it. Nonetheless, you will go free, without payment, at the prayers of his wife; she will thoughtfully order the belt to be released from your loins at once by a salutary decree. You will barely escape another storm: whatever duty you have hitherto neglected to fulfil for your aged parent,

ante praestare officii, rependes
      fratribus actus.
Tu pie patrem excipias fouendum,
quamlibet munus graue iudicetur,
75 septimo corpus sepelitur ortu
      patris abinde.
Quin parem matri pietatis actum
denuo fratres adigent rependi,
te minor natu bonus hocce frater
80   fasce leuabit.'
Fatus haec Uates gladium Conachto
dat, recedentem benedixit addens,
'Cum potes liber, memor huc reuerte
      uerna Tonantis.'
85 Uatis impleto penitus relatu
iure deuenit Domini solutus
fratribus pace et genetrice missis
      Robur ad ore.
Qua maris feruor furit estuosi,
90 euripo curuas celerante puppes,
scinditur tractu procul a Britanno
      cespes Iberus.
Uiderat uelum ratis Albionem
uersus intensum prope littus, orat
95 clamitans, 'Christi uel amore, uector
      me cape tecum.'   [f. P 43v; A 270v]
Sed nec illius redeunt miserti
remiges, moestus gemuit Conachtus,
orat aduersos merito superbis
100   Alitis Euros.
Protinus uerso tumet unda uento,
aduolant littus pelagi uolucres,
fit fragor, pontus uomitur per altas
      spumeus oras.
105 Nauta consultat reuehi clientem
Alitis, clamans ait, 'Appropinques.
Num putas uentum fore, te secundum
      naue recepto?'
'Prosperos,' inquit, 'pius obtinebit
110 Foelemi gnatus Zephyros, recepto
me, peregrinans adeo beatae
      limen Ionae.'
Tum ratis curuae tabulis uehendus

you will now repay that action to your brothers. You will kindly take in your father to be cared for, however heavy this duty may seem; on the seventh morning thereafter, your father's body will be buried. Your brothers will indeed again require the same deed of kindness to be paid to your mother; but your younger brother, a good man, will relieve you of this burden.'

Having said this, the Prophet gave the sword to the man of Connacht, and blessed him in parting, adding, 'When you are able, return here free, a mindful servant of the Thunderer.'

When the Prophet's narration had been completely fulfilled, set free, having dismissed his brothers and mother in peace, he came by the Lord's will to the Oakwood by the shore (Derry).

Where the fury of the angry sea rages, as the narrow channel quickens the curving prows, the soil of Ireland is divided afar from the British land. He saw the sail of a ship close to the shore, heading towards *Alba*; crying out he begged, 'For the love of Christ, take me with you as a passenger!'

But the sailors did not return having pity for him; the sorrowful man of Connacht groaned, he prayed by the Dove's merits for contrary east winds for the proud ones. At once the seas swelled as the wind turned, the sea-birds flew towards the shore, there was a crashing as the foaming sea was thrown up on the high shore.

A sailor asked for the Dove's associate to be carried across; calling out, he said, 'Come near! If we take you into the ship, do you really think that there will be a favourable wind?'

He said, 'The pious son of Fedlimid will obtain a favourable south-west wind when you take me on board, travelling thus to the entrance of blessed Iona.' Then the passenger was placed on board the curving ship;

sistitur, nautis ait et uiator
115 quem, Dei nutu, recolit Columba,
      'Tendite uela.'
Supparum dicto citius retensum
turgidant mites animae Fauoni,
praepeti cursu ratis et Britannam
120   appulit oram.
Mox cliens Uatis benedixit illis
impiger, Septem procul in Trionem
limen ad Sancti ueniens penates
      laetus Yaeos.   [f. P 44r; A 271r]
125 Ales excepit reducem benigne
audiens illo referente prorsus
omne completum proprio recentum
      carmen ab ore.
Indidit nomen monacho Conachto
130 atque 'Libranus uocitaris,' inquit:
      'liber es, summi famulus Tonantis
      Ethicam adito.
Tu diu uiues pius, et senecta
in bona uitam bene terminabis,
135 sed nec in terris Britonum resurges
      carne recinctus.
Nilque tristeris, quod in Albione
conderis nunquam, tumulum relinques
cum meis sanctis alibi serenus
140   lumine surges.'
Ille perrexit benedictione
Uatis accepta, pietate multos
Campilungaei monachusque phani
      fulsit in annos.
145 Unde prouectus senio, uetustum
in solum uenit Scotiae, caterua
cepit aegrotum pia Roboreti
      corpus humantes.
Hactenus Clyo cecinit Columbae
150 nostra ueraces Deicosque uisus,
fata Librani, meritisque uersos
      Alitis Euros.

and the traveller, whom Columba remembered by the will of God, said to the sailors, 'Hoist the sails.'

As soon as he had said this, the gentle spirits of the west wind swelled the taut sail, and the ship reached the British shore by a swift course. Then the Prophet's associate blessed them quickly, coming joyfully to the Saint's home, far away in the northern lands, his dwelling on Iona.

The Dove received him gladly on his return, hearing, as he described, his tale of the recent events, from his own mouth, everything fulfilled. He gave a name to the monk from Connacht, and said, 'You are called Librán: you are free; a servant of God the Thunderer, you will go now to Tiree. You will live in piety for a long time, and will end your life well in good old age; but you will not rise again clothed in flesh in the lands of the Britons. And do not be sad because you will not be buried in *Alba*: you will leave your burial-place and arise in light in another place, serenely with my saints.'

Having received the Prophet's blessing, he set out; and as a monk he shone for many years in piety in the sanctuary of Magh Luinge. Having grown old there through advanced age he came into the ancient land of *Scotia* (Ireland); he took ill, and the pious troop of the Oak grove buried his body.

Thus far our own muse, our Clio, told these truthful and godly visions of Columba: the fortunes of Librán, and the east wind turned about by the merits of the Dove.

(*See notes, p. 313–14*)

[f. P 44v; A 271v]

[2.31] Muliercula parturiens S<ancti> precibus liberatur

Una lucinam queritur proteruam
Mithlia quondam mulier propage,
qua rubet sero spaciosa Iberis
    Munya Phoebo.
5 Notuit Sancto querulus Columbae
foeminae fletus parili momento
stanti Ionaeo et gradienti in aruo,
    unde misertus,
ingredi fratrum iubet ille coetum
10 sancta delubri loca, 'Nunc Iberis
inuocat,' dicens, 'mulier precatum
    anxia nostrum.
Edidit sospes mulier gemellos
nunc,' ait, 'nostra prece,' perbeauit
15 quem Deus Uatem patriae, Columba
    praesul et abbas.

[f. P 44v; A 271v]

[2.32] De Nauigatione Sancti Cormachi S<ancto> Columbae caelitus ostensa

Cormachus uastum uice dum secunda
nauigat pontum gelidam sub Arcton
quaeritans olim uacuas eremi
    uisere sedes.   [f. P 45r; A 272r] M
5 Notuit Sancto status hic Columbae
coelitus Regi simul et Brudaeo
taliter praesens loquitur Prophaetes
    omine scitus:
'Uir bonus, sanctus, Superumque cultor
10 Cormachus de gente nepos Lethani
Mithlia, coetus hominum prophanos
    taesus aberrat.
Iam uagus solam cupiens eremum,
frigidum Septem procul in Trionem
15 pellitur monstris socius marinis
    flatibus Austri.
Orchadum quare cito maximati

[2.31] A woman in labour is freed by the Saint's prayers (*VC*, ii, 40)

Once a woman of the race of Míl complains of a painful childbirth, where spacious Munster of Iber turns red with the evening sun. The woman's doleful tears became known to St Columba in the same moment, as he dwelt and walked in the fields of Iona; moved to pity by this, he orders the assembly of brothers to enter the holy places of the church, saying, 'Now an Irish woman in distress invokes our prayers. The woman has now safely brought forth twins by our prayers,' said Columba, priest and abbot, whom God has greatly blessed as Prophet of his homeland.
(*See notes, pp. 314–15*)

[2.32] The Voyage of St Cormac, revealed to St Columba in heavenly fashion (*VC*, ii, 42)

Once, when for a second time Cormac sailed the empty sea to the frosty northern regions, seeking to visit empty spaces of a wilderness, this circumstance became known to St Columba in heavenly fashion, and at the same time the knowing Prophet, then present, spoke thus by foreknowledge to King Bridei: 'A good and holy man, worshipper of the Most High, Cormac Úa Liatháin, of the race of Míl, weary of the earthly company of men, is wandering abroad. Now the wanderer, seeking a lonely hermitage far away in the cold northern lands, as a companion to sea monsters, is driven by the south wind. Wherefore, good lord, may you quickly command the lord of the Orkneys

Cormachum mandes, foueat tegatque,
flante iactatum Borea per oras,
20   optime princeps.'
Affuit praesens simul imperanti
regulus, iussum celer et capessit
liberans actum Mithlii nepotem
          morte, periclis.
25 Tertia uastum uice dum peragrat
Cormachus pontum, pia consulebat
sic cohors Uatem: 'Quid agit latentis
          quaestor eremi?'
'Cormachus,' Uates ait, 'hoc die mox
30 has Ionaeas adigetur oras
plurimis functus[24] uarie periclis
          morte minante.   [f. P 45v; A 272v]
Ille quindenos properante soles
nauigat uento, totidemque noctes,
35 septimum linquens, ab Hyberto in Arcton
          post paralelum.
Luce quindena decimam sub horam
monstra terrebant truculenta passim,
obtegunt pontum, latus et carinae
40   impete quassant.
Sed polo fixis oculis precatur
Cormachus Numen sociique adorant,
crebriter cuncti manibus leuatis
          ore supino.
45 Compati fratres ita nauiganti[25]
nos decet, Christum rogitemus ergo,
quo suos seruet famulosque Cauro
          flante reuectet.'
Nubilus sancti prece cessit Auster,
50 impedit fluctus Aquilo serenus,
laetior clari facies Olympi
          mox aperitur.
Inde quindenos Aquilone soles
flante decliui Octipedi tot umbras
55 Cormachus recto rediit meatu
          littus Hiberti.
Unde transactis aliquot diebus

---

[24] fuuctus, Blado.
[25] uauiganti, Blado.

to care for and shelter Cormac, when he is cast upon his shores by the gusting north wind.' The subject-king was present with the ruler at the same time; quickly he undertook the command, freeing the descendant of Míl, when he was driven (there), from death and danger.

When for a third time Cormac travels across the empty sea, the pious company asked the Prophet thus: 'How is he faring, the seeker of a hidden hermitage?'

The Prophet said, 'Soon today, Cormac will be driven to these shores of Iona, having endured many dangers in various ways, with death threatening him. For fifteen days and as many nights with the wind driving him, he has sailed from Ireland, towards the northerly region, leaving behind the seventh parallel. At the tenth hour on the fifteenth day fierce monsters everywhere were terrifying them; they covered the sea, and angrily buffeted the sides of the ship. But Cormac prayed to God with his eyes fixed on heaven, and all his companions praised God insistently, with hands raised and upturned faces. It is fitting for us brothers to feel sympathy for such a voyager; therefore let us beg Christ that He may save His servants and bring them back, when the north-west wind blows.'

The cloud-bearing south wind ceased at the Saint's prayer, a serene north wind held back the waves; the more cheerful face of the clear heavens was presently revealed. Then, as the declining north wind blew to Cancer for fifteen days and as many nights, by a straight course Cormac returned to the shore of Ireland. After a few days had passed,

Cormachus, Diuo referens Columbae
cuncta quae Uates cecinit penates
60   uisit Yaeos.   [f. P 46r; A 273r] M ii
Pende Neptuni tumidas procellas
huius oratu domitas, canoros
labier uentos, nocuasque pestes
        cedere ubique.
65 Sed mihi Clyo memora supernae
ciuis aulai modo quanta uirtus
sit, solo carnis trabeam tenente,
        quanta potestas.
Nam licet toto studiosus aeuo
70 coelicam duxit Deitate uitam,
carne plus sancta tamen ille dempta in
        aethere pollet.

[f. P 46r; A 273r]

[2.33] Quomodo liber manu S\<ancti\> exaratus sub aquis diu latitans nil damni pateretur

Saeculis iam pluribus a Beati
transitu quondam iuuenis peribat
amne submersus, latuitque in imo
        luce uigena.
5 Huius ascella iuuenis uolumen
infuit tantis madidum diebus,
cuius insignit folium Columbae
        forte character.
Uanuit lymphis penitus solutum
10 caeterum libri, calamo at beati
scripta seruantur, patitur nec ullum
        pagina damnum.

[f. P 46v; A 273v]

[2.34] Simile miraculum

Sic et hymnorum liber exaratus
litera Diui graphiceque pictus,
ponte delapsus penetrauit imam
        gurgitis undam.

Cormac visited the household of Iona, relating to St Columba everything that the Prophet had foretold.

Consider the swelling storms of Neptune tamed by his (Columba's) prayers, how the noisy winds drop, and injurious plagues give way everywhere. But remind me, O muse, how great is the strength of a citizen of the heavenly court, now while he wears a garment of flesh on earth, and how great is his power; for although he eagerly led a heavenly life with the Godhead's help through all his lifetime, yet, having laid down the flesh, he is stronger in the sacred heavens.

(*See notes, p. 315*)

[2.33] How a book written by the Saint's hand suffered no damage lying in water for a long time (*VC*, ii, 8)

Once, many years after the Saint's passing, a young man died, drowned in a river, and he lay at the bottom for twenty days. Within this young man's armpit there was a book, moistened for as many days, of which it happened that Columba's writing had distinguished (one) page. When freed, the remainder of the book was completely erased by the waters; but the writings from the Saint's pen were preserved, and the page suffered no damage at all.

(*See notes, pp. 315–16*)

[2.34] A similar miracle (*VC*, ii, 9)

Thus, also a book of hymns, written in the Saint's writing and ornamented with pictures, dropped from a bridge, fell into the deep waters of the stream.

5 Pridie nonas cecidit Decembres
fluminis codex, reperitur omnis
nescius, labis liquidaeue, apertus
    quum reperitur.

[f. P 46v; A 273v]

[2.35] Quomodo uestibus et libris Sancti sub dio productis pluuia elicitur tempore siccitatis

Uector Hellaeus, Bouis atque sydus
sedecem plusquam rigidantur annos,
ut queat tellus sitibunda nullos
    ducere foetus.
5 Uere durescit cereale et aruum,
stirpitus syluae, fruticesque arescunt,
graminum uenae uolitant solutae
    flamine sicco.
Torpet effoeto cinerosa tellus
10 puluere, exhausta pecudes palude
iam siti cunctae pereunt, arenae
    lumina turbant.
Nullus aeoo rigat imber ortu
gramen, aut sero pluuiosa nubes,   [f. P 47r; A 274r] M iii
15 nulla Thaumantis sinuata curuo
    rorat ab arcu.
Tum putes uere Domini minantis
uerba compleri, populo scelesto
sic quibus fatur, 'Superet malignos
20   aeneus aether.'
'Aeneum uobis superaddo caelum,
terra ferrescet, nihil et labores
proderunt uestri, neque germinabit
    glaeba, uel arbor.'
25 Hanc timescentes trepidare plagam
cepimus phani uigiles Yaei,
unde consulto placuit senatus
    cingere campum,
Utque lustrantes, tunicam niualem,
30 qua fuit tectus Uolucer beatus
uentilent et chyrographum per agros
    aruaque passim.

The book fell on the fourth of December; it was found, innocent of all stain of the river or of its waters, lying open, when it was found.
(*See notes, p. 316*)

[2.35] How rain was brought forth in time of drought when the Saint's clothing and books were taken out into the open air (*VC*, ii, 44)

More than sixteen years ago, the Bearer of Helle (Aries) and the stars of Taurus were made rigid, so that the thirsty earth could not bring forth any young growth. The cornfield also turns hard in spring, trees and shrubs become dry to the root; detached stems of grass fly about in the dry breeze. The scorched ground becomes useless with unproductive dust, all the flocks perish of thirst in the marsh, now dried out; the sands disrupt the daylight. No rain at sunrise in the east or rain-bearing clouds at evening moisten the crops; no bending rainbow distils moisture from its curving bow.

Then you might think the Lord's threatening words to the wicked people had been truly fulfilled, to whom it was spoken thus, 'Let a bronze sky be over the wicked:' 'I will set a sky of bronze over you, the earth will become like iron; your labours will profit you nothing, neither the earth will sprout, nor trees.'

Fearing this affliction, we watchful ones of the sanctuary of Iona began to be afraid; so our elders decided advisedly to circle the fields, so that as they traversed they could expose to the air in scattered places through the fields and plains a white tunic which had covered the blessed Dove, and a manuscript (written by him).

Protulit uestem niueam Columbae
coetus anfractu graditurque longo,
35 Angeli Cliuo reserans uolumen
          legit ibidem.
Mox polus nubes, nimis ante purus
contrahit, laetos liquefecit imbres,
perdius, pernox pluit, unde potus
40   parturit orbis.
Tum pecus cunctum uegetatur, arbos
gemmeas ridet paritura frondes   [f. P 47v; A 274v]
et Pales magno Ceres atque damnum
          foenore pensant.
45 Unde mirantes inopinus imber
tam cito coeli faciem tegebat,
gloriam summo dederant Tonanti
          Numini Ionae.

[f. P 47v; A 274v]

[2.36] Uaria alia miracula his nostris temporibus per S\<anctum\> Columbam declarata

Signa, uirtutes, uarieque mira,
quae per auditum capimus uetustum,
iam fide praesens bene firmat aetas
          fulgida signis,
5 uisus auditum docuit fidelem,
uidimus nostro tribus alteratum
protinus uentum uicibus fauente
          Alite uoto.
Forte quercetum metimus lacustre
10 aedibus dum materiem struendis,
atque secessu mare flexuoso
          grande subimus,
pinea robur tabula uehentes
nautilem[26] rostro facimus recuruo
15 machinam quernis grauidam dolatis
          littoris unda.
Ponimus tusas acie secures,
dum domum lassi petere auspicamur,   [f. P 48r; A 275r]

---

[26]   natilem, Blado.

The assembly took Columba's white tunic, and walked on a long circuitous route; opening his book they read (from it) at *Cnoc Aingeil*, the Angel's hill.

Soon the sky, hitherto completely clear, draws together the clouds, moistens the welcome rains; it rains all day and all night, and then the earth brings forth liquid to drink. Then all our flocks flourish, the tree smiles to bring forth leafy branches like jewels, and Pales and Ceres also redress the damage with a high return. The unexpected rain covered the face of heaven so quickly; the astonished people gave glory to the Thunderer, to the God of Jonah. (*See notes, pp. 316–17*)

[2.36] Some other miracles shown by St Columba in our own times (*VC*, ii, 45)

The present age, resplendent with miracles, now confirms fully the signs, powers, and wonders which we variously receive in faith from hearing from a long time ago; our sight teaches us what we have heard in faith; we have seen three times the winds changed immediately by our prayer with the help of the Dove.

It happened that when we were harvesting a lakeside oakwood for timber for building a house, and went to the wide sea to a remote sinuous place, carrying the oak on a platform of pine, we made a nautical craft with a curving prow, loaded up with the hewn oaks, on the seashore. We lay aside our axes, beaten in the blade, when, being tired, we begin to make for home;

occupat ponto fluitante portum
20   coedua quercus.
Crispat horrentes laceratque uultus
Aphricus saeuo pelagi fragore,
durus aduersam minitatus auram
          tempore longo.
25 Hispidus uasto tumuit uolutu
fluctuum Naereus, ater occidentem
nimbus obfuscat, monuit bimestrem
          turbo procellam.
Tum pio nobis calet ara thure,
30 sobrii uestes simul et uolumen
ponimus Sancti, canimusque psalmos,
          cantica et hymnos.
Poscimus uentos meritis Columbae
prosperos, non a grege fabuloso
35 numinum, sola at sobole a Tonantis
          talia fantes,
'Una supremi soboles Tonantis,
cui solum seruit, polus aether unda,
quem colunt, uentos adhibe secundos
40   nomine Ionae.
Legimus sicco pluuiam sub astro
elici tactu tunicae, librique,
posse, nec uentum minus alterari
          credimus isdem.
45 Obtine sanctis precibus fauentes
huic rati flatus, sinuosa surgens   [f. P 48v; A 275v]
per freta aeoo Nothus halet axe,
          diue Columba.'
Nil more, mox Euronothus nitentes
50 explicat pennas, dedimusque uela,
littus alterno Lybe fluxuosum et
          legimus Euro.
Congruit uentus sinibus, Boraeus
tendit antennas rigor, hinc Iapyx,
55 inde Uulturnus, tepidusque et Auster
          more Meandri.
Luce per flatus uarios eadem
prospere Sancti meritis Columbae
uenimus, sospes subit atque Yaeos
60   machina portus.
Altera lapsis aliquot diebus

the oak ripe for felling enters the harbour while the sea is flowing. The south-west wind tears and lacerates the bristling face of the sea with fearful crashing, harshly threatening adverse breezes for a long time (to come). Shaggy Nereus swelled up with vast rolling of the waves, a black cloud darkened the west, a whirlwind threatened a great storm of two months' duration.

Then the altar burns for us with pious incense; prudently we place (there) the clothes and book of the Saint, and we sing psalms and songs and hymns. We ask for favourable winds by Columba's merits, not from the fabled flock of the gods, but only from the child of God the Thunderer, speaking thus: 'O one child of God the Thunderer, whom the earth serves, whom sky, air, and sea revere, summon favourable winds in the name of Jonah! We have learned that it is possible to summon rains under a dry star by the touch of his tunic and his book; and we believe no less that the wind can be changed by these same things. Obtain favourable winds for this boat by your holy prayers, O Holy Columba! let the south wind rising blow from an eastern sky, through winding channels.'

At once without delay a south-easterly wind spreads its shining wings, and we raised the sails; we skirted the winding coast as the south-west wind changes to the east. The wind was agreeable to our bending course: the strength of the north wind filled our sails, then the northeaster, then the southeaster, and the warm southerly, in meandering fashion. We came fortunately that day by these various winds through St Columba's merits, and the craft came safely to the harbour of Iona.

Another time, after some days had passed,

dum strue ilignas uehimus dolatas,
obstat aduersus Zephyrus maligno
   flamine nautis.
65 Uocibus patrem querulis Columbam
cimus, et tali uelut increpamus
poene lamento, 'Libet hicce uentus
   siccine, Iona?
Esse te magni meriti supremis
70 sedibus num re sine uel potentem
remur? An uirtus tua iam senescit?
   An furit ira?
Te potem lapsum memorauit aeuum
primitus, terrae, maris, atque coeli,   [f. P 49r; A 276r]
75 saepius nosmet uariis leuasti
   fascibus ante.'
Hisque uix dictis cecidit Fauoni
murmur, aurorae foribusque apertis
loene Uulturnus dat iter carinis
80   littus ad Yuum.

[2.37] Post Euernensis synodi recessum
dum domo uentis prohibemur, inque
ploebe tardamur generis Loerni, et
   coeperat aestas.
85 Iunias sextoque diescit Idus
pridie Natalicii Columbae
Sainea tristes remoramur ora
   flamine Cauri.
Idque ieiuni, querimur precantes,
90 'Crastinus spiret Nothus ut secunde,
quo domi fas sit, celebrare tantae
   orgia lucis.
Num decet uulgo monachos prophano
sic tuos tali, Pater, interesse
95 luce nec festos cecinisse ritus
   domate Yaeo?'
Clara Tithoni thalamum relinquens
Matua aeoo modo rorat ortu,
ecce uelata rate cardinalis
100   crebruit Auster.
Uenimus quinta modo iam diei
praepetes hora, manibusque lotis   [f. P 49v; A 276v]
pangimus sexta sociis iugati
   limine sacro.

when we are carrying hewn oaks in a heap, a contrary west wind opposes the sailors by a malign breeze. We rouse our father Columba with complaining voices, and almost chide him with a lament, like this: 'Is this wind thus pleasing to you, O Jonah? Are we not indeed to esteem you to be powerful, of great merit in the highest places, or are you without purpose? Has your strength now grown weak? Or is your anger aroused? The past age remembered you as once having power over the earth, sea, and sky; often before you have relieved us of various burdens.'

We had hardly finished saying these things when the noise of the west wind dropped, the gates of the east were opened, the southeast wind gently gave our ships passage to the shore of Iona.

[2.37] After our departure from the Irish synod, while the winds kept us from home, we were delayed among the people of the race of Lorn, and summer had begun. The eighth day of June dawned, the day before Columba's birthday; we were sadly delayed on the shore of *Saine* by the blowing of the north-west wind. Fasting and praying, we asked this: 'May the south wind blow tomorrow favourably, so that it may be right to celebrate at home the rites of such a great day! Surely it is not right, Father, for your monks to be here thus among secular people, and not to sing your festive rites this day in your house on Iona?'

Bright Aurora now distils dew from the eastern sunrise, leaving the bedchamber of Tithonus; lo, the prevailing south wind grew strong as the ship was given sail. Coming by a straight course, we arrived then at the fifth hour of the day; having washed our hands, at the sixth hour we sang (hymns) in the sanctuary, joined with our companions.

(*See notes, pp. 317–19*)

[f. P 49v; A 276v]

[2.38]

Poene terrarum miseranda pesti
bis lues omnem uitiarat orbem
qua patet tellus habitata terno
      clymate secta.
5 Utque iam tractus taceam remotos
Ausonas, Gallos, Britones, Suaeuos,
Teuthones, fines quoque Celtiberos
      plaga peremit.
Insulas hinc Oceani per omnes
10 serpit, et totam necat Albionem,
nec tamen Pictos tetigit, Gathaeli
      nec genus usquam.
Sint duo quamquam populi feroces,
criminum quamuis aliquando mole
15 Numen irritant, patiens pepercit
      at Deus illis
nempe tutela fuerant Columbae
sospites, sacro ueneranda cultu
cui tot in cuncta Scotia dicantur
20   templa, sacella.
Hanc quoque acceptam ferimus salutem
praesuli nostro, populante circum
peste, quod bina uice tunc amicos
      uisimus Anglos.
25 Carmen hoc nostras cape nunc Iona
et memor uestri miseresce uatis,   [f. P 50r; A 277r]
ut simul tecum uolet et quiescat
      suffice pennas.

ΤΕΛΟΣ

[2.38] [The plague] (*VC*, ii, 46)

Twice miserable pestilence has afflicted almost all the lands of the world with plague where the inhabited land stretches, cut off from the third region. To say nothing of remote regions, the plague devastated Italians, French, Bretons, *Suevi*, Germans, and also the Spanish lands. From there it crept through all the islands of the Ocean, bringing death to the whole of *Alba*; but it did not touch the Picts, neither the Gaelic race anywhere. Although they be two savage nations, although sometimes they anger God by the immensity of their crimes, yet merciful God spares them both; surely they have been kept safe by the protection of Columba, to whom so many ancient churches and shrines are dedicated in all of *Scotia*.

We also credit this health which we received to our ruler, while the plague around us was devastating, both times when we were visiting our English friends.

Accept now this song, our own native Jonah, and be merciful, mindful of your poet; give him wings, that he may fly away and rest together with you.

The End

(*See notes, p. 319*)

Paraphrasis elegiaca of Psalm 1

[f. P 50r; A 277r]

Ne pagina remaneret uacua, adiicitur paraphrasis elegiaca in Psalmum primum, quam idem Rodericus, ut pleraque alia, ex tempore cecinit.

O pius, O foelix, O uir sine fine beatus
    uitat iniquorum qui mala facta uirum:
perfida nec stolidae uaecors in compita ploebis
    labitur erronum triste secutus iter.
5 Sed nec pestiferas zelat conscendere sedes,
    coetus nugonum quas numerosus habet.
Illius in uera at crescet pietate cupido,
    lex amor illius, semper et ardor erit.
ut uiret irriguis arbor contermina riuis,
10   quo debet foetus tempore fertque suos,
cuius nec folium tristis rapit aura Nouembris,
    seu cuius nullo frons erit acta Notho,
omnia successus illius facta secundos
    semper habent, quoniam tentat inane nihil.
15 Non ita, sed dispar sceleratis exitus instat,
    quos leuis a supero proiicit aura solo.
Non igitur iustum stabit impius ante tribunal,
    et neque cum sanctis pars erit ulla malis.
Semita iustorum quoniam preciosa Tonanti
20   claret, iter scelerum stirpitus omne perit.

FINIS

Paraphrase of Psalm 1

In order to fill the page, here is inserted a paraphrase in elegiac verse of Psalm 1, which Roderick composed *ex tempore*, as with many of the other (Psalms).

O holy, O happy man, and a man joyful without end, is he who avoids the evil deeds of wicked men, and does not like a madman wander into the treacherous crossroads of the stupid *plebs*, following the gloomy ways of vagabonds. But neither does he yearn to ascend to the pestilential seats which the numerous throng of triflers occupies. But in true holiness his longing will grow; his love will be the law, and it will always be his burning desire. As a tree flourishes adjacent to irrigating streams, and bears its fruit at the time when it should, whose leaves neither the wind of dull November snatches, or whose foliage will be driven by no south wind. All his deeds always have favourable success, since he attempts nothing that is vain. Not so with the wicked, but a different end hangs over them, whom a light breeze sweeps away from the surface soil: the unholy therefore will not stand before the just tribunal, and neither will there be any place with holy men for the wicked. For the path of the just is well known, precious to the divine Thunderer; the whole way of crimes perishes utterly.

The End

(See notes, pp. 319–20)

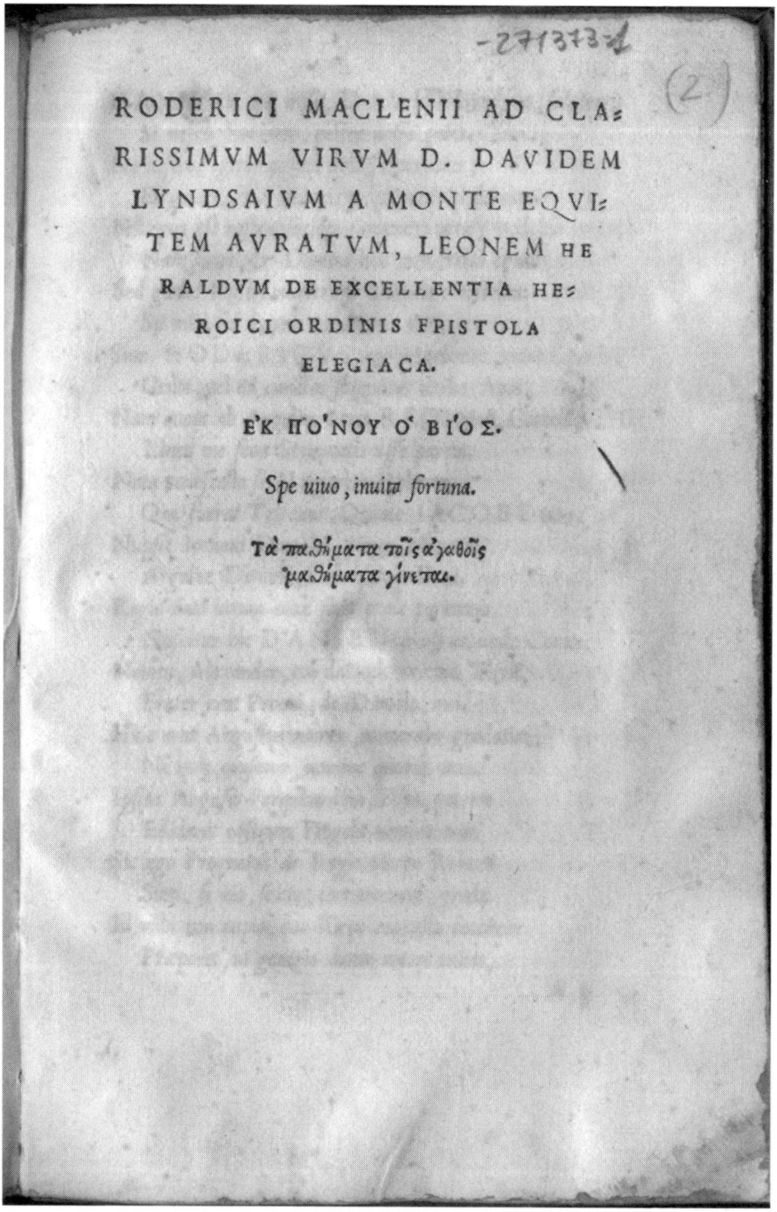

(2)

RODERICI MACLENII AD CLA=
RISSIMVM VIRVM D. DAVIDEM
LYNDSAIVM A MONTE EQVI=
TEM AVRATVM, LEONEM HE
RALDVM DE EXCELLENTIA HE=
ROICI ORDINIS EPISTOLA
ELEGIACA.

Ε'Κ ΠΟ'ΝΟΥ Ο' ΒΙ'Ο Σ.

Spe uiuo, inuita fortuna.

Τὰ παθήματα τοῖς ἀγαθοῖς
μαθήματα γίνεται.

Figure 7. Title page of *Perugia, Biblioteca communale Augusta*, I-L-66 (2), a letter in elegiac couplets addressed to Sir David Lindsay of the Mount. By kind permission of the Biblioteca communale Augusta, Perugia.

Epistola elegiaca to Sir David Lindsay
of the Mount

RODERICI MACLENII AD CLARISSIMVM VIRVM D\<OMINVM\> DAVIDEM LYNDSAIVM A MONTE EQVITEM AVRATVM, LEONEM HERALDVM DE EXCELLENTIA HEROICI ORDINIS EPISTOLA ELEGIACA

ἘΚ ΠΌΝΟΥ Ὁ ΒΊΟΣ.

Spe uiuo, inuita fortuna.

Τὰ παθήματα τοῖς ἀγαθοῖς
μαθήματα γίνεται.

The Excellence of the Heroic Order:
a Letter in elegiac Verse
to the most noble Man
Sir David Lindsay of the Mount, Knight, Lyon Herald
by Roderick MacLean

Our life is from hard work.

I live in hope, while fate is against me.

For good men,
suffering becomes a lesson.

[f. 2r] Aii

Hanc tibi qui misit, Dauid Lyndsaie, salutem,
    si nescis hominem, postea nosse potes.
Ne nostros igitur pigeat nouisse parentes,
    et genus, et patriam, meque, meamque domum.
5   Nil opus est nostrae seriem contexere uitae,
    nam fama et Domini lux manifestat opus.
Sed genus illustri numero si stemmate nostrum:
    sit mihi fas humili conditione uiro.
Sum Rodericus ego Maclenius, ortus equestri
10   gente, uel ad cunctos sanguine clarus auos.
Nam quota ab Argolico uenit Regina Gathelo,
    linea me fecit stemmatis esse parem.
Nata Senescallo si Margareta Roberto
    qui fuerat tritauus, quinte Iacobe, tuus,
15 nupsit Ioanni[1] Danielis, uirgo, nepoti
    Argaliae domino, Hebridicoque duci.
Regia nata uirum mox fecit prole parentem,
    nascitur hic Daniel Rossius unde comes.
Nomen, Alexander, cui dat celeberrima Thyle,
20   frater erat proaui, de Daniele, mei.
Huic erat Angusius nomen, numerabo gradatim,
    ne quis causetur, nomine quemque uoco.
Ipsius Angusii Ferquhardum, filia, patrem
    ediderat nostrum Fingola nomine erat.
25 Sic ego prognatus de regis stirpe Roberti
    sum, si uis, sexto, connumerare, gradu.
Id mihi non cupio, quo stirps augusta fauorem
    praeparet, ut generis dante nitore uehar,   [f. 2v]
quicquid id est, nostrum non est, nisi quatenus horum
30   assequimur mores, ingenuosque uiros.
Quamuis[2] illustres uirtus imitata penates
    eminet, et raro limen agreste petit,
solum nobilitat uirtus, nec clara parentum
    hac sine origo ualet, nec status amplus, opes.
35 Nostri namque[3] lares ibi sunt, patriique penates,
    qua lacus illimi gurgite Noesus abit.
Terra sub occidui gelido sita cardine coeli
    quam cingit rabidis Ennosigaeus aquis.

---

[1]   Ioannni, Blado.
[2]   Quanuis, Blado.
[3]   nanque, Blado.

[f. 2r]

If you do not know the man who has sent you this greeting, David Lindsay, you may get to know him hereafter; may it therefore not be irksome to know my parentage and my race, my homeland, myself, and my family. It is not needful to put together the course of my life, for reputation and the light of the Lord show forth my works; but if I enumerate my race from an illustrious lineage, let it be right for me, a man of lowly state.

I am Roderick MacLean, born of knightly race, and noble by blood all the way back to my ancestors. For by what number (of generations) the Queen descends from Gathelos of Argos, the line of my succession makes me equal, if Margaret, daughter of Robert Stewart (Robert II), who was your great-great-great-great-grandfather, O James the Fifth, as a virgin married John MacDonald, grandson of the lord of Argyll and ruler of the Isles. This royal child soon made her husband a father with offspring; from them Donald earl of Ross was then born. Alexander, to whom celebrated *Thyle* (Islay) gave his name, was brother of my great-grandfather descended from Donald. His name was Angus; lest anyone should object, I will count by steps, and call each of them by name: the daughter of the same Angus gave birth to my father Farquhar; she was called Finguala. Thus I am descended from the royal stem of King Robert (II), if you will count it up, in the sixth degree.

I do not want this for myself, that august ancestry should procure favour, (or) that I should progress with the help of distinguished race; [f. 2v] whatever this (lineage) is, it is not mine, except insofar as I match these generous men and their ways. However much virtue, when it is followed, makes illustrious houses distinguished, and rarely seeks out a peasant house, only virtue ennobles; without it, neither noble parental origin, nor distinguished status and wealth, have any value.

My place of origin and parental home is in the place where Loch Ness runs out in an unmuddied flood, the land which Neptune encircles with raging waters,

Hanc Danieligenum duro mauorte tenebat
40   progenies, armis, nobilitate, potens.
Nunc postquam fato concesserat illa propago,
        constat in audaci plurimus ense furor.
Id melius lator referet, formamque, modumque,
        tu mihi quam dederis, huic adhibeto fidem.
45   Te mihi notificat tua uirtus, carpis iniquos
        qua semper mores, euehis atque bonos.
Te ueges aethereum dulci facundia uatem
        ore docet, sermo Nestoreusque lepor.
Est tibi libertas mores taxare prophanos,
50   alter ut et Momus credier ipse queas.
Sic uiret ingenium, sic nempe cadentibus annis
        te fouet in proprio sancta Minerua sinu.
Fouit Iessaeum prius ista iuuencula psaltem,
        ipsa solet gelidi corporis esse comes.
55   Has ego uirtutes nitido tam pectore natas
        osculor, has tota denique mente colo.   [f. 3r] Aiii
Altius humanas et quod transcenderis artes,
        est laus, et uitam sic statuisse tuam,
cunctus ut agnoscat Numen, uereatur, adoret,
60   sic Euangelica clangis ubique tuba.
Nunc honor ingeniis fieri cum cessat, inique
        cum status hic studium turbidus omne premit,
te tua Tempe fouent, et amica silentia Musis,
        unde sit, ut uideas, publica tuta salus.
65   Ut uetus eloquio Nestor plus iuuit Achiuos,
        quam manus Aeacidae, Myrmidonumque uigor,
sic tua maiores potuisset habere triumphos
        gens, si consilii res ageretur ope.
Te tua secessu tantum sapientia firmat,
70   et solidat recto tramite tantus honor.
Est honor eximius, quo fulges, ardua regum
        arma geris princeps, unde uocare Leo.
Syluius Aeneas heroibus aequat heraldos,
        hoc nomen Teutho, Graecus at illud habet.
75   Nil secus heiraldus, quam priscus miles in armis,
        significat, talis saepe senecta ualet.
Quis melius belli uel pacis dulcia nouit
        munia? Quam miles, quam ueteranus homo?
Nam deus author erat Liber, qui primus, ut Indos
80   subdidit, heroas iusserat esse uiros.
'Uos ego militia soluo, bellique labore,'

situated under the frosty pole of the western sky; the race of Clan Donald, powerful in arms and nobility, held this land by hard warfare. Now, after that race has yielded to fate, much fury becomes established with raging sword. The bearer will tell this better, in both form and manner; give the same credence to him that you would give to me.

Your virtues make you known to me, by which you always criticise evil ways and exalt those that are good. Lively eloquence and the language and grace of Nestor imbue you, an ethereal poet, with sweet speech. There is freedom for you to criticise profane ways, and so you can be considered to be another Momus himself. Thus your genius flourishes, thus holy Wisdom nurtures you in her own bosom as the years pass by. As a young woman she (Wisdom) once nurtured the harpist, the son of Jesse; she herself was accustomed to being the companion of his cold body. I embrace these virtues, born from such a splendid breast, I cherish them, indeed, with all my heart. [f. 3r] And it is praiseworthy that you have highly transcended human arts, and that you have so established your life, that all may know the Godhead, worship, and adore Him, as you sound forth everywhere by the trumpet of the Gospel. Now, as honour is no longer paid to men of talent, as this disturbed condition unfairly prevents all study, your Valley of Tempe and silence friendly to the Muses nurture you, so that you can see whence public security comes. As old Nestor aided the Greeks more by his eloquence than did the hand of Achilles and the vigour of the Myrmidons, so your nation might have had greater triumphs if affairs were being directed by the help of wise counsel. Your wisdom alone strengthens you in your seclusion, and such great honour makes you strong in the right path. Special is the honour by which you shine; as a prince you bear the lofty arms of kings, wherefore you are called the (Lord) Lyon.

Silvius Aeneas equated heralds with heroes; the one name is Germanic, while the other is Greek. 'Herald' signifies nothing other than an ancient knight in arms; such venerable men are often very worthy. Who knows better the sweet duties of war or peace than a knight, than an experienced veteran?

For the god Bacchus was his maker, who first commanded men to be heroes, when he subjugated the peoples of India. He said, 'I release you from military service and the labour of war,

dixit, 'et heroas nomino, iusque dabo.
Uestrum munus erit, communi instare saluti,
    consulere et regno, publicitusque coli.   [f. 3v]
85 Arguere et sontes, mores laudare benignos,
    esse aliis uacuos semper, ubique uolo.
Suppeditent uictum reges, decus auctius omnes
    ferte apud illustres, xoenia duxque dabit.
Stetque fides uestris (soboles Heroica) dictis.
90   Exhorrete malos proditione reos.
Uos mendax hominum genus exhorrete, perennis
    uobis libertas sit, uia, tuta, mora.
Si uos aut aliquem uestrum ferus anxerit hostis,
    angentis stricto decidat ense caput.'
95 Rex Macedum mundi uictor uos purpura, et auro,
    ornari uoluit, primus et arma dedit.
Iulius et Caesar, Romana monarchia postquam
    constitit, hos tali lege beauit auos.
'Quisquis,' ait, 'belli decimum peruixeris annum,
100   si tibi quadragies ante December abit,
siue pedes fueris, siue ordine clarus equestri,
    aes liber mereas, militiaque uaces.
Postmodo sis heros ueteranus miles, ab aula,
    te uetet a phano nemo uel urbe, foro.
105 Nemo tibi asscribat crimen, nec pondere onustet
    quis, petat aut censum, nemo magister erit.
Si modo delinques, a solo Caesare mulctam
    spectato, Caesar solus et ultor erit.
Censorem timeant homines te, si quid honesto
110   quod modo non quaderet forsan inerter agant.
Arguat et falsi nemo, quod dicis, apertum
    sit tibi iter, tutus sit quoque ubique locus.   [f. 4r]
Mensa, cibus, potus tibi regis in aede parentur,
    teque, tuamque domum, bursa quotennis alat.
115 Quam quoque legitima face duxeris, illa uenusto
    femina sit cultu, sit ueneranda thoro.
Is, quem demerito forte exprobraueris, atque
    dixeris infamem, semper honore uacet.
Quae dederint reges insignia, nomina, et arma,
120   et cultus, heros rex ueterane, feras.
Quodque uoles, facias, dicas, et ubilibet orbis
    gens te nulla uetet, natio, siue lares.
Qui sine iure tibi noceat, ceruice careto,
    iudicium omnimodae nobilitatis habe.'

and call you heroes, and I will give you authority. Your function will be to stand up for the common weal, give counsel to the kingdom, and be honoured at public expense; [f. 3v] I wish you everywhere to expose criminal ways, to praise good behaviour, to be always free for others. Let kings supply your livelihood; bear increasing honour among all illustrious men, and the ruler will give you presents. May trust be given to your words, offspring of heroes; abhor the wicked and guilty for their treachery. Abhor the lying sort of men; may constant freedom, may safe journeying and safe dwelling, be yours. If a fierce enemy has oppressed you or anyone of yours, let the oppressor's head fall by an unsheathed sword.' The king of the Macedonians, conqueror of the world, first wished to ornament you with purple and gold and gave you arms.

Julius Caesar also, after the Roman Empire was established, blessed these veterans with such a decree: he said, 'Whosoever lives through ten years of war, if December has previously gone past you more than forty times, whether you are a foot soldier or distinguished in the cavalry ranks, you should, as a free man, earn payment, and be discharged from the army. Afterwards you are to be a veteran soldier, a hero: let no one bar you from the palace, temple, city or marketplace; let no one accuse you of a crime, nor anyone lay a burden on you, or demand money; no one shall be your master; if you do wrong in any way, expect your penalty from Caesar alone, and Caesar alone shall be your judge. Let men fear you as a judge, if perchance they do anything in lazy fashion that does not square with what is honourable. Let no one claim that what you say is falsehood; let the way be open to you, let everywhere also be a safe place for you. [f. 4r] Let your board, your food, and drink be provided in the king's hall, and let him maintain you and your household annually from his purse. Let that woman whom you take in legitimate marriage also have gracious respect; let her be respected in her marriage. Let him whom you perchance reproach and denounce as disreputable for his faults be without honour. O veteran hero king, may you bear those insignia, titles, arms, and respect that kings have given you. You may do or say whatever you wish, and in all the world let no race, nation, or household forbid you anything. Whoever harms you unjustly, let him lose his head; have judgement over every degree of nobility.'

125 Non minus hos Carolus Magnus donauit honore:
     'Uos,' ait, 'heroes, regibus este pares.
  Uos, socii regum, imbelles seruate pupillos,
     parcite foemellis, pauperibusque probis.
  Consulite, o uigiles ueterani, regibus, atque
130   turpia corripite, et munera habete ducum.
  Munera qui renuet uobis, inglorius esto,
     is nequit ingenuus rure, uel urbe frui.
  Intulerit damnum si quis, uel mouerit iram,
     se maiestatis nouerit esse reum.
135 Utilis heroas decet ergo cautio, tanti
     ne cadat indignis tantus honoris apex.'
  Non tamen haec memoro[4] tibi tam notissima, Dauid,
     ut nouus officii quid doceare tui:
  sed penitus rarum uideo, cui tanta potestas
140   sit, nulla officii parte deesse sui.   [f. 4v]
  Ardua res, tantum meritis attingere honorem[5]
     Plus tamen est ipsum nobilitare gradum.
  Quantum splendorem dedit hic heroicus ordo
     tam tuus heroas luminat ipse decor.
145 Quare age, clare parens, facundum Naestora, regni
     et sociis rectam consule saepe uiam.
  Et qui semper amas, uerumque fateris aperte,
     te praecor, in causa parce tacere mea.
  Nam seriem nostrae non hic recitabo querelae.
150   Me tamen immeritum fors inimica premit.
  Post obitum fratris Sodorensis praesulis olim
     nominor ad uacuum praesulis ipse locum.
  Inuidus ast alius nimia ambitione superbus,
     instat, et hoc nomen quaerere raptor auet.
155 Plura sed huic obstant, ne sit uel praesbyter, ortus
     prostibulo, moecha matre, petulcus, atrox,
  maiestate reus laesa, bastardus, adulter,
     caupo, rapax praedo, prorsus amusus, iners.
  Ter semel addictum patribus puto nomen adeptum,
160   ut sit Patricius, tot satus arte patrum.
  Nona sed huic placido praecessit olympias aeuo
     totque nouos habuit, quot tria lustra, patres.
  His modo tam multis patribus, totiesque patratus
     nomine plus matris, quam patris inde refert.

---

[4]   momoro, Blado.
[5]   houorem, Blado.

Charlemagne gifted them with honour in no less degree: he said, 'You heroes are to be the equal of kings. You, associates of kings, protect defenceless wards, be sparing towards women and the honest poor. O watchful veterans, give counsel to kings, and correct wrongdoing, and have the office of rulers. Whoever denies you your office, he is to be without honour, he cannot freely enjoy countryside or town. If anyone has done harm, or aroused anger, let him know that he is guilty of *lèse majesté*. Therefore helpful prudence is becoming to heroes, lest so great a pinnacle of such great honour should fall to the undeserving.'

I do not, however, remind you of these very well-known things, David, so that, like a newcomer, you may be shown anything that belongs to your office; but I see that it is very rare for those who have so much power not to be deficient in some part of their office.

[f. 4v] It is a hard thing to attain to so much honour by merit, but yet more so to ennoble the office itself. This same grace of yours illuminates heroes with as much splendour as the heroic order has given (you). Wherefore, distinguished father, act like eloquent Nestor, and often advise your companions in the kingdom of the right way.

And, I beg you, you who always love and openly acknowledge the truth, do not keep silent in my cause. For I will not recount here the course of my complaint, although adverse fortune oppresses me undeservedly. But after the death of my brother, the late bishop of the Isles, I myself was nominated to the vacant position of bishop; but then another, envious and proud with excessive ambition, intervened, and as a robber desired to obtain this title. But many things stand in his way, so that he should not even be a priest: he is born of a whore from an adulteress mother, wanton, savage, guilty of *lèse majesté*, a bastard, an adulterer, a huckster, a rapacious thief, totally uncultivated, slothful. I reckon the name given to him once is acquired by those who are thrice fathers, so that he may be 'Patricius', sired by the art of so many fathers: but the ninth Olympiad (i.e., thirty-six years) has passed for him in pleasant age, and he had as many new fathers as three *lustra*. Having now been brought about by so many fathers, and so often, he bears more of his mother than of his father in his name;

165 Sic bene 'Matricius' fiet tam spuria proles,
       quod pater ignotus, cognita mater erat.
    Multorum capitum si pressit belua matrem
       turba, decet natum patribus esse parem.   [f. 5r]
    Dunlopius, Conygham, Maclaenius, Hayus, [et]⁶ Hepburn,
170   Campbel, Barre, Beton, nascitur omnis homo.
    Is, uelut Hesperidum glaucus draco limina seruat,
       praesulis usurpat iure uetante locum.
    Cumque crucem potius metuisset, culmina Regni
       non dubitat stolida poscere mente, nephas.
175 Sed tuus haud candor patitur fortasse tenebras
       audire has, taceo, ne piger ista legas.
    Quod superest, lator referet me, corpore mente,
       hanc, mihi quam⁷ dederis, huic adhibeto fidem.
    Si mortalis habet nil, quo persoluere grates
180   pro merito poterit, Numen abunde dabit.
    Non haec grandisono taxabis uerba boatu,
       dum legis, aut dices haec decuisse parum.
    Uecors et stolidum generis iactare nitorem,
       quem dotes animi destituere, scio.
185 Nec minus esse tui scio muneris arma, genusque
       quam dotes animi noscere, siue bonum.
    Ad quemuis alium sic scribere praeter heraldum
       dedecuit, uitium sic tamen esse nego.
    Nosse tuum titulos, natales, arma, triumphos,
190   est, aeque, ut bene sint omnia, uelle tuum.
    Tu quoque, Pieridum columen Lyndsaie sororum,
       quaeuis longaeuae dona salutis habe.
    Atque ego seu fuero, qua uespertinus Iberno
       Tytan flammigeros aequore tingit equos,
195 luthea seu roseas aperit qua Aurora fenestras,
       urget ubi aeoos torrida zona lares,
    pectore inhaerebis nostro, nec lumine, possum,
       dum fruar, herois non memor esse mei.   [f. 5 v]
    Haec⁸ tibi Noesaeo scripsit Rodericus ab agro
200   Idibus Octobris, perlege, uiue, uale.
       MDXLVIII.

---

⁶ omitted, Blado.
⁷ qnam, Blado.
⁸ Hec, Blado.

so such a false offspring will rather become 'Matricius', because his father was unknown, and his mother has been (thoroughly) known. If a many-headed monster, a crowd, has copulated with his mother, it is fitting that the child is the same as his parents: [f. 5r] each man is born Dunlop, Cunningham, MacLean, Hay, Hepburn, Campbell, Barrie, or Beaton. He usurped the place of the bishop while the law forbade it, just as the blue-grey dragon guards the threshold of the Hesperides. While he should rather have feared punishment – horror! – stupidly he does not hesitate to aspire to the highest place in the kingdom.

But perchance your goodness cannot bear to hear this darkness, so I am silent, lest you be reluctant to read these things. The bearer will tell what remains about me, of body and soul; give the same credence to him as you would give to me. If a man has nothing for which he can give thanks deservedly, the Godhead will supply it abundantly. You will not reproach these words for high-sounding bellowing, or say while you read them that they are unbecoming of me: I know that it is mad and stupid to boast of splendour of family when mental qualities have abandoned you. I know no less the arms of your office, and you are known to be such a talented soul. It would be unfitting to write thus other than to a herald, but I nonetheless deny that this is a fault. It is yours to know titles, births, arms, triumphs, and equally it is yours to wish that all should be well: may you also, Lindsay, pillar of the Muses, have whatever gifts of long-lived health you may wish.

And whether I be where Titan at evening dips his flame-bearing horses in the Irish Sea, or else where golden Dawn throws open her rose-coloured windows, where the torrid region scorches the eastern homes, you will be dear to my heart; neither can I, while I enjoy the light, be unmindful of my hero. [f. 5 v] Roderick has written this to you from the fields of the Ness on 15 October. Read it through; live long; farewell.

1548.

(*See notes, pp. 321–5*)

Hec tibi Noesæo scripsit Rodericus ab agro
Idibus Octobris, perlege, uiue, uale.
M. D. X L V I I I.

AD ILLVSTRISS. MAECOENATEM
D. Iacobum ab Hamylton Comitem Aranyæ Sereniß.
Mariæ Scotorum Reginæ Tutorem, & Regni Gu=
bernatorem D. Roderici Maclenij Stræna gra=
tulatoria de reditu Clarißimi ac incliyti D.
Comitts Huntlij &c. Mæcœnatis sui spe=
ctatißimi primo Iannuarij M. D.
X L I X.

NATE Gathæliadum claro Dux sanguine Regum,
   Qui cum Cælitibus par moderamen habes.
En modo nascentis promittit Ianitor anni
   Iste dies Scotiæ cuncta serena tu æ.
Albion irato lugebat Numine, longos
   Et meruit fletus, quos meruitq; luit.
Ecce nouo rerum series noua nascitur anno,
   Omnia pro uoto nunc habet illa suo.
Placantur Superi, cœpit fauor, ira quieuit,
   Auctior amissus fœnore uenit honos.
Ecce per armatos redit ille Georgius hostes,
   Patria quo, doluit, dum uiduata fuit.
Scottia quem reducem sic amplexata salutat,
   Tu postliminy iure beatus aue.

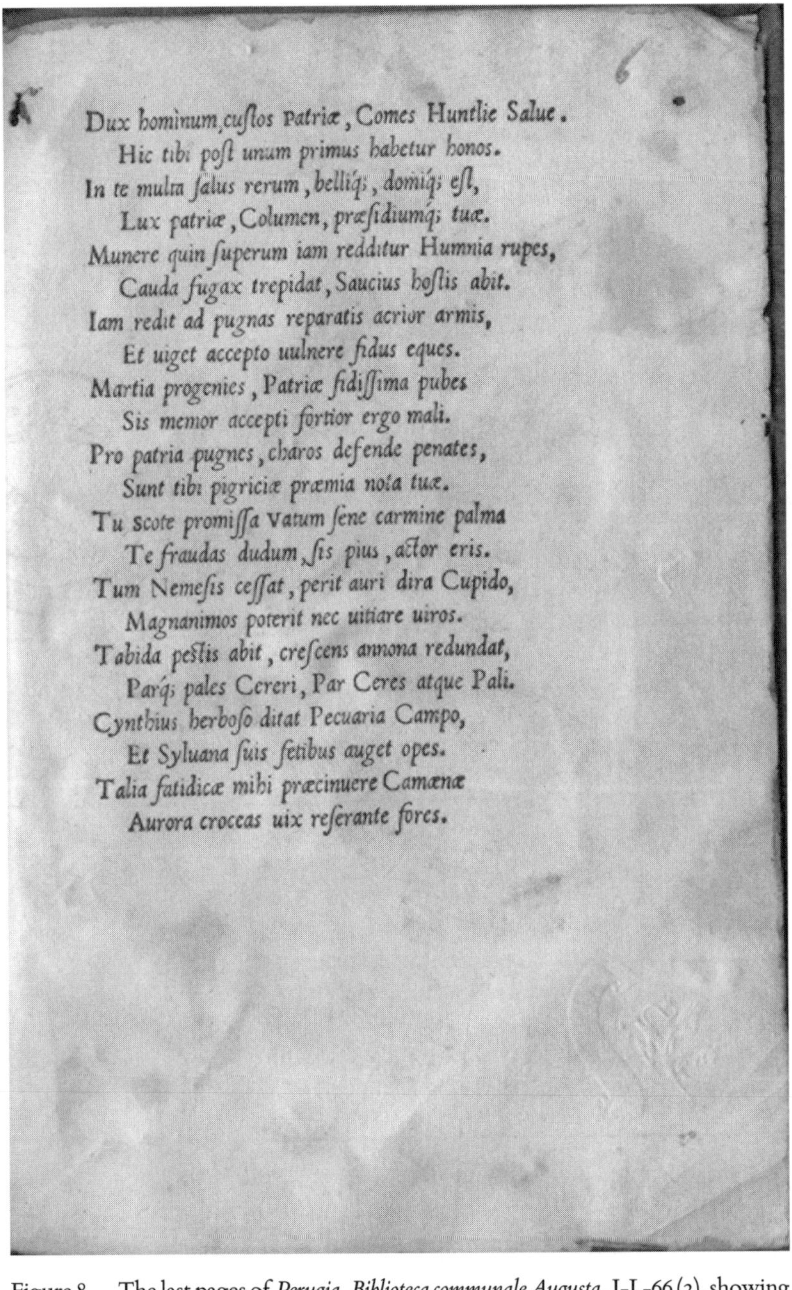

Dux hominum, cuſtos Patriæ, Comes Huntlie Salue.
  Hic tibi poſt unum primus habetur honos.
In te multa ſalus rerum, belliq́, domiq́; eſt,
  Lux patriæ, Columen, præſidiumq́; tuæ.
Munere quin ſuperum iam redditur Humnia rupes,
  Cauda fugax trepidat, Saucius hoſtis abit.
Iam redit ad pugnas reparatis acrior armis,
  Et uiget accepto uulnere fidus eques.
Martia progenies, Patriæ fidiſſima pubes
  Sis memor accepti fortior ergo mali.
Pro patria pugnes, charos defende penates,
  Sunt tibi pigriciæ præmia nota tuæ.
Tu Scote promiſſa Vatum ſene carmine palma
  Te fraudas dudum, ſis pius, actor eris.
Tum Nemeſis ceſſat, perit auri dira Cupido,
  Magnanimos poterit nec uitiare uiros.
Tabida peſtis abit, creſcens annona redundat,
  Parq́; pales Cereri, Par Ceres atque Pali.
Cynthius herboſo ditat Pecuaria Campo,
  Et Syluana ſuis fetibus auget opes.
Talia fatidicæ mihi præcinuere Camænæ
  Aurora croceas uix reſerante fores.

Figure 8. The last pages of *Perugia, Biblioteca communale Augusta*, I-L-66 (2), showing the *Straena Gratulatoria* addressed to the governor, the earl of Arran, in elegiac couplets. By kind permission of the Biblioteca communale Augusta, Perugia.

AD ILLVSTRISS<IMVM> MAECOENATEM

D<ominum> Iacobum ab Hamylton

Comitem Aranyae

Sereniss<imae> Mariae Scotorum Reginae Tutorem,

et Regni Gubernatorem

D<omini> Roderici Maclenii

Straena gratulatoria de Reditu Clarissimi ac Incliti D<omini>

Comitis Huntlii, etc.,

Maecoenatis sui Spectatissimi

primo Ianuarii MDXLIX

A New Year's Gift

to the most illustrious Patron of Letters Lord James Hamilton,
Earl of Arran,

Guardian of her Serene Highness Mary Queen of Scots, and
Governor of the Kingdom,

celebrating the Return of the most famous and noble Lord the
Earl of Huntly,

his most proven Patron of Letters,

by Sir Roderick MacLean

1 January 1549

Nate Gathaeliadum claro dux sanguine regum,
    qui cum caelitibus par moderamen habes.
En modo nascentis promittit Ianitor anni
    iste dies Scotiae cuncta serena tuae.
5 Albion irato lugebat Numine, longos
    et meruit fletus, quos meruitque, luit.
Ecce nouo rerum series noua nascitur anno,
    omnia pro uoto nunc habet illa suo.
Placantur Superi, coepit fauor, ira quieuit,
10   auctior amissus foenore uenit honos.
Ecce per armatos redit ille Georgius hostes,
    patria quo, doluit, dum uiduata fuit.
Scottia quem reducem sic amplexata salutat,
    tu postliminii iure beatus aue.   [f. 6r]
15 Dux hominum, custos patriae, Comes Huntlie salue.
    Hic tibi post unum primus habetur honos.
In te multa salus rerum, bellique, domique est,
    lux patriae, columen, praesidiumque tuae.
Munere quin Superum iam redditur Humnia rupes,
20   cauda fugax trepidat, saucius hostis abit.
Iam redit ad pugnas reparatis acrior armis,
    et uiget accepto uulnere fidus eques.
Martia progenies, patriae fidissima pubes
    sis memor accepti fortior ergo mali.
25 Pro patria pugnes, charos defende penates,
    sunt tibi pigriciae praemia nota tuae.
Tu Scote promissa uatum sene carmine palma
    te fraudas dudum, sis pius, actor eris.
Tum Nemesis cessat, perit auri dira cupido,
30   magnanimos poterit nec uitiare uiros.
Tabida pestis abit, crescens annona redundat,
    parque Pales Cereri, par Ceres atque Pali.
Cynthius herboso ditat pecuaria campo,
    et Syluana suis fetibus auget opes.
35 Talia fatidicae mihi praecinuere Camaenae
    Aurora croceas uix reserante fores.

Ruler born of the famous blood of the kings of the Gael, you who have power equal with the heavenly ones: this day the gatekeeper of the new-born year now promises that everything will be serene for your Scotland. Having angered the Godhead, *Alba* was in mourning, and deserved long weeping, and has atoned for what it deserved.

Lo, a new succession of events is born with the new year: now it has everything in accordance with its prayers. The Heavenly ones are placated, favour has begun, anger has cooled; honour, having been lost, has come (back) greatly increased with interest. Lo, George returns, passing through armed enemies, for whom his homeland lamented while it was bereft of him. Scotland, thus cherishing him, salutes him as he returns: you are blessed by right of restoration, hail! [f. 6r] Leader of men, guardian of your homeland, greetings, Earl of Huntly! At this time the first honour is held to be yours, after one man. In you there is much well-being in affairs of state, in war and at home, light, pillar, and protection of your homeland.

Now indeed, by gift of the Heavens the rock of Hume Castle is restored, the fleeing tail trembles, the wounded enemy flees away. Now he returns to the fight more fiercely, his arms restored, and a faithful knight grows stronger in spite of receiving a wound. Child of Mars, most faithful son of your homeland, may you then, now stronger, remember the ill-treatment you received. May you fight for your homeland, defend your dear home, the noteworthy rewards of your idleness are yours. O Scotsman, you have long cheated yourself of the pre-eminence promised by an old song of the poets: be faithful, and you will be the one who acts.

Then retribution ceases, a deadly lust for gold abates, neither will it be able to corrupt great-hearted men. Wasting disease departs, yield abounds increasingly; Pales is equal to Ceres, and Ceres equal to Pales. Apollo enriches flocks in grassy fields, and Silvana increases resources with her produce. The prophetic Muses have foretold these things to me, as Dawn has barely reopened her saffron doors.

(*See notes, pp. 325–7*)

Notes and Commentary

NOTES

IONIS

Preliminaries

[Title Page] A f. 231r; P1 f. 1r

Roderici Maclenii, etc.: the title of the poem is *Ionis*, gen. *Ionidos*, formed on the model of naming classical poems from their subject + *-is*, *-idos*. An obvious example is the *Aeneid*, 'the song of Aeneas'. MacLean's title contains a pun on the name of Iona and that of Jonah (Vulg. *Iona*) the prophet. His poem is divided into two books, Book I, *De Intuitu Prophetico D. Columbae*, and (starting on A f. 249 r, P1 21r) Book II, *De Virtutibus et Miraculis D. Columbae*. Together, these make up the *Ionid*, 'the Song of Iona' (or 'Song of Jonah'). They are derived from Books i and ii of Adomnán's *Vita Columbae*. MacLean did not paraphrase Adomnán's Book iii, although he was familiar with its contents. Possible reasons for this are discussed in the Introduction, pp. 25–7.

ἸΑΚΩΒΟΥ, etc. See Introduction, pp. 19–20.

συλλαίνει: read σιλλαίνει (cf. Sharpe, 'MacLean', 114).

μήποτε: this word is not correctly used with an indicative verb. Sharpe (loc. cit.) suggests that οὔποτε would be grammatically better.

[P1] A f. 231v; P1 f. 1v Metre: Elegiac couplets.
7–8. *Dira neotericae … uenena Mineruae*: this is unlikely to be a reference to Lutheranism, which was not new, was not hostile to the cult of saints, and which MacLean had experienced at first hand in Wittenberg in the 1530s. It may allude to the rise of Calvinism in the 1540s, or some other 'new learning'. See the Introduction, pp. 27, 51.

[P2] A f. 231v; P1 f. 1v Metre: Elegiac couplets.
2. *Ionis*: 'the Song of Iona', or 'the Song of Jonah', punning on the Hebrew form of Columba's name. See Introduction, pp. 29–30.

[P3] A f. 232r; P f. 2r Metre: Iambic trimeter.
It is clear from this that MacLean has been subject to criticism, but it is not clear who his critics are. Presumably they include the φίλεχθρος ἀνήρ attacked on the title page. See Introduction, pp. 20–1. These verses are in iambic trimeter, a rapid and aggressive metre often used for polemic and invective.

4. *Nil infaceto arridet isti saeculo*: cf. *saeclum ... infacetum* (Catullus, *Carmina* 43.8).

5. *Experirier*: An archaic pres. inf. pass. form found in early verse, esp. in Plautus = *experiri*. Other examples are: *consinuarier* (P5.47), *perdier* (P5.54), *perdier* (2.2.11), *tingier* (2.6.6), *prendier* (2.18.14), *tingier* (2.23.3), *labier* (2.32.63).

10. *Cicutipota*: possibly coined by MacLean; from *cicuta*, 'hemlock' + *potare*.

12. *Alphabeticus*: This is not a classical word; it has possibly been coined by MacLean. Cf. *Hoc discunt omnes ante apha et beta puellae* (Juvenal, *Satires*, 14, 209). *Alphabetum* is found in Gildas, Bede, and in ML.

15. *Uegrandi Tonitruo*: obscure. It is not clear who or what is the 'puny thunderer' or 'little thundering god' to whom those who have bought their degrees profess their arts. MacLean had matriculated at Wittenberg *gratis inscriptus*, presumably the equivalent of gaining a scholarship.

18. *Pars pro bonis accipiunt saepe pessimas*: On the title page, MacLean's supporter James Thorntoun attacks someone who ἀγαθόν τε κακοῦ, μήποτε μᾶλλον ἔχει ('never holds to the good rather than the bad').

30–1. *Nam sunt agrestes*: 'for they are rustics'. Perhaps MacLean's critics had accused him of rusticity? *Sororum coetus*: the Muses.

35. *Philautia*: a Greek word, very rare in Latin of any period (cf. *DMLBS*, s.v.).

[P4] A f. 232v; P1 f. 2v Metre: Elegiac couplets.
Io. Formannus Scotus: The identity of John Forman is discussed in the Introduction, p. 21. The fact that a Scottish writer made comments on MacLean's poetry before *Ionis* was published in Rome in May 1549 indicates that poems of his (whether psalm paraphrases, or drafts of *Ionis*, or other poems now lost) were circulating in Scotland earlier.

[P5] A f. 233r–234 v; P1 f. 3r Metre: Modified third Asclepiad: four Asclepiad lines + one Glyconic.
The introduction proper to the poems. The verse form is unusual. Cf. Sharpe, 'MacLean', 120; *Horace*, ed. Rudd, p. 13; Green, 'Paraphrases', 262–3.

1–20. MacLean begins with a catalogue of classical deities, first of the sea, then of the land, and finally of the heavens; he rejects these deities as immoral in favour of Christian monotheism.

17. *Cypria*: Aphrodite.

29. *Sarae genito*: Isaac.

31. *Uates Solimi*: from LL adj. *Solimus*, 'of Jerusalem': cf. *DMLBS*, s.v.

37. *Flumine et Halitu*: cf. John 3: 5: *quis renatus fuerit ex aqua et Spiritu*.

47. *Consinuarier*: from *con* + *sinuare* ('to bend'). Cf. *consinuacio* in one MS of *Chron. Pluscarden*, x, 20 (ed. F. J. H. Skene, i, 346). For the present infinitive passive form in -*ier*, cf. note on P3.5 above (p. 270).

49. *Ira remissior sanctorum precibus*: This statement is not compatible with Lutheran theology, in which prayers to the saints are not admitted, and they are not seen as mediators of salvation.

61–4. *Uarios ... ortus, ... lares, dicta prophetica, uisus angelicos, craebraque proelia, et magnalia*: Adomnán's Book iii explores Columba's origins, his childhood, and his angelic visions. Books i and ii cover his prophecies and deeds of power. Perhaps MacLean's original intention had been to include Book iii in his paraphrase as well. Cf. *Columbe merita et signa singula, / facta prophetica, clara miracula*, etc., in the hymn at Lauds in his office in the Inchcolm fragment and the Aberdeen Breviary: Macquarrie, *Legends of Scottish Saints*, 138–9.

69. *Eoae foliis arboris*: possibly an allusion to the tree of life in the Garden of Eden: cf. Gen. 2: 8–9.

73-5. *Amathi filius ... siue Peristhera*: Columba's father was Fedlimid, *VC*, 2nd Preface. MacLean frequently refers to Adomnán's pun on the name Columba in different languages: Hebrew *Yona*, name of the prophet Jonah, and Gk περιστερά ('pigeon') (spelt πηριστηρα in the A MS of *VC*). He is called 'son of Amathi', from LXX Ἰωνᾶς υἱός Ἀμαθὶ, Vulg. *Iona filius Amathi*, Jonah son of Amittai (2 Kings 14: 25; Jon. 1: 1). Amittai = 'my truth'.

79. *Qui missus Niniuen*, etc.: Jonah.

82. *Cuius imagine*, etc.: obscure. Perhaps *iura* is a misprint, but one hesitates to suggest an emendation. There is perhaps an allusion to Jonah becoming penitent during his time in the belly of the whale: cf. Jon. 2. MacLean may

also be thinking of the dove (*columba*) sent out over the waters by Noah in
Gen. 8: 8–12.

84–5. *Sareptidos*: the gen. of a Gk adj. σάρεπτις, 'of Zarephath', a place near
Sidon mentioned in 1 Kings. The son of the widow of Zarephath was revived
by Elijah, cf. 1 Kings, 17: 10–24. He is not named in 1 Kings. Jerome, however,
in the Prologue to his Commentary on Jonah, recounts a Jewish tradition that
the son of the widow of Zarephath was called Jonah and was identifiable with
the prophet Jonah son of Amittai (2 Kings, 14: 25; Jon. 1: 1): *Tradunt autem
Hebraei hunc esse filius viduae Sareptanae, quem Elias propheta mortuum suscitavit*
(Migne, *PL*, xxv, cols. 1117–20, at 1118). For Jerome's commentary on Jonah,
cf. J N D Kelly, *Jerome: His Life, Writings, and Controversies* (London, 1975),
220–1. The widow's son is also mentioned by MacLean below, on f. 238 v, and
again on f. 262 v. Cf. *VC*, ii, 32. *Uera et nomen habet*: cf. 1 Kings 17: 24::*Verbum
Domini in ore tuo verum est. Hospite*: Elijah.

89. *Polyhymnia*: muse of song.

[P6] A f. 234v; P1 f. 4v
The queen's genealogy. Professor Sharpe ('MacLean', 120) suggests that
including this was a way of impressing the pope and cardinals as well as of
filling a blank folio (without it the page has only five lines of verse). Also
very significant for MacLean will have been his belief that many of the
kings in the list were buried at *Reilig Odhráin* on Iona: he has mentioned in
P2 that Iona is *uetus Scotorum regum sepulchrum*. The genealogy also contains
some important points of reference for the poems. MacLean mentions that
Columba was a descendant of Gathelus, eponym of the Gael (1.3.8, 2.1.7),
and Gathelus is frequently mentioned. Other kings from the list are named
in the poems: Iber Scot was ancestor of the *Iberides*, the Irish (1.7.11, 1.10.1,
1.35.8); MacLean mentions the *Mithlia gens* and *Mithlii nepotes*, descendants of
Mithlius (= Míl Espáne) (2.31.2, 2.32.11, 2.32.23). The historical kings Áedán
mac Gabráin and Eochaid Buide (Aedanus and Eugenius I), contemporary
with Columba, are mentioned in the poems (1.10). It is also to be borne in
mind that the Hamiltons were descendants of James II, and a reference to
his ancestors will have been flattering to the governor, who was Mary's heir
presumptive and who promoted MacLean's career in the early 1540s, and to his
half-brother the archbishop of St Andrews (elect from 1546). It was common
practice to include genealogical material in Irish and Scottish manuscript
compilations and anthologies.

Most of the names from Ferchardus and Fergusus onwards can be related to
names in the catalogue of kings in the prefatory material to Boece's *Scotorum
Historiae*. From Ferchardus back to Symon the names can be found in Boece,
SH, i, 13, and from Symon back to Mithlius (i) they can be found in Boece,

SH, i, 7. The earliest part of the list, from Mithlius back to Gathaelus son of Neolus, appears to have been cobbled together from more than one source with little regard for chronological direction. Wherever MacLean may have found it, it cannot accurately be described as *ex uetustissimis Gathaelicae nationis hystoriographorum libris decerptam.* (I am grateful to Professor Dauvit Broun for his comments and advice on this section. A convenient edition of Boece's *Scotorum Historiae*, to be used with caution, is edited by Dana F Sutton and is available at http://www.philological.bham.ac.uk/boece/, 26 February 2010.)

The genealogy's main interest is that it shows the sort of genealogical material which was circulating in mid-sixteenth-century Scotland, and which was being passed off as 'very ancient historical writings of the Gaelic race'. MacLean presumably accepted it as such in good faith. It is also of interest in that it shows MacLean was influenced by the writings of Hector Boece.

Hic habes apodixin: lit., 'here you have a demonstration', addressed to the reader. The word is rare. Cf. Aulus Gellius, *Noctes Atticae*, 17.5.5: *Argumenta autem censebat* (Cicero) *aut probabilia esse debere aut perspicua et minime controversa, idque 'apodixin' vocari dicebat, cum ea quae dubia aut obscura sunt, per ea quae ambigua non sunt inlustrantur.* Cf. also Quintilian, *Inst.* 5.10.7.

Chennethus I: from Kenneth mac Alpin onwards names have been anglicised in the translation.

Book 1

[1.1] A f. 235r; P1 f. 5r (*VC*, i, 1) Metre: Hexameter.
Phanaloga: obscure. Either from φαίνω ('disclose'), or (perhaps less likely) from *fanum* ('church, temple'), + λόγος ('discourse, narrative').

1. *En Falbaee* ...: Sharpe ('MacLean', 121) calls this section 'the most original part of the work', an imaginary conversation between Adomnán and his predecessor Faílbe (d. 674). Although MacLean says it is taken from the Second Preface, such a conversation is in fact mentioned briefly in *VC*, i, 1. The modern chapter numbers are not in the MSS, and in MacLean's MS the Second Preface may possibly have led without a break into the chapter labelled i, 1 in modern editions of *VC*. In MS A the list of chapter headings comes in between.

3. *Popelli*: cf. Hor., *Epistles* 1.7.65; Persius Flaccus, *Satires* 4.15, 6.50.

4. *Seginaeo*: Ségéne, fifth abbot of Iona, 623–52. *Ostualdus*: Oswald was king of Northumbria 634–42.

14. *Laedae … proles*: the sons of Leda by Zeus were Castor and Pollux. The sun is in Gemini from 21 May to 21 June each year, so the feast of Columba's death (9 June) falls under Gemini. The conversation between Faílbe and Adomnán is thus envisaged taking place after Matins/Lauds on the feast of St Columba (cf. *natalis quoque lux aderit nunc illius*) during Faílbe's abbacy (669–79).

16. *Ronanus*: according to the Book of Leinster and other Irish sources, Adomnán's father was Rónán son of Tinne. (Anderson, *ESSH*, i, 210; Ó Riain, *CGSH*, nos. 340, 662.15, 733.1) Rónán (from a diminutive of Gaelic *rón*, 'seal') was the name of a number of Irish saints. (Ó Riain, *Dictionary*, 538–41) A Rónán who was active in Northumbria in the 650s is mentioned by Bede. (*HE*, iii, 25) St Rónán figures prominently in the Irish tale *Buile Shuibne* (Dillon, *The Cycle of the Kings*, 69–74). In Scotland, the best-known Rónán was Rónán of Kingarth and Kilmaronock (Macquarrie, *Legends of Scottish Saints*, 56–7, 410–11). The parish church on Iona was *Teampull Rónáin*, and MacLean will certainly have known this. Here, however, MacLean associates Rónán father of Adomnán with the Isle of (North) Rona: see following.

20. *Ultra Leusiacas cautes*: *Leusiacus* is an adjectival form, apparently corresponding to Gaelic *Leòdhasach*, 'of Lewis'. This is MacLean's Latinisation of the name of the Isle of Lewis, Gaelic *Leòdhas*. The reference is to the Isle of (North) Rona, the island of St Ronan, seventy-one kilometres off the Butt of Lewis. MacLean held the parsonage of Barvas in Lewis (*RSS*, ii, 2045, where it is spelt *Leous*), in which parish North Rona lies. Clearly he associates Rónán, father of Adomnán, with the dedicatee of the chapel of St Ronan on the Isle of Rona, though we do not know if this association had been made earlier. The *Leusiacae cautes* were presumably the skerries and stacks at the Butt of Lewis. (On the early Christian remains on Rona, see Canmore, 1472 ff.: http://canmore.rcahms.gov.uk/en/site/1479/details/rona/.) The vividness of MacLean's description might imply that he had visited the Butt of Lewis. His nephew and successor as archdeacon, Donald Monro, provides detailed descriptions of Lewis (*Leoʒus*) and Rona. See Munro, *Monro's Western Isles*, 86–8.

21. *Delphinum socius*: Seals, dolphins, and killer whales occur in the waters between Lewis and Rona. Donald Monro comments concerning Rona: 'In this ile thay use to tak mony quhaillis and utheris great fisches' (Munro, *Monro's Western Isles*, 88).

29. *Auricomos Tytanis Lucifer ortus*: the morning star preceding sunrise. The Titan Hyperion was equated with the sun. For *auricomos* referring to the dawn, cf. Valerius Flaccus, *Argonautica* 4.92; in a different context, cf. Verg., *Aen.* 6.141. Given his predilection for Greek forms, MacLean might have been

expected to use the Gk gen. *Titanos*, but gen. *Titanis* is found in medieval writers (cf. *DMLBS*, s.v.).

31. *Haec, ubi phana … fundamen Ionida dixit*: cf. Adomnán, *VC*, i, 1, p. 12, lines 8–11.

39. *Atque … terrae*: MacLean refers several times to a pun on the name Iona, linking it with Hebrew *Yona* (Jonah), 'pigeon, dove', equivalent to Latin *columba*. Here he is suggesting that Columba changed its name from *Ia* to *Iona* when Columba expelled the demons, consecrating it by the Hebrew version of his own name. In fact, the form Iona was a much more recent innovation: cf. Sharpe, *Adomnán*, n. 56, 257–9. It may be that MacLean played an important part in popularising the form *Iona* alongside the older *Ì*. See above, Introduction, pp. 29–30.

41. *Fecit multoties … natitare per undas*: cf. *VC*, i, 1, p. 12, lines 22–6.

44–53. *Qua ferus hesperio … seuisse Prophetam*: This passage of ten lines, interrupting the narrative, refers to a legend about Columba's arrival on Iona which is not in *VC*, which purports to explain the origin of the large number of stone cairns on the shore at Port na Curaich and Port an Fhir-bhreige at the south end of Iona. One of the mounds can be fancifully thought to resemble an upturned *curach*. Cf. RCAHMS, *Argyll*, iv, *Iona*, 257, http://canmore. rcahms.gov.uk/en/site/21634/details/iona+port+na+curaich/ . The cairns were noticed by Pococke in 1760 (*Tours*, 87) and by Pennant in 1777 (*Tour*, i, 298), both of whom conjectured that they were constructed as penitential exercises. MacLean's description is the earliest written evidence we have for their existence and confirms that they are medieval.

47. *Insuetum per iter*: cf. Verg., *Aen.* 6.16. *Saxa latentia*: cf. Verg., *Aen.* 1.108. If Columba is envisaged approaching *via* the southern shore of Mull, he will have passed the tooth-like cliffs and arches at Carsaig and the Torran Rocks.

49. *Undisonum*: cf. Valerius Flaccus, *Argonautica*, 1.363–4: *hic patrium frangit Neptunius aequor qui tenet undisonam Psamathen* (note the allusion to Neptune); cf. ibid., 4.44.
Sancta comitante caterua: cf. Verg., *Aen.* 2.40 and 2.370.

50. *Fessam … cymbam*: cf. Verg., *Aen.* 1.168, for *fessus* with reference to ships.

54. *Hincque leuans unum*, etc.: Here MacLean returns to the narrative of *VC*, i, 1, which he has interrupted 10 lines earlier.

77–8. *Sed caeleste iubar ... depulit umbras*: cf. *VC*, i, 1, p. 12, last two lines, and p. 14, line 1. *De uertice sacrificantis*: cf. the Inchcolm Antiphoner Fragment (EUL MS 211.iv), in one of the antiphons at Lauds: *Sancto de uertice sacrificantis lux resplenduit diuine claritatis* (quoted in Macquarrie, *Legends of Scottish Saints*, 343). The wording of the corresponding antiphon in the Aberdeen Breviary is less close (ibid., 128). Cf. *VC*, iii, 17: *Sanctus Brendenus ... quendam criniosum igneum globum et ualde luminosum de uertice sancti Columbae ante altare stantis et sacram oblationem consecrantis tamdiu ardentem ... uidit* ('St Brendan saw a radiant and very bright fiery ball glowing from St Columba's head while he stood at the altar and consecrated the sacred oblation').

80–1. *Bathinaeus atque Diormitius*: MacLean has slipped up here. Baithéne, second abbot of Iona, died in *AU* 598, and so cannot have spoken to Faílbe (d. *AU* 679). The date of Diarmait's death is not recorded, but he is named as one of Columba's original twelve companions in 563 (*VC*, 238), so is unlikely to have been young at the time of Columba's death. According to Adomnán, he survived Columba by many years (*VC*, ii, 30).

87. *Uisu ... meridiano*: cf. *VC*, iii, 19: *Et sicut nullus aesteum et meridianum solem ... potest intueri*. MacLean here and in the preceding lines is echoing language from Adomnán's Book iii, with which he was clearly familiar although he does not include it in his paraphrase.

90. *Posteriora Tonantis*: cf. Ex. 33: 23: *Videbis posteriora mea*. *Tonans* (also found at 2.1.17, 2.16.29, 2.18.58, 2.24.29, 2.30.84, 2.30.131, 2.35.47, 2.36.35, 2.36.37, Ps19) and *tonitruus* (P3.15) were originally epithets for Jupiter, later applied to the Christian Deity.

96. *Nemo Deum uiuens cernit*: cf. John 1: 18.

97. *Mors ante Deum nimium preciosa piorum*: cf. Ps. Vulg. 115: 15 (116: 15): *pretiosa in conspectu Domini mors sanctorum eius*.

100. *Spiritus artus*: cf. Verg., *Aen.* 4.336.

102–3. *Tyrannis cornua deiecit*: cf. Ps. Vulg. 74: 11 (75: 10): *omnia cornua impiorum confringam*.

108. *Cathalone Britanno*: called Catlo (acc. Catlonem, abl. Catlone) by Adomnán in *VC*, i, 1, Caedualla by Bede in *HE*, ii, 20 and iii, 1. The Battle of Heavenfield near Hexham was fought in 634.

112. *Cum docuit nostra Christum leue uulgus in aula*: if MacLean is here implying that Oswald (born *c.* 603) had seen Columba (d. 597) in person, he has slipped up. But he may only be implying that Oswald remembered him in his vision as he envisaged him preaching. MacLean may have had in mind Bede's description of Oswald's participation when St Aidan preached to his court in Northumbria: *HE*, iii, 3. *Leue uulgus*: cf. Ovid, *Met.* 12.53.

113. *Sis animosus*, etc.: cf. 1 Cor. 16: 13.

119–21. *Barbarus ense cadet ... armis*: cf. Hor., *Odes* 2.7.9–12.

121. *Inglorius armis*: cf. Verg., *Aen.* 10.52.

124–5. *Nostramque camaenam ... memorent pugiles et certatura iuuentus.* Perhaps a reference to *VC*, i, 1, fo. 9b, where Adomnán describes how some warriors escaped from their enemies in battle after they had sung songs praising and commemorating Columba.

127. *Hora ... octaua*: MacLean appears here to be treating the day as consisting of twenty-four equal hours. The conversation is interrupted by the summons to Prime at about eight o'clock.

129. *Iambis*: This might seem to imply that MacLean was intending the next section to be composed in iambic metre. In fact the next twelve poems (1.2 – 1.13) are in a variety of Horatian lyric metres, mostly derived from Book i of Horace's *Odes*. Not until 1.14 ff. does he start using iambic dimeter.

[1.2] A f. 237r–v; P1 f. 7r–v (*VC*, 2nd Preface) Metre: Sapphic stanzas.
For St Maucte or Mochta of Louth (d. *AU* 535), cf. R Sharpe, 'Saint Mauchteus, *discipulus Patricii*', in A Bammesberger and A Wollman (eds), *Britain, 400–600: Language and History* (Heidelberg, 1990), 85–93; cf. also Sharpe, *Adomnán*, 244–5. *VC*, MS A has Maucteus; the B MSS have Macteus. Presumably the MS from which MacLean was working had *Mauteus* or *Maucteus*, which he misread by confusion of minims. Cf. Sharpe, 'MacLean', 121. See Introduction, p. 54.

1–2. *Praescius ... nascituri dixerat uates*: cf. Verg., *Aen.* 6.65–6: *sanctissima uates praescia uenturi.* Adomnán has *filius nasciturus est* (*VC*, 2nd Preface).

9. *Amathite*: earlier Columba is called *Amathi filius*, from the LXX Gk form (Ἀμαθί) of the name of Jonah's father Amittai (Vulg. Amathi).

13–14. *Eius et nostrum ... separantur*: cf. *Mei et ipsius duorom monasteriolorum aggelluli unius sepisculae interuallo disterminabuntur, VC*, 2nd Preface. The church traditionally associated with Maucte, at Louth, is not near any Columban monastery. Cf. Sharpe, *Adomnán*, 244–5.

[1.3] A f. 237 v; P1 f. 7v (*VC*, iii, l) Metre: Second Asclepiad.
Ethnae Parentis Uaticinium: MacLean's version of Eithne's vision departs considerably from Adomnán's account in *VC*, iii, 1.

4. *Tum mundo rediere aurea saecula*: cf. Verg., *Ecl.* 4.9: *toto surget gens aurea mundo*. Vergil's *Eclogue* 4 was much read and studied in the Middle Ages, as it was thought to prefigure the birth of Christ. Eithne's prophecy shares its spirit, though (except here) MacLean does not borrow much of its language.

21. *Arae et thure calent sacro*: cf. Verg., *Aen.* 1.416–7: *ture calent arae*. (Cf. also 2.36.29 below.)

23. *Haelian*: the prophet Elijah. Called Elia (MS A) and Helia (MSS B) in *VC*, ii, 32. Columba is likened to him because he revived a dead child (1 Kings 17). MacLean mentions the son of the widow of Zarephath, who became identified with the prophet Jonah, several times.

26. *Bisseptena ... triaeteris*: Columba was born in 521 and left Ireland in 563, at the age of forty-two.

35. *Coelo dux populis erit*: cf. *VC*, iii, 1: *innumerabiliumque animarum dux ad caelestem a Deo patriam est praedistinatus*.

43–4. *Gratus nemo sit in sua cum uates patria*: cf. Mat. 13: 57: *non est propheta sine honore nisi in patria sua*.

49. *Nil mortale feret bonum*: cf. *Nil mortale loquar* (Hor., *Odes* 3.25.18).

54ff. *Ut Sarae puer*, etc.: A list of children born to their mothers late in life: Isaac son of Sarah, the son of the widow of Zarephath (identified with Jonah), Samuel son of Hannah, John the Baptist son of Elizabeth.

60. *Manteus, Mantei*: see above, 1.2.

61. *Sic uisus iubet Angelus*. The angelic vision is the central theme of *VC*, iii, 1, but it finds only a very brief mention in MacLean's poem.

[1.4] A f. 238v–239r; P1 f. 8v–9r Metre: Fourth Archilochian.
5. *Centaurus*: the name of a large ship. The extended metaphor that follows connects poetry with ships and sailing, a metaphor that MacLean has used

before at P5.90. The *Centaur* was one of Aeneas's fleet: Verg. *Aen.* 5.122 ff.; 10.195. In *Aen.* 5, it sails too close to shore and runs aground.

11. *Cymbola*: cf. *DMLBS*, s.v. cymba, cymbula, symba; *OLD*, s.v. cumbula.

[1.5] A f. 239r–v; P1 f. 9r–v (*VC*, i, 2) Metre: Fourth Asclepiad.
1. *Ista colonia*: Columba's physical body. Cf. *VC*, i, 2: *Statim namque post meum de hoc ad Christum saeculo exspectatum et ualde desideratum transitum* ('Immediately after my expected and much wished-for passing from this world to Christ'). Elsewhere in the poem, MacLean uses *colonia* to mean a monastery dependent on Iona (1.26.8, 1.35.7), but that cannot be its meaning here. Cf. 2 Cor. 5: 1: *Scimus enim quoniam si terrestris domus nostra huius habitationis dissolvatur quod aedificationem ex Deo habeamus...* ('For we know that if our earthly dwelling-house is destroyed, we have a building from God...').

2. *In decimis orbibus*: a reference to Ptolemaic cosmology. The tenth sphere was the sphere of the *Primum mobile*, with the Empyrean beyond it.

5. *Fintenum*: St Fintén or Munnu was eventually abbot of Taghmon, County Wexford. He died in *AU* 635. He had a cult in Argyll as St Mun, but MacLean may not have known of the connection. Cf. R Butter, 'St Munnu in Ireland and Scotland: an exploration of his cult', in S Boardman and E Williamson (eds), *The Cult of Saints and the Virgin Mary in Medieval Scotland* (Woodbridge, 2010), 21–42.

16. *Albion*: MacLean uses this word, used by Bede and popularised by Geoffrey of Monmouth, as a name for northern Britain. He is doubtless influenced by the Gaelic word *Alba*, 'Scotland'. Cf. Watson, *CPNS*, 10–13; A L F Rivet & C Smith, *The Place-Names of Roman Britain* (1979), 247–8.

20. *Abbatique Ronanidae*: Adomnán himself. Cf. *VC*, i, 2, where in the last paragraph Adomnán claims to have heard the story directly from Oisséne.

21ff. *Foelix exilium*, etc.: The tone of these lines is similar to that of the 'Refrain' section, *O mors beata uisio*, first encountered after 1.19 and then repeated frequently. These lines could be regarded as an adaptation of the 'Refrain' section to the Fourth Asclepiad stanza. Both are based on a passage from Adomnán's iii, 23 (ed. Anderson, 232), which may have been the original ending of Adomnán's work: cf. note on 1.19 below, p. 284.

29. *Quis mihi det pennas*: cf. Ps. Vulg. 54: 6 (55: 6).

[1.6] A f. 240r; P1 f. 10r (*VC*, i, 3) Metre: Third Asclepiad.

10. *Clecense*: Clonmacnoise, called by Adomnán *in Clonoensi cenubio*. MacLean's form is unusual and not easily explained. In his bull of provision to the bishopric of the Isles in 1550, after *Ionis* was written, Clonmacnoise is called *ecclesia Cluanen'*: Rome, VA, RV 1791, 114r–116v; below, Appendix, p. 338.

17. *Tu Diuine gregis ductor Ionii*: Ernéne son of Craséne is here addressing Faílbe. According to *VC*, i, 3, Ernéne told this story to Ségéne in the presence of Faílbe, who heard it and later related it to Adomnán. Ernéne mac Craséni died in *AU* 635; cf. Sharpe, *Adomnán*, 259, n. 58.

[1.7] A f. 240r–v; P1 f. 10r–v (*VC*, i, 4) Metre: Alcmanic.
Coennicus: for Cainnech of Achad Bó, cf. Sharpe, *Adomnán*, 262, n. 68. His cult centre was originally at Aghaboe in Ossory; Kilkenny (*Cill Chainnig*) was also an important dedication. Cainnech died in *AU* 600.

[1.8] A f. 240v; P1 f. 10v (*VC*, i, 5) Metre: Greater Sapphic.
Columbanum, etc.: Adomnán's *Carubdis Brecani* is the strait between mainland County Antrim and Rathlin Island. MacLean, on the other hand, was probably thinking of the Corryvreckan Whirlpool between Jura and Scarba (NR 6902).

10. *Et salutabit … sodales*: presumably he will greet the monks of Iona upon his safe arrival. Adomnán has *ad nos transnauigare incipiens*.

[1.9] A f. 240+ 1r; P 11r (*VC*, i, 6) Metre: Alcaic.
1. *Tercio iam mense*: Adomnán has *tribus non minus vicibus* ('no less than three times'). It is not clear why MacLean changes this.

[1.10] A f. 240 + 1r–v; P 11r–v (*VC*, i, 9) Metre: Hipponactean.
1. *Aedeane Iberidum*: Áedán mac Gabráin, king of Dál Riata 574–c. 608. His reign was undoubtedly very important, but historical and legendary accounts of it (including Adomnán's) are problematic and difficult to reconcile. Cf. Sharpe, *Adomnán*, 270–1, n. 84. This section is addressed by Columba to Áedán. His family claimed descent from Iber Scot: cf. P6.

7. *Artur atque Ethodius*: *ATig.* records the death of *Eochaid Finn 7 Artúr* s.a. 596, but there may have been a conflation of accounts of more than one battle in the Annals, as they are not mentioned in *AU* 596, which mentions only Bran and Domangart at this point. Cf. Charles-Edwards, *The Chronicle of Ireland*, i, 118–9 and n. Adomnán places the death of Domangart at a different time *in Saxonia*, and does not mention Bran at all. Áedán had two sons called Eochaid.

8. *Miathei*: Adomnán calls this people *Miathi* (gen. plu. *Miathorum*) in *VC*, i, 8 & 9. MacLean's form is gen. sing. of an adj. *Miatheus* ('of the Miathi'),

in agreement with *hostis*. Dio Cassius mentions a people called the *Maeatae* during the reign of Septimius Severus (193–211). Cf. Rivet & Smith, *Place-Names of Roman Britain*, 404; Sharpe, *Adomnán*, 268–9; Macquarrie, *Saints of Scotland*, 103ff.

10. *Belgicorum*. Adomnán has *in Saxonia bellica in strage* ('in a warlike carnage in England' –the word-order is typical of Adomnán's style). MacLean has apparently misread or misunderstood Adomnán's *bellica* as *Belgica*, which would yield *in Saxonia Belgica in strage* 'in a carnage in Belgian Saxony'.

15–16. *Eugenes Ethodius Minerua*: Eochaid Buide ('yellow': king of Dál Riata *c.* 608–29). Minerva was traditionally portrayed with blond hair. The epithet *Minerva flava* is found in Ovid (*Amores*, 1.1.7–8; *Met.* 8.275). It was later used by George Buchanan: cf. McGinnis & Williamson, *Buchanan*, 109.

20. *Trecenta lustra*: 300 x 5 years = 1,500 years. MacLean was writing about 940 years after the accession of Eochaid Buide (called Eugenius I in P6).

[1.11] A f. 240 + iv; P1 f. iiv (*VC*, i, 11) Metre: Ionic *a minore*.
Scanlani, etc.: The story of Scandlán mac Colmáin, cryptically abbreviated from *VC*, i, 11. MacLean omits Adomnán's introductory and concluding sentences, and only paraphrases Columba's speech to Scandlán. On Scandlán mac Colmáin, king of Osraige (Ossory), cf. Sharpe, *Adomnán*, 272–3. Scandlán died *c.* 643 (*ATig.*). Áed mac Ainmirech, king of northern Uí Neill, died *AU* 598. Here the Irish name *Áed* is latinised as *Oedo*, gen. *Oedonis*; but cf. note on 1.29 below.

8. *Tria uiues*: MacLean deliberately does not say for three 'whats' Scandlán will live. Adomnán says that Columba predicted he would reign again *per tria ... breuia tempora*, from which Scandlán assumed he would live for three years, but he in fact died after three months.

[1.12] A f. 240+iv; P1 f. iiv (*VC*, i, 13) Metre: First Archilochian.
Áengus mac Áeda mhic Chommáin was king of Cenél Coirpri in County Longford until his death in *AU* 649, more than half a century after Columba's death: cf. Sharpe, *Adomnán*, 275. There is no obvious reason why MacLean should have included this story about an obscure kindred in the west Midlands of Ireland while omitting stories about the much more prominent Irish kings Domnall mac Áeda (*VC*, i, 10) and Áed Sláine mac Diarmata (*VC*, i, 14), both of whom were overkings of the Uí Néill. He also omits the story of Roderc son of Tothail king of Petra Cloithe (*VC*, i, 15), even though one would have expected him to recognise that *Cloithe* = Clyde (Gaelic *Cluaidh*), and that therefore the story is of Scottish interest, concerning a king of Dumbarton.

[1.13] A f. 241r; P1 f. 12r (cf. *VC*, i, 43, and i, 50) Metre: Third Asclepiad. This poem begins with another conventional apology for the author's use of lyric verse for an exalted subject. It is intended to prepare the reader for the simpler treatment of the material (in iambic dimeter) in 1.14 – 1.37. The last of these, 1.37, is based on the first half of *VC*, i, 43, while the latter part of 1.13 (lines 29 ff.) is loosely based on the second half of *VC*, i, 43 (see below), and the last three stanzas (lines 41 ff.) are based on the last paragraph of *VC*, i, 50. The point, made rather obscurely, is that these simple poems only scratch the surface of Columba's greatness, while some more high-sounding poetry exaggerates the quality of its subject matter.

7. *Digito*: Is it possible that MacLean is here playing on the word *digitus* ('finger'), as a pun for *dactylus*, the metrical foot dactyl (δάκτυλος = finger), and by extension heroic dactylic verse? In 1.4 he has already apologised for using lyric verse for a subject better suited to epic verse.

10. *Calamo*: Here as elsewhere MacLean uses *calamus* to mean a pen (1.1.12, 1.1.88, 1.1.126).

14. *Ductio*: obscure. Perhaps 'drawing' in the artistic sense, or perhaps in the sense of drawing a veil or covering over a picture? See the following note.

15–16. *Cerne ... contegunt*: obscure. Cloths could be used to cover unfinished paintings, or to make erasures. It is not clear what MacLean has in mind here. Cf. *hanc uelamine teximus* in line 40 below.

21. *Thersites*: a minor character in the *Iliad*, notably ugly and foul-mouthed.

23. *Paelion*: Mount Pelion, a high mountain in Thessaly.

29ff. *Iam digne poterit*, etc. Derived from the second half of *VC*, i, 43 (as noted by Sharpe, 'MacLean', 123).

30. *Sacramenta*: cf. *obscurissimum sacramentum*, *VC*, i, 43.

36. *Gentis doctor apostolus*: St Paul, mentioned by name in *VC*, i, 43, was 'the Apostle of the gentiles'. Adomnán refers here to 2 Cor. 12: 2 ff. MacLean may also have been thinking of 1 Cor. 13: 12.

41ff. *Quin Sancti ... arbore*: cf. *VC*, i, 50: ... *quasi quaedam parua aliquando stillicidia ueluti per quasdam rimulas alicuius pleni uassis fermentissimo nouo distillabant uino ... Deus nonnulla ex eis, uellint nollint ipsi deuulgat* ('as it were like some small drops

dripped through the cracks in a vessel full of strongly fermented new wine
... willy-nilly God makes some of them known').

49. *Foco ... Sycano*: the flames of Mount Etna in Sicily, where Hephaestus
had his forge.

[1.14] A f. 241 + 1r; P1 f. 13r (*VC*, i, 16) Metre: Iambic dimeter.
The characters named in this chapter are unidentified.

[1.15] A f. 241 + 1r–v; P1 f. 13r–v (*VC*, i, 18) Metre: Iambic dimeter.
9. *Occurret unus obuiam*: Adomnán names this man in *VC*, i, 18 as Laisrán mocu
Moie, a gardener.

[1.16] A f. 241 + 1v; P1 f. 13v (*VC*, i, 19) Metre: Iambic dimeter.
De ceto magno, etc. A very literal paraphrase of *VC*, i, 19. Both journeys
described are from Iona to *Ethica insula*. This is Adomnán's name for Tiree.
Donald Monro calls it *Thiridh* (*Western Isles*, 65). Cf. Watson, *CPNS*, 85–6.

16. *Cete*: elsewhere in 1.16 and in P5.80, MacLean treats *cetus* as second dec.
masc.; but in this instance it looks like a Gk fem. noun, presumably for metrical
purposes. For the form *cete* as neut. plu., cf. *OLD*, s.v. *cetus*.

[1.17] A f. 241+1v–242r; P1 f. 13v–14r (*VC*, i, 21) Metre: Iambic dimeter.
5. *Cathyrida*: Adomnán calls him *Nemanus filius Cathir*; MacLean's form is a
classicisation of *Mac Cathir*.

7–8. *Equinam ... carnem*: For the taboo on eating horseflesh, cf. Sharpe,
Adomnán, 282–3, n. 118. Cf. also Giraldus Cambrensis, *Topographia Hiberniae*,
lib. iii, cap. 25; ed. J F Dimock (RS, 1861–91), v, 169.

10. *Hymba*: Adomnán mentions an island called Hinba, containing an important
Columban monastery, a number of times. It was (like his monastery in Tiree,
though not necessarily at the same time) a place to which penitents were sent.
On MacLean's identification of Hinba with the Colonsay/Oronsay group, see
notes on 1.35 below. MacLean's spelling *Hymba* may be of interest: in modern
Scots Gaelic orthography the nasal *n* is regularly changed to *m* before the labial
consonants *b, f, m, p*, and he may be applying that rule here.

[1.18] A f. 242r–v; P1 f. 14r–v (*VC*, i, 22) Metre: Iambic dimeter.
This is a very literal paraphrase of Adomnán's chapter.

18. *Horresco ... cogitans*: cf. Verg. *Aen*. 2.204.

20. *In continentem*: Adomnán says explicitly *in Maleam insulam* ('onto the Isle of Mull').

44. *De Turtreis nepotibus*: the *Uí Thuirtri*, one of the kindreds of the Airgialla (Oriel), dwelling west of Lough Neagh.

[1.19] A f. 242v; P1 f. 14v (*VC*, i, 23) Metre: Iambic dimeter.
17ff. *O mors beata uisio*, etc. MacLean indicates that these twenty lines are to be used as a refrain after many of the following poems until the end of Book 1. Cf. Introduction, p. 56; Sharpe, 'MacLean', 124. These lines are based on a passage in *VC*, iii, 23 (134b, ed. Anderson, p. 232): *Hic itaque nostro praedicabili patrono uitae terminus fuit, ista meritorum exordia; qui, secundum sententias Scripturarum, aeternis comes triumphis, Patribus additus, Apostolis et Prophetis consertus, numero aggregatus albatorum millium agnino in sanguine suas Sanctorum qui lauerunt stolas, agnum ductorem comitatur, uirgo immaculatus, ab omni integer labe, ipso domino nostro Iesu Christo dignante: cui est cum Patre honor, uirtus, laus, gloria, et imperium sempiternum in unitate Spiritus Sancti, per omnia saecula saeculorum.* This may have been the original ending of Adomnán's work: the Metz MS and some of the derived versions end at this point (cf. *VC*, ed. Anderson, pp. lxii f., 233 n.). Adomnán's passage is derived in turn from passages in Evagrius's life of St Antony, Sulpicius's life of St Martin, and Rev. 7: 14 (cf. Anderson, loc. cit.; Sharpe, *Adomnán*, 377, n. 420). This is another example of MacLean echoing material from Adomnán's Book iii, even though his work does not include a paraphrase of that book. Cf. also the second part of 1.5, beginning *Foelix exilium*, which could be regarded as a paraphrase of this passage in the Fourth Asclepiad stanza.

[1.20] A f. 242v; P1 f. 14v (*VC*, i, 24) Metre: Iambic dimeter.
1. *Lugbeus*: In *VC*, Adomnán mentions frequently a monk called both Luigne and Luigbe (Lugneus, Lugbeus), whose family name is given as both mocu Blai and mocu Min. MacLean assumes, probably correctly, that these are different manifestations of a single person. He was an eyewitness to a number of Columba's prophecies and miracles. In MacLean's poems he is mentioned in 1.13, 1.20, 1.23, 1.37, and 2.18. But cf. Sharpe, *Adomnán*, 288–9.

[1.21] A f. 243r; P1 f. 15r (*VC*, i, 25) Metre: Iambic dimeter.
2. *Fretum*: The Sound of Iona (*Caol Ì Chaluim Chille*), frequently mentioned by Adomnán.

4. *Atramentarium*: Not CL, but cf. *atramentarium scriptoris*, Vulg. Ez. 9: 2, 9: 3, 9: 11.

12. *Atramen*: CL is *atramentum*. Perhaps MacLean has coined a third declension neuter noun for metrical reasons.

[1.22] A f. 243r; P1 f. 15r (*VC*, i, 26) Metre: Iambic dimeter.
1. *Luce Martis*: Tuesday. Adomnán has *die iii feriae*. Wednesday and Friday were normally fast days in Celtic monasteries: cf. Sharpe, *Adomnán*, 287, n. 129.

6. *Aedanus ortus masculi*: Adomnán calls him *Aidanus ... filius Fergnoi*. MacLean has analysed the father's name *Fergnoi* (gen.) as OI *fer* ('man') + *geinnae* ('born'), i.e. as if it were Latin *virogenus*. The second element in *Fergnoi* may in fact be from a root which conveys ideas of knowledge or wisdom (cf. Latin *gnosco*, Gk γιγνώσκω, γνῶσις, etc.). It is unusual for MacLean to analyse a name in this way. He may also have been thinking, consciously or unconsciously, of the biblical 'son of man', Gaelic *mac an duine*, Latin *filius hominis*, Greek υἱὸς τοῦ ἀνθρώπου, Mat. 8: 20, etc.

8. *Lautius*: In CL, *lautia* (nom. plu.) was a banquet offered to foreign dignitaries by the state. *Laute* = 'splendidly'.

[1.23] A f. 243r–v; P1 f. 15r–v (*VC*, i, 28) Metre: Iambic dimeter.
The destructive volcanic eruption mentioned in *VC*, i, 28 has not been identified. Today there are three active volcanoes in Italy, of which Vesuvius is the only one on the mainland. Sharpe (*Adomnán*, 289, n. 134) points out that Notker Balbulus (*c.* 890) speaks in his *Martyrologium* of *subversionem quoque civitatis, quae nunc Nova dicitur, in Italia* ('a city in Italy which is now called New') (Migne, *PL*, cxxxi, col. 1102), i.e. Neapolis, Naples: he viewed it as an eruption of Vesuvius. It is not impossible that Notker at St Gallen knew of a destructive eruption of Vesuvius in the sixth century; it is more likely, however, that this is just a guess on his part. No known eruption of Vesuvius can be linked to the period 563–97. There was a great eruption of Vesuvius in 512 and another in 787, and there may have been eruptions during Notker's lifetime (cf. the Smithsonian Institute National Museum of Natural History Global Volcanism Program information: http://www.volcano.si.edu/world/ volcano.cfm?vnum=0101-02=&volpage=erupt). Notker will also have known the account of the eruption of 79 AD by Pliny the Younger.

18. *Oenotriae*: originally Apulia, but applied poetically to Italy in general.

[1.24] A f. 243v–244r; P1 f. 15v–16r (*VC*, i, 29) Metre: Iambic dimeter.
1. *Capricorni*: the sun passes from Capricorn into Aquarius on 20–21 January.

13. *Ora ... Conalliae*: Tír Conaill, Tirconnell, the north-western part of County Donegal.

16. *Dryas*: strictly speaking, Δρυάς is a wood-nymph. The word MacLean is thinking of here is δρῦς, acc. pl. δρύας ('oak tree'). *Doeria*: Adomnán's *monasterium roboreti campi* ('monastery of the plain of oakwoods'), is in fact Durrow in County Offaly. MacLean has mistakenly identified it with Derry on the borders of Tirconnell, which was also a Columban monastery. MacLean's confusion is understandable: the names 'Durrow' and 'Derry' both contain an element derived ultimately from an Indo-European root meaning an oak tree. It is hard to believe that MacLean might be speculating on a relationship between Greek and Gaelic words. For George Buchanan's discussion of the relationship of the Celtic languages (written nearly 30 years after MacLean's death), cf. W Ferguson, 'George Buchanan and the Picts', *Scottish Tradition*, xvi (1990–91), 24–8.

17–18. *Domum … peramplam*: Adomnán has *in alicuius maioris domus fabrica*. Elsewhere (iii, 15) he speaks of a *magna domus* at Durrow; but cf. Sharpe, *Adomnán*, 292, n. 138.

[1.25] A f. 244r; P1 f. 16r (*VC*, i, 30) Metre: Iambic dimeter.
Faechnus: unidentified. The Irish name was Féchna or Fiachnae. Unusually, MacLean quotes almost verbatim Adomnán's chapter heading: *De Fechno sapiente quomodo paenitens ad Sanctum Columbam ab eodem praenuntiatus uenit.*

3. *Solis cubile uesperum*: cf. Hor., *Odes* 4.15.15–16: *ad ortus solis ab Hesperio cubile*.

4. *Mons Ionius*: the highest point on Iona is now known as Dùn Ì (NM 2825). This is certainly the hill MacLean has in mind here. The Andersons and Sharpe think Adomnán may in fact have had in mind Cnoc Mòr, further south near the modern village (*VC*, pp. 56–7, n.; Sharpe, *Adomnán*, 292, n. 140). We have no way of knowing whether MacLean is perpetuating an earlier tradition.

6. *Ministro*: Adomnán names him as Diarmait, Columba's constant companion in his last years.

27. *Boethenaeum*: Adomnán adds that Baithéne was at the time prior of the monastery of Magh Luinge in Tiree, to which penitents were sent.

[1.26] A f. 244 r–v; P1 f. 16r–v (*VC*, i, 31) Metre: Iambic dimeter.
1. *Oram … Gathaelicam*: Argyll; a Latinisation of *Airear Gaidheal*, later *Earra-Ghàidheal*, the 'Gaelic shore'.

1–3. *Lacus … unda piger … praeceps Abae*: the still waters of Loch Awe are contrasted with the rapid flow of the River Awe as it enters Loch Etive at Bonawe (*Abae … hostia*).

6. *Uetusta cellula*: Adomnán calls it *Cella Diuni*, named after Cailtan's brother Diun. It is unidentified. If MacLean's *adhaeserat* implies that he envisaged it clinging to a steep slope, then he might be thinking of a place on the north-west shore of the loch under the steep slopes of Ben Cruachan, perhaps near the present village of Lochawe.

18. *Uisum*: acc. supine, expressing purpose with a verb of motion. Here MacLean uses it with a direct object (*coloniam*). Cf. *uenit … lauatum*, 2.7.10; *abactum uenerat*, 2.13.1; *oratum … intrat*, 2. 17.9; *confluunt uisum*, 2.25.27.

24. *Uocarim*: for *uocauerim*.

[1.27] A f. 244v–245r; P1 f. 16v–17r (*VC*, i, 32) Metre: Iambic dimeter.
2. *Solis die iam septimo*: Correctly, Sunday was the first day of the week. Adomnán has *quadam dominica die*. Cf. 1.33 and n. below.

4, 6. *Fretum*: The Sound of Iona: cf. 1.21.2 above.

20. *Fratres stupent instantia*: as printed, this line is awkwardly placed, inter-rupting Columba's speech. It has probably been misplaced by a compositor, and should belong rather two lines lower, between Columba's speech and the brothers' reply. The passage does (just) make sense as Blado has printed it, but it is bumpy and awkward, and uncharacteristic of MacLean's usually smooth narration, so we have emended. Cf. the misplacing of a stanza in 2.25.9–16.

25–7. *Ciues … domestici … non hospites*: cf. Eph. 2: 19: *non estis hospites et advenae, sed estis cives sanctorum et domestici Dei.*

29–30. *Hostiam uiuam Deo*: cf. Rom. 12: 1: *ut exhibeatis corpora vestra hostiam viventem sanctam Deo placentem.*

33–4. *Nam sena uix per sydera Diana complet cornua*: cf. Verg. *Aen.* 3.645: *tertia iam Lunae se cornua lumine complent.* MacLean seems to mean that they both lived for six months; Adomnán states clearly that they died within less than a month of their arrival.

35. *Heri talento duplices*: obscure. Cf. the parable of the talents in Mat. 25: 14–30. Adomnán has *duo proselyti … longaque in breui Christianae tempora militiae complentes* ('two strangers completing in a short time a long period of Christian service'). *Heri*: gen. of *herus* < *erus* ('master, lord').

[1.28] A f. 245r; P1 f. 17r (*VC*, i, 33) Metre: Iambic dimeter.

Arbranano Norico: Adomnán makes it clear that Artbranán is a pagan and not a Gaelic speaker, as Columba requires an interpreter to preach to him. MacLean has assumed from this that he is Norse, and that the northern Hebrides were occupied by Norse before the more recent Gaelic settlement (*neoteri Gathaelici*). The misprint *Nori-rico* obscures the point. Read *Norico*, with -ri- repeated by dittography before and after the hyphen. Fordun also believed that there were Norse in Scotland in the sixth century (*Chron. Fordun*, iii, 27). Boece claimed that the Norse and the Danes had aided the Scots against the Roman invasion (Boece, *SH*, iv, 40 ff). In fact, Artbranán was probably Pictish.

1–2. *Arctous … sinus* = the Minch. In Gaelic this is *an Cuan Sgìth* ('the Sea of Skye'). *Haebrida*: Gk accusative, in agreement with *unam … poenextimam*. Pliny (*HN* 4.103) calls them *Hebudes*; Cf. Watson, *CPNS*, 37, and Rivet & Smith, *Place-Names of Roman Britain*, 354–5, for other classical forms of the name. Boece, *SH*, has *Hebrides*. *Poenextimam* has either been coined by MacLean or is a misprint for *poene extimam*.

3. *Uocarat* = *uocauerat*.

7–8. *A rege … portum uocant*: MacLean locates the incident at the place named *portus a rege*, i.e. Gaelic *Port Rìgh* ('king's harbour'), Portree (Sharpe, 'MacLean', 125). He says that Artbranán was baptised in a stream or river (*lauatur flumine*). There are three substantial streams flowing into Portree Loch, the rivers Leasgary and Chracaig near the harbour, and the River Varragill farther south; MacLean could have been thinking of any one of these. He makes no mention of Artbranán's cairn beside the seashore. Perhaps its location had been lost, together with all memory of the Picts who had once dwelt on Skye. MacLean was parson of Kilmaluag in Trotternish; he may have known a local tradition which located this incident at Portree, or the idea may come from his own imagination. An early dedication to Columba on Skye was at Skeabost on the River Snizort.

10. *In parte terram*: Cf. *VC*, i, 33, *alicuius loci terrulam mari uicinam baculo percutiens*.

12. *Res mira*: The exclamatory expression *mira res* is common in medieval hagiography (e.g. Macquarrie, *Legends of Scottish Saints*, 160, 238, 272, 294). Adomnán has *mirum dictu* ('amazing to tell'). MacLean uses the expression *mira res* again at 2.24.69.

18–19. *Primarium Geon cohortis*: Adomnán's *Geonae primarius cohortis*. *Noricum* is an addition by MacLean. Cf. Anderson, *VC*, xxxii; Sharpe, *Adomnán*, 294, nn. 148 and 149; D N Dumville, '*Primarius cohortis* in Adomnán's Life of Columba', *Scottish Gaelic Studies*, xiii (1978–81), 130–1. Dumville draws attention to *AU* 588.3, *Mors nepotum Geno* ('death of the grandsons of Giun [?])'. An adjectival form of the name of the Pictish region *Cé* has also been suggested (Sharpe, *Adomnán*, 136 and 294, n. 149). MacLean clearly had no idea for either *primarius cohortis* or for *Geonae*.

28. *Salicta … annua*: there are to this day thickets of deciduous woodland around Portree Loch, including alder, birch, and rowan. Willow trees are not obvious among them. Trees are shown around Portree Loch in Blaeu's map (Stone, *Illustrated Maps of Scotland*, Pl. 43). Cf. *palus huic est, densis obsessa salictis* (Ovid, *Met.* 11.363).

[1.29] A f. 245r–v; P1 f. 17r–v (*VC*, i, 36) Metre: Iambic dimeter.
4. *Oedum*: from OI *Áed*. MacLean seems to be uncertain how to Latinise it. We find acc. *Oedum*, nom. *Oedus* (6); dat. *Oedo* (20); but also nom. *Oedo* (40), which would imply gen. *Oedonis*. In 1.11 above, *Oedo* (nom.) has gen. *Oedonis*.

8. *Regem peremit Scotiae*: cf. *AU* 565: *Occisio Diarmato m. Cerbuill. i. la hÁedh nDubh mc Suibhne.*

21. *Nigellides*: i.e. Columba, of the northern Uí Néill.

33–6. Cf. Sharpe, *Adomnán*, 297–8, n. 158. MacLean has missed the point of Áed's 'triple death' by piercing, falling, and drowning.

34–5. *Tanquam canis reuertitur ad faeditatem*: cf. Prov. 26: 11; 2 Pet. 2: 22.

40. *Iugulatus*: In *VC*, i, 36, MS A has *iugulentus*, probably influenced by *sanguilentus* in the previous line. The B MSS have *iugulatus*.

[1.30] A f. 245v–246v; P1 f. 17v–18v (*VC*, i, 37) Metre: Iambic dimeter.
1–2. *Horas Bilanx*, etc.: MacLean assumes that harvesting on Iona was carried out around the autumn equinox (22/23 September). This is not mentioned by Adomnán in *VC*, i, 37. In *VC*, ii, 3, Adomnán implies that harvesting could take place as early as the beginning of August, though only with miraculous intervention. Cf. Sharpe, *Adomnán*, 345, n. 335.
Bilanx = Libra, 23 September–22 October. Elsewhere MacLean associates early harvesting with Virgo (*Innuba* (2.3.15)).

7–8. *Auena, faba, triticum, ceresque et ordeacea*: these were presumably plants grown on Iona in MacLean's time. These homely crops make an effective contrast with the exotic plants listed below.
Faba: in CL, the first syllable is short. In MacLean's iambic verse, the fourth syllable of each line is normally heavy, and that is what we would expect

here. Here he treats the *a* as long, perhaps thinking of words like *fabula*, etc., with long *a*.

33ff. *Thus, myrra*, etc. Sharpe, 'MacLean', 116, describes MacLean's catalogue of aromatic plants as 'an exercise in virtuosity'. The starting point for this excursion is Adomnán's simple sentence, *quandam miri odoris flagrantiam acsi uniuersorum florum in unum sentio collectorum* ('I sense a fragrance of a marvellous smell, as if of all flowers gathered together in one'). (Interestingly, Adomnán had previously used this sentence in his *De Locis Sanctis*: cf. *miri odoris flagrantia ac si omnium florum inibi collectorum mirabili plena suauitate exoritur*: D Meehan, *Adamnan's De Locis Sanctis* (Dublin, 1958), III. 3, 12, p. 110.) Most of these names of plants can be found in Pliny, *HN*, Books 12, 13, 15, 16, 19, 20, 21 and 24. There was also a Latin version of Theophrastus' *Historia Plantarum* at Wittenberg in 1536 (Kusukawa, *Wittenberg University Library Catalogue*, 109). Some of the language echoes Vergil's *Georgics*. Cf. also Vulg., Song, 4. We have not attempted to trace MacLean's sources for all his names of plants. See p. 37.

33. *Thus, myrra*: cf. Mat. 2: 11: *aurum, tus et murram.*

38. *Pinus, uirorque buxeus*: cf. Isaiah 60: 13: *abies et buxus et pinus.*

43. *Aiax flosculus*: after the death of Ajax, flowers blossomed where his blood was spilt. The legend is similar to that of Hyacinthus, and the flower is identified as either the hyacinth or the iris.

44. *Sabaea cuncta aromata*: cf. 1 Kings 10: 10: *non sunt adlata ultra aromata tam multa quam ea quae dedit regina Saba regi Salomoni.*

46. *Tempe*: the valley of Tempe in Thessaly was famed for its beauty. Hor., *Odes* 3.1.24; Verg., *Geor.*, 2.469. Cf. also *Epistola*, 63, below.

48. *Tmolus ... odorifer*: Mount Tmolus is in Lydia in western Anatolia. Cf. Verg., *Georg.* 1.56–7: *Nonne uides croceos ut Tmolus odores ... mittit?*

50. *Mala Maedica*: a citrus tree, possibly the orange. Media was the mountainous country south-west of the Caspian Sea. Cf. Pliny, *HN*, 12.15: *Malus Assyria, quam alii Medicam vocant*; ibid., 15.47: *Malorum plura sunt genera: de citreis cum sua arbore diximus, Medica autem Graeci vocant patriae nomine.*

51. *Mella Hymaetia*: Mount Hymettus in Attica was famous for its honey. Cf. Hor., *Odes* 2.6.14–15: *Ubi non Hymetto mella decedunt.*

52. *Fistula*: obscure. Cf. Vulg., Song, 4: 13–14: *Emmissiones tuae paradisus malorum punicorum, cum pomorum fructibus Cypri cum nardo, nardus et crocus, fistula et cinnamomum, cum universis lignis Libani murra et aloe cum omnibus primis unguientis.*

62. *Aeous ... hortulus*: cf. *paradisum ... a principio*, Gen. 2: 8; cf. παράδεισον ἐν ἐδὲμ κατὰ ἀνατολάς.

64–5. *Superstites Enoch*, etc.: Enoch and Elijah are the two figures in the Old Testament who did not die a natural death, but were carried off to heaven alive, presumably making them *superstites* (Gen. 5: 24; 2 Kings 2: 11). Elijah (1 Kings 17 ff.) is recipient of several divinely sent refreshments. Enoch and Elijah are also linked in a story included by Maghnus Ó Domhnaill: cf. B Lacey, *Manus O'Donnell: the Life of Colum Cille* (Dublin, 1998), 201.

74–5. *Urania*, etc.: the Muses.

80. *Sed Cherubicosque Seraphicos*: unusually, this line as written appears to have ten syllables. Also -*que* following *Cherubicos* is unexpected. It is not clear how MacLean has intended it to be scanned. Some sort of syncope or adjustment is required to make the words fit the metre.

81. *Cantus* has a long first syllable, where we would regularly expect a short syllable.

98ff. *Beata fratrum*, etc. Here MacLean alters the first four lines of the refrain and indicates that the normal pattern (at 1.19.21) is to be resumed at 102.

[1.31] A f. 246v–247r; P1 f. 18v–19r (*VC*, i, 37) Metre: Iambic dimeter.
De tonitruo ... uaticinium: Strictly speaking this chapter does not contain a prophecy. MacLean may have used the word by force of habit.

17–18. *Collegium matrum*: 'council of mothers'. Obscure. Adomnán has only *quidam magi ad eos propius accedentes*. Perhaps MacLean envisages a council of priests of Proserpina and other mother-goddesses. Or possibly this is a misprint for *collegium atrum* ('dark council')?

[1.32] A f. 247r; P1 f. 19r (*VC*, i, 39) Metre: Iambic dimeter.
1. *Cruthneum ... Nemanum*: The Cruithne were one of the principal kindreds of north-east Ireland, but Adomnán does not associate Nemán with them. This is probably derived from a misreading by MacLean of Adomnán's *Nemanus filius Gruthriche* ([sic] in MS A of *VC*; Anderson, 72, has *Gruthrice*).

15–16. *Aquae Stygis, Cocytia fluenta*: cf. Verg. *Aen.* 6.323–7: *Cocyti stagna ... Stygiamque paludem ... rauca fluenta.*

20. *Canile*: *Cainle* is unidentified. Cf. Sharpe, *Adomnán*, n. 174, 300–1.

[1.33] A f. 247r–v; P1 f. 19r–v (*VC*, i, 40) Metre: Iambic dimeter.
1. *Sabbati*: Adomnán makes it clear that the incident took place on a Sunday. In *VC*, i, 16, Adomnán uses *sabbati dies* to mean Saturday, and MacLean's 1.14 follows him. In 1.27 (f. 244 v), on the other hand, MacLean has *Solis die iam septimo*, implying that he regarded Sunday as the seventh day of the week.

2. *Triorithi*: Sharpe ('MacLean', 126) points out that MacLean's form *Triorithi* is 'somewhat removed' from Adomnán's *trioit* (in MS A). It is even further removed from the form *triota* in the B MSS.

7. *Commercio*: Often commercial dealing or trafficking, but *commercium* can also mean sexual intercourse. Adomnán does not specify the nature of the man's sin.

[1.34] A f. 247v; P1 f. 19v (*VC*, i, 44) Metre: Iambic dimeter.
On the liturgical implications of this story, see Sharpe, *Adomnán*, 306.

4. *Pontifex*: Adomnán (in the chapter heading) calls him Crónán. He is not otherwise known.

[1.35] A f. 247v–248r; P1 f. 19v–20r (*VC*, i, 45) Metre: Iambic dimeter.
1–2. *Qua fessus undas aureus Phoebus colorat hesperas*: cf. Verg. *Aen.* 11.913–4: *roseus fessos iam gurgite Phoebus Hibero tingat equos.*

3. *Imba*: Adomnán mentions the island of *Hinba* several times in *VC* as the place of an important monastery. Its location is uncertain: a natural reading of Adomnán suggests that it was on a direct sea-route between Ireland and Iona. We may guess that its original Gaelic name has been covered over by a Norse name. The most likely possible identifications are either Jura or Colonsay-Oronsay (Watson, *CPNS*, 81–4; Sharpe, *Adomnán*, 306–8, n. 194; Macquarrie, *Saints of Scotland*, 91ff.), though a number of other suggestions have been advanced. MacLean's identification of *Hinba* is not in itself certain proof of its true location but may indicate that there was a medieval tradition linking it with a particular island. In 1.35 he gives us four pieces of information about *Hinba* (the first three are not taken from Adomnán):

1. It is a prominent island in the open western sea, *qua fessus undas aureus / Phoebus colorat hesperas* (1–2).

2. Columba's uncle Ernán went there from Iona with *Boraeum flamen*, the north wind (18).
3. Ernán later returned from there to Iona with *Auster*, the south wind (24).
4. It is implied that *Hinba* was not far from Iona: Ernán was able to travel from Hinba to Iona when *in extremis*.

From the above data there can be no doubt that MacLean was thinking of the Colonsay-Oronsay group, and perhaps in particular of Oronsay Priory. This is certain evidence of a tradition in MacLean's time linking *Hinba* with Colonsay-Oronsay; but how far back it stretches is unknown. Oronsay Priory was founded for Augustinian canons by John Lord of the Isles 1325 x 1353, probably on a site which was believed to have ancient associations (RCAHMS, *Argyll*, v: *Islay, Jura, Colonsay and Oronsay*, 253; Steer & Bannerman, *Sculpture*, 215; G Ritchie & M Harman, *Exploring Scotland's Heritage: Argyll and the Western Isles* (Edinburgh, RCAHMS, 1985), 113). Bower records a tradition that St Columba had founded a monastery on Oronsay (*Chron. Bower*, i, cap. 6; ed. Watt, i, 15). Donald Monro in 1549 speaks only of 'ane Ile callit Orvansay ... quhairin thair is ane Monasterie of Channonis' (Munro, *Monro's Western Isles*, 60), without providing any further information. Manus O'Donnell, whose *Beatha Colaim Chille* was written some fifteen years before MacLean's poem, does not attempt to identify *Hinba* (B Lacey, *Manus O'Donnell: the Life of Colum Cille* (Dublin, 1998), 130, 139, 169, 212). No traces of early Christian remains from before the fourteenth century have to date been found at Oronsay Priory. By contrast, there are copious early Christian remains on Colonsay.

5. *Lares priusquam deserens*: Adomnán does not say that *Hinba* was Columba's first foundation in Scotland. He does say (in i, 45) *ante plures fundauerat annos* ('he had founded it many years before'). It was certainly in existence by 574 at latest (*VC*, iii, 5). MacLean may be recording a tradition that *Hinba* was the first, or a very early, foundation of Columba's in Scotland.

15–16. *Sis talento fructifer, non est procul solutio*: Cf. the parable of the talents, Mat. 25:14–30. Cf. also *conamine abest procul non terminus ... Heri talento duplices*, above in 1.27.32–5. Although he does not quote from it directly, MacLean may have had in mind Gregory the Great's homily on Mat. 25:14–30 (Migne, *PL*, lxxvi, 1105–9).

33. *Duae cruces*: These were presumably south of the monastery: cf. Anderson, *VC*, lii; Sharpe, *Adomnán*, 195–7. MacLean does not make clear whether or not they were still identified in his time.

[1.36] A f. 248r; P1 f. 20r (*VC*, i, 47) Metre: Iambic dimeter
Adomnán calls the subject of this prophecy *Goreus filius Aidani* of the *Korku Reti*, i.e. Guaire mac Áedáin of the Corcu Réti or Dál Riata. It is possible that he was an otherwise unknown son of Áedán mac Gabráin, who may have died relatively young, before the discussion of the succession to Áedán mentioned in *VC*, i, 9 (MacLean's 1.10).

10–11. *Incinet / herbis ... nocentibus*: Adomnán has *maleficio*. The Andersons translate 'by magical art', with a footnote suggesting '"sorcery", or possibly "poison"'. Sharpe translates 'by witchcraft'. MacLean's *incinet* (a rare word) might imply singing incantations over noxious plants.

15. *Iugis*: *u* in the first syllable is long, where we would expect a short syllable.

18–20. *Hastae ... aeruginem ... fricabat*: this is MacLean's attempt to explain Adomnán's (very puzzling) *cristiliam de astili eradebat*. *Cristilia* is probably < *crustula* ('bark'), showing Adomnán's characteristic predilection for diminutives (Anderson, *VC*, 84–5, n.; but cf. also Sharpe, *Adomnán*, 311, n. 201; J-M Picard, 'The strange death of Guaire mac Áedáin', in D Ó Corráin, K McCone & L Breatnach [eds], *Sages, Saints and Storytellers: Celtic Studies in Honour of James Carney* [Maynooth, 1989], 370–1). The alternative suggestion, < *cristula* ('plume', 'crest'), seems less likely: one would not *eradere* a *cristula* to make a *hastile*. MacLean, on the other hand, may have been thinking of an iron spear or spear-point, on which the only possible kind of *crustula* would be rust (cf. Steer & Bannerman, *Sculpture*, plate 22, A & B). Presumably Guaire was envisaged sitting in the shelter of an upturned boat which restricted his movement, causing him accidentally to stab himself as he rose quickly.

[1.37] A f. 248r–v; P1 f. 20r–v (*VC*, i, 43) Metre: Iambic dimeter.
This is almost the only part of MacLean's Book 1 which is misplaced. It paraphrases the first half of Adomnán's *VC*, i, 43, but follows his paraphrase of *VC*, i, 47. Otherwise in Book 1 he mostly follows Adomnán's order strictly. The second half of Adomnán's *VC*, i, 43 is paraphrased in 1.13.29–40.

[1.38] A f. 248v; P1 f. 20v Metre: Third Asclepiad.
Haec utcunque, etc. A final peroration to end Book 1. MacLean describes himself as 'an exile where Ness flows into the sea in a bright stream.' This is a poetical Latin rendering of Gaelic *Inbhir Nis*, Inverness. He seeks to return *postliminio* ('to his rightful place'; cf. Sharpe, 'MacLean', 113, 127). His exile presumably did not begin until after he resigned his benefices and archdeaconry in 1547–48, in anticipation of his promotion to the bishopric of the Isles. We know that at some point in 1547–48 the commissary of St Andrews 'caused him to be removed and perhaps excommunicated' (Appendix, p. 335). We know also

from his *Epistola elegiaca* that he was in Inverness in October 1548. He did not finally gain peaceful possession of the bishopric until January 1552. See the Introduction, p. 11.

7. *Pater*: Columba.

Soli Deo honor et gloria: cf. 1 Tim., 1: 17. The following line is obscure and cannot be made sense of without emendation.

Book 2

Many of the poems in Book 2 have no headings. The headings in square brackets in the translation are adapted from Adomnán's chapter headings.

[2.1] A f. 250r; P1 f. 22r (*VC*, ii, 1) Metre: Sapphic stanzas.
1–3. *Christus orditur*, etc.: cf. John, 2: 1–11.

3. *Meraces*: for this ML variant, cf. *DMLBS*, s.v. *meracus*.

5. *Clari soboles Nigelli*: Columba's kindred, the Cenél Conaill, were of the Northern Uí Neill. Adomnán mentions in *VC*, i, 49 that Columba was of the *Nellis nepotes*. In 1.29.21, MacLean calls Columba *Nigellides*.

14. *Lyaeus*: Bacchus.

18. *Monefactus* [*sic*]: presumably from *moneo* + *facio*. Adomnán has *quo cognito*.

21–4. Cf. Adomnán's *Huius inquam libelli quasi quaedam lucerna inlustret exordium … miraculum*, *VC*, ii, 1.

22. *Lyra Sapphus*: a reference to the fact that all the poems in Book 2 are composed in Sapphic stanzas.

[2.2] A f. 250r–v; P1 f. 22r–v (*VC*, ii, 2) Metre: Sapphic stanzas.
1. *Sacras prope phana quercus*: Durrow, County Offaly.

14. *Bipotentis*: the word is unusual. Presumably it refers to Christ's divine and human natures.

[2.3] A f. 250v–251 r; P1 f. 22v–23r (*VC*, ii, 3) Metre: Sapphic stanzas.
7. *Aestuo … astro*: The Zodiacal constellations of late summer were Cancer (22 June–22 July) and Leo (23 July–22 August). Or MacLean is possibly thinking of Sirius, the Dog Star, prominent under Leo.

10–12. *Serenti ... Yaeo*: 'someone on Iona who sows'. MacLean is assuming that the farmer lived on Iona. But Adomnán says explicitly that the wattle was brought to Iona by ship, and that the peasant lived in a place called *Delcros*. Sharpe suggests that this unidentified place was nearby, possibly on the Ross of Mull (Sharpe, *Adomnán*, 318–9, n. 214). MacLean's assumption reflects the conditions of his own time, when there was a secular population on Iona.

15. *Innubae*: lit. 'unmarried woman'. The sun is in Virgo 23 August–22 September, the period of harvest.

17. *Martias ... sub Calendas*: the season of sowing in MacLean's time.

[2.4] A 251r–v; P1 f. 23r–v (*VC*, ii, 4) Metre: Sapphic stanzas.
1. *Collis ... Yaei*: Dùn Ì. MacLean has earlier (1.25) referred to *Mons Ionius*, by which he clearly means Dùn Ì. Adomnán calls it *Munitio magna*, a literal translation of OI *dún mór*. There are no man-made fortifications on Dùn Ì.

6–8. *Albioni usque qua praeceps Dya de niuoso uertice torret*: Adomnán has (MS A) *riuulo ... Ailbine usque ad uadum Clied* ('from the river of Ailbe to the ford of Clíath'), i.e. from the River Delvin to Dublin. The B MSS have *cléeth* and *déeth*, from which MacLean's form could not be derived. MacLean has apparently taken the first name to be *Alban*, the oblique form of *Alba*, 'Scotland'. The second name is more problematic. If MacLean's MS of Adomnán had *clied* with the first two letters close together, this could certainly be misread as *died*: the same confusion of *cl* and *d* has occurred in the B MSS. Later on, in 2.16, MacLean mentions that *Clyathus ... Amnis* (the Liffey) is in Leinster. Here, however, MacLean seems to have interpreted *clied* or *died* as the name of a river which he apparently identifies with the Dee in Aberdeenshire: its sources at Wells of Dee high up on Braeriach could certainly be described as *qua praeceps Dya de niuoso uertice torret*. (The other River Dee in Scotland, flowing out of Loch Dee in Galloway [NX 4679] and entering the sea at Kirkcudbright Bay, with its much lower and less snowy sources, is less likely.) Later on, in 2.22, he sets an incident *in Monte Scarsiaco*, on Beinn Sgarsoch, in the same area. Perhaps MacLean had at some time made a journey in winter across the Mounth *via* Glen Tilt and the headwaters of the Dee. It is implied that he saw the Mounth as dividing northern from southern Scotland: cf. Bede, *HE*, iii, 4. Perhaps this is how he understood Adomnán's *dorsum Britanniae*. For *praeceps* used of a fast-flowing river, cf. also *praeceps Abae* for Bonawe in 1.26.

26. *Aer*: the nom. normally has two long vowels, *āēr* < ἀήρ. In the oblique cases, *e* is short. MacLean is scanning it here as a trochee.

[2.5] A f. 251v–251 + 1r; P1 f. 23v–24r (*VC*, ii, 5) Metre: Sapphic stanzas.

9. *Celer O Lugoede*: Adomnán has: *Lugaidum ... cuius cognomentum Scotice Lathir dicitur* (also *Lugaidus ... Laitirus* in ii, 38). Cf. Gaelic *làidir* ('strong'). MacLean's *celer* does not translate *làidir*.

10–11. *Benedictionem hanc*: a sacred object which Columba had blessed. Adomnán says that the *benedictio* was placed in a *pinea capsella* ('little box of pine wood'). Cf. *VC*, 103, n.; Sharpe, *Adomnán*, 321, n. 226.

13. *Calculum uitae legat exigendae*: Adomnán says that Columba wrote the number *xxiii* on the lid of the box to indicate how many years she would live.

[2.6] A f. 251 + 1r; P1 f. 24r (*VC*, ii, 10) Metre: Sapphic stanzas. At this point MacLean skips over a number of Adomnán's chapters (ii, 6–ii, 9). Later, he includes Adomnán's ii, 8 and ii, 9 as 2.33 and 2.34.

1. *Ante*: MacLean uses *ante* with the meaning 'previously' or 'hitherto' here and at 2.7.2, 2.16.43, 2.25.44, 2.30.71, 2.35.37, 2.36.76. Cf. *DMLBS*, s.v. *Horeboea*: Mount Horeb in Sinai. Cf. Ex. 17: 6.

3. *Dubiae ... uirgae*: *Dubius* is a strange word ('doubtful, uncertain, changeable') for MacLean to use to refer to the rod of Moses. There is nothing in Ex. 17: 5–6 to prompt such a description. On its first appearance, however, Moses's rod changed shape, transforming into a serpent and back again (Ex. 4: 2–4), and it is possibly this that MacLean is referring to here. Later (Ex. 7: 9–10), a rod held by Aaron is changed into a serpent and back again.

13. *Lugoede*: Adomnán calls the child *Ligu Cenn Calad*, *VC*, ii, 10. MacLean may have assumed that it is a form of the name Lugaid, found in his previous poem (2.5). Adomnán locates this miracle in *Artda Muirchol*, Ardnamurchan, but MacLean does not mention this.

[2.7] A f. 251 + 1r–v; P1 f. 24r–v (*VC*, ii, 11) Metre: Sapphic stanzas. 10. *Lauatum*: acc. supine.

12. *Oppido suadent*: the final *–o* of *oppido* should strictly be long; but final *–o* is 'frequently scanned short in Silver Latin' (*OLD*, xxxiii). For treatment of final *–o* in Buchanan's verse, cf. R P H Green, 'George Buchanan, chieftain of neo-Latin poets', in L B T Houghton & G Manuwald (eds), *Neo-Latin Poetry in the British Isles* (London, 2012), 149.

13–16. *Sustulit ...Uolucerque ... ter manus, signum crucis effugitque ... doemon*: cf. *ter ... manus effugit imago ... uolucrique simillima somno*, Verg. *Aen.* 2.793–4.

[2.8] A f. 251 + 1v–252r; P1 f. 24v–25r (*VC*, ii, 15) Metre: Sapphic stanzas.
3. *Campilungaeos*: i.e. pertaining to *Magh Luinge*, the (unidentified) site of
Columba's monastery on Tiree. Cf. also 2.30 below. Adomnán always calls
it *Campus Lunge*.
Penates: Sharpe ('MacLean', 129) draws attention to this word. MacLean uses
it here and elsewhere (2.13, 2.15, 2.24, 2.30, 2.32) as synonymous with *lares*.
It is used frequently in Verg. *Aen.*

f. 252 r
13. *Aurora rutilante*: cf. *Aurora rutilat lucis prenuncia*, etc. the opening of the
hymn at Lauds for St Columba's feast day in the Inchcolm Fragment and
the Aberdeen Breviary: Macquarrie, *Legends of Scottish Saints*, 138, 340–1.
There was an early Christian hymn beginning *Aurora lucis rutilat*, sometimes
attributed to St Ambrose.

19–20: *Sole iam seros recreante currus egit ad oras*: cf. Hor., *Odes.*, 3.6.41–4: *sol …
amicum tempus agens abeunte curru.*

[2.9] A f. 252r–v; P1 f. 25r–v (*VC*, ii, 16) Metre: Sapphic stanzas.
2. *Atrii ad limen*: Adomnán has *ad ianuam tegorioli* (*tugorioli*, B). Adomnán calls the
small central domed structure in the Church of the Holy Sepulchre a *tegorium*
or *tegoriolum*: cf. D Meehan, *Adamnan's De Locis Sanctis* (Dublin, 1958), I.2
(pp. 42ff., and plate facing p. 47). Adomnán was probably thinking of a quite
modest hut, possibly circular. Cf. CL *tugurium*, with its (very rare) diminutive
tuguriolum. In ecclesiastical Latin, *atrium* could also mean a churchyard or
enclosure (*DMLBS*, s.v.). It is not clear what MacLean is thinking of here. If
he found Adomnán's word puzzling, perhaps he is being deliberately vague.

3. *Bubalo*: MacLean may have been thinking of the shaggy ancestors of
modern Highland cattle.

6. *Crucis signum quadriforme uitans*: The B MSS mentions that Columba invokes
the name of God as he blesses the vessel (*et invocato Dei nomine vas benedixit*),
a detail which is not in MS A; there is no trace of these words in MacLean's
version, but his paraphrase is not very close at this point.

[2.10] A f. 252v; P1 f. 25v (*VC*, ii, 17) Metre: Sapphic stanzas.
Goetus: see note on 2.24.12 below.

[2.11] A f. 253r; P1 f. 26r (*VC*, ii, 20) Metre: Sapphic stanzas.
5. *Trimales*: this word appears to be extremely rare, if not unique; it is
presumably connected with *trimulus* ('three years old'). Cf. *duālis*, etc.

16. *Longa supersit*: In the B MSS of *VC*, the story of Nesán (*VC*, ii, 20) is followed by a contrasting tale about a rich miser who refused the saint hospitality and became poor as a result of Columba's malediction. MS A proceeds straight to the story of Colmán in ii, 21. MacLean's version here, linked by *similiter* in the chapter heading and *sic* in the first line of the poem itself, follows A rather than B; it seems very likely (though perhaps not absolutely certain) that his MS did not have the addition in B. Cf. Introduction, p. 56.

[2.12] A f. 253r–v; P1 f. 26r–v (*VC*, ii, 21) Metre: Sapphic stanzas.
Similiter: see the previous note.

4. *Album*: in Gaelic mythology (e.g. in the *tána*), white cattle were much prized. There is no mention in Adomnán of white cattle. This may be an example of the influence of Celtic lore in MacLean's version.

[2.13] A f. 253v–254r; P1 f. 26v–27r (*VC*, ii, 22) Metre: Sapphic stanzas.
1–2. *Trux ... praedo*: Adomnán names the thief as Ioan son of Conall son of Domnall of the Cenél nGabráin. MacLean does not name him. *Abactum*: acc. supine.

2–3. *Rabies habendi dira*: cf. Verg. *Aen*. 8.327: *belli rabies et amor ... habendi*.

17. *Hebraeos Phariumque regem*: an allusion to Pharaoh's inflexibility, Ex. 5 ff.

25. *Aquilone*: Adomnán in *VC*, ii, 22 provides some geographical details for this story which MacLean has not included. He sets the incident in *Artmuirchol*, Ardnamurchan, and says that the thieves sailed from a bay called *Aithchambas* ('sharp bay') in Ardnamurchan. Their ship then sank between *Malea*, Mull, and *Colosus*, Coll. *Aithchambas* is unidentified, but must have been towards the west end of Ardnamurchan. (Cf. Sharpe, *Adomnán*, 328, n. 260) MacLean is correct in stating that *Aquilo*, the north wind, was required to carry a ship from Ardnamurchan to the Sound of Coll between Coll and Mull.

41. *O Pater*, etc.: MacLean becomes passionate when he touches upon the unjust detention of church property. This uncharacteristic outburst probably reflects his own position, exiled in Inverness and denied access to what he saw as his rightful place. Cf. the anger he expresses in the *Epistola*. *Pater ... aliger* = Columba, whom he has invoked in 1.38.

[2.14] A f. 254r–255r; P1 f. 27r–28r (*VC*, ii, 23) Metre: Sapphic stanzas.
Thylaei praesidis, Praesidi Thyles: Adomnán names him as Feradach, a rich man *qui in Ilea insula habitabat*. This is certainly Islay. In the *Epistola*, 19, MacLean calls Alexander of Islay (lord of the Isles *c*. 1423–49) *Alexander, cui dat nomen*

celeberrima Thyle. Clearly, MacLean is using *Thyle* as a name for Islay. Ptolemy equates Thule with Shetland, and Tacitus equates it with either Fair Isle or Shetland (cf. Rivet & Smith, *Place-Names of Roman Britain*, 473). In modern Gaelic, *Innis Tîle* = Iceland. *Thylaei* is gen. masc. of an adj.; *Thyles* is gen. of a Gk first dec. noun.

1–2. *Nitidus ... exul*: Adomnán calls him *quendam de nobili Pictorum genere exsulem Tarainum nomine*. There was a Pictish name, *Tara(i)n*: cf. *AU* 697, 699; Anderson, *KKES*, 90, 248, 262–3, etc.

8. *Cyclopis*: a reference to Polyphemus the Cyclops. When Odysseus and his crew sought refuge with him, he imprisoned them and ate several of them.

13–14. *Nemeaeus ... Leo*: the constellation Leo. The sun is in Leo from 23 July to 22 August. There may be an allusion here to the 'Dog Days', when Sirius is in the southern sky.

16. *Scorpius*: 24 October–22 November.

19. *Auernas*: an Italian lake surrounded by dense woods, which was believed to lead to the underworld. Cf. Verg., *Aen.* 6.201, etc.

30. *Par luci tenebrescit hora*: i.e. the autumn equinox, 22/23 September.

31–2. *Luna cornutos fericida ceruos, etc.*: *fericida* ('killer of wild animals') has apparently been coined by MacLean as an epithet for Diana. The implication is that the hunting of deer was discontinued during the rut.

37–40. *Christe sanctorum*, etc. MacLean may here be echoing an early Christian hymn in sapphic metre:

> *Christe, sanctorum decus Angelorum*
> *Rector humani generis et auctor,*
> *nobis aeternum tribue benigne*
>   *scandere caelum.*
> ... ...
> *Praestet hoc nobis Deitas beata*
> *Patris ac Nati pariterque Sancti*
> *Spiritus, cuius resonat per omnem*
> *gloria mundum.*

[2.15] A f. 255r–v; P1 f. 28r–v (*VC*, ii, 24) Metre: Sapphic stanzas.
Landers: Adomnán calls this person *Lám Dess* ('Right Hand') and also Latinises his name as *Manus dextera*. MS A has *lam dess* and *lam des*. The B MSS have

lamdhes, lamdes, laudes. Sharpe ('MacLean', 129) comments that 'if MacLean's copy was corrupt, he was evidently unable to correct it from the Latin form "Manus dextera"'. If MacLean read the name as a single word, he is perhaps applying the Gaelic orthographic convention of writing *n* before another dental consonant. (Elsewhere he applies the rule of writing *m* before a labial consonant, e.g. *Imba, Hymba,* for Adomnán's *Hinba.*) In MacLean's Gaelic, 'right hand' would be *làmh dheas.* In Insular minuscule script *s* could be mistaken for *r.* See Introduction, p. 55.

1. *Hymbaeos ... penates*: for Hinba, see notes on 1.35 above.

19. *Exangues ... artus*: cf. Baebius Italicus, *Ilias Latina,* 5.

38. *Altis ... quadrigis*: lit. 'in a high chariot'; possibly in the sense 'in triumph'? Cf. note on *quadrigis ... albicatis,* 2.29.69–70 below, and on *triumphat* in 2.16.79. There is no equivalent of the last three lines (38–40) in Adomnán (*VC,* ii, 24). It is not clear where MacLean intended Columba's reported speech to end, whether after line 36 or after line 40.

[2.16] A f. 255v–257r; P1 f. 28v–30r (*VC,* ii, 25) Metre: Sapphic stanzas.
1. *Germano*: in *VC,* ii, 25 Adomnán has *Gemmanus,* from OI *Gemmán.*

5. *Metropolis*: If MacLean knew Dublin, he may have been thinking of Christ Church, with its high tower near the Liffey.

5–6. *Columbae Patribus quondam lar amenus*: Columba's family were of the northern Uí Neill; the southern Uí Neill dynasties occupied lands in the Irish Midlands as far as the Liffey plain, where they bordered on the Laigin dynasties of Leinster. MacLean seems to have thought of the northern Uí Neill migrating away from the lands of the southern Uí Neill.

6–8. *Ortu ... prono*: the Liffey rises in the Wicklow Mountains south of Dublin. *Per undas ... Iberas*: It is not clear what waters MacLean is thinking of here: the lakes on the Liffey at Blessington, County Wicklow, are the result of modern damming. Other Irish rivers, most obviously the Shannon, flow through lakes.

7–8. *Clyathus ... amnis*: the Liffey at Dublin. Strictly speaking, the name *Áth Cliath* ('ford of hurdles') refers to a crossing point on the Liffey (*Life*) at Dublin rather than to the river itself. Adomnán sets this incident *in parte Laginensium ... in campi planitie.*

17. *Nisus ut Scyllam*: Nisus king of Megara and his daughter Scylla were transformed into an eagle and its prey respectively after she betrayed the city to his enemies.

18. *Acris*: here masc.

34. *Cypriae*: i.e. of Aphrodite or Venus.

43–4. *Ante germanam perimit quadrimam / trux inimicus*: It is not clear where MacLean has got this idea from. There is nothing in Adomnán corresponding to it.

51. *Sexies*: lit. 'six times', perhaps in the sense of 'about half a dozen times'. Adomnán says only *filiam ... lancea iugulauit*, without specifying the number of blows.

73. *Falsa ... Petro stipulante coniunx*: cf. Acts, 5: 4–11. A husband and wife are both struck down suddenly after lying to the Apostles.

77–8: *Templa ... latreiam*: cf. Acts, 5: 11: *et factus est timor magnus in universa ecclesia, et in omnes qui audierunt haec*, and also the end of *VC*, ii, 25. *Latreiam*: *latria* is a rare word from patristic Latin, < λατρεία.

79. *Triumphat*: cf. the reference to a *quadrigae* in the last stanzas of 2.15 and 2.29.

[2.17] A f. 257r–v; P1 f. 30r–31r (*VC*, ii, 26) Metre: Sapphic stanzas.
Uenenoso: in Celtic heroic literature wild boars could be poisonous and supernatural. In Gaelic literature the most celebrated hunter of boars was Diarmaid Úa Duibhne, and in the *Book of the Dean of Lismore* his fatal boar was poisonous: cf. D E Meek, 'The Death of Diarmaid in Scottish and Irish tradition', *Celtica*, xxi (1990), 335–61. Cf. also J MacInnes, 'Gaelic poetry and historical tradition', in *The Middle Ages in the Highlands*, ed. L MacLean (Inverness, 1981), 160; N K Chadwick, 'The lost literature of Celtic Scotland', *Scottish Gaelic Studies*, vii (1953), 142–5; for a Welsh example of a poisonous boar, see P K Ford, *The Mabinogi and Other Medieval Welsh Tales* (Los Angeles, 1977), 152. Adomnán does not mention poison. Cf. *uenena* in line 21 below.

3–4. *Insulas Galdi*: a Latinisation of *Innse Gall*, the Gaelic name for the Western Isles. MacLean's form is gen. sing. of a personal name: Galdus is a mythological king of Scots mentioned in Boece, *SH*, iv. Boece says that Galloway is named after him (*SH*, iv, 70). *Gall* is in fact gen. plu., 'of foreigners'. *Cynosura*: Ursa Minor, the Little Bear. *Mergi nescia*: because these isles are so far north, the northernmost stars do not set in the sea.

6–7. *Nemorosa … Schya*: MacLean will have known Skye from visits to his parsonage at Kilmaluag. Bleau's map of Skye (based on Timothy Pont's survey) shows woodlands around Portree Loch and Loch Ainort, opposite Scalpay, and between Kyleakin and Kylerhea. The last named may be the area MacLean had in mind: *qua … finditur … Schya continente … ab ora* (J Stone, *Illustrated Maps of Scotland from Blaeu's Atlas Novus* [London, 1991], Pl. 43, pp. 88–9). Donald Monro writes of 'mony woods, mony forrests' in Skye (Munro, *Monro's Western Isles*, 68). Parts of eastern Skye are still heavily wooded, including areas of indigenous woodland. The B MSS have *sua insula* for A's *scia insula*, so MacLean agrees with A against B. See Introduction, pp. 54–5.

8. *Hebris*: nom. in apposition to *Schya*. Elsewhere we find: abl. *Hebride*, 1.3.40; Gk acc. *Haebrida*, 1.28.1. MacLean never uses the word in the plural.

9. *Oratum*: acc. supine.

15ff. *Trux aper*: In lines 17–22 MacLean considerably elaborates Adomnán's description of the boar. In ii, 26 Adomnán simply has *mirae magnitudinis aprum*. MacLean does not mention that the boar was being pursued by a hunt (*quem forte venatici canes persequebantur* ['which it happened that hunting-dogs were pursuing']), a detail which is in MS A but not in B. Since he speaks of the boar emerging from a cavern (see following note), these words may not have been in his MS.

16. *Ab antro*: Adomnán does not mention a cave, but the wild boars of Celtic literature sometimes dwelt in caves. Cf., for example, the magic pigs of Mag Macruma, which emerged from the cave of Cruachain and blighted the land: see M Dillon, *The Cycle of the Kings* (London, 1946, reprinted 1994), 19, n. 2.

21. *Uenena*: cf. note on the chapter heading above.

[2.18] A f. 258r; P1 f. 31r–32r (*VC*, ii, 27) Metre: Sapphic stanzas.
Hippopotamus: Sharpe ('MacLean', 130) points out that this corresponds to the Gaelic *each uisge* ('water-horse') of Celtic lore. Much of MacLean's vocabulary here implies a horse-like creature: cf. *hinnus aquosus* (16, 51) and *caballus* (37) below; also *dorso … equino* (27). *Hinnus* strictly speaking is the offspring of a she-ass and a stallion; MacLean may use the word to indicate that his *each uisge* is a hybridised horse-like monster. Adomnán only calls it *aquatilis bestia* and *bilua* (= *belua*); the equine imagery is MacLean's. As in the previous chapter, he elaborates considerably.

3. *Noesus*: MacLean was familiar with the River Ness and its *amena … hostia* at Inverness.

6–7: *Ad leuum Boream*: cf. *Cauro … sinistro*, 2.22.3. *Reflexus … sinuosa*: the Ness flows north-east in meandering fashion, then turns sharply north to enter the sea at South Kessock.

18. *Copallus*: MacLean has taken this unusual word from Adomnán: cf. *caupallus* in *VC*, ii, 27. The (rare) CL form is *caupulus*, which would not fit MacLean's prosody. Cf. *Shorter OED*, and *CSD*, s.v. *coble*; *DMLBS*, s.v. *caupulus, cobellus*. *NCLCL* offers no examples except Adomnán.

26ff. *Monstrum exitiale*, etc.: cf. Pliny the Elder's description of the Nile hippopotamus (*HN*, 8, 95): *Maior altitudine in eodem Nilo belua hippopotamus editur, ungulis binis quales bubus, dorso equi et iuba et hinnitu, rostro resimo, cauda et dentibus aprorum aduncis.*

29. *Bicolis*: from *bi* + *caulis* ('stalk').

30. *Apriceps*: from *aper* ('boar') + *-ceps* < *caput*. This word has possibly been coined by MacLean.

33. *Asellum*: Luigbe is likened to a 'little donkey', by contrast with the great water-horse towering over him. Cf. Gaelic *asal* ('donkey, ass').

f. 258 v
41. *Non opus …est* = 'it is not needful'.

f. 259 r
51–2. *Lingua … pelasga*: Greek. *Hyppopotamos*: ἱπποπόταμος = 'river horse'. MacLean treats the α in the penultimate syllable of ἱπποπόταμος as long, to make it fit the metre.

54. *Lepus a Molosso*: cf. Verg. *Georg.* 3.405–10: *Molossum pasce … et canibus leporem … uenabere.* Here and at 2.29.49 MacLean regards the Molossian hound as a hunting hound.

60. *Noesicolum = Noesicolarum*.

[2.19] A f. 259r–v; P1 f. 32r–v (*VC*, ii, 28) Metre: Sapphic stanzas.
1. *Castor et Pollux*: the stars of Gemini, transited by the sun 21 May–21 June each year. This incident is thus set in late May–early June 597, a few days before Columba's death on 9 June. In *VC*, iii, 23 Adomnán states that this visit took place *quadam die mense maio*.

7. *Rossiae ... ad oram*: the Ross of Mull. This implies that nursing animals and their young were taken from Iona to shielings on the Ross of Mull in early summer while the fields of Iona were given over to agriculture – presumably a reflection of farming practice on Iona in MacLean's time. In the 1560s the Ross of Mull pertained to Iona Abbey: cf. *Collectanea de Rebus Albanicis* (Edinburgh, 1847), 1.

f. 259 v

15–16. *Conditor ... benedicat altus ... ex Monte Syone*: cf. Ps. (Vulg.) 127: 5: *benedicat tibi Dominus ex Sion*. (Also Ps. (Vulg.) 133: 3.) There may also be an echo of the opening words of the early Iona poem *Altus prosator*, attributed to St Columba (T O Clancy & G Márkus, *Iona: the earliest Poetry of a Celtic Monastery* [Edinburgh, 1995], 44).

18–19. *Ceres ... Pales*: Latin deities of agriculture and herding respectively.

28. *Uipera mordax*: it is believed that there are no snakes on Iona. By contrast, the adder is found on the Ross of Mull. Cf. Sharpe, *Adomnán*, 330–1.

30. *Incolamur*: obscure. Adomnán's ii, 28 ends with the words *Quandiu Christi mandata eiusdem commorationis incolae obseruauerint* ('as long as the inhabitants of that dwelling-place shall observe the commandments of Christ').

[2.20] A f. 259v–260r; P1 f. 32v–33r (*VC*, ii, 29) Metre: Sapphic stanzas.
1. *Moluag*: Adomnán calls this monk *Molua nepos Briuni*, Molua Uá Briúin. He is not otherwise known. MacLean has assimilated him to St Moluag of Lismore (Sharpe, 'MacLean', 130). MacLean had been parson of Kilmaluag in Trotternish in Skye, a dedication to St Moluag. There was also a chapel of St Moluag (Teampull Mholuaigh) at Eoropie in Lewis, in the parish of Barvas, of which MacLean was also parson. For his cult in Scotland, cf. Macquarrie, *Legends of Scottish Saints*, 148–59, 395–8.

2–3. *Rude ... frustulum ferri*: Adomnán only has *ferrum*, which does not necessarily imply unfinished iron. MacLean may have jumped to this conclusion because of the mention of reworking the iron later in *VC*, ii, 29.

9. *Sic ait*: MacLean does not make clear who is the speaker here. According to Adomnán, Columba did not look up when Molua presented the iron dagger to be blessed, and he then asked Diarmait what it was that he had blessed. When he was told it was a dagger, he remarked that it would be useless for killing anything from then on.

25ff. On metalworking on Iona, cf. Mrs Anderson's note in *VC*, pp. 136–7 n.; Sharpe, *Adomnán*, 332, n. 282. It may be a reflection of conditions in MacLean's times that he assumed that iron could be forged on Iona.

27–8. *Secta per phani sacret aera nostri / lamina sparsim*: obscure. Cf. the last sentence of *VC*, ii, 29: *Quod monaci scientes experti eiusdem pugionis ferrum ignis resolutum calore per omnia monasterii ferramenta liquefactum diuiserunt inlinitum* ... ('When they knew this, skilled monks melted the iron of that dagger in the heat of a fire, and distributed it, divided up, spreading it upon all the iron tools throughout the monastery...').

[2.21] A f. 260r–v; P1 f. 33r–v (*VC*, ii, 30) Metre: Sapphic stanzas. In *VC*, ii, 30, the monk is named as Columba's servant and confidant Diarmait.

1–2. Cf. Verg., *Geor.* 3.458: *cum furit atque artus depascitur arida febris* ('when a dry fever rages and feeds on the limbs'). *Repasta*: dep., like Vergil's *depascitur*.

f. 260 v
4. *Habebat*: without a direct object.

8. *Machaon*: a legendary physician and healer of the Trojan War, son of Asclepius and grandson of Phoebus; Phoebus was also associated with medicine and healing.

10. *Mea fata cernes*: Adomnán does not mention in *VC*, ii, 30 that Diarmait was the chief witness to Columba's last hours; this only emerges in iii, 23. So MacLean must have been familiar with this part of Adomnán's Book iii, even though he does not include it in his paraphrase.

15. *Charitum*: < χάρις.

[2.22] A f. 260v–261v; P1 f. 33v–34v (*VC*, ii, 31) Metre: Sapphic stanzas. *In Monte Scarsiaco*: Adomnán only says that this incident occurred while Columba was travelling *trans Britannicum Dorsum*, across *Druim Alban*. There is a hill called An Sgarsoch (NN 9383), with Druim Sgarsoch beside it, above the heads of Glen Feshie and Glen Tilt and above Linn of Dee. Although now quite remote, at one time it was the site of an annual cattle-fair called *Feil Sgarsaich* (cf. C McNeish, *The Munros: Scotland's Highest Mountains* [Broxburn, 1996], s.v. An Sgarsoch). On Mercator's map of northern Scotland (1595), *Scarschioch* and *Scarschioch hilles* are shown above the heads of Glen Muick and Glen Clova. They may be misplaced: on Robert and James Gordon's map of eastern Scotland (*c.* 1636–52), *Scairsoch Mons* is shown further west, above the sources of the rivers Dee and Feshie (the true location of An Sgarsoch). On

Blaeu's map of *Braid-Allaban*, etc. (1654, based on information supplied by Robert Gordon, and possibly ultimately by Timothy Pont), *Mountayns of the Scairsoch* are also shown above the sources of the rivers Dee, Feshie, and Tilt. There is nothing in Adomnán to suggest this identification, so it appears to be a flight of poetical fancy by MacLean: perhaps he envisaged Columba travelling through Rannoch and Atholl and up Glen Tilt either to Braemar or to Glen Feshie. It may be that MacLean interpreted travelling *trans Britannicum dorsum* as travelling on a south-north route across the Mounth. In 2.4 MacLean has referred to *qua praeceps Dya de niuoso uertice torret*, apparently the sources of the Dee high up on Braeriach, so he may have passed through this area himself; certainly, his description in the first two stanzas is quite vivid. Cf. Scotiae Regnum (north sheet) per Gerardum Mercatorem, NLS, http://maps.nls.uk/view/00000589; A map of Eastern Scotland, including basins of Rivers Don, Dee, Tay, Forth, and Tweed, by Robert Gordon, NLS, http://maps.nls.uk/joins/gordon06.html; J. Stone, *Illustrated Maps of Scotland from Blaeu's Atlas Novus* (1991), 68–9. (My thanks are due to Dr Peter Drummond for much of this information.) Dr Simon Taylor points out to us that An Sgarsoch is near the boundary of Insh parish, a medieval dedication to St Adomnán. See S Taylor, 'Seventh-century Iona Abbots in Scottish place-names', in D Broun & T O Clancy, *Spes Scotorum: Hope of Scots* (Edinburgh, 1999), 66–7.

2. *Alpibus*: MacLean had travelled to Rome in 1542, possibly crossing the Alps; he was to do so again in 1549.

f. 261 r
5. *Capricorna*: the sun is in Capricorn for the month following the winter solstice, 22 December–20 January. *Capricorna* here is abl. sing. fem. of an adj.

6. *Aquis urnae Ganymaedis astro*: i.e. Aquarius, 21 January–19 February. There is nothing in Adomnán to locate this story at midwinter; this is an elaboration of MacLean's.

10. *Quidam comitantis*: Adomnán in ii, 31 names him as Fintén mac Áedo. He is not otherwise known.

13. *Ignea flauet*, etc. This verse alludes to other miracles of Columba: the ripening of a parched harvest (2.35) and the calming of a raging sea (2.26). Since he can do these things, Columba is able to alleviate the harshness of the winter journey.

f. 261 v
32. *Callianinde*: MS A of *VC* has *Kailli au inde*; the B MSS have *Kailli anfinde* and *Kailli anfind*. It is unidentified: cf. Anderson, *VC*, 138–9 n.; Watson,

CPNS, 93; Sharpe, *Adomnán*, 333, n. 284. Clearly MacLean had no idea where it was, and he did not attempt an identification. His form, without *f* (which was lenited), is closer to that in MS A; see Introduction, p. 55.

[2.23] A f. 261v–263r; P1 f. 34v–36r (*VC*, ii, 32) Metre: Sapphic stanzas.
3. *Tingier*: pres. inf. pass. = *tingi*.

6. *Mantae*: from μαντεία ('prophesying').

7. *Triuia*: Diana, goddess of the meeting of ways. *Litarant* = *litauerant*.

9. *Plutho*: god of the Underworld.

20. *Erynnin*: < Ἐριννύς, one of the Furies.

21. *Megaeram*: one of the Furies.

32. *Auspice Iona*: i.e. Columba.

38. *Sacramen*: ML, for *sacramentum*: *DMLBS*, s.v.

58. *Factu*: abl. supine.

61. *Helias … uiduae Sareptae*: Elijah and the widow of Zarephath (1 Kings, 17: 8–24), mentioned by MacLean several times. Here again MacLean alludes to the identification of the widow's son with Jonah, and the equation of the names Jonah and Columba. This is the first of a list of resuscitations of the dead. Adomnán (ii, 32) mentions Elijah and Elisha, Peter, Paul and John.

65. *Sunamitis … Helisaeum*: Elisha revived the child of a Shunamite woman (2 Kings, 4: 8–37).

66. *Exangues … artus*: cf. 2.15.19, above, and n.

69. *Lazarus*: cf. John, 11: 1–44.

73. *Petrus*: the revival of Dorcas by Peter (Acts 9: 36–41).

74–5. *Ioannes …Drusianam*: the story of Drusiana of Ephesus is told in the apocryphal 'Acts of John', caps. 62–86. See M R James, *The Apocryphal New Testament* (Oxford, 1924), 243–50; J K Elliott, *The Apocryphal New Testament* (Oxford, 1993), 328–35.

76. *Perscius ales*: the symbol of St John the Evangelist was the eagle. *Perscius* has perhaps been coined by MacLean; *perscītus* is rare in CL and ML, but it would not fit the metre.

83. *Sed nephas credo*: strangely, having said he thinks it would be wrong to do so, MacLean proceeds to repeat Columba's words in verse.

86. *Nosti = nouisti.*

87. *Noteas signo*: from ML *noteo* ('to become known').

100. *Munere duplo*: i.e. both physical and spiritual.

[2.24] A f. 263r–264v; P1 f. 36r–37v (*VC*, ii, 33) Metre: Sapphic stanzas.
5. *Melconis*: Bridei son of Mailcon. Adomnán names Bridei five times in *VC*: in i, 1, i, 37, ii, 33, ii, 35, and ii, 42. He always calls him *Bru(i)deus rex* without a patronymic: MacLean has not got *Melconis* from Adomnán. Bede (*HE*, iii, 4) calls him *Bridius filius Meilochon*; Fordun and Bower use similar forms derived from Bede, possibly influenced by king lists. *Chron. Bower*, iii, 26 (ed. Watt, ii, 68) has *Brudeo filio Mealochon*. The Pictish king list in the Poppleton MS calls him *Bridei f. Mailcon*. Boece, *SH*, ix, 46, mentions *Melothon* as father of *Brudeus*. Cf. Anderson, *KKES*, 144 n., on the forms of the father's name.

5–8. *Pedagogus ... ludimagister*: MacLean has got the idea that Bridei was young and Broichan was his schoolmaster from Adomnán's *nutricio eius* ('his foster-father'). As the Andersons point out (*VC*, ii, 33, 142 n.), *nutricius* translates OI *aite* ('foster-father') and does not imply that the king was of immature age. Cf. also Sharpe, *Adomnán*, 334, n. 291.

12. *Goeto*: the meaning is clear from *Augures, mantae, druidae, goeti, saga, medeae, quoque nicromantae*, 2.25.57, f. 265 v. Sharpe ('MacLean', 128–9) points to a Gk word γοήτης ('sorcerer'), and comments: 'I have no idea where MacLean may have learnt it'. The word seems to be extremely rare. St Augustine, in *De Civitate Dei* 10.9, speaks of *goetia* ('sorcery, necromancy').

16. *Renatam*: i.e. baptised.

19. *Ad pedem collis uiridesque ripas*: MacLean may have been thinking of the hill on which Inverness Castle stands. Since Adomnán states that Bridei's messengers came from his hall to the banks of the Ness on horseback, implying a site at some distance from the Ness, some modern writers have suggested the site of Craig Phadrig, 2.5 kilometers west of Inverness. This hill was the site of

an Iron Age hill fort, with evidence of a major secondary occupation during the Pictish period. There is no consensus. Cf. Sharpe, *Adomnán*, 335, n. 294.

33. *Equites*: this is the word used by Adomnán, probably used by him to mean 'riders on horseback'. MacLean may mean 'soldiers, knights'.

54. *Scotis*: nom. of a noun, cf. *Scotide* (abl.), line 36, *Scotidem* (acc.), line 42. Cf. *Scotidos* (gen.), 1.3.10. *Paciali* = *pacali*.

[2.25] A f. 264v–265v; P1 f. 37v–38v (*VC*, ii, 34) Metre: Sapphic stanzas.
8. *Austri*: Adomnán makes Columba come to the north end (i.e. the outflow) of Loch Ness (*ad lacum Nisae fluminis longum*), having been staying near the royal residence beside the River Ness, presumably at or near Inverness. To sail south, he will have needed a north wind (*Boreas*) to carry him up the loch. But MacLean says he was hoping for *Auster*, the south wind, while Broichán conjured up *Boreas* against him. Adomnán does not name the winds in question. MacLean knew Inverness well and is usually very careful in naming the winds, and a mistake of this kind would be most unusual for him. He seems to have envisaged Columba sailing north into the Moray Firth, in spite of what Adomnán says: the reference to *Neptuni ... aquas* in line 15 implies a journey into the open sea. Elsewhere (e.g. 2.4, 2.22) MacLean has a very free and imaginative interpretation of geographical details in Adomnán.

f. 264 v–265r
9–16. *Mitis aiebat ... Carbasa uentis*: the order of these two verses has been reversed, as they make more natural sense in this order. Blado's text reads: ... *austri? // Dum uelit Christus, comitante uita, / tertio solis dabimus sub ortu / nostra Neptuni per aquas secundis / carbasa uentis. // Mitis aiebat Uolucer, Brochane / ut modo ueris pius acquiescas / quod uiae nostrae rogitas dietam / certus habeto. // Improbus ...* The only other example of a similar kind is the awkward line *Fratres stupent instantia* in 1.27.20, which appears to have been misplaced.

27. *Uisum*: acc. supine.

A f. 265v; P1 f. 38v
43. *Monaeis ... popellis*: the name *Mona* was applied both to Anglesey and the Isle of Man. MacLean here apparently applies it to all of Great Britain.

46. *Pelagi periclum*: probably 'dangers of the sea', rather than 'dangers of Pelagius'. Adomnán does not mention that Germanus was coming to Britain to combat the Pelagian heresy, though it has been noted that his account in *VC*, ii, 34 contains language lifted from Constantius's Life of Germanus (Anderson, *VC*, 145 n.; Sharpe, *Adomnán*, 336, n. 298). Constantius says that Germanus's

first visit to Britain was intended to combat Pelagianism, and his account is quoted more fully by Bede, *HE*, i, 17 (who does mention Pelagianism). It is not in Fordun or Bower.

[2.26] A f. 265v–266r; P1 f. 38v–39r (*VC*, ii, 12) Metre: Sapphic stanzas. This is a paraphrase of *VC*, ii, 12, and is out of position here. MacLean has placed it next to his paraphrase of *VC*, ii, 34 because they both show Columba's control over the elements of nature during seafaring. The vividness of MacLean's description reminds us that he too spent his life in a seafaring society. The biblical model for Adomnán's story in *VC*, ii, 12 is in Mat. 8: 23–27, Mark 4: 36–40.

3–4. *Quassae ut tabulae fathiscant aere soluto*: cf. Verg. *Aen*. 1.122–3: *laxis laterum compagibus omnes / accipiunt inimicum imbrem rimisque fatiscunt* ('When the fastenings of the sides were loosened, they all let in hostile waters and gape at the seams').

6. *Tethys*: a sea-goddess, consort of Oceanus.

8. *Aeolus*: god of the winds, which he kept in a cave.

11, 18. *Uacuare, uacuans*: Sharpe (*Adomnán*, 163 and n. 236, 323) suggests reading *exinanire* ('to empty') in *VC*, ii, 12 at 62b (rather than the Andersons' tentative alternative, *ex inani re* ['from a vain thing']). MacLean's *uacuare* is synonymous with *exinanire*, possibly suggesting that that was what he read in his MS. Cf. Anderson, *VC*, pp. 110–11, n 139. Adomnán's *aquam ... amaram exinanire hi nin glas* ('to empty bitter water *hi nin glas*, into the green wave') is perhaps a proverbial expression for a futile action, echoed by MacLean's *resultans ... salum disco uacuans*, ('emptying out the returning sea with a shallow bowl').

23. *Silet uentus*: cf. *In sermone suo siluit uentus* in the office for St Columba: Macquarrie, *Legends of Scottish Saints*, 138.

26. *Galathaea*: Galatea, a sea-nymph.

27. *Repandrostro*: i.e. dolphins. From an extremely rare CL word *repandirostrus* ('having a turned-up snout'), with syncope to make it scan. Cf. Quintilian, *Inst*. 1.5.67, quoting Pacuvius (second century BC): *Nerei repandirostrum incurvicervicum pecus*.

28. *Naereus*: Nereus, a sea god, mentioned also in P5 (the Introduction). Scanned as a dissyllable.

[2.27] A f. 266v; P1 f. 39v (*VC*, ii, 35) Metre: Sapphic stanzas.

[2.28] A f. 266v–267r; P1 f. 39v–40r (*VC*, ii, 36) Metre: Sapphic stanzas.
1. *Duum ruris ... coenobitas* [*sic*]. Adomnán (*VC*, ii, 36) has *in monasterio duum ruris ... riuulorum* ('in the monastery of the land of two streams'), i.e. *Tír dá glas*, now Terryglass, County Tipperary. Rather uncharacteristically, MacLean's paraphrase at this point makes poor sense. He may have been misled by *duum* in Adomnán: in prose *duorum* would normally be expected. On the other hand, MS A has *duorum* in the chapter heading, which should have given MacLean the correct sense. MS B1 has *duorum* both in the chapter heading and in the text, and so cannot have been MacLean's source.

f. 267 r
10. *Ianuis clausis et inire*: cf. John 20: 26: *uenit Iesus ianuis clausis*. Cf also John 20: 19.

[2.29] A f. 267r–268v; P1 f. 40r–41v (*VC*, ii, 37) Metre: Sapphic stanzas.
This curious story may contain folk-tale elements: a poor man acquires an artefact with supernatural properties which makes him wealthy, then becomes poor again when he mistakenly destroys it out of fear of its power.

3. *Rogulam*: a diminutive of LL *roga* ('alms') (*DMLBS*, s.v. *roga*). Adomnán has *elimoysinam*. MacLean may have coined the diminutive.

7, 11. *Contuli, contulum*: taken from Adomnán, *VC*, ii, 37. Cf. Latham, *MLWL*, s.v. *contulus*; also in *NCLCL*. Cf. *contum* below. Adomnán has already used this word in *VC*, ii, 27, in the sense of 'the length of a pole'.

A f. 268r; P1 f. 41r
33. *Coniugis primum*: cf. Gen. 3.

49. *Utilis ... molossus*: a hunting hound. Adomnán has *domesticus ... canis*. The death of a useful domestic animal on the stake seems to contradict Columba's promise in lines 14–15 above, and is an inconsistency in the story; but MacLean is here following Adomnán (*VC*, ii, 37, f. 84a).
A f. 268v; P1 f. 41v

68. *Unguem*: Adomnán has *ueru ... adsumpta securi in plures concidens particulas in ignem proicit*. ('Taking an axe he chopped the stake into many small pieces and threw it into a fire.' [*VC*, ii, 37].) MacLean has apparently misread *in ignem* as *unguem*, missing the point that the stake was burnt up. Adomnán does not say that the peasant injured himself while cutting up the stake. In MS A, *in ignem* is very clearly written as two words, but perhaps in MacLean's copy they were run together. In the Office for St Columba in the Aberdeen Breviary, which must, to some extent, reflect traditions which were current

on Iona in the early sixteenth century, this story is alluded to in one of the responsories at Matins: *A beato uiro pauper petens alimoniam, sudem aptat manu sancta, qua pauperi preparantur omnia. Palo per se posito, necdum igne combusto, pauperi preparantur omnia.* ('When a poor man begged alms from the saint, he prepared a stake by his holy hand, whereby all things were provided to the poor man. When the spike had been set up by him, before it was burnt up by fire, all things were provided to the poor man.') See Macquarrie, *Legends of Scottish Saints*, 136–7.

69–70. *Quadrigis ... albicatis*: obscure. Perhaps in the sense 'in triumph'? Cf., however, *numquam ... quadrigis albis indipiscet postea* ('he will never thereafter overtake, [even] in a white chariot'), Plautus (*Asinaria* 2.2.13), as an image of something fast. It is not clear where MacLean can have got this. He has used a similar expression at 2.15.38. Cf. also the last stanza of 2.16.

[2.30] A f. 268v–271r; P1 f. 41v–44r (*VC*, ii, 39) Metre: Sapphic stanzas. The story of Librán 'of the reed bed' is one of the longest and most involved narratives in *VC* (only iii, 23 is longer). In MacLean's *Ionis* 2.30 is by some way the longest poem in Book 2. For commentary on the details of the story, cf. the notes in Sharpe, *Adomnán*, pp. 338–40.

1–2. *Conachtus gente*: Adomnán has *de Connachtarum regione oriundum*.

19. *Cunctum facinus piandum*: Adomnán says that he confessed all his sins (*omnia sua ... peccata*) before going on to mention that he had committed homicide and oath-breaking: so MacLean is paraphrasing accurately. Cf. Anderson, *VC*, 154 n.; Sharpe, *Adomnán*, 338, n. 311. As Sharpe remarks, it is only a 'slight flaw' in Adomnán's narrative, and clearly MacLean was not concerned to change it.

25. *Algedo*: the meaning, 'cold', from CL *algidus, algeo*, is not in doubt, but MacLean's form is unusual and not classical. Cf. Cicero, *Tusculanae Dispitationes* 2.34: *leges ... Lycurgi laboribus erudiunt iuuentutem, venando, currendo, esuriendo, sitiendo, algendo, aestuando*.

27. *Expianto*: third person plural future imperative, a rare form.

31. *Campilungeis*: Adomnán's *Campus Lunge*, for Gaelic *Magh Luinge* ('plain of the ship'), was the site of Columba's monastery in Tiree. It is unidentified.

54. *Maceratus*: an unusual word. The vowel in the first syllable is short, connecting it with *macer* ('thin'), *macresco*, etc. Cf. ML *macerativus* ('that involves fasting') (*DMLBS*). Possibly influenced by *mācero* ('to make wet'), which, however, has a long vowel. If Librán worked in reed beds as a penitent for

seven years, he will have become both thin and wet. Cf. *quaderet*, *Epistola*, 110, where MacLean has added an extra syllable for metrical reasons.

88. *Robur ad ore*: Derry. Adomnán has *daire calcig*.

90. *Euripo*: if MacLean knew Derry, he possibly has in mind the narrowing of the River Foyle between Derry and Lough Foyle. *Curuas ... puppes*: cf. Verg. *Aen.* 6.4–5; Ovid, *Fasti* 4.131. MacLean uses *curuas ... carinas* at 2.13.10, and *ratis curuae* (gen.) at 2.30.113. MacLean will have been thinking of the late medieval West Highland galley, with its high bow and stern curving upwards from below the waterline. Cf. Steer & Bannerman, *Sculpture*, 180–4, and illustrations on 181, Plates 5 B & C, 6 C, 16 A, 18 B & C, 24 D, 26 C, 32 A.

110. *Foelemi gnatus*: Columba. Cf. *Felemitides*, P 5.74; *Fedhlaemita*, 1.3.5.

122. *Septem procul in Trionem*: i.e. *Septentrionem* in tmesis; the 'seven stars' of the Plough, almost the most northerly constellation. Cf. the same phrase at 2.32.14 below.

147. *Roboreti*: MacLean has assumed that this is the same place that he has recently mentioned as *robur*. Adomnán calls it *roboreus campus* and says that Librán travelled through the plain of Brega (in Meath) to get to it: he means Durrow in County Offaly. MacLean's confusion is understandable. In 1.24 he has previously identified *monasterium roboreti campi* with Derry, where Adomnán (*VC*, i, 29) means Durrow. When giving their names in Old Irish, Adomnán calls Durrow *Dair mag* (oakwood plain) and Derry *Daire Calcig* (oakwood of Calgach).

149–50. *Clyo ... nostra*: 'our muse of historical narrative', i.e. Adomnán.

[2.31] A f. 271 v; P1 f. 44v (*VC*, ii, 40) Metre: Sapphic stanzas.
1–4. *Una Lucinam*, etc. Both *Mithlia* and *Munya* are puzzling; there is nothing in *VC*, ii, 40 from which MacLean can have got them. There is no doubt that *Munya* is Munster. The reference to the setting sun implies that it is in the west of Ireland. In 1.34 MacLean refers to the *Munenses* ('People of Munster'). In the corresponding passage in *VC* (i, 44) Adomnán calls it *Muminensium prouincia*. Since Columba's family is not connected with Munster in Adomnán or any other early source, this appears to be a flight of fancy by MacLean. All that Adomnán says is that Columba said *mihi est cognitionalis de meae matris parentella genitorem habens progenitum* ('she is related to me having a father born of my mother's kindred'). On the pedigree of Columba's mother Eithne, cf. Ó Riain, *Dictionary*, 211, 293. *Mithlia* is an adj. from Mithlius, the name of an early mythological king mentioned by MacLean in P6. In MacLean's

genealogy the first Mithlius is father of Erimon; in the *Lebor Gabála*, Míl (Espáne) is father of Éremón. The race of Mithlius is mentioned again in 2.32 in connection with Cormac Úa Liatháin (see below), who was born in Munster. On the family of Míl, cf. O'Rahilly, *EIHM*, 195 ff.

13. *Gemellos*: another imaginative development by MacLean. Adomnán does not mention twins but speaks of *prolem*.

[2.32] A f. 271v–273r; P1 f. 44v–46r (*VC*, ii,42) Metre: Sapphic stanzas.
11. *Mithlia*: See note on 2.31.2 above. Cormac Úa Liatháin's pedigree connects him with County Cork in south Munster (Ó Riain, *Dictionary*, 226). He eventually became abbot of Durrow, and has important dedications in the Irish Midlands, especially in Offaly and Westmeath. By *gens mithlia* MacLean apparently means the descendants of Míl Espáne.

13. *Solam ... eremum*: *eremus* can be fem. in the Vulgate, e.g. Deut. 1: 19: *per heremum terribilem et maximam.*

14. *Septem procul in Trionem*: MacLean has already used this phrase, referring to the stars of the Plough, at 2.30.122.

17. *Maximati*: an unusual ML word, formed on the analogy of *magnates*, and very rare in the sing.

35–6. *Septimum ... paralelum*: obscure. Perhaps the Arctic Circle?

54. *Octipedi*: the Zodiacal sign of Cancer, the 'eight-footed' crab. The sun is in Cancer 22 June–22 July.

61ff. *Pende Neptuni*, etc.: based on the closing words of *VC*, ii, 42: *Perpendat itaque lector quantis et qualis idem uir beatus, qui talem profeticam habens scientiam uentis et ociano Christi inuocato nomine potuit imperare.*

63. *Labier*: archaic pass. (dep.) inf.: cf. note on P3.5.

65. *Clyo*: muse of history and narrative: here a reference to Adomnán.

66. *Aulai*: from *aulaeum*, originally a curtain or covering, but in ML attracted to *aula* ('hall'): *DMLBS*, s.v. *aulaeum*, 2. MacLean treats it as fem.

69. *Studiosus*: Columba.

[2.33] A f. 273r; P1 f. 46r (*VC*, ii, 8) Metre: Sapphic stanzas.

Here again MacLean departs from Adomnán's order, including some material from earlier in Book ii.

5. *Ascella*: MacLean has taken this strange word from Adomnán, *VC*, ii, 8. The CL word is *axilla* or *ala* ('oxter, armpit'). (Cf. *NCLCL*, s.v.) Cf. Gaelic *achlais*.

[2.34] A f. 273v; P1 f. 46v (*VC*, ii, 9) Metre: Sapphic stanzas.
2. *Pictus*: Adomnán says (*VC*, ii, 9) that the book had been the property of, and was returned to, *Iogenanum prespiterem gente Pictum*. This must be where MacLean got *pictus* from, but he has misunderstood and deviated a long way from Adomnán's meaning. Adomnán says nothing about illustrations. He sets this incident in Leinster, however, so MacLean will not have been expecting a reference to a Pict. Eoganán the Pict was presumably a monk of the *familia* of Iona. There was an important Columban church at Moone (*Maoin Choluim Chille*) in County Kildare.

5. *Pridie nonas ... Decembres*: Adomnán says the book was submerged *a natalicio Domini usque ad Pascalium consummationem dierum* ('from Christmas until the end of the days of Easter'). The fourth of December is three weeks before Christmas, and it is not clear why MacLean has changed this. Confusion may have arisen because Christmas Eve is the ninth day (inclusive) before the Kalends of January (*ante diem nonum kalendas Ianuarias*). MacLean says nothing about the date of the finding of the missing book, which is odd after he has been so specific about the date of its loss.

[2.35] A f. 273v–274v; P1 f. 46v–47v (*VC*, ii, 44) Metre: Sapphic stanzas.
1. *Uector Hellaeus*: Helle, daughter of Athamas, was riding on a ram with a golden fleece, in flight from her stepmother Ino, when she drowned in the Hellespont. Ino, out of jealousy of her stepchildren, had caused Athamas's seed corn to be roasted so that it would not sprout, then feigned that the Delphic oracle demanded the sacrifice of Helle and her brother Phryxus. The sun is in Aries (the Ram) 21 March–20 April. MacLean thus locates his narrative at the season of sowing, while alluding very obliquely to seed corn which would not sprout due to drying heat. *Bouis ... sydus*: Taurus, 21 April–21 May.

2. *Sedecem ... annos*: MacLean is not saying that it did not rain for sixteen years. Adomnán says *Ante annos ... ferme xuii* ('nearly seventeen years ago'). The B MSS have *quatuordecim*, presumably having misread *xuii* as *xiiii*. So here MacLean is closer to A than to B. The B MSS also have an additional sentence which is not in MS A that makes clear that Adomnán is describing a contemporary event as an eyewitness (*Miraculum quod nunc Deo propitio describere incipimus, nostris temporibus factum propriis inspeximus oculis*).

10. *Exhausta ... palude*: There is marshy ground on Iona around Loch Staoineig (NM 2622) near the south end.

15. *Thaumantis*: Iris, daughter of Thaumas, was goddess of the rainbow. Cf. Ovid, *Met.* 11.647.

19. *Aeneum*: cf. Lev. 26: 19–20, quoted by Adomnán: *Daboque caelum vobis desuper sicut ferrum et terram aeneam; consumetur in cassum labor vester; non proferet terra germen nec arbores poma praebebunt.* MacLean has adapted the wording slightly to fit the metre.

35. *Angeli Cliuo*: Adomnán calls this hill *colliculus angelorum* ('the angels' hill'), here in ii, 44 and in iii, 16, where he adds that its Gaelic name is *cnoc angel*. It is traditionally identified with a knoll at Sìthean farm overlooking the western machair of Iona which is now called *Cnoc nan Aingeal*. (Cf. Sharpe, *Adomnán*, n. 385, 368) MacLean's word *clivus* ('gentle slope'), is a good descriptor for *Cnoc nan Aingeal*. *Sìthean* = 'fairy hill'.

40. *Arbos* = *arbor*. Cf. Verg. *Georg.* 4.24: *obviaque hospitiis teneat frondentibus arbos*.

43. *Pales ... Ceres*: the classical deities of herding and agriculture. Cf. 2.19.18–19.

[2.36] A f. 274v–276r; P1 f. 47v–49r (*VC*, ii, 45) Metre: Sapphic stanzas.
In this chapter MacLean shows off his knowledge of the names of the winds. His starting point is Adomnán's words in *VC*, ii, 45: *Tum deinde per longas et oblicas uias tota die prosperis flatibus Deo propitio ... peruenit* ('Then it [the boat] came through long and tortuous routes with favourable winds by God's favour'). The winds mentioned in 2.36 and 2.37 are: *Aphricus, Nothus, Euronothus, Lybs* (= Λίψ), *Eurus, Boraeas, Iapyx, Uulturnus, Auster, Zephyrus, Caurus*. The impression given is that the raft was intending to sail from a point on the mainland south-east of Iona through various island channels but was at first prevented by the prevailing south-westerly. This dropped and was replaced by a variety of winds from other directions which brought them through the islands of the Firth of Lorn and eventually to Iona. For another example of MacLean expanding a short phrase in Adomnán into an elaborate showcase for his extensive vocabulary, cf. 1.30.

3. *Praesens ... aetas*: i.e. Adomnán's own time.

9. *Lacustre*: a very rare ML word: cf. *DMLBS*, s.v.

14. *Natilem ... machinam*: probably a misprint for *nautilem* or *nautilam*, from Gk ναυτίλος ('of a ship, nautical'). The first syllable is long.

17. *Tusas acie secures*: from *tundo* ('to beat'), either in the sense of axes with blades of beaten metal, or possibly blades blunted by repeated blows. From the context, it is not clear which. Cf. Pliny, *HN*, 34, 43, 149: *Ferrum ... rubens non est habile tundendo, neque antequam albescere incipiat.*

26. *Ater*: the vowel in the first syllable of this word is always long in CL. This is a rare slip by Maclean.

29. *Calet ara thure*: cf. Verg., *Aen.* 1.416–17: *ture calent arae.* (Cf. 1.3.21 above.)

41–2. An allusion to the miracle recounted in 2.35.

56. *Meandri*: i.e. like the twisting River Maeander in Phrygia. MacLean has adjusted the spelling, and consequently the scansion, to make this word fit his prosody.

75. *Leuasti* = *leuauisti*. Cf. Adomnán, *VC*, ii, 45: *huc usque a te ... praestari sperauimus consulatorium adiuentum* ('until now we have hoped for consoling help to be given by you').

79. *Loene* = *lene*.

[2.37] A f. 276r–v; P1 f. 49r–v (*VC*, ii, 45) Metre: Sapphic stanzas.
In Adomnán, the equivalent passage follows as part of *VC*, ii, 45 without a break. MacLean does not have a chapter heading here, but he capitalises the first word as if beginning a new section. This edition follows Sharpe's numbering system.

81. *Post Euernensis synodi recessum*: the Synod of Birr, 697, in which Adomnán played a very prominent part. This was the centenary of Columba's death, but it is not clear how conscious of this Adomnán will have been, if indeed at all.

87. *Sainea*: unidentified. Possibly one of the many islands of the Firth of Lorn whose original Gaelic name has been overlaid by a Norse name. MacLean does not attempt to identify it. His form is adjectival, like Adomnán's. Cf. Sharpe, *Adomnán*, 347–8, n. 343.

96. *Domate*: cf. Gk δῶμα ('house').

97–8. *Matua*: The usual name for the goddess of the morning is Aurora; she is also known as *Matūta*, but the vowel in the second syllable is long and would not scan here. She was the spouse of Tithonus.

99. *Cardinalis ... Auster*: cf. Adomnán, ii, 45: *Auster cardinalis qui et Notus.*

101–2. *Quinta ... hora*: Adomnán, ii, 45, has *post horam diei tertiam.*

[2.38] A f. 276v–277r; P1 f. 49v–50r (*VC*, ii, 46) Metre: Sapphic stanzas.
3–4 *Terno ... clymate*: obscure.

6. *Britones*: MacLean probably does not mean the people of Britain here:
he mentions *Albion* ('*Alba*, Britain'), in the following stanza. Adomnán has
*Europae regionibus, hoc est Italia et ipsa Romana ciuitate et Cisalpinis Galliarum
prouinciis, Hispanis quoque Pirinei montis interiectu disterminatis, Ociani insulae ...
uidelicet Scotia et Brittannia.*
Suaeuos: in classical writers, the *Suebi* were a group of eastern Germanic
peoples. It is not clear what MacLean is thinking of here: possibly either
eastern Europe or Scandinavia.

19–20. *Tot ... templa, sacella*: Adomnán speaks in *VC*, ii, 46 of Columba's
monasteria ... ualde honorificata among the Picts and Scots. By MacLean's time
the number of his dedications in Scotland had actually increased.

24. *Anglos*: Adomnán visited England twice, in 686 and 688. Cf. *VC*, ii, 46;
AU 687; Bede, *HE*, v, 15.

25. *Nostras*: a reference to the fact that Adomnán's *Vita Columbae* was composed
on Iona.

28. *Suffice pennas*: a last echo of Ps. 55: 6.

PARAPHRASE OF PSALM 1

A f. 277r; P1 f. 50r Metre: Elegiac couplets.
Ne pagina remaneret uacua: Although MacLean says the elegiac paraphrase
of Ps. 1 is only included to fill a blank page, and it is not part of *Ionis*, his
psalm paraphrase in fact forms a fitting and satisfying close to the book as a
whole. It is easy to identify Columba as the *beatus uir qui non abiit in consilio
impiorum*, while MacLean's enemies could be identified with the wicked men
mentioned in the Psalm. For a detailed commentary on this poem, cf. R P
H Green, 'Poetic Psalm Paraphrases: Two Versions of Psalm 1 compared',
in R Schnur, ed., *Acta Conventus Neo-Latini Budapestinensis: Proceedings of the
Thirteenth International Congress of Neo-Latin Studies, Budapest, 6–12 August 2006*
(Tempe, 2010), 261–70.

Ut pleraque alia: This is the only psalm paraphrase by MacLean which is known to have survived. If, as he claims, he had composed paraphrases of 'many of the others', then large quantities of MacLean's verse have been lost, or await discovery. In P3 he complains that he has been criticised, presumably for his earlier poetry. In P4, his advocate John Forman challenges his critics to do better themselves. It might speculatively be suggested (Introduction, p. 22) that MacLean could have published a volume of psalm paraphrases on his previous trip to France and Rome in 1542–43, which had a poor reception on his return to Scotland. On the *genre* of psalm paraphrase, cf. R P H Green, 'George Buchanan's Psalm Paraphrases in a European Context', in T Hubbard & R D S Jack (eds), *Scotland in Europe* (Amsterdam, 2006), 25–38, esp. 32; and R P H Green, *George Buchanan: Poetic Paraphrase of the Psalms of David* (Geneva, 2011).

Ex tempore: On the meaning of this expression cf. Green, 'Poetic Psalm Paraphrases', 262. The psalm could have been added after MacLean saw the final layout of the book with an almost totally blank folio at the end: he could then have added an appropriate psalm paraphrase which he had previously composed, which he jotted down quickly from memory. That could perhaps be described as *ex tempore*, while also explaining that it was included *ne pagina remaneret uacua*. On the other hand, it may be that MacLean was able to compose poetry fairly quickly: the *Straena Gratulatoria* was dated 1 January 1549, describing events that had taken place in the far south of Scotland on 22–23 and 26 December 1548. That news must have been very fresh on 1 January 1549. Cf. the use of this expression with reference to MacLean's poems in P4.

4. *Erronum*: although perhaps not as rare as *nugo* (see below), *erro* (a wanderer or runaway), is a very uncommon word. Cf. Green, 'Poetic Psalm Paraphrases', 266.

6. *Nugonum*: this word (from *nugae*, 'trifles') seems to be extremely rare, possibly found only in Appuleius, *Metamorphoses*, 5.29 and 30. Cf. Green, 'Poetic Psalm Paraphrases', 266.

17. *Stabit*: Professor Green ('Poetic Psalm Paraphrases', 268) points out that *stabit* has a long *a* 'and so the metre is faulty'. This is 'a strange mistake … since MacLean's prosody here and as a rule elsewhere is careful.' He suggests that MacLean may have been thinking of words like *stabulum* with short *a*.

EPISTOLA ELEGIACA

PI, f. 2r–5v
Sir David Linsday of the Mount (*c.* 1486–1555) was a prominent courtier of James V, Lyon Herald, and an ambassador to the emperor and the kings of England and France in the 1530s and 1540s. After the king's death in 1542 he remained influential with the governor the earl of Arran and Mary of Guise. He wrote highly original poetry in Scots, including anti-clerical satires. MacLean here appeals to him to use his influence at court on his behalf, although it is implied that Lindsay has by this time retired to his estates in Fife. His best known (and most anti-clerical) poem, *The Thrie Estaitis*, was not published until after MacLean's address to him was written.

2. *Postea nosse potes*: clearly MacLean was planning a visit to court in late 1548 or early 1549 to curry favour with the governor, and these verse letters were part of his preparation.

6. *Fama*: Little is known of Roderick MacLean's reputation before the later 1540s. He had been on a diplomatic mission from the crown to Ireland and Rome in 1542 (cf. Introduction, pp. 6–7), and he had been appointed archdeacon of the Isles about the same time. He appears to have published poetry, perhaps Latin psalm paraphrases, in the 1540s. In 1544 the governor told Cardinal Carpi that Roderick had a good reputation for Gaelic scholarship (cf. Introduction, pp. 46–7). He was nominated by the governor to the vacant bishopric of the Isles in 1545.

11. *Regina*: Mary Queen of Scots, born 8 December 1542, was approaching her sixth birthday when MacLean was writing.

14. *Quinte Iacobe*: James V had died on 14 December 1542.

15. *Ioanni Danielis*: John MacDonald, son of Angus Óg MacDonald, lord of the Isles 1336–87. He married Margaret Stewart, daughter of Robert Stewart who became Robert II in 1371. Robert II was indeed *tritauus* of James V.

15, 17, 20. *Danielis, Daniel*: MacLean's classicisation of Gaelic *Dòmhnall*, Donald. Cf. note on 39 below. John MacDonald's name in Gaelic was *Iain Dòmhnallach*.

18. *Daniel Rossius . . . comes*: Donald, lord of the Isles 1387–c. 1423, and earl of Ross by his marriage to Mariota Leslie some time before 1403.

19. *Nomen Alexander cui dat celeberrima Thyle*: Alexander of Islay, lord of the Isles *c.* 1423–49. In his charters (*ALI*, 34–76) he is always called *Alexander de*

Ile, Alexander of Islay. MacLean here is equating *Thyle* or *Thule* with Islay.
Cf. *Ionis* 2.14, where Adomnán's rich man *qui in Ilea insula habitabat* (*VC*, ii,
23) is rendered *Thylaei praesidis* (gen.). Perhaps MacLean thought, wrongly,
that Islay (Gaelic *Íle*) was a lenited form of *Thyle*. On forms of the name Islay,
cf. Steer & Bannerman, *Sculpture*, 126–7. (The *s* in the modern English name
Islay is intrusive, from a false connection with English *isle*.)

23–4. *Ipsius Angusii Ferquhardum, filia, patrem ediderat nostrum Fingola nomine erat.*
Fingola must represent the Gaelic female personal name Finguala or Fionghuala.
According to MacLean, she was daughter of Angus, brother of Alexander
of Islay, lord of the Isles. She must have been married to Hector MacLean,
father of Farquhar, who was in turn father of Farquhar and Roderick, the
successive bishops of the Isles.

31. *Imitata*: here in a passive sense. Cf. *OLD*, s.v. *imitor*.

36. *Qua lacus illimi gurgite Noesus abit*: a branch of the MacLeans of Kingairloch
settled at Urquhart on Loch Ness, and it has been argued (Dilworth, 'Iona
Abbey and the Reformation', 91–4) that Farquhar and Roderick belonged to
this branch. This family also had an association with Contin in Easter Ross.
This could explain why Roderick was spending his 'exile' at or near Inverness,
and why in papal documents he is often called 'clerk of the diocese of Ross',
indicating the diocese of his birth.

38. *Ennosigaeus*: A Homeric name (the 'earth-shaker') for Poseidon or Neptune;
very rare in Latin writers.

39. *Danieligenum*: the *Clann Dhòmhnuill* or Clan Donald. The MacDonald
lords of the Isles were forfeited by the crown in 1493, but Dòmhnall Dubh's
rebellion in 1544–45 had widespread local support. The form is gen. plu.

48. *Nestoreus*: in the *Iliad*, Nestor was an elder who gave traditional sage
advice to the Greeks.

50. *Momus*: the personification of fault-finding.

52. *Minerua*: as well as being the goddess of wisdom and crafts, Minerva was
also a patron of writers and actors.

53. *Iessaeum . . . psaltem*: David son of Jesse was an accomplished harpist: 1
Sam. 16: 16–18. He is also described as *prudens*. See 1 Sam. 18: 5, 14, etc.

59–60. *Cunctus ut agnoscet Numen*, etc. Lindsay's poems, especially *The Thrie Estaitis* (which, however, was published later than MacLean's poems), are anti-clerical and reformist in tone. MacLean is here expressing approbation for his evangelical opinions.

62. *Status . . . turbidus*: following the Battle of Pinkie in September 1547, English troops garrisoned south-east and eastern Scotland and attempted to establish a 'Scottish Pale'.

63. *Tua Tempe*: the valley of Tempe in Thessaly was famed for its beauty, and the name was applied by extension to any rural place removed from the cares of war or public service: Hor., *Odes* 3.1.24; Verg., *Geor.* 2.469. Cf. also *Ionis* 1.30.46, above.

65. *Nestor*: see note on l. 48 above.

66. *Aeacidae*: Aeacus was grandfather of Achilles. *Myrmidonum*: Achilles' soldiers.

69. *Tua secessu*: David Lindsay 'was born, at the latest, in 1486' (Lyall, *Thrie Estaitis*, xiv). He must then have been at least sixty-two when this poem was written. He still held the post of Lyon Herald, and was on a diplomatic mission to Denmark in 1549 (*TA*, ix, 347). It is recorded that messages from the court were sent to Lindsay in Fife in 1547 and 1550: *TA*, ix, 96, 381. Thanks to Dr Janet Hadley Williams for this information.

73. *Syluius Aeneas*: an ancestor of the royal house of Alba Longa, mentioned by Livy (1.3) and Verg. (*Aen.* 6.769–70): *Siluius Aeneas pariter pietate uel armis / egregius*. He is the first in a list of rulers who, in MacLean's view, encouraged the order of heralds, followed by Alexander, Caesar, and Charlemagne.

79–80. *Liber*: a name for Bacchus. *Ut Indos subdidit*: Alexander the Great invaded India in 326 BC.

88. *Xoenia duxque dabit*: cf. Ps. 68: 29 (V. 67: 30): *tibi offerent reges munera*.

110. *Quaderet*: for *quadret*.

151ff. *Post obitum fratris Sodorensis praesulis olim / nominor ad uacuum praesulis ipse locum*: Roderick's brother Farquhar was bishop of the Isles 1530–45. On his death in June 1545 Governor Arran nominated Roderick. Dòmhnall Dubh's supporters, however, nominated a rival candidate with support from Henry VIII. See the Introduction, pp. 9–11.

155ff. *Plura sed huic obstant*, etc. The virulence of Roderick's attack on Patrick MacLean and his mother is striking. It perhaps has something in common with the invective of Gaelic bardic satire.

157. *Maiestate reus laesa*: presumably a reference to his participation in Dòmhnall Dubh's rebellion against the Governor and Mary Queen of Scots in 1544–45.

159. *Ter semel addictum*, etc.: obscure. The *Ius trium liberorum* of Augustus granted certain privileges, originally limited to patricians (*patricii*), to families with three or more children. The ironic point may be that Patrick has the name 'patrician' undeservedly, while he is himself part of a large family of illegitimate children. Thanks to Dr Betty Knott-Sharpe for her guidance through this obscure passage.

160. *Patricius*: Patrick MacLean, an illegitimate half-brother of Hector MacLean of Duart, was appointed 'bailie of Iona' by Dòmhnall Dubh's Council of the Isles in 1545. In August 1547 the governor granted the temporalities of the abbacy of Iona to Patrick MacLean until such time as the pope should make provision to it. See the Introduction, p. 10.

161. This passage is obscure. If this interpretation is correct, Patrick MacLean was thirty-six years old: but since the minimum age for consecration as a bishop was thirty, this was no disqualification. Roderick was probably in his mid-forties, so could have regarded Patrick as a young upstart. Cf. *ephoebus* in *Ionis*, P3.6, which, however, does not fairly describe Patrick MacLean. Patrick's father had died at Flodden (9 September 1513). In 1565 Patrick MacLean declined the bishopric in exchange for a pension when Queen Mary offered it to him, on grounds of infirmity (Maclean-Bristol, *Warriors and Priests*, 151–4). It is implied below that his mother had remarried several times, or had had various sexual liaisons.

162. *Lustra*: the word has several meanings. *Lustrum* can mean the purification ceremony for a new-born infant, or a ceremonial period of (usually) five years. The point may be that three further children have been born to Patrick's mother by different fathers, each requiring a *lustrum*. The couplet is obscure.

164. *Nomine plus matris, quam patris inde refert*: Patrick MacLean's father was Lachlan MacLean of Duart, who was married several times and had legitimate issue. 'He also had a bastard son, Patrick, by one Catherine Kay (*sic: recte* Hay)' (J P MacLean, *A History of the Clan MacLean from its early Settlement at Duard Castle in the Isle of Mull to the present Period* [Cincinnati, 1889], 72–3). Cf. Maclean-Bristol, *Warriors and Priests*, 119: 'Mr Patrick was Lachlan Cattanach's

son by one Catherine Hay. He had evidently been educated at a lowland university.' Roderick here is claiming that she was promiscuous.

165. *Matricius*: presumably because his paternity is in doubt. There may be a secondary play on the word *meretricius*.

166. *Pater ignotus*: if Patrick was indeed thirty-six, he was born in 1512, a year before his father's death. So his father will have been 'unknown' to him in this respect at least.

167. *Pressit belua matrem*: MacLean's strong language here is striking. The influence of Gaelic bardic satire may be suspected. Cf. D S Thomson, *Companion to Gaelic Scotland* (Glasgow, 1994), 135–6, 293.

169. *Dunlopius*, etc.: obscure. The accusation may be that Patrick's mother had borne children with all these surnames. As printed by Blado, the line is a syllable short: read *Hayus et Hepburn*.

171. *Hesperidum glaucus draco*: Ladon, the dragon which guarded the apple tree of the Hesperides. Heracles slew the dragon and took the apples.

189. *Titulos, natales, arma, triumphos*: the basic subject matter of the Lindsay Armorial, written by Sir David Lindsay in 1542. *Natales*: in the sense of family origins.

191. *Pieridum . . . sororum*: the Muses.

193–4. *Qua uespertinus Iberno Tytan flammigeros aequore tingit equos*: cf. cf. Verg. *Aen.* 11.913–4: *roseus fessos iam gurgite Phoebus Hibero tingat equos*. Cf. also *Ionis* 1.35.1–2.

193–6. *Atque ego . . . zona lares*: that is, whether MacLean is in his rightful place on Iona in the far west, or in the heat of Italy, litigating for his right to the bishopric and commendatorship at the papal *Curia*. He was in Rome by April 1549, when he arranged for publication of the *Ionis*. His legal battle dragged out for nearly a year, and he did not secure his final legal victory in Rome until March 1550.

STRAENA GRATULATORIA

P1, f. 5v–6r
The poem is addressed to James Hamilton, earl of Arran and governor of Scotland (d. 1575). He was Queen Mary's heir presumptive and the most

powerful man in the kingdom during the regency. His policy was to try to remain independent of both England and France, but this attempt collapsed after a heavy defeat at the Battle of Pinkie (10 September 1547), when he was forced into a French alliance to expel the occupying English forces. His attempt at religious reform in 1543 had also been a failure.

The subject of the poem is the return to Scotland in December 1548 of George Gordon, fourth earl of Huntly (d. 1562). He had been captured at Pinkie, but escaped the following year and made his way back to Scotland. According to a very circumstantial account in Lesley's *History*, he was being conveyed to Morpeth so he could have a conjugal meeting with his wife when he slipped away from his guards on the night of 22–23 December and was in Edinburgh for Christmas. See *The History of Scotland . . . by John Lesley, Bishop of Ross* (Edinburgh, 1830), 220–2; cf. also *Scottish Correspondence of Mary of Lorraine* (Edinburgh, 1927), 280–1.

1. *Nate Gathaeliadum*, etc.: James Hamilton, earl of Arran, was a direct descendant of James II.

5. *Albion . . . lugebat*: probably a reference to the defeat at Pinkie and subsequent English occupation of the south-east.

11. *Georgius*: George Gordon, fourth earl of Huntly, d. 1562. He was the most powerful nobleman in the north-east and in the central Highlands. He had a good military reputation after his victory over the English at Haddon Rigg in 1542, and for his gallantry at Pinkie.

16. *Tibi post unum*: the only 'one' who deserved honour ahead of Huntly was the governor, the earl of Arran.

19. *Humnia rupes*: the rock on which Hume Castle stands (NT 7041). Hume Castle changed hands several times during the Rough Wooing. It surrendered to the English after Pinkie (*Diurnal of Occurrents*, 45), but was recovered by the Scots in December 1548. It is the latter event that MacLean is celebrating here. Cf. *The History of Scotland . . . by John Lesley*, 222–3, giving 26 December; *Diurnal of Occurrents* (49) has 16 December. It is possible that the former date is correct, and the *Diurnal* has mistakenly written *xvj* instead of *xxvj*: cf. *Scottish Correspondence of Mary of Lorraine*, 280–1, 283, supporting the later date.

20. *Cauda fugax trepidat*: There was a persistent rumour in the later Middle Ages, at least among their enemies, that Englishmen had tails. Cf. Watt, *Bower's Scotichronicon*, ii, 90–92, and nn., 234; v, 98.

26. *Pigriciae*: probably a reference to the enforced idleness of the earl's captivity.

33. *Cynthius*: Apollo.

36. *Aurora croceas uix reserante fores*: the morning of 1 January 1549. If Lesley's date is correct, news of the events on the Border just six days earlier must have been very fresh. This has implications for discussion about how quickly MacLean could compose his poetry.

APPENDIX:
MATERIAL IN THE VATICAN ARCHIVES
RELEVANT TO THE CAREER OF
RODERICK MACLEAN

1. MATERIAL IN THE *REGISTRUM SUPPLICATIONUM*

During his two visits to Rome in 1542–43 and 1549–50, Roderick MacLean submitted a number of legal supplications to the pope of which record has survived in the *Registrum Supplicationum*. He is also mentioned in the supplications of others. The calendar of abstracts below is taken from the microfilm collection of Scottish entries from the Vatican Archives held at Glasgow University.

Abbreviations: d. = diocese, diocese of; OClun = Cluniac Order; OSA = Order of St Augustine; OSB = Order of St Benedict; ster. = sterling. Christian names have been standardised, but not surnames or place names.

RS 1981, f. 278v–279r   *Perinde valere*   11 July 1529
It is shown for the part of Charles Makelan, clerk, d. Sodor, that the parsonages of the parish churches of St Columba de Knokis in Kynnellwedanech, d. Lismore, of St Columba, Skerechoyr, and of St Peter in Kannedes3 in Wist, d. Sodor, are vacant, and have been for so long that by the Lateran statutes their collation has devolved on the apostolic see, although Roderick Hectoris Johannis *alias* Makilan, clerk, d. Sodor, has detained that of Knok, as have the abbot and convent of the monastery of Iona (*Ione Insule*), OSB, d. Sodor, the two others, without any title or support of law in respect of them but of their own temerity and *de facto*, for a certain time, as they still do. Charles therefore supplicates that the pope would commit to some good men in these parts to investigate, and if they find the churches to be vacant, would provide him thereto (£6 sterling combined), vacant as above, or howsoever, notwithstanding defect of birth.[1]
Concessum. Rome, St Peters.

---

[1]   There is a corresponding papal letter with the same date: cf. *CPL* xxiii, part 1, no. 447, pp. 267–8.

RS 2158, 93r   *Indultum*   4 December 1531
Farquhard, bishop of Sodor, professed OSB, supplicates that the pope would licence him to wear a white rochet or *pallium*, and other vestments of decent colour, such as other bishops in the kingdom of Scotland wear, as the late George [Hepburn], bishop of Sodor, his predecessor, did, and as the late George [Learmonth], coadjutor and successor in the church of Aberdeen, OSB, did, and also black clothes (*vestes*) of the form of secular priests and prelates under his cloak or mantle (*sub clamide seu mantello*), or the black clothes of a secular priest, without apostasy from his order, and without ecclesiastical censure or scruple of conscience, and without laying aside his rochet or *pallium* at the canonical hours by day or night, or other offices of the use of the church of Sodor, and to remain in his order, etc.
Fiat. Rome, St Peters.

RS 2471, f. 80r–81r   *Commissio per breve*   15 November 1542
A case between Richard Lauson, then archdeacon of Sodor, and John Campbell, asserted clerk, his adversary, over the archdeaconry of Sodor, and one-third of the fruits of the parish church of St Mary (Kilmorie) of Arran, perpetually annexed thereto, was pending in the first instance before the ordinary or his vicar, and a sentence was correctly given in favour of Richard, whereupon John appealed to the archbishop of St Andrews against the decision giving Richard the third part; and the archbishop correctly confirmed the decision, whereupon John appealed to the apostolic see, and the pope appointed judges in those parts to determine the case. Richard then, weighed down with age, resigned into the hands of the ordinary, who admitted this resignation and provided it to Roderick Ferquhardi, clerk, d. Ross, by ordinary authority, vacant by this resignation or otherwise, now archdeacon of Sodor, and he was assecuted and had corporeal possession. Since, however, Roderick, present archdeacon of church of Sodor, doubts the certainty of this provision, he supplicates that the pope would appoint some good men in d. St Andrews, metropolitan to the church of Sodor and the rest of Scotland, and in d. Dunkeld where John dwells, jointly and severally, to hear and determine the case, etc.
Concessum. Rome, St Peters.

RS 2472, f. 235r   *De horis*   9 December 1542
Since Roderick Ferquhardi, archdeacon of Sodor or the Isles, and William Munro, priest, d. Ross,[2] desire to use the divine office recently published by Francis, cardinal priest of Sta Croce in Gerusalemme, they supplicate that the pope would grant them indult to read the canonical hours, breviary, etc., alone or with familiars, outwith the choir.
Concessum. Rome, St Peters.

---

[2]   Cf. 2486 f.259r–v *Ad duo*. William Munro, clerk d. Ross, that the pope would dispense him to hold two incompatible benefices. 4 April 1543.

RS 2474, f. 32v–33r   *Nova provisio*   14 January 1543
Formerly the parish churches of St Mary the Virgin in Barvass in Lewess, and of Kilmolwok in Throutness (= Kilmaluag in Trotternish) and Kilcomian in Watterniss, which are perpetually united, d. Sodor, were vacant by the death of Martin Makgillewartyn, parson thereof, and by presentation of James king of Scots Roderick Ferquhardi Hectoris, clerk, d. Ross, was provided and instituted by ordinary authority; but some have doubted this presentation and provision, and assert that the parsonages are still vacant: therefore Roderick supplicates that the pope would provide him anew thereto (£9 ster.), vacant as above or howsoever.
Concessum. Toscanella, d. Viterbo.

RS 2476, 87r–v   *Nova provisio*   25 January 1543
Formerly the archdeaconry of Sodor being vacant by free resignation of Richard Lawson into the hands of the ordinary, Roderick Ferquhardi, clerk d. Ross, was provided by ordinary authority, had possession and received the fruits; but for certain reasons he doubts the validity of this provision and fears that it may be claimed by some that it is still vacant: he therefore supplicates that the pope would provide him anew thereto (£12 ster.), vacant as above or howsoever; also that he may hold another incompatible benefice.
Concessum. Cornetto.

RS 2478, f. 23r   *Per obitum*   19 February 1543
Since the parish church of St John the Evangelist (Kildalton) in the island of Ile, d. Sodor, is vacant by the death of John Ebrolchan (= Ó Brolcháin):[3] Roderick Ferquhardi Hectoris, MA, clerk, d. Ross or another d., of noble birth on both sides, supplicates that the pope would provide him thereto (£8 ster.), vacant as above or howsoever.
Concessum. Rome, St Peters.

RS 2486, f. 258v   *Per obitum*   4 April 1543
Since the parish church of Kilchoman, isle of Ile, d. Sodor, is vacant by death of Donald Makdufy:[4] Roderick Ferquhardi, clerk, d. Ross, supplicates that the pope would provide him thereto (£12 ster.), notwithstanding Archibald Mackarbry[5] or any other detaining it unlawfully.

[3] Cf. *RSS*, iv, 28: sir John Obrolchane, late parson of Kildalton: 8 January 1549.
[4] Donald MacDuffie, canon OSA, was provided to the priory of St Columba of Oronsay on the resignation of Donald MacPhail on 28 April 1538: RS, 2285, f. 131r–132r; Reg. Vat., 1510, f. 14r–15r.
[5] There may be confusion between two persons, one called Archibald MacGillvray and the other called Archibald MacCairbre. Cf. *RMS*, iv, no. 800: per D. Arch. Makgilwray de Kilcomman. But cf. also RS 2469, 216v: 'Perugia, 10 September 1542. Since the perpetual vicarage of the parish church of Killenan, d. Lismore, which Archibald Makcarbre, its last vicar, held, is vacant by his death last July, therefore John Campbell, clerk d. Dunkeld, supplicates that the pope would provide him thereto (£7 ster.), vacant as above or howsoever,

Concessum. Reggio.

RS 2486, f. 258v–259r   *De quarto*   4 April 1543
Roderick Ferquhardi, clerk, d. Ross, MA, of noble birth on both sides, previously dispensed to hold three incompatibles: now supplicates that the pope would dispense him to hold four incompatible benefices.
Concessum. Reggio.

RS 2486, f. 259r   *Per obitum*   4 April 1543
Since the parish church of St Mary of Kilmorie in Arran, d. Sodor, is vacant by the death of Donald or Augustinus (= Angus?) Makdonall; therefore Roderick Ferquhardi, clerk, d. Ross, supplicates that the pope would provide him thereto (£12 ster.), vacant as above or howsoever.
Concessum. Reggio.

RS 2639, f. 56v–57r   *Resignatio*   25 August 1548
Since Roderick Maclan, archdeacon in the church of Sodor, resigns the same into the hands of the pope: therefore Donald Munro, priest, d. Ross, supplicates that the pope would provide him thereto (£6 ster.), vacant as above or howsoever.
Concessum. Rome, St Marks.

RS 2657, 246r   *Per obitum*   7 April 1549
Since the perpetual chaplaincy at the altar of St John the Baptist in the parish church of Invernes, d. Moray, is vacant by death of John Scott, its last possessor, in a month which may be stated in letters, Roderick Maclen, clerk d. Ross, supplicates that the pope would provide him thereto (£6 ster.), vacant as above or howsoever.
Concessum. Rome, St Peters.

RS 2664, f. 151r[6]   *Per obitum*   8 June 1549
Motu proprio. It is supplicated for the part of Mary Queen of Scots, for Roderick Maclen, clerk d. Ross, MA, of noble birth on both sides, that the pope would provide him to the monastery of St Columba of the island of Iona *alias* Ycolumkill, OSB, d. Sodor, vacant by the death of the late Ferquhard Hectoris or Maclen, who died in the month of June 1545 (*in mense Iunii anno*

---

etc.' Archibald MacCairbre, called 'clerk of Dunkeld or another diocese', also appears in a supplication dated 28 April 1538 (RS 2285, 153r–154r). Since Archibald MacCairbre died in July 1542, and Archibald MacGillvray is consistently linked with Kilchoman in Islay, this supplication must relate to Archibald MacGillvray.

[6] The supplication is difficult to read because writing on the reverse side of the page shows through.

millesimo quingentesimo quadragesimo quinto), or by the death of John Campbell or of George Hepburn, or howsoever (£100 ster.), or by free resignation of the said Ferquhard, provision resting specially with the holy see, to hold it *in commendam.*
Concessum. Rome, St Marks.

RS 2664, f. 155v[7] *Per obitum*   22 July 1549
Alan Macaulosi, parson of the parish church of St Coman in Valternes, d. Sodor or the Isles, supplicates that the pope would provide him to the chancellorship of the church of Sodor, a non-major dignity after the pontifical therein, while the dignities, canonries, and prebends annexed to the said church have been detained and occupied by the English for about one hundred years, vacant by death of James Carmure,[8] last chancellor (£9 ster.), or howsoever, etc.
Concessum. Rome, St Marks.

RS 2667, f. 298v *Per obitum*   2 August 1549
Ferquhard Macneyll, parson of the parish church of St Columba of Euinort, d. Sodor or the Isles, supplicates that the pope would provide him to the deanery or *archipresbyterium* of the church of Sodor or the Isles, a non-major dignity after the pontifical therein, while the dignities, canonries, and prebends annexed to the said church have been detained and occupied by the English for about one hundred years,[9] vacant by the death of Christopher Archi' or another, dean while he lived and last possessor, perhaps in a reserved month which may be stated in letters, (£12 ster.), vacant as above or howsoever, etc., and to retain his parish church (£10 ster.), as prebend of the deanery.
Concessum. Rome, St Marks.

RS 2667, f. 299r *Per obitum*   2 August 1549
Patrick Martin, parson of the parish church of St Mary in Barvas in Insula de Le3us, d. Sodor or the Isles, supplicates that the pope would provide him to the subdeanery of the church of Sodor or the Isles, a non-major dignity after the pontifical therein, while the dignities, canonries, and prebends annexed to the said church have been detained and occupied by the English for about one hundred years and more, vacant by death of Simon Magowl

---

[7] The supplication is difficult to read because writing on the reverse side of the page shows through.
[8] Cf. Watt & Murray, *Fasti,* 270–1
[9] Sic: *que inibi dignitas non tamen maior post pontificalem seu personatus administratio vel officium et cum aliis dignitatibus ac canonicatibus et prebendis annex' eiusdem ecclesie ab Anglis per centum annos detenta et occupata extitit.* The deanery of a cathedral church would normally be classed as the major dignity after the pontifical. But cf. the following supplications for other dignities in the cathedral of the Isles, which were non-major: the phrasing of this supplication may have been attracted to them.

or another, subdean while he lived and last possessor (£8 ster.), vacant as above or howsoever, etc., with dispensation to hold with the parish church the vicarage of the parish church of St Peter Prince of the Apostles of Nes, said d. Sodor or the Isles (£4 ster.) as prebend of the subdeanery.
Concessum. Rome, St Marks.

RS 2667, f. 299r–v   *Per obitum*   2 August 1549
Donald Munro, parson of the parish church of Hy in Leʒus (= Eye in Lewis),[10] d. Sodor or the Isles, supplicates that the pope would provide him to the precentorship ([*prec*]*entoria*)[11] of the church of Sodor or the Isles, a non-major dignity after the pontifical therein, while the dignities, canonries, and prebends annexed to the said church have been detained and occupied by the English for about one hundred years, vacant by death of Duncan Maconiel or another, precentor while he lived and last possessor (£9 ster.), vacant as above or howsoever, etc. together with his parish church (£10 ster.), as prebend of the precentorship.
Concessum. Rome, St Marks.

RS 2667, f. 299v   *Per obitum*   2 August 1549
Archibald Macgillevray, parson of the parish church of St Coman in Ile,[12] d. Sodor or the Isles, supplicates that the pope would provide him to the treasurership of the church and d. of Sodor or the Isles, a non-major dignity after the pontifical therein, while the dignities, canonries, and prebends annexed to the said church have been detained and occupied by the English for about one hundred years, vacant by death of John Macgernian or another, perhaps in a reserved month (£9 ster.), vacant as above or howsoever, etc., and to hold with it the parish church of St John the Evangelist in Ardnis and the chaplaincy of Ellenfinlagan, d. Sodor or the Isles (£9 ster.), as prebend of the treasurership.
Concessum. Rome, St Marks.

RS 2667, f. 299v–300r   *Per obitum*   2 August 1549
Finlay Tormoti,[13] parson of the parish church of St Brigit in Byaray,[14] d. Sodor or the Isles, supplicates that the pope would provide him to the succentorship of the church of Sodor or the Isles, a non-major dignity after the pontifical therein, while the dignities, canonries, and prebends annexed

---

10 Cf. D. Donaldo Munro rectore de Y, *RMS*, iv, no. 750.
11 There is an ink-blot on the paper at this point.
12 On 18 September 1542 Archibald Maklewray, priest, d. Sodor, had dispensation to hold three incompatibles for life.
13 Tormod was 'a favourite name with the Macleods' (Black, *Surnames*, 775). Cf. also *OPS*, ii, pt 1, 377: 'sir Finlay Termatsone rector of Hary'.
14 *lege* Hyaray, i.e. *Hearadh*, Harris.

to the said church have been detained and occupied by the English for about one hundred years, vacant by death of Donald Indecis[15] or another (£7 ster.), vacant as above or howsoever, etc., and to retain the parish church (£5 ster.) as prebend of the succentorship.

Concessum. Rome, St Marks.

RS 2668, f. 185r   *Reformatio*[16]   16 August 1549

Since John Hay, clerk d. St Andrews, for whom Mary Queen of Scots had supplicated by her letters for the monastery, considering that Roderick is of more usefulness to the monastery because of his skill in the local language, which John lacks and Roderick has (*ob idiomatis loci peritiam que ab ipso Ioanne abest ac dicto Roderico inest*): John therefore supplicates for an annual pension of 200 merks Scots (£23 ster.) from the fruits of the abbatial *mensa*, not exceeding half its value.

Concessum. Rome, St Marks.

RS 2672, f. 38r   1 October 1549

Since, in a case before John Spittal, asserted commissary of the vicars-general of the church of St Andrews,[17] the archbishopric of St Andrews being then vacant, between the prior and convent of Ycolmkill, OSB, d. Sodor, actors, and Roderick Maclain, clerk d. Ross, over certain moveable goods and other matters, at the instance of the prior and convent he (Roderick) was summoned personally before the said John Spittal, and doubting his competence, he refused, and because of his non-appearance John caused him to be removed and perhaps excommunicated. It was then appealed by Roderick to the pope within due time: He therefore supplicates that the pope would commit and give mandate to some good men in these parts to hear and determine the case, citing himself and John Spittal and whomsoever else, as needful.

Concessum. Vetralla, d. Viterbo.

RS 2704, f. 203r–v   *Nova provisio*   14 April 1550

The parish church of St Nicholas (*recte* St Moluag)[18] in Trouternes, d. Sodor, being vacant by free resignation of Roderick Maclan into the hands of the ordinary, David Lauson, clerk d. St Andrews, was provided by ordinary authority. Since, however, for certain reasons he doubts the validity of this

---

[15] Sic. If *indecis* is a misreading of a Gaelic surname, it could begin *mcl-*. For *mclecis* (?) perhaps read Gaelic *MacLucais*, or something similar?

[16] Sic: read *Pensio*.

[17] Official of St Andrews, 1546 53. See Watt & Murray, *Fasti*, 420. The vacancy lasted from May 1546 to June 1549 (ibid., 386–7).

[18] That is, Kilmaluag in Trotternish. The original probably read *sancti moloci*, which the scribe has misread as *nioloci* and then rationalised as *nicolai*.

provision, he supplicates that the pope would provide him anew thereto
(£4 ster.).
Concessum. Rome, St Peters.

RS 2704, f. 210r–v   *Alternatim*   9 September 1550
Motu proprio. To Roderick elect of Sodor, that while he is bishop of Sodor, and
to whatsoever cathedral church he may be transferred, the pope would grant
him the right of collation and provision to all benefices within the diocese
which become vacant in the months of May, July, September, November,
January, and March each year.
Concessum. Rome, St Peters.

RS 2850, f. 180r   *Per obitum*   4 March 1555
Since the monastery of Ycolmkill, d. Sodor, OSB or OClun, which the late
Roderick Maclane, clerk Glasgow or another d., held *in commendam*, is vacant
by his death: therefore Alexander [Gordon], archbishop of Athens, supplicates
for provision to the monastery (£70 ster.).
Concessum. Rome, St Peters.

RS 2867, f. 72r   *Nova provisio*[19]   3 October 1555
Since the monastery of Ycolmkill, d. Sodor, OSB or OClun, which the late
Roderick Maclane, clerk Glasgow or another d., held *in commendam*, is vacant
by his death: therefore Alexander [Gordon], archbishop of Athens, supplicates
for provision to the monastery (£70 ster.).
Concessum. Rome, St Peters.

2. BULL OF RODERICK MACLEAN'S PROVISION TO THE
BISHOPRIC OF THE ISLES BY POPE JULIUS III

This document has not been previously published, so even though it is largely
formular, a full transcript is included here because of its inherent interest. There
is a brief abstract in W M Brady, *The Episcopal Succession in England, Scotland
and Ireland, A.D. 1400 to 1875* (Rome, 1876), citing the 'Barberini collection'
(i, 163). This transcript, with editorial punctuation and capitalisation, is from
Registrum Vaticanum, 1791 (114r–116v), taken from the microfilm collection at
Glasgow University. Square brackets [ ] indicate missing words or tentative
readings; pointed brackets < > indicate marginal and other alterations made
within the MS.

---

[19] The wording is very similar to the foregoing supplication granted by Julius III; this one
was granted by Paul IV. Strictly speaking, the rubric should be *Per obitum*.

Abstract

Rome, St Peters, 5 March 1550.

Pope Julius III to Roderick Maclen, clerk d. Sodor. Formerly Pope Paul III reserved to his own disposition provision to all churches then vacant and to be vacated, and the church of Sodor or the Isles, which Farquhar Hectoris held, being vacant by his death outwith the Roman *curia*, was still vacant when Pope Paul died, and for the avoidance of ambiguity the present pope declares that it is still reserved to his disposition. Not wishing the church to experience a long vacancy, in consultation with the cardinals the pope, considering his many virtues, has focused upon Roderick, elect of Clonmacnoise, of noble race on both sides, considering that he has today ceded the church of Clonmacnoise into the pope's hands without apostolic letters thereanent having been drawn up, and, having admitted this cession, he hereby provides him as bishop to the rule and administration of the church of Sodor. With admonition to the clergy and people of the diocese, the vassals of the church, the chapter, Mary Queen of Scots, and the archbishop of St Andrews. The grant is made *motu proprio*. He may retain any benefices which he holds, including the Monastery of St Columba, OSB, d. Sodor, *in commendam*, and his pensions and rights in the churches of St Coman in Ila (Kilchoman in Islay) and St Mary in Arania (Kilmorie in Arran), the fruits of the parish churches together not exceeding £25 ster. and the fruits of the monastery not exceeding £70 ster. With the proviso that divine service and the customary number of monks and servants in the monastery shall not be reduced, and the parish churches shall not be defrauded in their obsequies or neglected in the cure of souls.

RV 1791, 114r–116v
Ecclesia Sodoren'

Julius episcopus seruus seruorum Dei dilecto filio Roderico Maclen clerico Sod<o>ren'[20] [diocesis] salutem et apostolicam benedictionem. Apostolatus officium meritis licet imparibus nobis ex alto commissum quo ecclesiarum omnium regimini diuina dispositione presidemus utiliter exequi coadiuuante Domino cupientes solliciti corde reddimur et solertes ut cum de ecclesiarum ipsarum regiminibus agitur committendis tales illis in pastores preficere studeamus qui populum sue cure creditum sciant non solum doctrina uerbi sed etiam exemplo boni operis informare commissasque sibi ecclesias in statu pacifico et tranquillo uelint et ualeant auctore Domino salubriter regere et feliciter gubernare. Dudum siquidem felicis recordationis Paulus papa tertius predecessor noster prouisiones ecclesiarum omnium tunc uacantium et inantea uacaturarum ordinationi et dispositioni sui reseruauit, decernens extunc

---

[20] At most occurrences the word is written *Sodren'* with a superscript *o* and a caret mark between the *d* and *r*. Towards the end of the document there are a few examples where the superscript o is not added.

irritum et inane si secus super hiis a quoquam quauis auctoritate scienter uel
ignoranter contingeret attentari. Postmodum[21] uero ecclesia Sod<o>ren' alias
Insularum cui alias bone memorie Ferquhardus Hectoris episcopus Sod<o>ren'
alias Insularum Hebridum dum uiueret presidebat per obitum eiusdem
Ferquhardi episcopi qui extra Romanam curiam diem clausit extremum
pastoris solatio destituta, nos uacatione huiusmodi fidedignis relatibus intellecta
ad ipsius ecclesie celerem et felicem prouisionem de qua nullus preter nos pro
eo[22] quod nos qui dicto predecessore per eum predicte ecclesie etiam tunc ut
prefertur uacanti non prouiso sicut Domino placuit ab hac luce subtracto
diuina fauente clementia ad summi apostolatus apicem assumpti fuimus. Cum
a nonnullis reuocaretur in dubium cui aliquis preter Romanum pontificem
de prouisionibus ecclesiarum tempore obitus predecessoris huiusmodi
uacantium quarum prouisiones dispositioni sue reseruauerat se intromittere
potuisset siue posset ad huiusmodi ambiguitatem / dictum collendum dubium
declaramus prouisiones ecclesiarum predictarum tempore premisso uacantium
propter reseruationem et decretum predecessoris huiusmodi remansisse et
remanere assertas nullumque in illis preter eundem Romanum pontificem
[h]actenus[23] se intromittere potuisse siue posse quoquomodo, ac irritum et
inane decernimus si secus super hiis per quoscunque quauis auctoritate scienter
uel ignoranter contigerit attentari se intromittere potuit siue potest reseruatione
et decreto obsistentibus supradictis. Ne ecclesia ipsa Sod<o>ren' longe uacationis
exponatur incommodis patentis et sollicitis studiis intendentes post delibera-
tionem[24] quam de preficiendo eidem ecclesie Sod<o>ren' personam utilem
et etiam fructuosam cum fratribus nostris habuimus diligentem demum ad
te electum Cluanen' de nobili genere ex utroque parente procreatum consideratis
grandium uirtutum donis quibus personam tuam illarum Largitor Altissimus
multipliciter insigniuit et quod tu qui hodie regimini et administrationi
ecclesie Cluanen' cui alias tunc certo modo uacante de persona tua apostolica
auctoritate prouisum fuerat literis apostolicis desuper non confectis in manibus
nostris sponte et libere cessisti omnisque cessionem huiusmodi duximus
admittendo eandem ecclesiam Sod<o>ren' fies uoles et poteris auctore Domino
salubriter regere et feliciter gubernare direximus oculos nostre mentis quibus
omnibus debita meditatione pensatis te a quibusuis excommunicationis etc
censentes de dicta persona tua de ipsorum fratrum consilio prefate ecclesie
Sod<o>ren' predicta auctoritate providemus teque illi in episcopum preficimus
et pastorem curam et administrationem ecclesie Sod<o>ren' predicte tibi in
ipsis spiritualibus et temporalibus plenarie committendo firma spe fiduciaque
conceptis quod dirigente Domino actus tuos dicta ecclesia Sod<o>ren' sub

---

[21]   Written twice in error, the first one is crossed out and initialed *B*.
[22]   The word *eodem* is written; then the last three letters are crossed out and initialed *B*.
[23]   *Sic.* The words *hac vice* sometimes appear at this point in similar documents.
[24]   A word is crossed out; it is initialed *B*.

tuo felici regimente regetur utiliter et prospere dirigetur ac grata in eisdem / spiritualibus et temporalibus suscipiet incrementa quocirca discretioni tue per apostolicam scriptam mandamus quatenus curam et administrationem predictas sic exercere studeas sollicite fideliter et prudenter quod exinde sperati fructus aduenant ac tue bone fame odor latius diffundatur necnon supradicta ecclesia Sod<o>ren' gubernatori prouido ac fructuoso administratori gaudeat se commissam tuque preter eterne retributionis premium nostram et apostolice sedis benedictionem ac gratiam exinde uberius consequi merearis. Ac clero et populo Sod<o>ren' ciuitatis et diocesis necnon uassales eiusdem ecclesie Sod<o>ren' quatenus capitulum tibi tamquam <patri et >[25] pastori animarum suarum humiliter intendentes exhibeant tibi obedientiam et reuerentiam debitas et deuotas, ac clerus te pro nostram et sedis predicte reuerentia benigne respicientes et honorifice pertractantes tua salubria monita et mandata suscipiant humiliter et efficaciter adimplere procurent. Populus uero <te>[26] tamquam patrem et pastorem animarum suarum deuote suscipientes et debita honor- ificentia prosequentes tuis monitis et mandatis salubriter humiliter intendant ita quod tu in eos deuotionis filios et ipsi in te pro consequens patrem beneuolum inuenisse gaudeatis. Uassali autem prefati te debita honore prosequentes tibi fidelitatem solitam necnon consueta seruitia et iura tibi ab eis debita integre exhibere procurent alioquin sententiam siue penam quam respectiue rite tuleris seu statueris in rebelles ratam habebimus et faciemus autore Domino usque ad satisfactionem condignam inuiolabiliter obseruari. Rogamus quoque charissimam in Christo filiam nostram Mariam Scotorum reginam illustrem et uenerabilem fratrem nostrum Archiepiscopum Sancti Andree ipsi archie- piscopo per eadem scripta mandantes quatenus te et prefatam dicte suam / dicti Archiepiscopi suffraganum habentes pro nostra et prefati sedis reuerentia propensius commendatos in ampliandis et conseruandis tuis ac predicte ecclesie Sod<o>ren' iuribus sic te et illam eorum benigni fauore auxilio prosequantur quod in illorum fultus presidio in commisso tibi cure pastoralis officio possis Deo propitio prosperari ac eidem Marie Regine adeo perennis uite premium et a nobis condigna promeruat actio gratiam, ipseque archiepiscopus prouide diuinam misericordiam ac nostram et eiusdem sedis benedictionem et gratiam ualeant uberius promereri et insuper ut statum tuum iuxta pontificalis dignibilis exigentiam decentius tenere valeas. Motu proprio non ad tuam uel alterius pro te nobis super hoc oblate petitionis instantiam sed et nostra mera liberalitate. [Volumus][27] tecum ut etiam postquam in uim prouisionis et prefetionis predictarum pacificam possessionem seu quasi regiminis et administrationis premissorum ac ipsius ecclesie Sod<o>ren' bonorum seu maioris partis eorum

---

[25] In margin.
[26] Superscript.
[27] Omitted: but some word of this kind is required here. The following *tecum*, however, is odd. A common formula, which we might expect here, is *Volumus etiam quod postquam*.

assecutus fueris ac munus consecrationis susceperis omnibus et singulis dispen-
sationibus apostolicis tibi hactenus etiam ad quecunque quotcunque et quali-
acunque curata seu alias inuicem incompatibilia secularia at cum cura et sine
cura quorumuis ordinum regularia beneficia ecclesiastica insimul quomodolibet
obtinenda qualitercunque qualificata concessis et litteris apostolicis desuper
confectis uel conficiendis cum permutando et commende cedendo ac omnibus
et singulis aliis in eis contentis clausulis uti (?)[28] necnon dicta sub illis compre-
hensa recipere et iuxta earum tenores ac Monasterium Sancti Columbe ordinis
Sancti Benedicti Sod<o>ren' siue Insularum diocesis / nuper seu alias certo
modo uacans tibi pro te quoad uiueres etiam unacum omnibus et singulis
compatibilibus beneficiis ecclesiasticis que obtineres necnon pensionibus
annuis quas perciperes imposterum dicta auctoritate commendatum si illum
assequaris in commendam quoad uixeris etiam postquam dictum munus
susceperis etiam unacum prefata ecclesia Sod<o>ren' quamdiu illi prefueris
ac omnibus et singulis etiam curatis seu alias inuicem incompatibilibus
secularibus et regularibus beneficiis necnon pensionibus supradictis retinere
ac ius tibi in Sancti Comani in Ila et Beate Marie in Arania predicte Sodren'
diocesis parrochialibus ecclesiis quarum insimul uigintiquinque et dicti
monasterii fructus redditus et prouentus septuaginta librarum sterlingorum
secundum communem extimationem ualorem annuam ut etiam accepimus
non excedunt utend' illas quomodolibet competeris prosequi et deducere
illasque etiam consequi et ut premittitur retinere libere et licite ualeas. Generalis
Concilii et quibusuis aliis constitutionibus et ordinationibus apostolicis ac
ecclesie Sodren' et monasterii necnon ordinis predictorum iuramento confir-
mationis apostolica uel quauis firmata te antea roboratis statutis et consuetu-
dinibus ceterisque contrariis nequaque obstantibus eadem auctoritate apostolica
de specialis dono gratie dispensamus decernentes propterea dispensationes
non expirare et commendam non cessare ac ius huiusmodi non uacare. Irritum
quoque et inane si secus super hiis quoquam quauis auctoritate scienter uel
ignoranter contingit attentari. Prouiso quod propterea in dicto monasterio
diuinus cultus ac solitus monachorum numerus et ministrorum nullatenus
minuatur et dicte parrochiales ecclesie debitis non fraudentur obsequiis nec
animarum cura in / eis nullatenus negligatur sed ipsius monasterii ac dilectorum
filiorum illius conuentus congrue supportentur onera consueta. Datum Rome
apud Sanctum Petrum Anno Incarnationis Domini Millesimo quingentesimo
<quadragesimo nono>[29] Tertio Non' Martii Pontificatus nostri anno primo.

At head: *Blo. El. Fulgin'*;
At end: *M. Car. Cris.*   *R. de Piscia:~* [30]

---

[28] MS looks like *ute*.
[29] *Quinquagesimo* is written in the text, scored through, and initialed *B*. The correction in the margin is initialed *B*.
[30] There is a blank space between the two names, where normally the taxation would be recorded.

BIBLIOGRAPHY

For classical authors cited, see the List of Abbreviations.

PRIMARY SOURCES

Aberdeen University Library, p3 92211 Col M (*Ionis*, copy A).

Cawdor Castle, Campbell of Cawdor Papers, 649/2 (Charter of the bishop of the Isles, 8 August 1532).

Edinburgh, NRS CH5/2/1, Liber Sententiarum Officialis S Andree Principalis 1541–53.

Edinburgh, NRS CH5/2/3, Liber Actorum Officialis S Andree 1546–48/9.

Perugia, Biblioteca communale Augusta, ANT I-I-1255 (8) (*Ionis*, copy P2).

Perugia, Biblioteca communale Augusta, I-L-66 (1–2) (*Ionis*, copy P1; *Epistola Elegiaca* & *Straena Gratulatoria*).

Rome, Archivium Apostolicum Vaticanum, Registrum Supplicationum (RS), 1981, 2158, 2471, 2472, 2474, 2476, 2478, 2486, 2639, 2664, 2667, 2668, 2672, 2704, 2850, 2867.

Rome, Archivium Apostolicum Vaticanum, Registrum Vaticanum (RV), 1791.

SECONDARY SOURCES

Acts and Proceedings of the General Assemblies of the Kirk of Scotland, 1560–1618 (Glasgow, 1839).

Anderson, A O, *Early Sources of Scottish History, AD 500–1286* (Edinburgh, 1922).

———, & M O Anderson, *Adomnán's Life of Columba* (2nd edn Oxford, 1991).

Anderson, M O, *Kings and Kingship in Early Scotland* (Edinburgh, 1973).

Bannerman, J W M, 'Literacy in the Highlands', in I B Cowan & D Shaw (eds), *The Renaissance and Reformation in Scotland* (Edinburgh, 1983).

Beavan, I P Davidson & J Stevenson, *Library and Archive Collections of the University of Aberdeen* (Manchester, 2011).

Bieler, L, 'Review of *Adomnán's Life of Columba*, ed. A O & M O Anderson (1961)', *Irish Historical Studies*, xiii (1962–3), 175–84.

Black, C F, 'Perugia and post-Tridentine Church reform', *Journal of Ecclesiastical History*, 35/3 (July 1984), 429–51.

Black, C F, *The Italian Inquisition* (New Haven, 2009).

Boece, Hector, *Murthlacensium et Aberdonensium Episcoporum Vitae* (Aberdeen, 1894).

———, *Scotorum Historiae*, ed. Dana F Sutton, http://www.philological. bham.ac.uk/boece/, 26 February 2010.

Book of the Thanes of Cawdor (Aberdeen, 1859).

Brady, W M, *The Episcopal Succession in England, Scotland and Ireland, A.D. 1400 to 1875* (Rome, 1876).

Brewer, J S, et al., *Letters and Papers, Foreign and Domestic, of the Reign of Henry VIII* (London, 1862–1932).

Broëti, Paschasii, et al., *Epistolae* (Madrid, 1903).

Broun, D, & T O Clancy, *Spes Scotorum: Hope of Scots* (Edinburgh, 1999).

Brown, M P, *A Guide to Western Historical Scripts from Antiquity to 1600* (London, 1990).

Burton, J H, et al., *Register of the Privy Council of Scotland* (Edinburgh, 1877–1908).

Butter, R, 'St Munnu in Ireland and Scotland: an exploration of his cult', in S Boardman and E Williamson (eds), *The Cult of Saints and the Virgin Mary in Medieval Scotland* (Woodbridge, 2010).

Caius, John, *De Canibus Britannicis* (London, 1570).

Cameron, Annie, *Scottish Correspondence of Mary of Lorraine* (Edinburgh, 1927).

Cecchini, G, *La Biblioteca Augusta del comune di Perugia* (Rome, 1978).

Chadwick, N K, 'The lost literature of Celtic Scotland', *Scottish Gaelic Studies*, vii (1953), 115–83.

Charles-Edwards, T M, ed, *The Chronicle of Ireland* (Liverpool, 2006).

Clancy, T O, & G Márkus, *Iona: The Earliest Poetry of a Celtic Monastery* (Edinburgh, 1995).

Colgrave, B, & R A B Mynors, *Bede's Ecclesiastical History of the English People* (Oxford, 1969).

Dickson, T, et al., *Accounts of the Lord High Treasurer of Scotland* (Edinburgh, 1877–1970).

Dictionary of Scottish Church History and Theology (Edinburgh, 1993).

Dillon, M, *The Cycle of the Kings* (Oxford, 1946; reprinted Dublin, 1994).

Dilworth, M, 'Iona Abbey and the Reformation', *Scottish Gaelic Studies*, xii (1971), 77–109.

Dimock, J F, *Giraldi Cambrensis, Topographia Hiberniae* (London, 1861–91).

Diplomatarium Norvegicum (Christiana, 1848–1972).

Donaldson, G, 'The Church Courts', in *An Introduction to Scottish Legal History* (Edinburgh, 1958), 363–73.

———, *James V to James VII* (Edinburgh, 1965).

———, *The Scottish Reformation* (Cambridge, 1960).

Dondi, C,& M A Panzanelli Fratoni, 'Researching the origin of Perugia's public library (1582/1623) before and after *Material Evidence in Incunabula*', *Quaerendo*, 46 (2016), 129–50.

Dowden, J, *The Bishops of Scotland* (Glasgow, 1912).

Dumville, D N, '*Primarius cohortis* in Adomnán's Life of Columba', *Scottish Gaelic Studies*, xiii (1978–81), 130–1.

Durkan, J, 'The cultural background in sixteenth-century Scotland', *IR*, x, 382–439.

———, 'Native influences on George Buchanan', in *Acta Conventus Neo-Latini Sanctandreani: Proceedings of the Fifth International Congress of Neo-Latin Studies*, ed. I D McFarlane (New York, 1986), 31–42.

———, 'Scottish evangelicals in the patronage of Thomas Cromwell', *RSCHS*, xxi (1981–3), 127–56.

———, *Scottish Schools and Schoolmasters, 1560–1633*, ed. J Reid-Baxter (Edinburgh, 2013).

———, & J Kirk, *The University of Glasgow, 1451–1577* (Glasgow, 1977).

Easson, D E, & A MacDonald, *Charters of the Abbey of Inchcolm* (Edinburgh, 1938).

Elliott, J K, *The Apocryphal New Testament* (Oxford, 1993).

Ford, P, & R P H Green, *George Buchanan: Poet and Dramatist* (Swansea, 2009).

Ford, P K, *The Mabinogi and Other Medieval Welsh Tales* (Los Angeles, 1977).

Fumagalli, G, et al., *Catalogo delle edizioni romane di Antonio Blado Asolano ed Eredi, 1516–1593*, 4 vols (Rome, 1891–1961).

Gildersleeve, R L, & G Lodge, *Latin Grammar*, 3d edn (London, 1895).

Graham, T W, Patronage, 'Provision and Reservation: Scotland and the Papacy during the Pontificate of Paul III' (PhD diss, Glasgow University, 1992).

Green, R P H, 'George Buchanan, chieftain of neo-Latin poets', in L B T Houghton & G Manuwald (eds), *Neo-Latin Poetry in the British Isles* (London, 2012).

———, *George Buchanan: Poetic Paraphrase of the Psalms of David* (Geneva, 2011).

———, 'George Buchanan's Psalm paraphrases in a European context', in T Hubbard & R D S Jack, *Scotland in Europe* (Amsterdam, 2006).

———, 'George Buchanan's Psalm paraphrases: matters of metre', in *Acta Conventus Neo-Latini Sanctandreani: Proceedings of the Fifth International Congress of Neo-Latin Studies*, ed. I D McFarlane (New York, 1986).

————, 'Poetic Psalm paraphrases: two versions of Psalm 1 compared', in *Acta Conventus Neo-Latini Budapestinensis*, Medieval & Renaissance Texts and Studies 386 (Tempe, 2010).

————, P H Burton, and D J Ford, *Scottish Latin Authors in Print up to 1700: A Short-Title List* (Leuven, 2012).

Gregory, D, & W F Skene, *Collectanea de Rebus Albanicis* (Edinburgh, 1847).

Hannay, R K, and D Hay, *Letters of James V* (Edinburgh, 1954).

Harvey, A, & J Power, *Non-Classical Lexicon of Celtic Latinity,* i, *Letters A–H* (Turnhout, 2005).

Herbert, M, *Iona, Kells and Derry* (Oxford, 1988; reprinted Dublin, 1996).

————, & P Ó Riain, *Betha Adamnain: The Irish Life of Adamnan*, Irish Texts Society, liv (Dublin, 1988).

Hogan, E, *Ibernia Ignatiana* (Dublin, 1880).

James, M R, *The Apocryphal New Testament* (Oxford, 1924).

Kelly, J N D, *Jerome: His Life, Writings, and Controversies* (London, 1975).

Knott, E, *Irish Syllabic Poetry, 1200–1600* (Dublin, 1928; reprinted 2011).

Kusukawa, S, *A Wittenberg University Library Catalogue of 1536* (Binghamton, 1995).

Lacey, B, *Manus O'Donnell: The Life of Colum Cille* (Dublin, 1998).

Laing, D, *A Diurnal of Remarkable Occurrents that Have Passed within the Country of Scotland* (Edinburgh, 1833).

Latham, R E, *Revised Medieval Latin Word-List* (London, 1965).

————, et al., *Dictionary of Medieval Latin from British Sources* (London, 1975–2013).

Lesley, J, *The History of Scotland . . . by John Lesley, Bishop of Ross* (Edinburgh, 1830).

Lindsay, W M, *Sexti Pompei Festi de Verborum Significatu quae supersunt* (Leipzig, 1913).

Livingstone, M, et al., *Registrum Secreti Sigilli Regum Scotorum* (Edinburgh, 1908–82).

Lorimer, P, *Patrick Hamilton, first Preacher and Martyr of the Scottish Reformation* (Edinburgh, 1857, reprinted 1957).

Lyall, R, *Ane Satyre of the Threi Estaitis, by Sir David Lyndsay* (Edinburgh, 1989).

MacCaffrey, J, *History of the Catholic Church from the Renaissance to the French Revolution* (Dublin, 1914).

MacDonald, I G, *Clerics and Clansmen: The Diocese of Argyll between the Twelfth and Sixteenth Centuries* (Leiden, 2013).

————, '"That uncouth dialect": English-speaking clergy in late medieval Gaelic Scotland', *RSCHS*, xliii (2014), 1–29.

MacInnes, J, 'Gaelic poetry and historical tradition', in *The Middle Ages in the Highlands*, ed. L MacLean (Inverness, 1981), 142–63.

Mackechnie, J, *The Clan Maclean: A Gaelic Sea Power* (Edinburgh, 1954).

MacLean, J P, *A History of the Clan MacLean from Its Early Settlement at Duard Castle in the Isle of Mull to the Present Period* (Cincinnati, 1889).

Maclean-Bristol, N, *Warriors and Priests: The History of Clan MacLean, 1300–1570* (East Linton, 1995).

Macquarrie, A, *Calendar of Entries in the Papal Registers Relating to Great Britain and Ireland: Papal Letters*, xxiii, 1 (Dublin, 2018).

———, *Legends of Scottish Saints* (Dublin, 2012).

———, *The Saints of Scotland* (Edinburgh, 1997).

Maitland Thomson, J, et al., *Registrum Magni Sigilli Regni Scotiae* (Edinburgh, 1882–1914).

Malcolm, N, *The Correspondence of Thomas Hobbes* (Oxford, 1994).

Martin, M, *A Description of the Western Isles of Scotland, 1716* (Edinburgh, 1981).

McFarlane, I D, *Buchanan* (London, 1981).

McGinnis, P J, & A H Williamson, *George Buchanan: The Political Poetry* (Edinburgh, 1995).

McNeish, C, *The Munros* (Edinburgh, 1996).

Meehan, D, *Adamnan's De Locis Sanctis* (Dublin, 1958).

Meek, D E, 'The death of Diarmaid in Scottish and Irish tradition', *Celtica*, xxi (1990), 335–61.

Migne, J-P, *Patrilogia Cursus Completus Series Latina*, (Paris, 1844–66).

Munro, J, and R W Munro, *Acts of the Lords of the Isles, 1336–1493* (Edinburgh, 1986).

Munro, R W, *Monro's Western Isles of Scotland and Genealogies of the Clans* (Edinburgh, 1961).

O'Kelleher, A, and G Schoepperle, *Beatha Colaim Chille* (Urbana, 1918).

Ollivant, S, *The Court of the Official in Pre-Reformation Scotland* (Edinburgh, 1982).

O'Rahilly, T F, *Early Irish History and Mythology* (Dublin, 1946; reprinted 1984).

Ó Riain, P, *Corpus Genealogiarum Sanctorum Hiberniae* (Dublin, 1985).

———, *Dictionary of Irish Saints* (Dublin, 2011).

Origines Parochiales Scotiae (Edinburgh, 1851–55).

Patrick, D, *Statutes of the Scottish Church, 1225–1559* (Edinburgh, 1907).

Pennant, Thomas, *A Tour of Scotland and Voyage to the Hebrides in 1777* (London, 1790).

Picard, J-M, 'The strange death of Guaire mac Áedáin', in D Ó Corráin, K McCone, & L Breatnach (eds), *Sages, Saints and Storytellers: Celtic Studies in Honour of James Carney* (Maynooth, 1989).

Pococke, Richard, *Tours in Scotland in 1747, 1750 and 1760* (Edinburgh, 1887).

Registrum Episcopatus Glasguensis (Edinburgh, 1843).

Ritchie, G, & M Harman, *Exploring Scotland's Heritage: Argyll and the Western Isles* (Edinburgh, 1985)

Rivet, A L F, & C Smith, *The Place-Names of Roman Britain* (London, 1979).

Robinson, M, *Concise Scots Dictionary* (Aberdeen, 1985).

Royal Commission on the Ancient and Historic Monuments of Scotland, *Argyll*, iii: *Mull, Tiree, Coll & Northern Argyll* (1980).

Royal Commission on the Ancient and Historic Monuments of Scotland, *Argyll*, iv, *Iona* (1982).

Royal Commission on the Ancient and Historic Monuments of Scotland, *Argyll*, v: *Islay, Jura, Colonsay and Oronsay* (1984).

Royal Commission on the Ancient and Historic Monuments of Scotland, *Inventory of the Outer Hebrides, Skye and the Small Isles* (1928).

Rudd, N, *Horace: Odes and Epodes* (Cambridge, Massachussetts, 2004).

Salmeronis, Alphonsi, *Epistolae, 1536–1565*, vol. 1 (Madrid, 1906).

Schoor, R van de, *Georgius Cassander's De Officiis pii Viri (1561)* (Berlin, 2016).

Sharpe, R, *Adomnán of Iona: Life of St Columba* (London, 1995).

———, 'Roderick MacLean's Life of St Columba of Iona in Latin verse (1549)', *IR*, xlii (1991), 111–32.

———, 'Saint Mauchteus, *discipulus Patricii*', in A Bammesberger and A Wollman (eds), *Britain, 400–600: Language and History* (Heidelberg, 1990).

Shorter Oxford English Dictionary, revised edn (London, 1983).

Sinclair, A Maclean, *The Clan Gillean* (Charlottetown, 1899).

Skene, F J H, *Liber Pluscardensis* (Glasgow, 1877–80).

Steer, K A, & J W M Bannerman, *Late Medieval Monumental Sculpture in the West Highlands* (Edinburgh, 1977).

Stokes, W, *The Annals of Tigernach* (reprinted Felinfach, 1993).

Stone, J C, *Illustrated Maps of Scotland from Blaeu's Atlas Novus of the Seventeenth Century* (London, 1991).

Taylor, S, 'Seventh-century Iona abbots in Scottish place-names', in D Broun & T O Clancy (eds), *Spes Scotorum, Hope of Scots: Saint Columba, Iona and Scotland* (Edinburgh, 1999).

Thomson, R L, *Foirm na n-Urrnuidheadh* (Edinburgh, 1970).

Thomson, T, & C Innes, *Acts of the Parliament of Scotland* (Edinburgh, 1814–75).

Watson, W J, *History of the Celtic Place-Names of Scotland* (Edinburgh, 1926; reprinted 1993).

Watt, D E R, & A Murray, *Fasti Ecclesiae Scoticanae* (SRS, 2003).

Watt, D E R, & N Shead, *The Heads of Religious Houses in Scotland* (SRS, 2001).

Watt, D E R, et al., *Scotichronicon by Walter Bower* (Aberdeen, 1987–98).

'William Dey: Obituary' in *Aberdeen University Review*, iii (1915–16), 185.

INDEX

.